FRANCE IN AMERICA

By W. J. Eccles

Michigan State University Press
East Lansing, Michigan
1990

Copyright © 1990 by Fitzhenry & Whiteside

Published by arrangement with
Fitzhenry & Whiteside
Markham, Ontario, Canada
L3R 4T8

Revised Edition.

All Michigan State University Press books are produced on paper which meets the require-
ments of American National Standard of Information Sciences — Permanence of paper for
printed materials ANSI 239-48-1984

Michigan State University Press
East Lansing, Michigan 48823-5202

Library of Congress Cataloging-in-Publication Data

Eccles, W.J. (William John)
  France in America/by W.J. Eccles. — Rev. ed.
    p. cm.
  Includes bibliographical references.
  ISBN 0-87013-284-9
  1. France — Colonies — America — History. 2. French — America — History.
  3. America — History — To 1810. 4. Canada — History — To 1763 (New France) I. Title.
E18.82.E25   1990
973'.0441 — dc20   90-33403
                                                         CIP

Contents

Illustrations

These illustrations, grouped in a separate section,
will be found following page 252.

1. Jean-Baptiste Hertel, seigneur de Rouville
2. The Marquis de Montcalm
3. Brigadier General James Murray, first British governor of Quebec.
4. Monseigneur François de Laval, Bishop of Quebec 1674–1688
5. The Desceliers Mappemonde, 1550
6. Seigneurial settlements at Trois Rivières, 1709
7. Section of map by Père François Joseph Bressani
8. De l'Isle map, 1750
9. View of Quebec from the northeast
10. The Hôtel-Dieu, Quebec
11. Eighteenth-century *habitant* home, Charlesbourg
12. Street scene, Quebec, at night
13. Eighteenth-century parish church, Saint-Laurent, Île d'Orléans
14. Fort St. Frédéric, Lake Champlain
15. View of Trois Rivières
16. Montreal, 1761
17. Plan of Fortress Louisbourg, 1744
18. Reconstructed barracks and King's Bastion, Louisbourg
19. French faïence excavated at Louisbourg
20. Canadian silver, eighteenth century
21. Superior Council Chamber, Louisbourg
22. Canadian *habitants*
23. Brigadier George Townshend cartoon of Major General James Wolfe
24. Canadian Indians
25. The Siege of Quebec, 1759
26. Destruction of lower town, Quebec, 1759
27. Interior, Jesuit Church, Quebec, 1759
28. Map, St Christophe
29. Map, St Domingue
30. Tobacco manufacture
31. Sugar mill
32. Jean Baptiste Le Moyne de Bienville, Governor of Louisiana
33. Pierre Le Moyne d'Iberville, founder of Louisiana
34. Don Alexandro O'Reilly, Governor of Louisiana, 1769–1770
35. Colonial regime house, New Orleans

MAPS

Preface

With a statue, it is the stone that is not there that counts. The same is true of this book. The main problem in writing it was the necessity to compress. The French West Indies and Louisiana had, therefore, to be dealt with rather summarily because the main emphasis had to be on Canada, since the latter colony played a much more vital role in the history of the Americas than did any other of the French colonies. Had Canada not been conquered by Britain — and that conquest was by no means foreordained or inevitable — the history of North America would have flowed in different channels. This is not true of either Louisiana, which could not have stood alone, or the Antilles.

Unlike the Spanish in the Americas, the French today are only a few million people, largely concentrated in the eastern part of Canada, struggling to preserve their separate identity. This was not their condition in the eighteenth century. Then, France and her Indian allies dominated most of North America, from the north Atlantic coast to the Rocky Mountains, from the sub-Arctic to the Gulf of Mexico, while the English held only the Atlantic coastal strip and a few isolated posts in Hudson Bay. Since the historian is concerned with the past for its own sake, and only incidentally with what developed out of it, he has to strive to be detached from the present and its claims. He has to view the past through the eyes of the people of the past age and culture he studies and depicts, to judge men and their actions by the values of their own time rather than his own. Thus, of necessity, this book views events and developments from the French rather than the English side of the hill. There would, however, be no history without change, and the present cannot help but impinge. Today questions that were not asked before are being put to our own society, our institutions, and our values; much that was for long taken for granted is presently being challenged. As a consequence the historian now asks questions of the past — and through research seeks the answers — that would never have occurred to historians one and more generations ago.

This book is based on research undertaken over several years. A great many people and institutions — archivists, librarians, colleagues, graduate students, the editors of the series, foundations — have given me aid. Without their help this work could not have been accomplished. To them all I express my sincere thanks. In particular I must acknowledge my indebtedness to the Canada Council for a Senior Killam Fellowship, which provided the financial assistance and freedom from academic duties needed to make the work possible.

W. J. ECCLES

Preface to the Revised Edition

Eighteen years have elapsed since this book was first written. During that time a great deal of research has been done by many scholars, including myself, which caused me to view several aspects of the history of the period in a new light. Several of the assumptions and premises, as well as those of other historians that I had accepted, began to appear dubious, indeed in some instances erroneous. New questions arose, demanding answers; previous answers to old questions had to be discarded and new ones sought. In addition there was the need to correct the inevitable minor errors that creep into every manuscript, like thieves in the night.

Hence this second edition. The framework remains the book that I was commissioned to write for The New American Nation Series, edited by Henry Steele Commager and Richard B. Morris. In some chapters, corrections and extensive revisions were made, but Chapter 8, Aftermath, 1760–1783, had to be completely rewritten from an entirely different perspective. The need for that particular revision became obvious as, over the years, I worked my way through the documents pertaining to French foreign policy for the period 1763–1783 at the Archives du Ministère des Affaires étrangères, Quai d'Orsay, Paris. There the understaffed, overworked archivists were consistently helpful, saving me many hours of fruitless searching. To them I offer my most sincere thanks. My thanks also go to the librarians at the Robarts Research Library and the Fisher Rare Books and Special Collections Library at the University of Toronto for their assistance and patience.

W. J. ECCLES
TORONTO, DECEMBER 1989

L'Amérique Septentrionale. From Georges Louis Le Rouge, *Atlas nouveau portatif. . . .* 2nd edition, Paris, c. 1759 (Courtesy of National Archives of Canada 6626)

Chapter 1

False Starts, 1500–1632

When the western European powers began their expansion overseas in the fifteenth century, France, like England, was left behind. Not until the kingdom had recovered from the Hundred Years' War was the monarchy able to take much interest in developments beyond its frontiers. By that time Spain and Portugal had, with the sanction of the Pope, divided the newly discovered territories in Africa, Asia, and the Americas between them. The Valois kings were more interested in Mediterranean trade than in the wider world beyond, and they did not challenge the Treaty of Tordesillas of 1494.[1] In fact, when the French Crown did intervene in the Americas, it was more a reaction against the growing colonial might of Spain and Portugal than an attempt to establish a French empire overseas.

French seamen and merchants, however, showed a keen awareness of the wealth to be derived from the new lands in both North and South America. In 1500–1502 the Corte-Real brothers had explored the southern coast of Labrador and of Newfoundland, claiming the area for Portugal. They were quickly followed by Breton, Norman, and Basque fishermen who reaped rich harvests of fish on the Grand Banks to satisfy a market created by the 153

---

[1] See bull *Romanus Pontifex* of Nicholas V, 1455; bull *Inter caetera* of Calixtus III, 1456; Treaty of Alcaçovas, 1479; bull *Inter caetera* of Alexander VI, 1493; Treaty of Tordesillas, 1494, in Francis Gardiner Davenport, *European Treaties Bearing on the History of the United States and its Dependencies (1648–1715)* (3 vols., Washington, 1917–34).

1

fish days a year of Catholic France.[2] In 1506 Jean Denys of Honfleur explored the Atlantic coast from the Strait of Belle Isle to Bonavista. Thomas Aubert of Dieppe was in the same region two years later, and it was likely he who brought seven Indians to Rouen in 1508.[3] It was, however, the Portuguese who established the first colony in the region, on Cape Breton, between 1520 and 1525.[4]

The interest of the French monarchy in this northern region was stimulated by Ferdinand Magellan's expedition, which added considerably to Spanish prestige and power. Between 1521 and 1559 Spain and France were in a virtually perpetual state of war. One way for France to challenge the emperor, Charles V, was to find a more direct route to the riches of the Far East than by circumnavigating South America as Magellan had done. Thus Francis I gave his support to the Verrazano expedition of 1524 which explored the east coast of North America from present-day Charleston to Maine; that is, between the Spanish-dominated territory of Florida and the Portuguese base on Cape Breton. Verrazano claimed these lands for France, and at the same time demonstrated that North America was a vast land barrier, a geographical nuisance, between Europe and the riches of Cathay. Moreover, it appeared to have much the same flora and fauna as did France: no spices, no exotic woods, no advanced civilizations surfeited with gold, silver, or precious stones. But even had he been so inclined, Francis I was unable to follow up this voyage. On February 26, 1525, he was taken prisoner by the Spaniards at Pavia and held in captivity for thirteen months.

In the southern hemisphere, Breton and Norman seamen had begun to invade the Portuguese-claimed coast of Brazil, establishing amicable relations with the natives and gathering rich cargoes of pepper and dye wood. In fact, the ports of northwest France were as much concerned with the Brazil trade as with the fishery of the Grand Banks.[5] The Portuguese had to countenance

---

[2] It is possible that Breton ships had fished along the coast of Newfoundland in the fifteenth century. See Ch.-A. Julien, *Les voyages de découverte et les premiers établissements (XVᵉ-XVIᵉ siècles)* (Paris, 1948), pp. 21–28.

[3] *Ibid.*, p. 25.

[4] H. P. Biggar, *The Precursors of Jacques Cartier, 1497–1534* (Ottawa, 1911), pp. 196–197.

[5] Julien, *Les voyages de découverte*, pp. 7–76, 177–184.

this trade lest the French Crown issue letters of marque against their galleons to the feared French privateers. The captivity of Francis I was, therefore, too good an opportunity to miss. King John III of Portugal quickly dispatched a fleet to Brazil. Most of the French traders along the coast were captured, brought to Lisbon, and executed as pirates. A few escaped and fled into the interior, throwing themselves on the mercy of the indigenous tribes; but from Bahia to Rio de Janeiro, an effective French presence had been eliminated.[6] A few years later, 1529–1530, the French moved further afield and attempted to dislodge the Portuguese in Sumatra, without success. When they again returned to resume their trading activities at Recife on the Brazil coast they were swiftly captured by the Portuguese and put to the sword. Clearly, the French were as yet unable to concentrate forces sufficient to hold their own in the parts of the world claimed by Portugal.

It was out of this position of weakness that the French began to evolve a new concept of colonialism, one that was eventually to be accepted by all the European powers. The Portuguese and Spanish claimed exclusive rights to the newly discovered lands overseas by virtue of papal decrees, confirmed by the treaties of Alcaçovas and Tordesillas. The French disputed the right of the Pope to partition the world in this fashion, claiming that a monopoly on trade in any area could be maintained only by permanent occupation of the region. Wherever Europeans had no fixed establishments, the trade had to be open to all. In short, sovereignty was to be based on occupation, not on a papal bull, and in 1533 Francis I succeeded in persuading Pope Clement VII that the bull *Inter caetera* of Alexander VI, which had divided the world between Spain and Portugal, governed only the then known lands, not those subsequently discovered by the subjects of other crowns.[7]

On the strength of this, one year later, the first French expedition commissioned and financed by the King set sail to explore the gulf far to the north, to be named St Lawrence by Mercator on his map of 1569. This expedition, commanded by an experi-

---

[6] *Ibid.*
[7] *Ibid.*, pp. 113–117, 145–147.

enced captain of Saint-Malo, Jacques Cartier, was not intended
to establish a colony or to convert the pagans to Christianity, but
to discover mineral wealth similar to that found in Mexico, and
also to seek out a sea route through the North American land
mass to Cathay. The Spaniards, and Verrazano, had established
that solid land existed between Florida and what was eventually
to be called Nova Scotia. Perhaps farther north, a strait would
be found leading to the Pacific. This, therefore, was the route
Jacques Cartier was ordered to take with his two sixty-ton ships.[8]

On this first voyage Cartier merely passed through the Strait
of Belle Isle and cruised about the coastline within the gulf, going
no farther than the western tip of Anticosti Island. A chance
encounter with a ship from La Rochelle and the attitude of the
Indians, who were eager to trade their furs for metal goods,
indicate that Cartier's were by no means the first ships to sail in
those waters. No great store of wealth was discovered, nor a
strait leading to Cathay. Yet there was a possibility that both lay
only a little way farther up the gulf. No one yet had any suspicion
of how broad North America was at that latitude. In any event,
the cupidity of Francis I was sufficiently aroused to commission
a more ambitious expedition. This time Cartier was to make a
thorough exploration of the gulf for the ardently desired strait,
and for the gold and silver of another Mexico or Peru.[9] There
was no intention to establish a permanent settlement, only to
winter in the country. Cartier and his men were to be the first
Europeans since the Vikings known to have done so.[10]

This expedition produced no great results. Nothing that was
worth transporting across the ocean was discovered, only infor-

---

[8] The best edition of Cartier's journal is contained in H. P. Biggar, *The Voyages of Jacques Cartier: Published from the Originals with Translations, Notes and Appendices* (Ottawa, 1924). See also H. P. Biggar, *A Collection of Documents Relating to Jacques Cartier and the Sieur de Roberval* (Ottawa, 1930). The best studies of Cartier's voyages by modern historians are Marcel Trudel, *Histoire de la Nouvelle-France*, Vol. I, *Les vaines tentatives, 1524–1603* (Montréal, 1963), and Julien, *Les voyages de découverte*. Julien gives an excellent brief critical bibliography, pp. 118–119.

[9] It might be noted that while Cartier was exploring the Gulf of St. Lawrence, Pizarro was completing his conquest of the Inca empire in Peru. The initial seizure of booty there amounted to 603 kg of gold and 1182 kg pounds of silver (13,265.4 pounds of gold and 26,000 pounds of silver). See F. A. Kirkpatrick, *The Spanish Conquistadores* (London, 1963 ed.), p. 163.

[10] The recent archaeological discoveries at L'Anse aux Meadows on the northern tip of Newfoundland have established the existence of a Viking community there in the late tenth century. See Helge Ingstad, *Westward to Vinland*, trans. from the Norwegian by Erik J. Friis (London, 1969).

mation, gleaned from the Indians and embroidered by the greedy imaginations of these Europeans, that gold, silver, spices, and a people with a very advanced civilization were to be found in the interior. Still, much geographical and ethnological knowledge about North America was garnered. Cartier had established that the great river of Canada drained a huge land mass and could not be a strait leading to Cathay. The natives he encountered both at Stadacona (Quebec) and at Hochelaga (Montreal) had nothing material to offer of any value. They had progressed beyond the nomadic hunting and gathering stage, practising a crude agriculture by raising corn — maize — in forest clearings, and they had learned to store food, but their implements and weapons were made of wood, stone, bone, and sinew; their houses and canoes of wood and bark; their clothing of fur and dressed buckskin. In short, a Stone Age civilization.

Cartier had also discovered that rapids barred navigation at Hochelaga. Even ships' longboats could go no farther. That was enough to send him back after spending less than twenty-four hours there. By then, early October, it was too late to risk the return voyage to France. Blissfully unaware of the length and severity of the Canadian winter, deceived by the heat of the past summer and a latitude more than two degrees south of Paris, Cartier wintered at Stadacona. By spring twenty-five of the crew were dead of scurvy, the remainder were in a very weak condition, and the Stadacona tribesmen had been alienated to the point that they had to be cowed by a salvo from the French cannon.

When the survivors arrived back in France, bringing with them several kidnapped Indians, they had to justify their meagre results to the King. They had nothing tangible to offer, only vague rumours of a mythical kingdom beyond where they had been, and vast stores of gold, silver, cloves, nutmegs, pepper, and tropical fruits within striking distance in the interior. It may well be that the Indians brought by Cartier, discerning what the French avidly sought in their country, assured them that all those things were there in abundance, in the hope that the French would be induced to return and take them back.[11] At all events, Francis I

---

[11] A few years later a Portuguese pilot, Joäno Fernando Lagarto, expressed grave doubts of such tales told by captive Indians in Europe for this very reason. See Lagarto to John III, Jan. 22, 1739, in Biggar, *Collection of Documents*, pp. 75–81.

was now convinced that another Peru was almost within his grasp; but the resumption of war with the Emperor in July, 1536, prevented him from taking active measures until 1540, after hostilities had ceased. Then, when queried by the Spanish ambassador on his intentions in the New World, he reiterated his right to exploit lands not previously occupied by other Christian powers. The Emperor and the King of Portugal were not in a position to dispute this claim effectively. They were obliged to acknowledge the new principle of imperialism: that title to territory in the Americas and elsewhere rested not on papal decrees but on prior exploration, conquest, and ultimately, on occupation and settlement.[12]

This concept required that the French, if they were going to garner the wealth of Canada and exclude other nations, had to establish a permanent colony as far up the great river as possible. To give the expedition that was now organized adequate stature, a nobleman rather than a simple sea captain, such as was Cartier, had to be placed in command. Thus Jean-François de la Rocque de Roberval was commissioned the King's "lieutenant-general in the country of Canada" and Cartier was given command of the fleet. Much was made of the intention to convert the Indians to Christianity, but this appears merely to have been an attempt to bolster the French claims against the anticipated protests of Spain.

As with Cartier's earlier expeditions, Saint-Malo and the other channel ports, fearing that their interests would be jeopardized, put every obstacle in the path of recruiting crews and colonists. Recourse again had to be had to the royal prisons.[13] While ships, crews, and supplies were being mustered, the Emperor was corresponding with John III of Portugal on the measures to be taken against this threat to their territories. It was at first feared that the expedition was intended for Brazil, Guinea, or the West Indies. Not until early April 1541, did the Spanish learn the true

---

[12] *Ibid.*, pp. 169–171, 239–244, 283–284. The genesis of this French doctrine of imperialism is succinctly explained in Julien, *Les voyages de découverte*, pp. 115–117, 145–147.

[13] An English report stated bluntly: "Yf . . . theye never returne agayne yet that be no grete losse of them specyally." Biggar, *Collection of Documents*, pp. 188–191.

destination. Then their fears abated somewhat, for, as the Emperor informed the council, "As regards settling in the Northern Sea, there is nothing to envy in this; for it is of no value, and if the French take it, necessity will compel them to abandon it." And the King of Portugal remarked that if Cartier and Roberval had gone up the river of Canada they "could not have gone to any place where they could do less damage to His Majesty [Charles V] or to himself." Yet the Emperor still feared that the French would settle these new lands, then go on to threaten the Spanish settlements to the south. He demanded exact information as to where the new land actually lay.[14]

Two years later the Emperor's fears were allayed. The first French attempt to establish a colony in North America was a total disaster. Neither Cartier nor Roberval proceeded any farther up the river than Cartier had done previously.[15] The Indians of Stadacona and Hochelaga were again alienated, and an army would have been required to make a permanent settlement secure against their attacks. The bitter winter that had claimed its victims in 1535 was found to have been no climatic freak. The gold and diamonds Cartier discovered near Stadacona proved, on better assay, to be worthless dross.

Great hopes had been riding on the enterprise. They had now been shattered. The disappointment was terrible. Suddenly, Canada had become a savage country, offering nothing of value, leading nowhere, and uninhabitable for Europeans half the year. French interest in the region vanished. Francis I abandoned all notions of establishing colonies overseas. He now claimed only the right for his subjects to trade peaceably in territories still unoccupied by Christians, more particularly along the coasts of Guinea and Brazil. This the Spanish and Portuguese would not allow. Yet, when Francis I died in 1547 European colonial sov-

---

[14] See Biggar, *Collection of Documents, passim*, for Spanish reaction to the Roberval expedition.

[15] There is no evidence to indicate that they proceeded above the rapids at Hochelaga; had they done so they could hardly have failed to discover that the site was on a large island at the juncture of what were later to be named the Ottawa and St Lawrence rivers. Neither the Harleian map circa 1542, an anonymous French map of 1543, the Vallard map of 1547, the Descelliers map of 1550, nor the Mercator map of 1569, all based on the knowledge gained by Cartier and Roberval, depict such an island at the juncture of the two rivers. See Marcel Trudel, *Atlas de la Nouvelle-France: An Atlas of New France* (Quebec, 1968).

ereignty no longer rested on old papal bulls, but on the principle he had enunciated: discovery, conquest, and settlement. The drastic failure of the Roberval expedition made it easier for Spain to accept, albeit grudgingly, this new doctrine of imperialism.

Regardless of such tacit accords between their monarchs — most likely in ignorance of them — the fishermen of northwest Europe harvested the never diminishing wealth of the sea off the coasts of Newfoundland; and French corsairs drove a rich trade, mingled with piracy, in the Gulf of Guinea and along the coast of Brazil. In the latter region the Portuguese had established several settlements and an administrative framework, but in doing so they had antagonized the native tribes. The French also reestablished their bases along the coast as far south as Rio de Janeiro. They, of necessity, maintained good relations with the Indians, and armed and encouraged them in their struggle with the Portuguese.[16] Some Norman sailors settled among the natives, became virtually assimilated in much the same fashion as French *coureurs de bois* were later to be in Canada, and acted as intermediaries between the French sea traders and the tribesmen.[17] By 1550 the area from Cape Frio to Rio de Janeiro was under French rather than Portuguese control.

It was, therefore, in this region rather than in Canada that Admiral Gaspard de Coligny, the Huguenot first minister of Henri II, determined to establish a French colony. His aims were threefold: to establish a base for eventual expansion into a vast colonial empire; to create a sanctuary for his coreligionists; and to weaken the Catholic powers by breaking their hold on the Americas. The man chosen to lead this ambitious undertaking,

---

[16] On French activities in Brazil in the sixteenth century see Julien, *Les voyages de découverte*, pp. 177–221; Paul Gaffarel, *Histoire de Brésil français au seizième siècle* (Paris, 1878); Jean de Léry, *Histoire d'un voyage fait en la terre de Brésil, autrement dite Amérique contenant choses curieuses et remarquable en ce pais-la* (La Rochelle, 1578).

[17] It is frequently stated that the French had a gift for conciliating native peoples, as displayed in Brazil and Canada. There is much truth in this, Jacques Cartier to the contrary. It may well be, however, that the Portuguese alienated the natives because they sought to settle the land, establishing plantations, thereby displacing their resident natives or enslaving them. The French showed no inclination to clear and settle the land. They were interested only in trade with the natives for exotic goods, in particular, emeralds and dye woods. The same distinction was to be made in North America in the next century between the French and English, the one coveting the Indians' land for settlement, the other only the trade in furs and a military alliance with the Indians. In both places, the one had to displace—that is, destroy—the Indians, the other preserve them, in order to achieve their aims.

Nicolas Durand de Villegaignon, had won renown for his bravery on several battlefields. He was quarrelsome, passionate, extremely opinionated; a worse choice for leader of the Brazilian enterprise could hardly have been made. As with Roberval's expedition, volunteers were scarce. A few Huguenots came forward, but recourse had to be had to human debris swept up off the streets of the northern ports.

In November 1555, Villegaignon's small expedition reached Rio de Janeiro, where he established his base on a small island that lacked fresh water at the mouth of the bay. To augment the food supplies brought by ship the expedition relied on trade with the Indians, but they were quickly provoked and moved away. Among the settlers, imprisoned on the island, there arose dissension leading to mutiny, which Villegaignon suppressed with a heavy hand.

The following year Coligny sent some three hundred reinforcements, but Villegaignon's oppressive rule, made worse by his newly found conviction that all heresy must be extirpated, ended in disaster. Several of the Huguenots made their way back to France, where their reports caused an expedition of some seven or eight hundred would-be colonists to be abandoned. Then Villegaignon himself returned to France, taking fifty natives with him. Two years later, in March 1560, a Portuguese force captured the French base after a savage engagement. Some of the defenders escaped to the mainland; those captured were sold into slavery. It was not until 1603, after the union of Spain and Portugal, that the Portuguese were finally able to eliminate the French from Brazil. For a century, French traders had challenged the Portuguese hold on this vast region, with little or no aid from the Crown. But for the religious dissension at Rio de Janeiro, and the unfortunate character of Villegaignon, France rather than Portugal might well have established a vast empire in South America.

Coligny, however, still refused to acknowledge Spain's monopoly over the New World. Defeated on the subcontinent, he decided to establish a Huguenot colony to the north, in Florida, but the Spanish were a much more ruthless and determined foe than the Portuguese. The first attempt, in 1562, ended in disaster without Spanish intervention. In 1564 another attempt was made, farther south; but as at Rio de Janeiro the colony was torn by internal conflicts, mutiny, and brutal reprisals. Reinforcements arrived from France the following year, but a Spanish force captured Fort Caroline and swiftly executed the 132 male defenders. Some others who had been absent at the time of the assault, or who managed to escape capture, were subsequently constrained to throw themselves on the mercy of the Spaniards. As heretics, in Spanish eyes they merited death by burning at the stake. But the officer commanding, Pedro Menendez de Aviles, was merciful; he merely put them to the sword.[18]

Driven out of the subtropical zones in both the northern and the southern hemispheres, all that remained to France in the New World was a tenuous claim to sections of the brutally inhospitable northern coast. Fortunately, no other power showed much interest in the area. Had that occurred, the French Crown could have done little about it. In 1572 the queen mother, Catherine de Médicis, sought to terminate the religious turmoil that was tearing the kingdom apart by massacring the Huguenot leaders, come to Paris for a royal wedding. The slaughter, begun on St Bartholomew's Day, August 24, 1572, claimed Coligny among its victims but failed of its purpose. The ensuing wars of religion, the chaos that they engendered, made it impossible for the Crown to give more than moral support to colonial ventures.

Yet the French presence in North America was maintained throughout these troubled years by fishermen of all the French ports from Bordeaux to Dieppe. Every spring they voyaged to the Grand Banks, to the Gulf of St Lawrence, and the coast of what had come to be known as Acadia. The attraction was the teeming stockfish—cod—and the seals, valuable for their oil and pelts. Three-quarters of the catch went to supply the French Lenten market. Every year it was a race to return to port on the eve of Lent. Half a cargo then was worth a full cargo later. A crew might complete their catch in four to six weeks, or it might take five months. The profits were small; 90 to 120 livres per man was considered good. The hardship and dangers from bitter

---

[18] Julien, *Les voyages de découverte*, pp. 239–248; Francis Parkman, *Pioneers of France in the New World* (Boston, 1874), pp. 119–139.

cold, fog, and icebergs were great; but it was a living.

Two quite different methods were employed in the fishery. On the Grand Banks large fish formed the bulk of the catch, while along the coast smaller fish were taken. The latter were filleted and spread on drying racks on the shore. This could not be done with the larger fish, since they took too long to dry and became maggoty; hence they were merely cleaned and salted down in the ships' holds. The wind-dried shore fish required only half as much salt as the larger "green" cod, but the labour costs were greater; twice as many crew members were needed and the voyage took much longer. Dry cod, however, brought a better price.[19] Moreover, the time spent waiting on shore for the fish to dry permitted sustained contacts with the Indians.

Trade with the Indians had come to have considerable economic importance as the demand for furs increased in Europe. A major factor here was the vogue for wide-brimmed felt hats. The best material for the felt was the soft underfur of the beaver, since each strand had tiny barbs which caused the felt to mat securely and gave a lustrous finish. The supply of European beaver was by this time exhausted; thus the beaver pelts brought to France by the fishing fleets fetched high prices, particularly since they were of far better quality than the European variety had been.[20] The coastal Indians were desperately eager to obtain the European metal goods that were starting to revolutionize their Stone Age culture. Furs were the only goods they had to offer in exchange. Thus the shore-based dry fishermen were able to drive a brisk trade. The costs of the voyage were paid for with the cargo of fish; the furs provided a tidy profit. Fur was, in fact, well on the way to becoming a viable staple in its own right.

As more ships engaged in the dry fishing, permanent shore bases became necessary. Men had to be left ashore over the winter to guard the more favoured sites and the drying racks, and to make things ready for the following season in order to catch the

---

[19] See Nicolas Denys, *The Description and Natural History of the Coasts of North America (Acadia)*, trans. and ed. by W. F. Ganong (2 vols., Champlain Society Publications, Toronto, 1908), I, pp. 257 ff.

[20] See Elspeth M. Veale, *The English Fur Trade in the Later Middle Ages* (Oxford, 1966), pp. 174–176. On the felt-making process and the mechanics of the trade see E. E. Rich, *The History of the Hudson's Bay Company 1670–1870* (3 vols., London, 1958), I, pp. 47–49.

Lenten market. These men, of necessity as well as for commercial reasons, had to maintain good relations with the Indians. Moreover, women were not brought out from France, which gave an added incentive for friendly attitudes.[21] Eventually the need arose to raise crops at these bases to feed the winterers and decrease dependence on supplies brought from France. Once these fishing and trading bases were well-established, the French ports came to depend on the profits they provided and to demand protection from the King. In 1578 Henri III named the Breton nobleman Mesgouez de La Roche governor, lieutenant general, and viceroy of the pagan lands in the New World. Nothing tangible resulted from this commission, but it did make manifest a renewed interest in the region by the Crown after a lapse of thirty-four years.[22]

In 1598, after Henri IV had acceded to the throne and the wars of religion had finally ended, La Roche obtained a fresh commission as lieutenant general of the King in the lands claimed by France; namely Canada, Hochelaga, Newfoundland, Labrador, the Gulf of St Lawrence, and Acadia. He was permitted to build forts, grant lands, and make laws, and, what was most significant, he was given a monopoly on the trade of these lands. For colonists, La Roche, like Roberval, had to have recourse to the jails, obtaining two hundred men and fifty women. For reasons that are hard to imagine, La Roche chose to establish his base on the sandy waste of Sable Island, out in the storm-swept Atlantic 144 km off the coast of Nova Scotia. It endured for five years. In 1603 the eleven survivors were repatriated to France.

The merchants and fishermen of the French ports were, understandably, bitterly opposed to the granting of monopolies that excluded them from the fur trade, but these monopolies were a cheap way for the Crown to maintain a claim to sovereignty and some degree of control over the region. In 1598 the Edict of Nantes granted the Huguenots equal civil status with Roman

---

[21] It has been suggested that the Malecite tribe of the St John River area were métis, deriving from liaisons between the fishermen of Saint-Malo and the local Abenaquis, the name Malecite being a corruption of the Abenaquis word *Malouidit*, signifying a man of Saint-Malo. See Lucien Campeau, S.I. (ed.), *Monumenta Novae Franciae*, I, *La première mission d'Acadie (1602–1616)* (Rome and Québec, 1967), p. 118.

[22] For a detailed account of the first settlements of Acadia see Trudel, *Histoire de la Nouvelle-France*, I.

Catholics. The following year La Roche's vast territorial monopoly was divided; the northern half, comprising the trade of Canada, was granted to a Huguenot merchant mariner of Honfleur, Pierre Chauvin de Tonnetuit, for a ten-year period. To protect his monopoly against the fierce opposition of the Saint-Malo fishermen-traders, in 1600 Chauvin established what he intended to be a permanent year-round base at Tadoussac where the Saguenay flows into the St Lawrence from the north. Again the cruel winter — far more severe than at Quebec — proved too much. Of the sixteen men who wintered, only five were still alive come spring. Although there had been no intention to establish a self-supporting colony at Tadoussac, only a permanent trading post, it appeared that the northern winter made even that impossible in the lower St Lawrence Valley. In any event the majority of the French traders had no inclination to invest capital in permanent posts. They preferred to send ships to Tadoussac each summer to meet the hundreds of northern Indians who foregathered for the trade, then return to France in the autumn when the Indians departed for the hunt. Profits, not imperialism, were their concern. Thus, at the beginning of the seventeenth century, France still did not have more than a foothold for a few months in the year on the continent. Compared to Spain and Portugal, as a colonizing power France had failed dismally.

Yet conditions in Europe at long last had made it possible for the French Crown to make a more determined effort to consolidate its claims to a large section of North America. It had required only a few years of peace and the determined efforts of Sully and Henri IV to restore the royal finances and to expand greatly the national economy. France had regained its breath. Moreover, Philip III, ruler of Spain and Portugal, now faced serious problems at home.[23] He could not extend his American empire farther north; he could not even hope to prevent other powers from occupying that region.

There was, however, a threat to French colonial ambitions from other quarters. The Dutch, while engaged in their struggle with Spain for independence, dominated European maritime trade and

---

[23] See John Lynch, *Spain Under the Hapsburgs* (2 vols., Oxford, 1969), II, pp. 1–13.

were beginning to establish commercial bases overseas. England too was in a position to challenge Spain in North America. The defeat of the Spanish Armada in 1588 had removed the immediate threat of invasion, and for the next half-century the country was to enjoy political stability. Unlike the continental powers, England had no need to maintain a large standing army to defend its frontiers; thus manpower could be exported overseas. It was, therefore, no accident that the three maritime states, France, the Netherlands, and England, now all began to make determined efforts to carve out empires in North America.

In 1603 the duc de Montmorency, admiral of France, commissioned Pierre de Gua, sieur de Monts, vice-admiral in the lands of Acadia, stretching up the Atlantic coast from 40 to 46 degrees of latitude, including the lands on both sides of the St Lawrence from the Gaspé Peninsula eastward, and stretching as far inland as could be explored and settled. This commission was confirmed by Henri IV, who appointed de Monts his lieutenant general over the same vast region, with the power to grant lands in seigneurial tenure, and a ten-year monopoly over the fur trade of the St Lawrence Valley and Acadia. A further term of the commission was that sixty persons, vagabonds if others could not be had, be transported to settle on the ceded lands.[24] There was, however, little hope of any extensive settlement. The main aim was still to discover workable mineral lodes and a navigable water route through the land mass to the western ocean.[25] Meanwhile it was expected that fish and fur would provide profits enough, and these products did not require a large supply of labor. The establishment of settlers in any numbers was an expensive proposition, requiring a heavy capital investment with little prospect of return for several years, if ever.

Both de Monts and one of his associates, Samuel de Champlain, had visited Tadoussac previously and had formed a very low opinion of its physical environment. They therefore turned their backs on the St Lawrence and chose to found their base of oper-

---

[24] See Marcel Trudel, *Histoire de la Nouvelle-France*, Vol. II, *Le Comptoir, 1604–1627* (Montréal, 1966), pp. 9–15.

[25] The Levasseur map of 1603, reproduced in Trudel, *Atlas de la Nouvelle-France*, p. 72, indicates how vague was the existing knowledge of the geography of Acadia.

ations on the Atlantic coast where the land was known to be fertile and the climate more agreeable. The wish being father to the thought, it was also believed that minerals were abundant in that more southerly region. This marked the real beginning of Champlain's career, spanning three decades, in North America. A devout man, with the intense curiosity of the born explorer, he more than anyone else kept alive French claims to these lands on the Atlantic and, subsequently, the St Lawrence Valley. More than that, without his published journals we would know very little of what transpired during those early years.

Champlain and de Monts maintained their base in Acadia for only three years. In 1607 the merchants of the northern French ports, who had bitterly opposed the monopoly trading rights granted to de Monts, succeeded in having the fur trade reopened to all the King's subjects. During the three years that Champlain and de Monts were in Acadia, although they failed in their main quest for mines and a navigable strait to the western ocean, they still accomplished much that was to be of lasting importance. Champlain produced excellent charts of the coast from Cape Breton to Cape Cod; and cereal grains and vegetables were sown at the main base of Port Royal, in the Bay of Fundy, and were found to flourish. Although the casualties from scurvy were heavy, it was established that, with proper care, Europeans could live all year round in that part of the world. Perhaps most important of all, good relations were established with the Micmac and Abenaquis tribes.

Port Royal during these years was never more than a base for exploration, with fish and fur paying the costs. Mineral wealth, rather than the establishment of a self-sufficient colony, was still the main objective. No women came from France. Perhaps some of the men had it in mind to bring their wives later and settle permanently on the land, but the majority of them most likely intended to return to France when their contracts expired. Supplies enough for only a year at a time were sent from France, and when spring came anxiety mounted lest the food stocks be exhausted before the ships arrived. The agonizing question was, then, whether to hang on, gambling that nothing had happened to prevent the ships from coming, or return to France while enough supplies remained for the voyage. This danger was very real, since de Monts had to raise fresh capital each year, gambling on the returns of the season's trade.[26] When word was received at Port Royal that the monopoly had been canceled, Acadia was abandoned. While the crews were loading the ships for departure in August 1607, far to the south 105 Englishmen were establishing a base at Jamestown. Another group was making a similar attempt to the north on the Kennebec River, well within the confines of the territory ceded to de Monts by Henri IV.

Back in France, de Monts salvaged what he could from the debacle. He succeeded in persuading the King to extend his fur trade monopoly for one more year to allow him to recoup at least part of his investment. De Monts, however, had learned from bitter experience that the rugged coastline of Acadia was impossible to police. Interlopers made a mockery of any monopoly. He therefore decided to establish a base on the upper St Lawrence, relinquishing Port Royal to one of his lieutenants, Jean de Biencourt de Poutrincourt.

Not until 1610 did Poutrincourt manage to raise enough capital to fit out a ship. With his expedition went a secular priest, Jessé Flesché, who within a few weeks of his arrival at Port Royal baptized more than eighty Micmacs after the bare minimum of instruction through the medium of an interpreter. This rather inauspicious beginning marked the commencement of the great missionary drive in North America by the French clergy.[27] It was hoped that the King would be favourably impressed by this evangelical enthusiasm, but a short time later it was learned that Henri IV had been assassinated, throwing France once again into turmoil, just as the threat from the English in America began to assume dangerous proportions.

The news that converts had, at last, been made among the pagans had more far-reaching effects than Poutrincourt would

---

[26] For the details of these hand-to-mouth financial arrangements see the relevant documents in *Nouveaux documents sur Champlain et son époque*, Vol. I, *1560–1622*, ed. by Robert Le Blant and René Baudry (Publications des Archives publiques du Canada, No. 15, Ottawa, 1967).

[27] Flesché was not the first priest to reside in Acadia. A Roman priest and a Huguenot pastor had been at Port Royal with Champlain, but they had served only the members of the trading venture and spent much of their time disputing with each other until they both succumbed to scurvy. They were buried in a common grave by the irreverent crew, who desired to see if they could abide each other in death, not having done so while alive.

have wished. The queen mother, Marie de Médicis, urged on by the very devout Madame de Guercheville, obliged him to accept the Society of Jesus, an order that he detested with pathological intensity, as his associate. The Society was willing to furnish the capital he lacked to maintain Port Royal, but he in France and his son Charles de Biencourt, in command in Acadia, leveled wild charges at the Jesuits and harassed the two resident missionaries without cease. This caused Madame de Guercheville to withdraw her support. In 1613 she sent a ship with a year's supplies and thirty men to establish a mission on the Penobscot, near present-day Bangor, which gave access to the interior and, by way of the Chaudière River, to the St Lawrence. Unfortunately, the crew of the ship refused to go farther than Mont Désert Island, and the mission of Saint-Sauveur had to be established on the mainland across from the island, all too vulnerable from the sea.

A month later it was destroyed. On July 2, 1613, Samuel Argall of Virginia on the fourteen-gun *Treasurer*, with sixty soldiers, came up in thick fog on the collection of tents at the edge of the forest. The French were taken completely by surprise. Argall did not even send a summons before launching his assault. Two of the French were killed and four were wounded in the brief flurry of resistance. Argall then declared the French to be pirates and pillaged their stores. Some of the survivors made their way to the Grand Banks in a bark and returned to France with the fishing fleet. The rest were taken to Virginia, where they came close to being hanged before they were released. In October, Argall sailed north again, to Port Royal. The men were absent from the fort, away trading or working in the fields. What Argall could not pillage, he burned. Then, after claiming Acadia for England, he sailed off. Once again the French presence had been eliminated in Acadia.

These attacks had occurred in time of peace. Admiral Montmorency immediately protested to the Court of St James's, demanding the release of the French subjects held prisoner, compensation of 100,000 livres for damages, and guarantees that the English would not again trouble French subjects going about their lawful occasions in New France. This availed them nothing. The

Council of Virginia maintained that it held title from James I to all lands from 34 to 45 degrees of latitude. Saint-Sauveur and Port Royal were both south of 45 degrees; therefore the French had usurped the territory of Virginia and had no grounds for complaint.

This was pure chicanery. The 1606 charter of the Virginia Company stated that the company could establish settlements between 34 and 45 degrees north, in areas "which are not now actually possessed by any christian Prince or People."[28] If, however, title were to be based on charters issued by monarchs, the French had the better claim. In 1603, Henri IV had granted de Monts title to the lands on the Atlantic coast between 40 and 46 degrees. A French title to lands explored, and to some degree exploited, by Frenchmen was every bit as good as, or better than, a subsequent English title to the same area.

Sovereignty over this part of the world, however, was going to rest less on the claims and charters of European monarchs than on the ability to seize, occupy, and hold the territory, by force if need be. The rights of the resident Indians were, of course, not taken into account. Given these conditions, French prospects in North America did not look good. In Acadia only a handful of their traders remained. Following Argall's attacks they had taken refuge with the Indians and subsequently returned to rebuild the post at Port Royal, and to man posts at Miscou and on the St John River. Madame de Guercheville, after her heavy financial losses, the destruction of the Jesuit mission at Saint-Sauveur, and the ensuing vicious attacks by Poutrincourt against the Jesuits, had abandoned her evangelical endeavours in Acadia. At the base established by Champlain up the St Lawrence at Quebec only fifteen to twenty men wintered. There was little likelihood that the number of year-round residents in Acadia or at Quebec would increase sensibly. The fewer the staff the better, in order to keep down the costs in what was still strictly a commercial endeavour.

In the parvenu English colonies, the situation was becoming very different. In 1614 John Rolfe shipped the initial cargo of

---

[28] For the relevant documents concerning Argall's attack see Campeau, *Monumenta Novae Franciae*, I, pp. 285–289, 296–313, 411–449; *Nouveaux documents sur Champlain et son époque*, I, pp. 326–329.

tobacco to London. After that Virginia never looked back.[29] Its population began to soar, reaching ten thousand in that first generation.[30] In 1620, Plymouth colony was established and religious dissenters began to flood across the Atlantic to create new settlements along the coast, well within the territory claimed by France north of 40 degrees latitude. Even the Dutch, despite their struggle with Spain, established a trading colony on the Hudson River without the French doing anything to prevent them. Prior to this, in 1606, the Dutch had garnered the bulk of the furs in the St Lawrence. They also provided much of the capital for the Rouen merchants engaged in the Canadian trade.[31]

It was to escape the ruthless competition of interlopers, who had even gone so far as to rob Indian graves to obtain furs,[32] that Champlain in 1608 had established de Mont's post at Quebec where the river narrowed sufficiently to allow cannon to dispute the passage. The site was, in fact, one of the best natural military strongpoints in North America. Whoever controlled it controlled access to the interior of the continent. Fortunately for Champlain and his men, the St Lawrence Valley was no longer occupied by the Iroquois, who had dominated the region in Cartier's day. Only a few clearings and rotting, fallen palisades marked where their villages had been. Why they had departed, and to where, cannot be stated with certitude.[33] Their absence, however, allowed the French to occupy the region from Tadoussac to Montreal without opposition and without negotiations, treaties, or purchase.

This is not to say that the nomadic Algonquin nations who voyaged through the region did not exact a price from the French. The sole purpose of the base at Quebec was the trade with these tribes for their furs. There was no alternative to it. Fishing, even

---

[29] Louis B. Wright, *The Cultural Life of the American Colonies, 1607–1763* (New York, 1957), p. 2.

[30] Marcus Lee Hansen, *The Atlantic Migration, 1607–1860* (Harper Torchbook ed., New York, 1961), p. 33.

[31] See Trudel, *Histoire de la Nouvelle-France*, II, pp. 66–67, 153; Thomas J. Condon, *New York Beginnings: The Commercial Origins of New Netherland* (New York, 1968), p. 15.

[32] Trudel, *Histoire de la Nouvelle-France*, II, pp. 66–67, 153.

[33] The most likely explanation is that the warriors were slaughtered by their arch-foes, the Hurons, their women and children assimilated by that nation. See J.V. Wright, *Quebec Prehistory* (Toronto, 1979) pp. 71–75.

as an adjunct to the fur trade, was not economically feasible. The St Lawrence teemed with fish, but the ice-free season was too short, and Quebec too remote from the European market, to compete with the Normands and Bretons fishing on the Grand Banks. They could take their catch and have it on the European market before the Canadians could put a boat in the ice-clogged river. Although the Indian nations to the north and west of Quebec were now spared the long trip downriver to Tadoussac to obtain European goods, they still had the option of trading there should they become dissatisfied with the goods and services offered them at Champlain's post. Operating as they were with very little capital, at the mercy of arbitrary decisions at the royal court, Champlain and his associates had to keep their costs low. One summer without a good trade at that stage could have spelled ruin. It was essential, therefore, that the Indian suppliers be humoured. This meant offering as much or more in goods for furs as did the freetraders downriver, the maintenance of good relations, catering to the suppliers' whims, and acceding to their demands for military aid on occasion against their foes. Moreover, the French were so few in numbers they could have been overwhelmed at any time that the Indians determined. That first year only twenty-eight men wintered at Quebec, and by spring only eight remained alive. Dysentery and scurvy had claimed the rest.

The following summer, Champlain, with two companions, was constrained to join a war party of Algonquins, Montagnais, and warriors of another nation whom the French had not encountered before, the Hurons, in a campaign against the Mohawks. The expedition enabled Champlain to explore the water route that led from the St Lawrence to the Hudson River by way of the Richelieu and the lake that today bears his name, and also to establish trade relations with the Huron confederacy that occupied the region between Lake Simcoe and Georgian Bay. These Hurons, numbering some eighteen to twenty thousand souls, were an Iroquoian people but enemies of the Five Nations Iroquois confederacy that occupied the territory south of Lake Ontario. Their importance to the French lay in their being sedentary agricultural tribes who bartered their corn and beans to the northern nomadic hunting

Algonquin tribes for venison and furs. They also acted as go-betweens with the northern tribes and the French. It has frequently been asserted that they became the middlemen of the fur trade during the period 1609–1649,[34] obtaining furs from the northern tribes in exchange for French goods. The latter tribes could, and did, take their furs directly to the French; they had no need for Huron intervention. Neither the Huron, nor any other Indian tribe, were capitalist entrepreneurs in moccasins, seeking to buy cheap and sell dear in order to make a profit. One must ask, if they sought to make a profit, what would they have done with it? The significance of this particular expedition was that it inaugurated a revolution in warfare in North America and heralded the bitter economic rivalry that was soon to develop between two geographic regions, that of the St Lawrence and that of the Hudson River. According to Champlain's account, which strains credulity, he with two French companions and some sixty Indians encountered two hundred Mohawks at the narrows of Lake Champlain. The Mohawks, terrified by the French firearms, clumsy matchlocks, promptly turned and fled after suffering heavy casualties. The entire episode as described by Champlain does not ring true. We know from many subsequent accounts that the Indians' mode of warfare bore no resemblance to that described by Champlain.[35]

Prior to this brief skirmish, intertribal warfare had been an extension of the family feud, with an element of blood sport. All men were expected to be hunters and warriors. The Iroquoian nations had long been dependent on agriculture for their sustenance rather than the produce of the hunt, and it was the womenfolk who tended the corn and bean crops. This left the men with time hanging heavy on their hands. Faced with this same dilemma, the ancient Egyptians, the American Aztecs and Mayans built massive pyramids, the medieval Europeans built cathedrals. The Iroquois men, no longer required to demonstrate their prowess as hunters to feed their families, turned to hunting

---

[34] See George T. Hunt, *The Wars of the Iroquois: A Study in Intertribal Trade Relations* (Madison Wisc., 1940) pp. 38–65, and Bruce G. Trigger, *The Huron Farmers of the North* (Toronto, 1969) pp. 36–40.

[35] See H.P. Biggar (ed.), *The Works of Samuel de Champlain* vol. II (Toronto, 1925. Reprinted 1971), pp. 82–106.

humans to display their martial valour and earn prestige. The northern nomadic hunting tribes were kept busy hunting, fishing, gathering in order to survive; they could not afford to lose their hunters in war, hence they were no match for the practised Iroquois warriors. Prisoners were usually subjected to ceremonial torture, intended to inflict the maximum degree of pain for the longest possible time. The warrior, being the epitome of courage, was expected to demonstrate it as effectively when his enemies had him at their mercy as he did when he put some of them to death. He had to submit to this long-drawn-out agony without flinching and without complaint. From childhood, the Indian warriors schooled themselves to bear excruciating pain in order one day, if need be, to meet a warrior's death in the correct manner. Although not all prisoners were treated in this fashion — sometimes they were kept as slaves, or on occasion adopted by their captor's family to replace a kinsman killed in battle — yet it happened with sufficient frequency to govern the nature of Indian warfare. There was no such thing as a sustained campaign. War consisted of a quick raid to inflict casualties, take enemy scalps as a sign of martial prowess, and capture the odd prisoner for the torture ceremony and sadistic pleasure. When these aims were achieved the attackers retired as swiftly as possible. Casualties were, therefore, rarely very heavy.

This mode of warfare was now to change drastically. The introduction of iron weapons and firearms was one factor. Of far greater consequence was the Indians' use of Europeans, with their advanced technology and economic motives, as auxiliary troops. At this stage, that is all the French were. Champlain felt obliged to aid the Algonquins and Hurons against the southern Iroquois to cement his commercial alliance. In 1610 he aided them in an attack on two hundred Iroquois at the mouth of the Richelieu River, destroying them all. The allies, thinking themselves invincible when they had French support, in 1615 demanded that Champlain and his men accompany them in an invasion of Iroquoia. He accepted the more willingly because he hoped, at the successful conclusion of the campaign, to voyage farther west and discover the western ocean, which he believed could not be far distant. This time, however, they were repulsed by the Oneidas. The Iroquois were encouraged by this victory to carry the war to the northern tribes and to the French.

This subordinate role of the European was not to endure for long. Within a few decades the roles were to be reversed. The first step in this change occurred just a few weeks after Champlain and his men had first taken part in the Algonquin-Iroquois war. In mid-September 1609, Henry Hudson's *Half Moon* sailed up the river named after him and carried on a good trade with the natives. Five years later the Dutch had a trading post, Fort Nassau, where Albany stands today. Rival European trading nations were now established on the two rivers that gave access to the interior of the continent. In those early years both were interested only in the fur trade, and the French had decidedly the better of the two locations. The Hudson and Mohawk rivers gave easy access to the St Lawrence and to Lake Ontario, but the French blocked the one and the Iroquois the other. The Dutch could obtain furs only from the Iroquois or the Algonquin tribes to the east. The French, on the other hand, could voyage up the St Lawrence and the Ottawa to the Great Lakes and from there — as they were to do — by way of the Mississippi, the Missouri, and the Saskatchewan across the Great Plains as far as the Rocky Mountains and the Gulf of Mexico. They also had river routes north through the forest and muskeg to Hudson Bay. Moreover, they had the means to do it: the birchbark canoe. An excellent means of transport, requiring only an axe and a knife to construct from material readily available in the northern forest, it could carry heavy loads and, weighing only one or two kilograms per foot of length, was easily transportable around river obstacles. Moreover, these canoes were hard to come by in the region occupied by the Dutch, for the white birch whose bark was the essential commodity did not grow there to the same extent as in the north. Finally, and most important of all, the furs of the cold northern regions were incomparably superior in quality to those from south of the Great Lakes.

The main threat to Champlain's base at Quebec was not the Dutch but rival French traders. With his feeble resources he could not exclude the Bretons, Normands, Rochelois, and Basques who made their way up the St Lawrence almost to Quebec every summer. Too often they obtained the lion's share of the trade. In an attempt to forestall this competition, Champlain and his men moved upriver each summer to the mouth of the St Maurice, one of the main routes from the north, and to the island of Montreal to intercept the northern and western tribes coming to trade. He also sent some of his young men to winter among the western Algonquins and Hurons to learn their language, explore their country, and wean them away from the other traders. In this way the French were drawn into the interior, ever farther westward, and their knowledge of the Great Lakes basin rapidly grew. The Indians, however, were the masters, and the French did their bidding. They were allowed to go only where the Indians permitted; they were the supplicants and had to be grateful for any small concessions the Indians deigned to grant them.

The maintenance of the permanent base at Quebec was rendered very precarious by the lack of adequate working capital. Each year's operations were dependent on the success of the preceding summer's trade. Overhead costs had to be reduced to the minimum, and thus the number of men maintained at Quebec could not be more than was absolutely necessary. The Crown regulation requiring the fur trading companies to establish agricultural settlements was evaded for economic reasons. There was also the fear that settlers would gain control of the trade with the Indians and oblige the company to purchase the furs from them rather than obtain them at first hand.[36] Despite this last danger, Champlain was anxious to see the French outpost on the St Lawrence become something more than a summer trading centre maintained by a corporal's guard the rest of the year. He had had grain sown, and the resulting yield had demonstrated that the country could sustain a sizable population by its own produce. Were farmers to be brought in, the forest cleared, and the land cultivated, the dependence on food supplies transported from France would be removed, and with it the terrible fear of starvation should anything prevent the ships from reaching Quebec.

In 1617 Champlain appealed to the French Chamber of Commerce to undertake a major colonization program. Submitting a

---

[36] Trudel, *Histoire de la Nouvelle-France*, II, p. 261.

detailed estimate of the products the country could provide — fish, fur, timber, minerals, grain, and leather — valued at 6,400,000 livres a year, he requested that three hundred families and a garrison of three hundred soldiers be sent to Quebec. He voiced the fear that unless this were done the Dutch or the English would seize control of the St Lawrence and go on to eliminate the six to seven hundred French ships from the fishery. The cost of this ambitious program, he estimated, would be a modest 45,000 livres a year, and once the water route across the continent to the Pacific was discovered, the customs duties on Asiatic goods using that shorter and safer route would flood the royal coffers. The Chamber of Commerce found this proposal very interesting but thought it something the Crown should undertake.[37] There was, however, no hope of that. In 1617 Louis XIII had taken power into his own hands and was immediately faced with the rebellious great lords now joined by the ousted queen mother. That faction had to be brought to heel. The power of the Huguenots, comprising almost a state within the state, also had to be curbed; and across the Rhine and religious war that was to endure for thirty years threatened to spill over into France.[38] Under these circumstances neither money nor manpower could be spared to convert a distant trading post into a colony.

The Crown could not, and the French business community would not, provide the backing Champlain sought. Only one other agency remained: the Church. When the French clergy had first been approached they had responded with some enthusiasm, but it was to be several years before they were to do anything really effective. Under the Regency, the Catholic revival had begun. The influence of the clergy at the court and throughout the kingdom was growing immeasurably. Prelates dominated the Council of State, the Jesuits had established their colleges to educate the upper classes, new teaching orders were founded, old ones reformed. Some of these orders, in particular the Jesuits and the Capucins, concentrated on bringing the Protestants back into the fold, but it was not long before they began to look farther afield, to dream of converting the pagan hordes of Asia and

[37] H.P. Biggar (ed.) The Works of *Samuel de Champlain*, II, pp. 326–357.
[38] See Ernest Lavisse (ed.), *Histoire de France* (9 vols., Paris, 1905), VI-2, pp. 133–234.

America. In America they had the example of the Spanish and Portuguese to challenge them.

In 1614 the Estates General had met at Paris and the clergy there assembled had approved the proposal that four Récollets, a branch of the Franciscans, be sent to Canada.[39] They had even provided 1,500 livres to defray their expenses. The following year, so eager were these Récollets to begin their work that as soon as they landed at Quebec two of their number left for the mission field, one to Tadoussac, the other to Huronia. Their brave hopes of converting the North American tribes were, however, quickly dashed. To travel with and live among the Indians proved to be almost too much for these mendicants. Sitting cross-legged all day in a canoe wielding a paddle was agony for unaccustomed muscles. Stumbling across a portage in a cassock with a heavy load amid a cloud of mosquitoes and black flies was bad enough, but the Indians showed no mercy. If the monks failed to keep up, they were left behind. Sleeping on the bare ground in all weather and, at the Indian village, in smoke-filled, drafty, flea-ridden bark lodges, racked their aching bodies. Indian food was hard to stomach. But worst of all were the problems of communication, mastering the language, and the Indians' indifference at best, hostility at worst, to the Christian message. They had a religion that sufficed very well for their needs and saw no need to abandon it. Moreover, the Christian religion incorporated a complex and strict moral code, and much of it conflicted with the Indians' own mores.[40]

For the first ten years after their arrival there were never more than four Récollets in Canada, and most of their time they spent at Quebec, making brief forays to the Montagnais at Tadoussac or to Huronia. Being a mendicant order, they lacked the financial resources to mount a great missionary effort. They also lacked the fanatical zeal and the iron-willed discipline that alone would enable a handful of men to come to grips with the task. They did, however, establish the presence of the Church in New France,

---

[39] On this initial missionary effort see Trudel. *Histoire de la Nouvelle-France*, II, pp. 317-351.

[40] See Gabriel Sagard, *The Long Journey to the Country of the Hurons*, trans. and ed. by George M. Wrong (Champlain Society Publications, Toronto, 1939), pp. 167-184, 211-214.

and once it was there it had to be maintained. The Church in France could not allow this foothold to slip away.

It was at this juncture of events that the Society of Jesus re-entered the North American mission field.[41] In 1625 five Jesuits were sent to Quebec, and the following year three more. Unfortunately, this order was the *bête noire* of the Huguenots who controlled La Rochelle and much of the shipping engaged in the Canadian trade. They hampered the Jesuits greatly by refusing to transport their supplies to Quebec. From the beginning of French attempts to establish commercial bases and colonies in both North and South America, the bitter conflict between Huguenot and Roman Catholic had caused trouble. It was becoming increasingly obvious that, huge though the regions claimed by France were, they were not large enough to contain both religions. The Huguenots had shown no desire whatsoever to establish permanent settlements in New France, nor had they made any attempt to convert the Indians to Christianity; instead they put every obstacle in the path of their Catholic compatriots who sought to accomplish these ends. Their obstructive tactics led Cardinal Richelieu, now the King's first minister, to exclude them from New France.[42] Future events were to justify this decision.

Richelieu's aims, however, went much further than mere negative religious measures. He had formulated a very ambitious colonial policy to expand and consolidate French possessions overseas. Whether his main aim was economic, the expansion of overseas trade, or rather a manifestation of *politique de grandeur* and an extension of his anti-Spanish policy is a moot point.[43] At all events, Spanish preoccupation with the religious war in Ger-

---

[41] See E. R. Adair, "France and the Beginnings of New France," *Canadian Historical Review*, XXV (Sept. 1944), pp. 246–278.

[42] In 1625 the wealthy and devout Henri de Lévy duc de Vantadour, on Jesuit urging, had purchased the title of Viceroy of New France and had immediately banned the exercise there of all religions except that of Rome. See Archives Nationales (Paris), Minutier Central des Notaires, Étude VI, p. 431.

[43] The well-documented case for Richelieu's policy's being economic is made by Henri Hauser, *La pensée et l'action économique du Cardinal de Richelieu* (Paris, 1944), pp. 121–142. That the Cardinal's colonial policy was not dominated by economic motives is argued by Bernard Schnapper, "À propos de la doctrine et de la politique coloniale de Richelieu," *Revue d'Histoire des Colonies*, XLII (1954), pp. 314–328.

many allowed the French to gain a foothold in the Caribbean. In 1625 Pierre Belain, sieur d'Esnambuc, established an *habitation* on Saint-Christophe (St Kitts) and, with Richelieu's support, formed a company to colonize the lesser Antilles. Despite the efforts of both the English and the Spanish to dislodge the four hundred French colonists, they managed to hang on, supported more by itinerant Dutch traders who extended them credit than by the French company which, through incompetence and inadequate capital, soon went bankrupt.[44]

It was, however, on Canada that Richelieu concentrated his main effort. Under his auspices, a new company, barred to Huguenots, was formed to develop and exploit the resources of New France, establish self-sufficient agricultural settlements, and foster missionary activity. More than a hundred persons — hence this Company of New France was frequently referred to as the Company of One Hundred Associates — were induced to invest 3,000 livres each to provide working capital. A third of the shareholders were government officeholders, twenty were merchants, the rest were nobles and clergy. Most of the associates were motivated more by religion than by the expectation of profits. The company became seigneur of the lands claimed by France in North America, with a monopoly on all trade except fishing, and the right to concede land in seigneurial tenure to settlers. In return it undertook to establish at least four thousand French and Catholic settlers in its territories within fifteen years. Once again the Crown had delegated to private parties the responsibility for securing French claims to Acadia and Canada. It was, however, a very ambitious undertaking, the greatest colonizing enterprise yet undertaken by France, and it had the full backing of the Crown.

In May 1628, the company sent four hundred settlers with the necessary supplies to Quebec, which still consisted of a small cluster of buildings, only a few of them of stone construction, less than eight hectares of cultivated land that had not yet been touched by a plow, and a population that during the preceding ten years had fluctuated between sixty and eighty-one, all depend-

---

[44] See S. L. Mims, *Colbert's West India Policy* (New Haven, 1912), pp. 14–23.

ent on annual shipments of food supplies from France.[45] The arrival of this initial convoy would have been of great consequence, but it failed to reach its destination. By the time it sailed, England and France were at war, following on the Duke of Buckingham's disastrous attempt to relieve the Huguenot port of La Rochelle, which was besieged by a Royal army. An English privateering expedition led by David Kirke, and with Huguenot aid, captured the convoy in the St Lawrence. Champlain and his men were reduced to grubbing in the forest for roots, and the charity of the Indians, to stave off starvation.

During the ensuing winter David Kirke and his brothers combined their resources with those of a Scot, Sir William Alexander, who in 1621 had obtained a grant of the lands from the St Croix River to the St Lawrence from James I and named his province Nova Scotia. Since the French in Acadia numbered only twenty, reputed to be living like savage beasts, Sir William encountered no opposition when he seized Port Royal in 1627. In July 1629, Lewis and Thomas Kirke were at Quebec with three ships and two hundred men. Champlain, cut off from France, his provisions long since exhausted, had no choice but to surrender.

After more than a century of rather half-hearted endeavour, French sovereignty had been eliminated in North America. First Brazil, then Florida, now Acadia and Canada; it seemed that France was to be denied a colonial empire in the Americas. Yet there was a significant difference this time. The loss of New France had resulted more from bad luck and poor management than overwhelming force. The event was more a conflict between rival business groups—one Anglo-Scots, the other French—than an example of Anglo-French imperial rivalry. Moreover, neither the Kirkes nor Alexander were much concerned with colonizing their acquisitions; commercial profits were all that interested them.

---

[45] The contrast between the French and the English and Dutch colonies is revealing. In 1627, Virginia had a population of some 2,000, New Netherlands 200, New England 310; New France, comprising Canada and Acadia, 107 all told. Trudel, *Histoire de la Nouvelle-France*, II, pp. 437–442.

Chapter 2

Merchants and Missionaries, 1632–1663

Some months prior to the surrender of Quebec to the Kirkes, England had abandoned the Huguenot cause. In April 1629, peace was arranged, and three years later the definitive Treaty of Saint-Germain-en-Laye was signed by Louis XIII and Charles I. One of the terms of that treaty was that all territory seized by the English from the French in North America be returned.

The original capital funds of the Company of New France had been lost in the ill-fated colonizing effort of 1628. Fresh capital in the amounts required could not be raised—certainly not from the Crown. The company was therefore obliged to lease its commercial rights to individuals who fitted out expeditions to retake possession of Acadia and Canada. Isaac de Razilly, one of the Associates of the Company of New France, formed a company for this purpose and in 1632 was appointed lieutenant general for Acadia. Before he was able to accomplish much he died, in 1635, and rival claimants to the trade of the region fought savagely for control, raiding each other's posts, seizing everything that could be carried off, and destroying what could not. The Crown exerted little influence and less control over individuals and events in this distant overseas wilderness.[1] By mid-century there were not more

---

[1] For this period in Acadian history the sources are very meagre; what there are consist largely of denunciations to the Crown by rival claimants. For a detailed account of the conflicts see Gustave Lanctot, *A History of Canada*, Vol. I: *From its Origins to the Royal Regime, 1663* (Cambridge, Mass., 1963), pp. 271–310.

than five hundred settlers in Acadia, but a beginning had been made at agriculture. The diking of the rich tidal marshlands had begun,[2] schools and mills had been built, and the Capucin order, on whom the task of serving the colonists and proselytizing the Indians of Acadia had been conferred, had twelve missionaries in the field.

The inability of the French government to protect its interests in North America was again made plain in 1655 when, in time of peace, a Boston expedition of four ships and five hundred men, raised to attack the Dutch at Manhattan, sailed instead to Acadia and captured Port Royal and the trading posts on the St John River and the Penobscot. The handful of French traders at the latter two posts was removed, but the terms of surrender of Port Royal allowed the French settlers to remain on their land with freedom of worship, and the Capucin monks were granted immunity. Once in possession, however, the New Englanders dishonoured the capitulation terms, thereby establishing a precedent they were religiously to follow in the future. They pillaged the church of all its valuables, killed the father superior, then burned the edifice, and also the fort, to the ground. That brave work done, they sailed back to Boston.

Whether or not Acadia was now an English possession, either de jure or de facto, is extremely doubtful. Since England and France were not then at war, the seizure of the French posts was an act of piracy. The estimated five hundred French settlers remained, and the Bostonians made no attempt to occupy the captured territory. Yet the French government under Cardinal Mazarin made no protest to England. Mazarin was desperately seeking Cromwell's military aid against the Spanish and the Frondeurs led by the Prince de Condé. The negotiations for an alliance proved difficult and drawn out.[3] Mazarin could not allow the dispute in Acadia, involving only a handful of French settlers and quarrelsome traders, to interfere with his plans to end the civil war in France. In fact, rather than demand redress from England,

---

[2] On this diking see Andrew Hill Clark, *Acadia: The Geography of Early Nova Scotia to 1760* (Madison, Wisc., 1968), pp. 161–163, and R. Cole Harris (ed.), Geoffrey J. Matthews (cartographer) *Historical Atlas of Canada* (Toronto, 1987), plate 29.

[3] See A. Cheruel, *Histoire de France sous le ministère de Mazarin* (3 vols., Paris, 1882), II, pp. 353–393.

Mazarin offered to pay Cromwell an indemnity of 600,000 livres for losses claimed to have been suffered at the hands of French privateers. On November 3, 1655, the Treaty of Westminster was finally signed. One of its twenty-nine articles stated that the question of the Acadian posts would be discussed and if agreement could not be reached by the two powers then recourse would be had to arbitration by the Republic of Hamburg. It was not, however, until 1670 that the English grudgingly relinquished their claims to the province and the French were able to reassert their sovereignty.

In the Caribbean the French fared much better. In 1635 the St Christopher plantation company was reorganized under the name Compagnie des Îles d'Amérique, with 75,000 livres in capital, Richelieu's blessing, and 3,000 livres of his private funds. This company, like the Compagnie de la Nouvelle France, was empowered to grant land under seigneurial tenure, raise troops, and build fortifications; it was required to build churches, support the missions, and convert the natives; and most important of all, it was to send to the islands four thousand French and Roman Catholic settlers or indentured workers within twenty years.[4] Unlike in Canada, there was no great missionary drive. The Carib Indians resisted the encroachment on their lands vigorously. By 1640 they had been expelled from Guadeloupe, but in 1653 they ravaged the plantations on some of the smaller islands and came within an inch of driving the French out of Martinique. By 1660, however, they were reduced to some six thousand and forced to come to terms whereby the French "attributed" the islands of St Vincent and Grenada to them in perpetuity.[5]

Meanwhile the islands' economy had developed rapidly. Tobacco and cotton proved profitable staple crops but, unlike the northern fur trade, required a great deal of unskilled labour. Within less than a decade the islands of Martinique, Guadeloupe, Dominica, and several of the smaller of the lesser Antilles had been occupied, and the total white population was estimated at

[4] See Nellis M. Crouse, *French Pioneers in the West Indies (1624–1664)* (New York, 1940); H. I. Priestly, *France Overseas Through the Old Regime: A Study of European Expansion* (New York, 1939).

[5] Gaston-Martin, *Histoire de l'Esclavage dans les Colonies françaises* (Paris, 1948), pp. 11–15.

seven thousand. In 1639 the cultivation of sugar was introduced from Brazil, and at the same time Negro slaves were imported. Very quickly slaves became almost as large an item in the plantation investment as land and buildings, two hundred slaves being required to produce 137 tonnes of sugar a year. They were the chief cargo to the islands. Indigo, tobacco, cotton, ginger, and dye woods were also raised, but sugar soon outstripped them all.[6]

The company, however, reaped little profit from this rapid expansion. Owing to the heavy customs and excise duties on island produce entering France—40 percent on sugar, 50 percent on tobacco, 240 percent on ginger—the islands' trade went to the Dutch who dominated the Atlantic sea lanes. It was they who had introduced sugar into the islands' economy, they who provided the capital for expansion, and they who owned most of the sugar mills. In fact these islands were much more a part of the Dutch empire than of that of France. Although the Crown appointed a lieutenant general for the islands, real power rested with the local governors, whose only concern was the augmentation of their family fortunes. In 1648 the company acknowledged its ineffectualness and sold its title to the governors, who were now recognized for what they had been all along: proprietors of the islands.[7]

Far to the north at Quebec, when the French returned in 1632, forty strong with three Jesuits, they were dismayed to find some of the buildings burned to the ground and others barely habitable. The English had not been good tenants. Yet the French did not have to start completely from scratch. During the two decades that they had held Quebec before its capture by the Kirkes they had established good relations with the northern tribes who alone could provide the better-quality furs; they had gained considerable knowledge of the land and its water routes as far west as Lakes Huron and Erie. Most important of all, they had learned how to survive and travel in the harsh northern environment. The

[6]*Ibid.*, pp. 117–128; F. de Vaux de Foletier, "Les Minutes des Notaires de Saint-Domingue aux Archives du Ministère de la France d'Outre-Mer," *Revue de l'Historie des Colonies françaises*, XXXIX (1951), pp. 295–299; Ch. Schnakenbourg, "Note sur les origines de l'industrie sucrière en Guadeloupe au XVIIᵉ siècle (1640–1670)," *Revue Française d'Histoire d'Outre Mer*, LV, p. 200 (1968), pp. 267–315.

[7] Gaston-Martin, *Histoire de l'Esclavage*, p. 14.

following year Champlain, now appointed governor of the colony for the King as well as for the Company of New France, arrived with three ships loaded with supplies, a squad of soldiers, and workmen, some of the latter accompanied by their families. Permanent settlement had really begun, but the French population at Quebec still numbered only a hundred. During the ensuing thirty years it was to increase to roughly 2,500. The Crown, however, contributed little to this modest growth. The Thirty Years' War raging in Germany, with France directly involved in the military operations from 1635 on, absorbed the energies and the resources of the government. Little time and less money could be spared for strengthening remote colonies when powerful armies threatened Paris.

What was accomplished for France on the mainland of North America was done under the auspices of private enterprise seeking commercial profits in the fur trade, and by the French branch of the Roman Church. To achieve their respective aims, both the merchant traders and the missionaries were completely dependent on the Indians, who alone could provide what each desired—furs and pagan souls for conversion. Fortunately, during the first few years the Indians provided furs in abundance, enough to meet the expenses and allow a profit sufficient to attract continued investment on an annual basis.[8] The trade was not, however, profitable enough to allow the vast expenditure of funds required to establish the minimum two to three hundred settlers a year called for in the company's charter.

The company, dependent on commercial profits in a very risky enterprise, was loath to sink the profits it did make in establishing settlers, at a cost of some 1,000 livres each, in significant numbers. But the danger remained that the Crown would revoke the company's title were it not to discharge this obligation. It therefore resorted to the expedient of granting subfiefs in Canada to

---

[8] In 1626 it was stated that the trade at Quebec amounted to as much as 22,000 furs, more usually 15,000 to 20,000, selling in France for an average 10 livres each. Costs, including a staff of forty at Quebec, two supply ships with a crew of at least 150 men at wages varying from 100 to 300 livres, plus the cost of the supplies and trade goods, must have been on the order of 100,000 livres a year. Financing being on an annual venture basis, there were no reserves, and if no furs were traded two years in a row the consequences were disastrous. For the figures on costs and prices see Reuben Gold Thwaites (ed.), *The Jesuit Relations and Allied Documents* (73 vols., Cleveland, 1896–1901), IV, p. 207.

seigneurs who were required to bring settlers, these settlers to be deducted from the number the company was required to establish in the colony. The first such grant was made in 1634 to Robert Giffard: four kilometres of frontage along the St Lawrence at Beauport near Quebec and nearly seven kilometres deep. Giffard brought out workmen and farm laborers and quickly brought part of his land into production. It was, however, very slow work; working full time, twenty men could clear only thirty arpents a year. Several other members of the lesser nobility accepted fiefs on the same liberal terms, and within thirty years some seventy seigneuries had been conceded to individuals and the Church.[9] By 1640 the population numbered sixty-four families: 158 men, 116 women, 29 Jesuits, 53 soldiers—a total of 356.[10]

To say that this land-tenure system was feudal is really to beg the question. It was accepted in northern France that there could be no land without a lord, that is, a seigneur. The company conceded land to seigneurs in the hope that they would bring settlers, clear the land, strengthen the fur trading base, and discharge the company's obligation to the Crown. Neither the seigneur nor the settlers on his seigneury bought their land, nor did they pay rent; there was no landlord-tenant relationship under the seigneurial system.[11] The seigneur was the vassal of the company and had to acknowledge this by declaring *foi et hommage* when he received his fief. Those to whom he granted lands on his seigneury rendered him *foi et hommage* in turn; they were also required to pay him *cens et rente, lods et vente.*[12] Although at the outset these dues were little more than nominal, their legal reality served to preserve the hierarchical framework of society. The seigneurs had to bend every effort to attract settlers to their concessions; thus they had to make the terms as attractive as

---

[9] Thwaites, *Jesuit Relations*, IX, pp. 153, 155–177; *Rapport des Archives du Québec*, Tome 41 (Imprimeur de Sa Majesté La Reine, Quebec, 1963), Journal des Jésuites, pp. 111, 113; R. C. Harris, *The Seigneurial System in Early Canada* (Univ. of Wisconsin Press, 1966), pp. 20–25.

[10] Dominion Bureau of Statistics, Demography Branch, Ottawa, *Chronological List of Canadian Censuses.*

[11] Until 1717 a seigneur was free to rent land, but there was little incentive to pay rent, except in the towns, when land could be obtained on very favourable terms as a seigneurial grant.

[12] For a succinct study of the seigneurial dues and the revenue derived from them, see Harris, *The Seigneurial System in Early Canada*, pp. 63–81.

possible in the hope that once the land was brought into production the modest seigneurial dues could be collected.

> In the early years the company was rather careless in the size and shape of the seigneurial grants it made, nor did it enforce the obligation to get them settled. In size the concessions varied from more than 330 square kilometres, with several exceeding a hundred, down to less than a hectare within the limits of the towns. The St Lawrence River, the Laurentian Shield, the fur trade, and the Iroquois dictated the area to which settlement was confined. The river was the only communication route, and every concession had to have access to it. The rolling hills of the Shield, with soil sufficient only to sustain poplar, birch, and coniferous trees, run almost parallel to the St Lawrence from the Ottawa River to near Quebec, at a distance of some sixty-five kilometres, but at Quebec the acid-soiled hills approach the river and a few kilometres downstream form a steep shoreline. Land suitable for agriculture was thus confined, on the north shore, to this rather narrow band of flat land, heavily forested with deciduous trees — mostly oak, maple, elm, and hickory, all of them markedly resistant to axe and saw. On the south shore the flat, alluvial plain was wider, but the menace of the Iroquois was an inhibiting factor. West of the island of Montreal there was a wide belt of suitable land, but the company — and after 1663, the Crown — would grant no concessions west of the island, on either the St Lawrence or the Ottawa, since an establishment there would have enabled the settlers to forestall the fur traders at Montreal by intercepting the Indians bringing the furs down from the west. Even without seigneuries in this western zone, forestalling became a serious problem. For all these reasons, therefore, down to the Conquest of Canada, settlement was confined to the St Lawrence Valley from Montreal Island to a point a few kilometres below Quebec.

Although the first concessions were all shapes and sizes, it early became apparent that the important element was river frontage. To avoid disputes over boundaries a main axis for all grants was established at right angles to the river. Seigneuries now became trapezoid in shape. The extent of river frontage was easily established, and the distance the grant extended back from the river was of little consequence until well on in the eighteenth century. Thus, as the land became settled and was divided through inheritance or, on occasion, sale, the seigneuries became narrower, the cultivated fields mere strips running back from the river, a configuration they have retained to the present day.[13]

This land settlement system evolved to meet purely Canadian conditions, and was radically different from anything in Europe. One feature of the European landholding system that would have served a vital purpose in Canada was conspicuously absent: namely, the village. For thirty years the settlements were under almost continual attack, or threat of attack, by the Iroquois and suffered heavy casualties. For security reasons alone the most sensible arrangement would have been to establish villages rather than to have settlers live in isolated homesteads scattered at wide intervals along the river. Although during these years settlement clustered about the three main posts, and the men went to the fields in armed bands, yet whenever there was a surcease from attack the families returned to their isolated farms. Attempts by the Crown in the 1670s and 1680s to establish villages with the fields radiating out from the centre, like spokes of a wheel, were a failure. The settlers, by that time Canadianized, would have none of it. Why this was so can only be guessed at. It may well be that these settlers had unpleasant memories of village life in France, with its constant surveillance by seigneurial, ecclesiastical, and royal authorities, with the attendant extortions, chicanery, and petty tyranny. They may well have regarded the chance to be done with all that as one of the great benefits offered by the colony, one that they certainly refused to relinquish. Then again, in France, villages were mainly inhabited by landless labourers. In Canada any man could have all the land he could work for the asking; there was no landless proletariat. The economic basis for villages was absent.

---

[13] The Coutume de Paris required that *censitaires* bequeath their land to their children equally; thus, over the years the concessions became ever more narrow, since the less enterprising preferred a small strip of cleared land in familiar surroundings to moving to a new seigneury where larger grants of forest land were available. In 1723 one *censitaire* held a strip four metres wide and more than five kilometres deep. In 1745 the Crown called a halt. An Ordonnance du Roi forbade anyone to build a house, stable, or barn on a concession measuring less than one and a half arpents (approximately 100 metres) frontage by thirty arpents depth (2 kilometres), on pain of a 100-livre fine and destruction of the buildings. See *Édits et ordonnances royaux, déclarations et arrêts du Conseil d'État du Roi concernant le Canada* (Quebec, 1854), pp. 585–586.

During the formative thirty-year period after 1632, self-preservation demanded compulsory military service. Most likely, many of the immigrants had never fired a gun before their arrival in Canada, but upon arrival they quickly had to master the art of musketry in order to survive. Moreover, they depended on hunting for much of their meat supply. In short order every Canadian male became an irregular soldier, an expert guerrilla fighter in a war that had a high casualty rate. By 1652, of the first forty settlers at Trois Rivières fewer than ten had survived the Iroquois assaults; and in that year, 1652, the governor of the fort, along with twenty-one settlers and garrison soldiers, were killed. The following year six hundred Iroquois laid siege to the post, launched assault after assault for nine days, but were eventually forced to retire by the garrison of forty, many of them lads in their teens.[14] But the French could not remain prisoners in their forts forever. When the enemy appeared nowhere in evidence and the French ventured out to hunt, to work their fields, or to voyage to the Indian villages in search of furs, too often they were ambushed. Some years later a governor of the colony described this manner of waging war from personal experience: "They are everywhere. They will stay hidden behind a stump for ten days, existing on nothing but a handful of corn, waiting to kill a man, or a woman. It is the cruelest war in the world. They are not content to burn the houses, they also burn the prisoners they take, and give them death only after torturing them continually in the most cruel manner they can devise."[15]

These were the rules of war that the Canadians had to accept. From the very early years they learned to fight with the utmost desperation, no quarter asked or given, with little regard for death, since it was infinitely preferable to being taken alive by the enemy. From 1633 until the end of the century the Canadians

---

[14] See *Dictionary of Canadian Biography*, Vol. II, *1701 to 1740* (Toronto, 1969), pp. 83–84; *Word from New France: The Selected Letters of Marie de l'Incarnation*, trans. and ed. by Joyce Marshall (Toronto, 1967), p. 209. Between 1608 and 1666, 191 settlers were killed by the Iroquois, out of a population that numbered 675 in 1650, and 3,035 in 1663. See John A. Dickinson "La guerre iroquoise et la mortalité en Nouvelle-France, 1608–1666," *Revue d'histoire de l'Amérique française*, v. 36, no. 1, juin 1982, pp. 31–54.

[15] *Rapport de l'Archiviste de la Province de Québec 1939–1940*, p. 445, MM de Vaudreuil et Raudot au Ministre, Québec, 14 Nov. 1708.

enjoyed fewer than fifteen years of peace. The first two generations of settlers became, of necessity, as skilled at guerrilla warfare as their Iroquois foe.[16] This military tradition early became
one of the dominant features of the emerging Canadian society.

During these years the situation was so grim that some settlers
gave up and returned to France. Fears were expressed that the
colony would have to be abandoned unless military aid were sent
from the mother country. All that kept many of the settlers in the
besieged colony was the reluctance to abandon everything that
they had worked and fought so hard to establish, to return to
France penniless, there to face misery and likely starvation.[17] The
company, from time to time, sent a few workmen to the colony,
but they would go only on short-term contracts and at high wages.
The queen mother, responding to appeals from the Jesuits, sent
out a few soldiers, but these reinforcements too often did not
match the casualties. In 1647 there were a hundred soldiers in
garrison at the three centres of settlement. The following year
their complement was reduced to sixty-eight.[18]

The agency mainly responsible for the development and expansion of the colony during these years was the Church. The company granted it almost twenty land concessions, ranging from
small building plots of a few arpents in the towns to very large
seigneuries outside. The Church also purchased a good deal of
property from time to time until it controlled a little more than a
quarter of the conceded land. Considering the services rendered
to the colony by the clergy, this landholding was by no means
excessive.[19] Unlike some who received seigneuries from the company, the Church made a determined effort to get their lands
cleared and settled. The Jesuits brought workmen to clear sections
before conceding it to settlers, thereby allowing them to begin
raising crops within a year of their arrival. This required the

---

[16] See D'Auteuil, Mémoire sur l'état présent du Canada, 12 déc. 1715, in *Rapport de l'Archiviste de la Province de Québec, 1922–1923*, p. 59.

[17] *Word from New France*, p. 182.

[18] Gustave Lanctot, "Les troupes de la Nouvelle-France," *Canadian Historical Association Report, 1926*, pp. 40–44.

[19] Harris, *The Seigneurial System in Early Canada*, p. 42; Marcel Trudel, *The Seigneurial Regime* (Canadian Historical Association, Historical Booklet No. 6, Ottawa, 1967). After the Crown took over the colony in 1663 the acquisition of land by the Church was actively discour-
aged, and in 1743 it was forbidden by royal decree.

investment of considerable capital with no prospect of an appreciable financial return for a good many years, but the Jesuits were able to obtain sizable donations from wealthy and pious individuals eager to further the missionary effort in the New World.[20]

One means employed to stimulate such donations and to recruit colonists was the publication of the annual Jesuit *Relations*, begun in 1632 and continued until 1673. Each year the missionaries in the Canadian field wrote reports of their activities to the superior at Quebec, who edited them for publication and added his own general report as introduction. The *Relations* were then submitted to the provincial of the order in Paris, who did the final editing before sending them to the printer. These *Relations* appear to have had a wide circulation among the devout of the small educated class. How many people the publication caused to contribute financially to Canada, or to emigrate to the colony, can never be known, but that it did have considerable effect cannot be doubted.[21]

All of this resulted from the religious revival that swept over France during the first half of the century. New orders, lay and religious, such as the Sulpicians, the Oratorians, and the Compagnie du Saint-Sacrement, were established to combat heresy, raise the religious and moral tone of society, and convert the pagan in all parts of the world. Canada was one of the chief beneficiaries of the movement, whose main purpose was, of course, the conversion of the pagan Indians to Christianity. The charter of the Company of New France declared this to be its main objective, and what is even more significant, Clause XVII declared that any Indians who embraced Christianity and became practising members of the Roman Church were, without any further formality, to be accepted as French subjects with all the

---

[20] Gustave Lanctot, *A History of Canada*, I, 218, states that between 1626 and 1655 the Jesuits received bequests and subsidies totaling 160,400 livres plus 90,000 livres specifically for defense. Unfortunately Dr. Lanctot cites a collection of sources to cover all the information given in a paragraph. It is thus very difficult to discover which of the eight sources cited refers to this particular statement. In any event I suspect that the amount cited is too low. Even so, given the colony's annual budget of 45,000 livres, the total of 250,400 livres expended by the clergy, spread over the thirty-year period, amounted to 20 percent of the budget.

[21] For the history of the Jesuit *Relations*, which is the most important single source for the history of Canada during the period of company government, see Joseph P. Donnelly, S.J., *Thwaites' Jesuit Relations, Errata and Addenda* (Chicago, 1967), pp. 1–26.

rights and privileges appertaining, including the right to settle in France whenever they wished and acquire and dispose of property there as would a subject born in the kingdom. Although this proved to be of no actual consequence, because the Indians were not interested in the offer, it was honestly meant. Certainly no other European colonizing power advanced such a civilized concept.[22] Moreover, in order to achieve this aim those settlers sent to the colony had to be carefully selected to prevent vice from gaining a foothold. What the directors and associates of the Company of New France were eager to establish was "a New Jerusalem, blessed by God and made up of citizens destined for heaven."[23]

The Jesuits declared that many of the settlers came to begin life afresh in the northern wilderness in order to lead more pious lives in greater freedom and to be far removed from the violence, chicanery, perfidy, cheating, and the grasping extortions of the law courts that were part and parcel of life in Old France.[24] Although the civil authority, in the person of the governor, seconded the efforts of the clergy to construct this new society on puritanical lines, it proved impossible to recruit enough settlers and indentured labourers of the desired high moral standard. The colony had to accept what it could get, and by 1636 the stocks at Quebec had their occupants, condemned for such crimes as blasphemy, drunkenness, or failing to attend Mass on a feast day.[25] Of more serious crimes, however, there is little mention, and the administration of justice appears not to have proved too onerous a task for the local governors to whom this responsibility was entrusted.

One concrete contribution of the Church was the establishment of urban institutions at a much earlier date, and of vastly superior quality, than the handful of colonists could ever have provided for themselves. In 1635 the Jesuits, having received an endow-

---

[22] Professor Marcel Trudel dwelt on this policy in his paper "Français et Algonquiens: Le choc des cultures," read to the International Colloquium on Colonial History at the University of Ottawa, November 1969.

[23] *Rapport des Archives du Québec*, Tome 41 (1963), pp. 109–110, premières pages du Journal des Jésuites, 1634–1635.

[24] *Ibid.*, p. 10.

[25] *Ibid.*, p. 43.

ment of 64,000 livres for the purpose, established a college to educate the sons of the colonists. Classes began that year, a year before Harvard was established, and the following year they moved into their own college building. The Jesuits claimed that some of the settlers had asserted that they would never have contemplated coming to the colony without the knowledge that their children would be afforded a good education.[26] The college was a pronounced success from the start, and for the ensuing 124 years it provided the Canadian upper class with as good an education for their sons as could have been obtained for them in France.

In 1639, largely under the stimulus of the Jesuits, the first women's orders established themselves at Quebec. In that year three Ursulines and three nursing sisters—to give the latter their proper title, Hospitalières de la Miséricorde de Jésus de l'Ordre de Saint Augustin—arrived to found a school and a hospital for Indian girls. It was believed that if they were educated and given proper care when sick, they would be persuaded to abandon their nomadic existence, adopt a sedentary mode of life, and eventually be assimilated into French Christian civilization. These hopes proved to be vain. The Indians did not regard the French way of life as superior to their own; just the reverse, in fact.[27] Indian children were particularly adamant. They refused to submit to school discipline; when left with the sisters by their parents they fled at the first opportunity and sought out their families in the depths of the forest. Those of them who fell ill preferred their own remedies to the French nostrums, bleeding and purges, and to being incarcerated in the hospital ward. The good sisters, despite their disappointment, did not despair.[28] Rather than admit failure and abandon their mission they remained to cater to the needs of the French settlers, soldiers, and workmen. The casualties inflicted by the Iroquois alone required the continuance of their work.

---

[26] *Ibid.*, p. 113, Journal des Jésuites de Québec, 1635–1636.

[27] On this "Frenchification" policy see Jean Delanglez, *Frontenac and the Jesuits* (Chicago, 1939), p. 36.

[28] A revealing commentary on the religious climate of the age — which did not endure much longer — is afforded by the desire of these nursing sisters to acquire grace by subjugating their senses in the undertaking of repulsive tasks. See *Word from New France*, p. 75.

The main purpose of this New Jerusalem on the banks of the St Lawrence was, however, to further the great work: the conversion of the Indian nations to Christianity. The Jesuits, upon their return to Quebec in 1633, had immediately set about establishing missions at Tadoussac, Miscou on the Gulf of St. Lawrence, and Huronia. It was at Huronia that they made their great effort. The Hurons, being a sedentary nation dependent largely on the raising of corn, beans, and squash and on fishing for their food supply, offered a much better field for proselytization than did the nomadic, hunting Montagnais and Abenaquis of the lower St Lawrence. In 1636 Father Charles Garnier wrote: "If Canada in my view is a holy and sacred temple built by God, the country of the Hurons is the *sancta sanctorum*. It is of all the country where we are, the field where our fathers hope to establish the most beautiful mission because they are a stable nation and not vagabonds like most of the others."[29] They were also much more numerous, estimated to be eighteen to thirty thousand souls residing in some twenty-five villages between Lake Simcoe and Georgian Bay.[30] Long before the French appeared on the scene they had been a trading nation, exchanging their surplus corn for tobacco, dried meat, native copper, and other goods from the surrounding tribes. Since their own immediate area was denuded of fur-bearing animals, they bartered corn and French goods with the northern Algonquin tribes for furs, which they then traded to the French.

Prior to the English interregnum, 1629–1632, the Récollet and Jesuit missionaries had experienced great difficulty owing to the presence in Huronia of French fur traders who, although popular with the Indians, were considered by the missionaries to be a great hindrance to their work of conversion. Many of these young men preferred Indian mores to Christian ones, bedded down with the Indian girls, who did not hold premarital chastity in any esteem, and were a living refutation of the way of life the missionaries espoused and wished to impose on the Indians. The

---

[29] *Rapport de l'Archiviste de la Province de Québec, 1929–1930*, p. 8.

[30] George T. Hunt, *The Wars of the Iroquois* (Madison, Wisc., 1940), gives an estimate of 30,000. Bruce G. Trigger, *The Huron Farmers of the North* (New York, 1969), pp. 11–13, in a careful analysis of the available evidence, suggests that 18,000 is a more realistic figure.

Associates of the Company of New France, with their deep concern for missionary work, decided to stop all that by entrusting the Jesuits with the maintenance of good trade relations with the Hurons. This led to accusations that they were more concerned with fur trade profits than with the conversion of savage souls, but these charges have no basis in fact. The Hurons showed little inclination to accept the religious beliefs of the French, but they were avid for their trade goods. They accepted the austere, vexing missionaries in their midst only because the French insisted on this as a condition of their trade alliance.[31] For their part, the Jesuits accepted the commercial responsibility because without the fur trade the entire French effort would have had to be abandoned. As Sister Marie de l'Incarnation of the Ursulines put it: "If there is no trade, no more ships will come here. If ships no longer come we shall lack all things necessary for life, such as cloth, linens, and the greater part of our food . . . if trade fails . . . the Savages, who stop here only to trade, will scatter in the woods."[32]

The Jesuits established missions in four of the principal Huron villages and in 1639 constructed a central mission, Sainte-Marie, on the Wye River near Midland Bay. This base, surrounded by a palisade with stone bastions, comprised a residence for the *donnés* — pious laymen who had contracted to serve the order as artisans or labourers — a chapel, a hospital, a forge, a mill, stables, and a hospice to which the missionaries in the field could return to rest and recuperate. By 1647 there were eighteen priests and twenty-four laymen in Huronia.[33] In addition to proselytizing, they gave shelter to all who asked, feeding as many as three thousand persons during the course of a year.

The task of converting the Huron nation to Christianity proved to be far more difficult than the Jesuits had imagined it would be. The Roman religion of the French was embodied in a complex liturgy that appealed to all the senses; the stations of the cross, music, incense, rich vestments for the priests, silver altar vessels,

---

[31] This aspect of the French presence in Huronia is succinctly explained by Trigger, "The French Presence in Huronia," *Canadian Historical Review* XLIX, 2 (June 1968), pp. 123–127.

[32] *Word from New France*, p. 185.

[33] Thwaites, *Jesuit Relations*, XXXIII, pp. 75–79.

all contained and displayed in massive buildings constructed for this sole religious purpose. The first French settlers therefore did not believe that the Indians had any concept of religion at all, only some silly superstitions at best, since they lacked all the physical manifestations that made European religious practices discernible. Mastering the language was no easy task for the missionaries. Eventually they came to realize that the Hurons were possessed of religious beliefs that were woven into the entire fabric of their culture.[34] To them all animate things were possessed of a spirit. Some spirits were good, some bad; the latter had to be appeased. The Hurons also had their priests, shamans, who communicated with the spirit world, gave advice, and healed the sick. Although they had a belief in a supreme being and of a life after death, they had no concept of a hell, and the abstract beliefs of the Christian faith were not easily conveyed. As Father Paul Le Jeune sadly remarked, "The Catholic teachings are newer to these barbarians than the operations of Algebra would be to a person who could only count to ten."

The Jesuits at first regarded the religious beliefs of all the Indians as the work of Satan, and every setback was attributed to his efforts. This made it very difficult for them to understand the Indians' point of view. The hostility they manifested toward these beliefs and social customs did not make the task of conversion any easier; just the reverse, in fact. Moreover, they had to be sure that those they succeeded in instructing and admitting to the faith by baptism would not become apostates. This problem they resolved in Manichean fashion by baptizing only the moribund, thereby ensuring that there would be no backsliding. When the Indians noted that baptism was closely followed by death, they were swift to attribute the loss of a member of their family to the ministrations of the priest. They therefore did their best to forfend the rite, and the Jesuits were obliged to render it surreptitiously. The brave hope of converting the entire Huron nation came to seem almost impossible of fulfillment without divine intervention. This led the missionaries to the conviction that they could hope to succeed only after some at least of their number

---

[34] See I. H. Kennedy, *Jesuit and Savage in New France* (New Haven, 1950), and André Vachon, "L'eau de vie dans la société indienne," *Canadian Historical Association Report, 1960*.

had suffered a martyr's death. Moreover, they craved immolation for personal reasons.[35]

The number of Hurons the Jesuits succeeded in baptizing rose astronomically between 1635 and 1640 when a European disease to which the Indians had no resistance swept through Huronia, reducing their numbers by half. The Hurons were quick to blame the Jesuits for this disaster. Only the need to maintain trade relations with the French prevented the Hurons from granting all the missionaries the martyrdom they each coveted.

This epidemic had no sooner run its course than the Iroquois began a concerted campaign to destroy the Huron nation. Their motives have long been a subject of controversy. To Francis Parkman, writing in the 1860s, it was insensate blood lust.[36] More recently, George T. Hunt and Bruce Trigger have maintained that the motive was economic; Hunt claimed that the Iroquois sought to divert the northern fur trade from Montreal to Albany, with themselves acting as middlemen.[37] Trigger maintains that they sought to obtain furs by pillaging the Huron and Algonquin fur brigades.[38] Both these hypotheses are refuted by the fact that, of 147 recorded Iroquois raids on the Hurons and French between 1626 and 1666, on only seven occasions were furs or other goods seized. On most occasions the furs were left to rot.[39] Allen W. Trelease disputes that the Iroquois fought mainly for trade, asserting instead that their real aim was to seize territory from the Hurons.[40] This hypothesis is more in accord with the evidence.

---

[35] That the Jesuits craved martyrdom is attested to by their own frequent and fervent declarations. See, for example, Thwaites, *Jesuit Relations*, XVII, XXV, XXXIV, XXXV, *passim*. In 1640 Marie de l'Incarnation wrote to her son: "It is possible that we shall have a martyr in his person [Father Joseph-Antoine Poncet de La Rivière] which will cause great jealousy to the others, who sigh incessantly after this high grace. We have an agreement with the Reverend Fathers that if this good fortune befalls them we shall sing the *Te Deum* and in return they will grant us a share in the merit of their sacrifice . . . they seek only to suffer for Jesus Christ and gain souls for him." *Word from New France*, pp. 83–84.

[36] See Parkman *The Jesuits in North America*, various editions, introduction.

[37] See Hunt, *Wars of the Iroquois*, p. 36.

[38] Bruce G. Trigger, "The French Presence in Huronia: The Structure of Franco-Huron Relations in the First Half of the Seventeenth Century," *Canadian Historical Review*, XLIX, 2 (June 1968); Trigger, "The Destruction of Huronia: A Study in Economic and Cultural Change, 1609-1650," *Transactions of the Royal Canadian Institute*, 33, No. 68, Pt. I, pp. 14–45.

[39] *Native Studies Review*, 2, No. 2 (1986), pp. 144–5, Review of Bruce G. Trigger, *Natives and Newcomers: Canada's "Heroic Age" Reconsidered*, by Conrad E. Heidenreich.

[40] Allen W. Trelease, *Indian Affairs in Colonial New York: The Seventeenth Century* (Cornell Univ. Press, 1960), pp. 118–20.

Certainly the Hunt-Trigger thesis has no evidence to support it, and it attributes European values and motives to the Indians, making of them capitalist entrepreneurs in moccasins, out to make a profit. That sort of behaviour was totally alien to the Indian character.

An explanation for Iroquois foreign policy, more in keeping with the evidence and the Indian psyche, is that the Five Nations Iroquois Confederacy sought, not furs, but security. Surrounded on all sides by hostile Indian nations who feared and hated them, and by the Dutch, the English, and the French, they sought to crush or scatter their Indian foes in order to establish territorial buffer zones.[41] This they did systematically, attacking their foes one by one. First the Mohawks drove the Mahicans eastward to the Connecticut valley, thereby securing Mohawk access to Albany. Then it was the turn of the Hurons, followed by the Eries and the so-called Neutrals. The Ojibway were driven far to the west and the Montagnais attacked at the watershed to James Bay.[42] In 1676 the Susquehannocks, weakened by treacherous attacks by large forces of Virginia and Maryland militia, made their peace with the Five Nations, and were assimilated by them.[43] In all these assaults the Iroquois took the scalps of those they had slain to prove their individual valour and prowess as warriors; more significantly, they always took large numbers of prisoners, some few for the torture ceremony, to appease the uneasy spirits of their own fallen warriors, but most were assimilated to replace their own heavy losses in this interminable war, and from the ravages of European diseases. Some of the Five Nations comprised fewer members of Iroquois descent than assimilated persons of other nations.[44] In an early campaign, the Oneidas lost so

---

[41] See *Historical Atlas of Canada*, plates 33, 35; Madeleine et Jacques Rousseau, "La crainte des Iroquois chez les Mistassins," *Revue d'histoire de l'Amérique française*, vol. 2, 1948–9, pp. 13–26; Thwaites, *Jesuit Relations*, vol. 47, pp. 125–243.

[42] Thwaites, *Jesuit Relations*, vol. 51, pp. 230, 242; vol. 58, p. 226; vol. 60, p. 172; *Calendar of State Papers Colonial and West Indies 1675–76*, # 936, p. 398.

[43] Thwaites, *Jesuit Relations*, vol. 49, p. 233; vol. 51, pp. 123, 186; vol. 52, pp. 52–54. On this policy of assimilation see the pregnant article by Susan Johnson, "Epidemics: The Forgotten Factor in Seventeenth Century Warfare in the St. Lawrence Region," in Bruce Alden Cox (ed.), *Native People, Native Lands*, (Ottawa, 1987).

[44] Thwaites, *Jesuit Relations*, vol. 27, p. 297 (Cited in Francis Jennings (ed.), *The History and Culture of Iroquois Diplomacy* (Syracuse University Press, 1985), p. 129.

many warriors that they had to ask the Mohawks to lend them some of their men to restock the nation. Thus, by adroit strategy and ruthless tactics, the Five Nations, in the second half of the seventeenth century, emerged as an Imperial Power in North America, the most powerful military force on the continent. Their Achilles heel was logistics; their increasing dependence on European firearms and iron weapons, obtained from the Dutch, then the English, traders at Albany.

The French were very fearful that a trade alliance would be established between the Iroquois and Hurons, fearing that it might lose them the bulk of the trade. Whenever any such overtures were made they did their best, with considerable success, to disrupt them. From Champlain's day to the Conquest, French policy was to preserve the Iroquois as a barrier between first the Dutch then the English on the Hudson River, and the northwestern tribes, for both economic and military reasons. They certainly did not, however, wish to see the Iroquois gain ascendancy. Yet when, in 1648, the Iroquois launched mass assaults on the Huron villages they could do nothing. By 1649 the Huron villages were destroyed, Sainte-Marie had to be abandoned and burned, hundreds of Hurons were slaughtered, and three Jesuit missionaries achieved martyrdom. Only ashes and charred corpses marked where the Huron confederacy and the great Jesuit mission had endured. Many of the Hurons were absorbed into the Iroquois tribes, and some three hundred made their way to Quebec, where they dragged out a bleak existence until they too were decimated by further Iroquois attacks and disease. Another remnant fled west and gained sanctuary among the Ottawas.[45] The Jesuits salvaged what they could. During the actual Iroquois assaults they baptized perhaps as many as five thousand of the Hurons, many of them en masse as they were slaughtered or consumed in the flames of their long houses. To a degree, therefore, the missionaries succeeded in their aim of saving the souls of at least half of the Huron nation and were satisfied that although the

---

[45] The most detailed and graphic account of these events is contained in the Jesuit *Relations*. Francis Parkman made good use of them in his *The Jesuits in North America* (Boston, 1867); in fact, much of this particular work is little more than a paraphrase. The most recent study of the destruction of the Hurons is contained in Bruce Trigger, *The Children of Aataentsic. A History of the Huron People to 1660* (Montreal & London, 1976) vol. II, pp. 725–826.

victims had been lost to this world they had been saved for eternity in the next. In all of this they saw the working of God's inscrutable will, and although Huronia was no more, they consoled themselves with the thought that the Hurons could no longer hinder them from voyaging farther west and south through the Great Lakes to nations even more numerous than the Huron. By the same token the route to the west was open to the French fur traders. Within a very few years they had voyaged to the western end of Lake Superior.

Another accomplishment, under clerical auspices and of far greater consequence than the Huronia mission, was the foundation of Montreal.[46] More specifically, it was the creation of the influential secret society, the Compagnie du Saint-Sacrement, composed of wealthy, powerful, extremely devout laymen and clerics dedicated to puritanical religious reform, charitable works, the extirpation of heresy, and the conversion of the heathen in foreign parts.[47] Taking counsel with Jesuits who had served in the colony, six members of the clandestine Compagnie (including Jean-Jacques Olier, founder of Saint-Sulpice), referring to themselves as "Messieurs les associés pour la conversion des Sauvages de la Nouvelle France en l'Île de Montréal," formed the Société de Notre Dame de Montréal.[48] On December 17, 1640, the Company of New France granted the greater part of the island of Montreal to the society, there to establish a mission settlement remote and independent from the main settlement at Quebec. It was believed that such a settlement, endowed with a church, a school, and a hospital, would induce the Indians to

---

[46] See E. R. Adair, "France and the Beginnings of New France," *Canadian Historical Review*, XXV (Sept. 1944), and "The Evolution of Montreal under the French Regime," *Canadian Historical Association Report, 1942*; Léon Gérin, *Aux Sources de Notre Histoire* (Montreal, 1946), pp. 162–191. A seventeenth-century account is Dollier de Casson's manuscript "Histoire du Montréal" at the Bibliothèque Mazarine, Paris. An accurate transcript was made by the Public Archives of Canada, then edited and translated by Ralph Flenley, *A History of Montréal, 1640–1672* (Toronto, 1928). Étienne-Michel Faillon, *Histoire de la colonie française en Canada*, (3 vols., Montreal, 1865–66), gives a very detailed account of events, citing his sources, some of which are no longer extant.

[47] On the role of the Compagnie du Saint-Sacrement see E. R. Adair, "France and the Beginnings of New France."

[48] Marie-Claire Daveluy, *La société de Notre-Dame de Montréal* (Montréal et Paris, 1965) A useful bibliographical and biographical study of the Company. Included is a facsimile reproduction of "Les véritables motifs de Messieurs et Dames de la société de Notre Dame de Montréal pour la Conversion des Sauvages de la nouvelle France." M.DC.XXXXIII.

settle permanently on the island in order to enjoy the benefits offered by these sophisticated institutions. They could then the more easily be converted to Christianity. Montreal was chosen specifically because of its remoteness and also because the island was located at the confluence of the two great water routes to the west, the Ottawa and the St Lawrence, making it easily accessible to a large number of Indian nations.

The society chose as the governor of the new colony Paul de Chomedey, sieur de Maisonneuve, a devout thirty-year-old army officer who was to demonstrate outstanding qualities of leadership for the ensuing quarter-century. He regarded the enterprise as a holy crusade, and his great piety was matched only by his courage. A young woman, Jeanne Mance, equally devout, volunteered her services to care for the sick, and seventy men of various skilled and unskilled trades were recruited to serve for a three-year term. When they arrived at Quebec in August 1641, it was too late in the season to proceed to Montreal. The people at Quebec were having a desperate time defending themselves against the Iroquois. They had suffered heavy casualties, and it was not easy to obtain replacements from France. To them, the advent of Maisonneuve and his followers appeared as God-sent reinforcements, but were they to proceed to Montreal it seemed certain they would be destroyed. The governor, Charles-Jacques Huault de Montmagny, and the settlers did their best to dissuade the newcomers from going upriver. Maisonneuve, however, was adamant. His orders were to establish a separate, independent settlement at Montreal, regardless of the danger. The following spring therefore they pushed on to their intended destination, and before the summer was out they had established themselves on the island in huts surrounded by a log palisade. Enough land was cleared to plant a little wheat and peas, and to graze the two oxen, three cows, and twenty sheep that had survived the voyage. The Iroquois, busy elsewhere, never anticipating such a daring move, failed to appear. This the settlers attributed to divine intervention.

This mission settlement, named Ville-Marie, was a unique endeavour. It came into being for purely altruistic reasons: to serve the Indian population in this world and gain entry for as many as possible into the next. For the first two decades a very puritanical religious way of life dominated the community. Commerce, and the commercial spirit, however, soon overtook religion as the main concern of the residents. The town's location was too well suited for the fur trade for it to be otherwise.

Perhaps the most interesting aspect of the experiment was that a small unit of seventeenth-century French society was successfully transplanted across the Atlantic and set down in the North American wilderness, three days' travel removed from the nearest French outpost, and with the Iroquois swarming all about. Both Quebec and Trois Rivières had begun as fortified commercial counters; settlement and such institutions as the Church, a school, and a hospital came later. Montreal incorporated all these institutions almost from the beginning.[49] Despite heavy losses suffered from Iroquois attacks, and a heavy turnover as indentured workers returned to France at the expiration of their contracts, the beleaguered settlement survived and managed to increase its numbers to 596 by 1663, including a goodly number of women and children.

What is even more remarkable is the way in which this fragment preserved the basic features of the hierarchical parent society. There is little evidence of the egalitarianism, or democracy, of the frontier. The only change in social structure is one of degree. French society in the seventeenth century was marked by considerable social mobility as members of the *roturier* class moved up the economic scale through commerce, and the commercial element clawed its way up the social scale into the *noblesse de robe*. In Montreal this social mobility tended to accelerate, and a few very talented men were able to move from the lowest order, that of soldier or indentured servant, into the ranks of the nobility in one generation.

From the outset, the three orders, clergy, nobles, commons, were represented. By 1663 the clergy numbered three priests, four nursing sisters on the staff of the Hôtel Dieu, and four teaching sisters of the Congrégation de Notre-Dame. There were thirty members of the lesser nobility, fourteen separate families,

---

[49] By 1655 it even had a prepaid medicare scheme. In that year surgeon Étienne Bouchard contracted with 26 families to provide them with his services for an annual fee of five livres.

who all enjoyed an elevated social status in the colony. When, in 1663, Maisonneuve formed the settlers into twenty militia companies of seven men each and ordered them to select their own officers by majority vote, the nobles were all elected; no noble served under the orders of a commoner.[50]

Among the third estate, social gradations reflecting those of France quickly developed. At the top of this part of the scale were the merchants, eight of them, a number made possible by, and indicating the extent of, the fur trade. Two of them, Charles Le Moyne and his brother-in-law Jacques Le Ber, both of humble origins, made sizable fortunes in this trade and were ennobled, the former for valiant service during the Iroquois wars, the latter by purchasing a *lettre d'annoblissement* for 6,000 livres. The other Montreal merchant families of this period took longer to move up the scale. Most of them held seigneuries, intermarried, and came to form the colonial dominant class, very conscious of their elevated economic and social status.

Beneath them was the lower order, made up of artisans professing all manner of trades, and common labourers. Many of them came to the colony on short-term contracts at relatively high wages, 60 to 100 livres a year, plus their food,[51] and they expected to return to France when their contracts expired. The Crown encouraged artisans to move to the colonies by promising that those who remained there ten years thereby acquired master's privileges and upon their return to France could set up shop as *maîtres de chef d'oeuvre*.[52] Some, however, chose to remain, and a distinction was made between the two groups. Anyone who cleared four arpents of land—three years' labour for one man—and declared his intention to settle permanently was given the civil status of *habitant* to distinguish him from the nonpermanent

---

[50] Marcel Trudel, *Montréal la formation d'une société 1642–1663* (Montréal, 1976), p. 39.

[51] See Roland-J. Auger, *La grande recrue de 1653* (Montréal, 1955), p. 15. Moreover, in France at least a third, perhaps one-half, of the product of a peasant family's labours was drained off in taxes of one sort or another. The colonists in Canada were not taxed. They paid only very modest seigneurial dues and were tithed at half the rate of northern France. For the economic condition of the French peasantry see Fernand Braudel and Ernest Labrousse, *Histoire économique et sociale de la France* (4 vols., Paris, 1970–), II, pp. 88–92.

[52] E. E. Rich and C. H. Wilson (eds.), *The Cambridge Economic History of Europe*, Vol. IV (Cambridge, 1967), p. 268.

wage earners.[53] Those who chose to become self-employed land-holders received a grant of thirty arpents and a gratuity from the Société varying in amount from 400 to 1,000 livres; enough for a family to live for a year, build a house, and furnish it with the essentials.[54] An added inducement was that only *habitants* were permitted to engage in the fur trade for their private profit. The sole stipulation was that they sell the furs they obtained in trade with the Indians to the charter company.[55]

Despite these favourable terms, in 1663 fewer than half of the *roturier* class, 284 of 539, were classed as *habitants*.[56] Conditions at Montreal — in fact throughout all of New France — at mid-century were hardly calculated to encourage people to opt for permanent residence. The Iroquois roamed about the settlements at will, from Montreal to Tadoussac, pouncing upon the unwary, dragging them off to be burned slowly to death in the villages of the Five Nations, slaughtering them on the spot if they put up too much resistance. Only the handful of reinforcements sent from time to time by the Company of New France, by the Société de Notre Dame, and on occasion by the Crown allowed the population to hold its own and even show a modest increase. By 1650 the total population was estimated to be two thousand, but the casualties were such that it was feared the colony would have to be abandoned unless help were sent from France.[57]

At Montreal the number of men capable of bearing arms was reduced to fifty.[58] Maisonneuve crossed to France to plead for aid. He succeeded in enlisting 153 recruits to serve for a five-year term, paying them a year or more wages in advance. Fifty of them thought better of it and failed to embark; eight died during the voyage; five met accidental death at Montreal; twenty-four were killed by the Iroquois; eleven returned to France; twenty-nine

---

[53] E.-Z. Massicotte, *Arrêts, édits, mandements, ordonnances et règlements, 1640–1760* (Montréal, 1919), p. 3. On the genesis of the peculiar Canadian usage of the term *habitant* see Konrad Fillion, "Essai sur l'evolution du mot habitant (XVIIᵉ-XVIIIᵉ siècles)," *Revue d'histoire de l'Amérique française*, XXIV, 3 (déc., 1970), pp. 375–401.

[54] Faillon, *Histoire de la colonie française*, II, p. 186.

[55] Thwaites, *Jesuit Relations*, IX, p. 171.

[56] Trudel, "Les débuts d'une société."

[57] *Word from New France*, p. 182.

[58] Gustave Lanctot, *Montreal under Maisonneuve, 1642–1665* (Toronto, 1969), p. 54.

of the men were still enrolled in the militia in 1663.[59] The settlers were well aware that the land had much to offer, could provide a much better life than most of the colonists had known in Europe, if only the Iroquois menace were to be removed. By 1659 some forty houses had been built at Montreal, but less than two hundred arpents of land had been cleared. Moreover, under these conditions there was no hope of fulfilling the main purpose of the settlement. Although during the early years an encouraging number of Indians, Algonquin for the most part, had been baptized, 78 in 1643 alone and 124 by 1647, there was no hope as long as the Iroquois war endured of persuading the Algonquins to settle on the island to emulate the French way of life and become Christian.

The settlement depended on supplies shipped from France, paid for by charitable donations raised by the Société de Notre Dame, and by the profits from the fur trade. These profits could be large, 200,000 livres in a good year, but they were at the mercy of the Iroquois blockade. Too often the supply ships had to sail back to France with bales of furs barely sufficient to pay the crews' wages.[60] Moreover, the early enthusiasm of the Société de Notre Dame for the Canadian mission field had faded. By 1650 its members had dwindled from forty to eleven. They now preferred to invest their funds in the Levant mission, rather than Montreal where the success obtained had been very meagre.[61]

The Company of New France also had abdicated its responsibilities. It was on the verge of bankruptcy, heavily in debt, and unable to provide the funds needed to maintain and defend the colony, let alone provide for its expansion. In 1645, therefore, the leading settlers took matters into their own hands. With the support of the Jesuits they formed the Communauté des Habitants and persuaded the proprietary company to cede to them the monopoly of the fur trade in return for an annual payment of one thousand prime beaver pelts. The Communauté also assumed the

---

[59] R. Auger, *La grande recrue de 1653*, p. 15.

[60] Faillon, *Histoire de la colonie française*, II, p. 33. Lanctot, *A History of Canada*, I, pp. 212, 216, 233–235, 247–248, 255, gives some random but revealing figures on the volume and profits of the trade. These rather meagre statistics were, for the most part, culled from the Jesuit *Relations*.

[61] Léon Gérin, *Aux sources de notre histoire* (Montreal, 1946), p. 180.

cost of administering the colony, some 45,000 to 50,000 livres a year, received the right to make land concessions on seigneurial tenure, agreed to bring out twenty families annually and get them established, and was allowed to appoint an administrative council at Quebec.[62]

The seat of colonial government had, in effect, been transferred from France to Quebec. It did not work well in practice. Within a year an appeal was made to the Crown resulting, in 1647, in the establishment of a new council composed of the governor of the colony, the local governor of Montreal, the superior of the Jesuits, and elected representatives of the people, syndics, to make known the views of the *habitants* of the three areas of settlement. This structure was modified further the following year and again in 1657, when it came to be composed of the governor of the colony and a financial director, both appointed by the Company of New France, and five councillors, two elected by the *habitants* at Quebec, one by Trois Rivières, two by Montreal.

The colony's framework of government was now rather complex. The King was sovereign over all, and the Company of New France was the seigneur; it appointed the governor, who, assisted by the council, which was composed of appointed and elected members, administered the colonial budget and the fur trade and in addition was responsible for defence. The weakness of this administration was that responsibility was too diffuse. The governor was responsible to the Crown and to the Company of New France; the local governor of Montreal was responsible to the Société de Notre Dame that had appointed him; the local councillors were responsible only to the electorate of their particular district. From the first establishment of a colonial council, its members displayed a lamentable lack of administrative talent, and the colony's financial affairs were soon in disarray. As a result they were subject to much hostile criticism, not all of it justified. In the times of continual crisis that faced New France during these years, this form of representative government was

---

[62] These, and the subsequent administrative arrangements, are briefly outlined by Gustave Lanctot in his doctoral dissertation, *L'administration de la Nouvelle-France* (Paris, 1929). He deals with the subject in more detail in his general narrative account, *A History of Canada*, Vol. I.

no substitute for competent and responsible administration.

One of the early problems that the council had to deal with was overtures from Boston, initiated in 1647, for a trade agreement between New France and the united provinces of New England. The only goods that New France could offer in any such arrangement were furs, for which they had a good market in France. The Quebec council was quite willing to enter into an agreement, but as a condition they demanded a military alliance to launch a combined assault against the Iroquois. In 1651 Father Gabriel Druillettes and a member of the council, Jean-Paul Godefroy, were sent to Boston to arrange the terms of a military-commercial treaty. New England, however, was not threatened by the Iroquois, and the Court of Commissioners, although proposing that the colonies remain neutral in the event of hostilities between their mother countries, saw no sense in bringing the wrath of that powerful confederacy down on their heads. In short, New England would have been foolish to accept the Canadians' terms, and free trade between Boston and Quebec did not, of itself, appear very attractive to the governor and council at Quebec. Negotiations therefore were broken off.[63]

That external problem, although resolved to no one's satisfaction — except unknowingly the Iroquois' — caused no dissension within the settlement. Other problems did. As though the Iroquois war were not enough, internal factional disputes racked the colony. In 1657 the question of appointing a bishop for New France caused a bitter struggle between the Jesuits and the Congregation of Saint-Sulpice. Each wanted its own nominee to receive the mitre. The Jesuits emerged victorious. Their nominee, the strong-willed, puritanical, and extremely devout François de Laval, not a Jesuit himself but educated by them and a member of the Compagnie du Saint-Sacrement, was appointed bishop *in partibus infidelium* and apostolic vicar in Canada. The colony now

---

[63] See Lanctot, *A History of Canada*, I, pp. 199–201. The records of the pre-1663 council have not survived, but in 1712 the governor general, Philippe de Rigaud de Vaudreuil, had the council records governing these negotiations transcribed and sent them to the minister. Likely this was done for the information of the minister of foreign affairs during the Treaty of Utrecht negotiations concerning the limits of Acadia and the status of the Iroquois. See Archives Nationales, Colonies, C11D, I, pp. 84–85.

had a bishop, but it was not yet a bishopric. Only in 1674, after much bitter wrangling among Rome, the French Crown, and the Gallican and Ultramontane factions in the French Church, was the problem of jurisdiction over the proposed Canadian bishopric resolved and the see at Quebec established.[64]

The Sulpicians had lost this struggle, but during it, to strengthen their case, they had agreed to take over responsibility for Montreal from the debt-ridden Société de Notre Dame. They acquired title to the island, becoming the seigneurs of Montreal, and their nominee for the bishopric, the wealthy Abbé Gabriel de Thubières de Lévy de Queylus, agreed to establish a seminary on the island. In the summer of 1657 he, with three other Sulpicians, arrived at Ville Marie and took charge of the parish from the resident Jesuit, who retired to Quebec. There was no love lost between these religious factions; the nascent rivalry between Montreal and Quebec was exacerbated, but Montreal did manage to maintain a large measure of independence. At the same time the danger that this western outpost of the French empire would be abandoned for lack of financial support was greatly reduced with the advent of the Messieurs de Saint-Sulpice.

The most controversial and divisive issue, one that was to rack the colony for several decades, was that of the sale of liquor to the Indians. Fermented and distilled beverages were unknown to them before the advent of Europeans, but once they became acquainted with *eau de vie*, they demanded it avidly. They drank purely for its intoxicating effect, believing that they were thereby transported to the exalted world inhabited by their gods, but with calamitous results in their mundane physical existence. When drunk they sometimes, if not frequently, lost all self-control and committed heinous crimes, assaulting, maiming, and even killing those about them. When they became sober they accepted no responsibility for their actions, claiming that they had not been themselves and that the alcohol was to blame, not they. Despite these effects, too many of them would do anything to obtain it, and unscrupulous fur traders took full advantage of their weak-

---

[64] The best study to date of this complex issue is that contained in the biography of Laval by André Vachon in *The Dictionary of Canadian Biography* (Toronto, 1969), II.

ness. More furs could be obtained in trade with a keg of brandy than with a canoe load of other goods.[65]

The clergy, particularly the Jesuits, were appalled by the effects of this trade and did everything they could to stop it, declaring it to be a mortal sin. They prevailed upon the civil authorities to make it a crime to give or sell liquor to the Indians, but this prohibition was easily evaded, and the fur traders protested the ban vigorously because it seriously reduced their profits. When Bishop Laval arrived at Quebec he needed little persuasion by the missionaries that the trade had to be stopped. He declared that anyone who engaged in it was automatically excommunicated, and he persuaded the governor, Pierre de Voyer d'Argenson, to support this action. In 1661 two men convicted of the offence were executed. Those traders who opposed the restriction refused to admit that what was permitted everywhere else should be regarded as a sin and a crime in Canada. The governor, who had begun to resent the pressure exerted by Laval, came to agree with them, and he withdrew his ordinance. This brought about a violent clash between the governor and the very determined bishop. The civil and the religious authorities were quickly at complete loggerheads. In 1661 d'Argenson asked for, and received, his recall to France. His replacement, baron Pierre Dubois Davaugour, a strong-willed veteran soldier, was also unable to work with the bishop, who in 1662 crossed to France on clerical business. His report on the governor's arbitrary actions brought about Davaugour's immediate recall.[66] It appeared that the clerical power ruled supreme in the colony; but this was more apparent than real, and even the appearance did not endure very long.

Both externally and internally the condition of the colony was

---

[65] Most of the accounts of the effects of alcohol on the Indians were written by the clergy and were highly coloured, likely exaggerated. Those who stood to profit from the trade denied that these accounts were true, claiming that the Indians were no worse than Englishmen or Dutchmen when in their cups. Some of the more responsible fur traders, however, agreed with the clergy that the effects of the trade were abominable and that it should be prohibited on pain of death. See W. J. Eccles, *Frontenac: The Courtier Governor* (Toronto, 1959), pp. 61–68; and André Vachon's perceptive article "L'eau de vie dans la société indienne," *Canadian Historical Association Report, 1960*. For the legal and constitutional aspects of this problem see W. J. Eccles, *The Canadian Frontier, 1534–1760* (New York, 1969), pp. 77–78.

[66] See Lanctot, *A History of Canada*, I, pp. 232–270.

now such that radical measures had to be taken to establish it on a more secure footing, or it might well collapse. It could not endure much longer in its uncertain state. Shortly after arriving at Quebec, Davaugour had appealed to the Crown for a strong force of regular troops to quell the Iroquois. He followed this up by sending Pierre Boucher, governor of Trois Rivières, to the court to explain in detail the desperate situation of New France, its potential, and what needed to be done to rectify the one and realize the other. Boucher proved to be an excellent advocate.[67]

Louis XIV, who had just taken the reins of power into his own hands upon the death of the cardinal minister Mazarin, decided to take over the French possessions in North America from the Company of New France. They were now to become a royal province, like the other provinces in the kingdom, with the Crown accepting full responsibility for security, finance, administration, justice, and economic development. Government by private company had proved a failure, a measure of self-government had proved no more successful, and the Church could do no more; but with the resources of the Crown and the direction of such a minister as was Jean-Baptiste Colbert, the colony could hope for big things. It was not to be disappointed.[68]

Yet despite the sad plight of New France prior to Louis XIV's intervention, a good deal had been accomplished upon which the royal administration could build. A firm economic base had been laid. The crops of northern Europe, cereal grains, vegetables, and some fruits, gave excellent yields. Cattle, sheep, and pigs had survived the long, harsh winters. With thirty arpents of cleared land an *habitant* could provide more than enough for his family. By 1652 three-quarters of the settlers produced enough for their needs and many families had a surplus.[69] Although not yet quite self-sufficient in the essential foodstuffs, it was clear that the colony soon could be.

Despite the fierce efforts of the Iroquois, the commercial alli-

---

[67] While in France, Boucher wrote a charming and valuable little book which he dedicated to Colbert, *Histoire véritable et naturelle des moeurs et productions du pays de la Nouvelle-France, vulgairement dicte le Canada* (Paris, 1664).

[68] See W. J. Eccles, *Canada under Louis XIV* (Toronto, 1964); S. L. Mims, *Colbert's West India Policy* (New Haven, 1912).

[69] *Word from New France*, p. 205.

ance with the Algonquin nations was firmly established, and when these tribes evaded the Iroquois blockage, 200,000 to 300,000 livres' worth of furs were shipped to France. French traders had now voyaged to the western limits of the Great Lakes, and north over the watershed to Hudson Bay, bringing more distant tribes into the French commercial orbit and giving promise of a great expansion of the trade were the Iroquois to be quelled. The fur trade had, in fact, superseded missionary activity as the dominant factor in the colony's existence.

The framework and the basic institutions of French rural and urban society had been established; but some, such as the crushing load of taxation, were mercifully lacking. Although this framework was hierarchical and status-ordered, there were, in addition to taxation, some other significant factors absent, and some novel ones present, that were to form this incipient colonial society into something markedly different in several respects from the parent society of France. Although the landholding system resembled that of northern France, the fact that settlers could have free all the land that they could till, with a secure title and only nominal seigneurial dues, precluded the emergence of an agricultural proletariat. The Canadians very quickly became conscious of the fact that they were *habitants*, not peasants. Capital for economic development was not to be obtained by exploiting them in the normal European fashion. Nor, unlike in the English colonies, could capital be raised by speculation in land; the seigneurial land-tenure system precluded it.

The constant state of guerrilla warfare with the Iroquois also had a profound influence on the Canadians. They had to become as adept at this most demanding type of war as was their foe. The martial spirit was early beaten into them. Forced to employ Iroquois tactics against the Iroquois and to combat this toughest of foes alongside Algonquin allies, they inevitably acquired Indian methods, learned in some measure to view things through the eyes of the Indian, and acquired some of the Indian's values, his stoicism, contempt for danger, incredible fortitude, savage ferocity, and lack of compassion for the enemy. These harsh conditions ensured that only the toughest survived and stayed on.

One of the more important elements in this emerging society was that the colony had not been used as a dumping ground for criminals and social outcasts. Although it had not become the New Jerusalem envisaged by the Jesuits and the *dévots*, a considerable number had emigrated for religious reasons; some to safeguard their own souls like the Puritans of New England, others from a genuine desire to help obtain entry into heaven for the pagans. Unlike the Puritans of Massachusetts Bay, who had set themselves the task of establishing a purified Christian state to bring about the reformation of all Christendom, the clergy and their lay followers of New France had set themselves more modest goals, not impossible to achieve, thereby sparing themselves much harrowing frustration. It had, however, proved impossible to recruit enough immigrants dedicated to proselytization. Many of those who came did so mainly to escape intolerable conditions in France, or from a spirit of adventure, or because they were lured by the prospect of high wages with only a three- to five-year contract, upon the completion of which they could hope to return to their familiar surroundings in France, money jingling in their pockets and tall tales to tell. The majority of the immigrants came with such contracts, which meant that they had not cut themselves off completely from the Old World. Those who chose to remain did so in the full knowledge of what it entailed, and of their own free will.

Moreover, the Roman Church provided the settlers during these trying years with a sensual and spiritual link to the world they had left, as well as assurance of recompense in the next. The liturgy, the consolation of confession, the other familiar rites, were exactly the same on both sides of the ocean. The Puritans, on the other hand, deliberately denied themselves the solace that the rich and evocative Roman ritual provided the Canadians, who thereby preserved their ties with the old civilization and did not feel themselves to be completely abandoned in the North American wilderness.

It has been asserted that ''the first experience of English settlers in America was one of crippling despair;'' that the English colonies were ''conceived and born in anxieties of a particularly

excruciating kind'' that have endured.[70] The Canadians occasionally knew despair during these early years, but it was caused
by external, physical factors, for which they knew there was a
remedy. Theirs was not the soul-searing spiritual despair that the
English colonists experienced; it was more intermittent frustration of hopes deferred. And this, they knew, was not beyond the
capacity of man's efforts to alter.

---

[70] See Page Smith, ''Anxiety and Dispair in American History,'' *The William and Mary Quart-erly*, 3d Ser., XXVI, 3 (July 1969), pp. 416–424.

Chapter 3

Colbert's Colonies, 1663-1685

The urgent appeal for aid to the Crown from the Jesuits, the bishop of Quebec, and the governor general of New France met with a positive response. Jean-Baptiste Colbert, the late Cardinal Mazarin's private secretary and Louis XIV's accomplice in the destruction of the too powerful and overly ambitious *surintendant de finance* Nicolas Fouquet, was entrusted with, among other things, the reorganization of the French colonial empire. Colbert's main aim was to increase the power of France by strengthening and expanding its economy on an imperial basis. The dominant position of the Dutch in French maritime trade was to be broken by the creation of a powerful merchant fleet. Population growth had to be encouraged to provide a larger labour force. The productive elements in society — the peasants, artisans, seamen, merchants, industrialists — were to be nurtured and stimulated to greater efforts. The non-productive elements, particularly the clergy, were to be curbed and their consumption of wealth reduced. The colonies were henceforth to provide the kingdom with the raw materials previously obtained from the Dutch, too often originating in the French colonies, and at the same time afford an expanding market for French manufactured goods. In short, Colbert intended that the French colonies should make the same contribution to the French economy as he saw the English colonies making to that of England.

Colbert wasted no time in initiating his plans. Some of them proved to be beyond the capabilities of the instruments available,

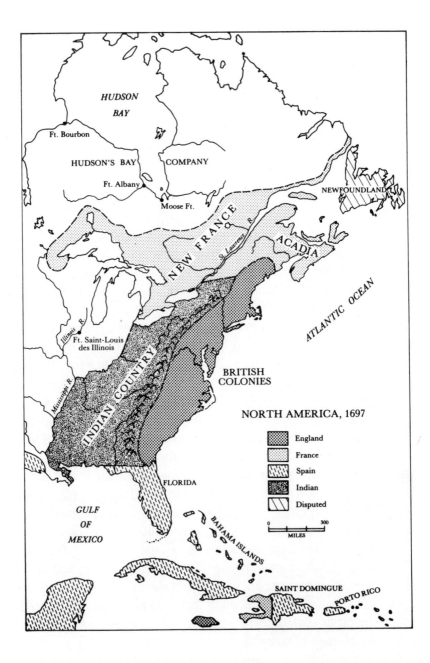

HUDSON
BAY

Ft. Bourbon

HUDSON'S BAY   COMPANY

Ft. Albany

Moose Ft.

NEWFOUNDLAND

NEW FRANCE

ACADIA

St. Lawrence R.

ATLANTIC OCEAN

Illinois R.

Ft. Saint-Louis
des Illinois

INDIAN COUNTRY

Mississippi R.

BRITISH
COLONIES

NORTH AMERICA, 1697

England
France
Spain
Indian
Disputed

FLORIDA

GULF
OF
MEXICO

BAHAMA ISLANDS

0   300
MILES

SAINT DOMINGUE

PORTO RICO

or were defeated by conditions which he had not foreseen or could not control, yet what he did accomplish in two decades was truly remarkable. Because he was in a hurry he employed the means used by the successful colonial powers, even though they were quite unsuited to the peculiar French social and eonomic conditions. He cancelled the charter of the moribund Company of New France and organized a new company modeled on the English and Dutch East Indies companies to take over the trade of all the American colonies. Unfortunately, Frenchmen with wealth to invest preferred to buy land, *rentes* (government bonds), or a public office. There was no confidence among the members of the French business community that this new company could compete successfully with the Dutch, and thus the needed capital was not provided in sufficient quantities from private sources; it had to come from the royal coffers. The Compagnie de l'Occident was never more than an agency of the Crown; therefore its demise in 1674 was without serious consequence for the colonies.[1]

While the new company was being organized, Colbert, always methodical and thorough, sent agents to the colonies to gather information upon which long-range plans could be made. As an interim measure, Alexandre Prouville, seigneur de Tracy, a senior officer noted for his past loyalty to the Crown and for his competence, was dispatched with four companies of troops, first to the West Indies to restore order, and from there to Quebec. His commission, dated November 19, 1663, appointed him "Lieutenant General in all the lands of our obedience situated in North and South America and in the islands of America." He was given supreme command of all French forces in the Americas on land and sea, and supreme judicial power.[2] His chief task was

---

[1] The initial capital subscribed in 1665 totaled 1,604,360 livres, of which the Crown put up 1,387,000 livres. The total capitalization over the years amounted to 5,522,345 livres, and the Crown furnished more than 3,000,000 of it. The rest was almost all provided by revenue farmers, tax collectors, and officials who were in no position to decline Colbert's invitation to subscribe. See Stewart L. Mims, *Colbert's West Indian Policy* (New Haven, 1912), pp. 75-81.

[2] André Vachon, in his admirable analysis of the administrative framework of New France, denies that Tracy was, in fact, a viceroy. It is true that he did not receive that appellation, yet it is difficult to see what additional authority he could have been given to act in the King's name; thus he was, in fact, a viceroy. See the article by Vachon in the *Dictionary of Canadian Biography* (Toronto, 1969), II, pp. xv-xxv.

to administer an oath of allegiance to all French officials and subjects "to establish the power of the King and to make all the people obedient unto him." Colbert stated that the Dutch obtained annually from the French islands two million livres' worth of sugar and one million of tobacco, cotton, and other goods. He was determined to break their hold on this trade. In short, Tracy was required to restore the islands to the French empire.[3]

Upon his arrival at Martinique in June 1664, Tracy wasted no time in restoring order. He made it very plain that he would accept no gifts from anyone, not even the customary perquisites. The administration of justice he took into his own hands and swiftly cleared away a backlog of cases. To show that he meant business, when fifty planters in a body protested his choice of tax collector, he committed the two leaders to prison and forbade on pain of death all such illegal assemblies. A form of representative government was inaugurated; each parish was permitted to select three persons, from among whom the governor of the island would nominate one, to serve as syndic to make representations concerning the desires and complaints of the people of the respective parishes. It was intended that this office would lead to the establishment of a magistrature, badly needed, it was stated, to bring the people back to a proper degree of subordination to authority.[4] Similar measures were enacted by Tracy on the other islands, St Christophe, St Martin, St Croix, St Bartholomew, Saint-Domingue, Marie Galante, Grenada, Guadeloupe, and Tortuga, after he had taken official possession for the Compagnie de l'Occident. Subsequently, sovereign councils were established on each island "to prevent the oppression of the poor by the strong and wealthy."[5] At the same time, 1667, the administration was centralized with a governor general and an intendant for the Antilles resident at Martinique.[6] Here, as in Canada, a main administrative problem was to be the all too frequent quarrels

[3] See Pierre Clément (ed.), *Lettres, instructions et mémoires de Colbert* (7 vols., Paris, 1861–73), II-1, p. cclix, Discours sur les manufactures.

[4] Paris, Bibliothèque Nationale, Mélanges Colbert, Vol. 128 bis, p. 1071, Du Lion à Colbert, Guadeloupe, 24 avril 1665.

[5] Clément, *Lettres, instructions et mémoires*, III-2, p. 408, Instructions à M. de Baas.

[6] See Alfred Martineau and L.-Ph. May, *Trois Siècles d'Histoire Antillaise: Martinique et Guadeloupe de 1635 à nos jours* (Paris, 1935), p. 120.

between these senior officials. For the defence of the islands at the onset of the Dutch war in 1672, six companies of regular troops raised for service in the colonies, the Troupes de la Marine, were sent out. Their main foe was not to be the Dutch, or the English, but ennui, and disease that constantly depleted their ranks.[7]

The company's monopoly of trade, and more particularly its energetic enforcement, which severed the old trade pattern with the Dutch, angered the planters, since the company was unable at first to supply the islands with enough goods of the desired sorts, and what it did provide cost far more than the Dutch had charged. The Dutch had been sending one hundred to one hundred and twenty ships a year to the French islands. In 1665 the Compagnie de l'Occident was able to send only a score, and to Canada only three. On Martinique some of the planters tried to stage a revolt, but it was quickly suppressed by the governor, Robert de Fichot des Friches, sieur de Clodoré. If nothing else, this abortive revolt indicates that the ban on foreign trade was hurting, hence was effective. The following year, the outbreak of war with England dealt the company, and the islands, a harsh blow. Ships laded for the West Indies were unable to sail from the French channel ports for fear of capture, and by the end of hostilities the director of the company estimated the losses attributable to the war at almost two and a quarter million livres. But the company, and the planters, survived these precarious years. By 1674 the islands' trade in cotton, tobacco, and sugar, with the latter crop predominating, was firmly in French hands. The company, although not a financial success, had achieved its main object, the exclusion of the Dutch.[8]

After 1674 the trade with the colonies was open to all French traders, and the number of ships sailing from Bordeaux, La Rochelle, and Nantes to the West Indies rose by leaps and bounds until by 1683 more than two hundred were engaged in the island trade.[9] The islands did not produce food enough to feed this population, and attempts were made to open up trade between

[7] Ibid., p. 50.
[8] Mims, Colbert's West Indian Policy, pp. 121, 142–175, 180–194, 223.
[9] Ibid., p. 236.

Canada and the islands, but with scant success. Colbert wanted Canada to provide fish, grain and other foodstuffs, lumber and barrel staves, and take sugar, molasses, and rum in exchange. Unfortunately, the length of the voyage, the short summer shipping season when hurricanes were prevalent, and the lack of salt in Canada made the cost of Canadian goods high, while the small population of Canada could not use enough sugar to make the return voyage profitable. Moreover, New England could provide all the things that Canada had at much lower cost, and with its larger population take enough French sugar and molasses to make the trade worthwhile for both parties. So profitable, in fact, that the laws of trade and navigation of both countries failed to stop it.

Acadia, the neglected colony, was not so easily recovered as the West Indies islands. Here too, trade with New England remained vital. Sir Thomas Temple refused to relinquish his hold on the province until 1670 when a regular army officer who had served briefly in Canada, Captain Hector d'Andigné de Grandfontaine, was appointed governor, subordinate to the governor general of New France. In July that year Grandfontaine called on Temple at his home in Boston and obtained his signature to the terms of transfer. That accomplished, with a company of fifty soldiers he was required to maintain the King's authority over a vast region stretching from the St George River to the Gulf of St Lawrence. The total French population, including a few score settlers sent out by Colbert, did not number more than five hundred, and they were dependent on Boston for the supplies they could not produce themselves. Given this condition of economic dependency, friendly relations had to be maintained with the New Englanders, and Grandfontaine was instructed to allow them to fish in Acadian waters, but not to permit them to trade for furs. His main tasks were to strengthen the provinces' defences and to discover the best overland communication route to Quebec, which proved to be up the St John River, over the height of land to the Chaudière, then down it to the St Lawrence across from Quebec.

The vulnerability of Acadia was made all too plain in 1673 when the posts at Pentagouet and Jemseg on the St John River were assaulted by Dutch pirates. Grandfontaine's successor, Jacques de Chambly, and two of his officers were taken prisoner to Boston and released only after the governor general of New France had paid their ransom. The contrast between the attention paid to Acadia and the effort made by Colbert to secure the French hold on the West Indies, as well as to develop and expand the colony of Canada, is indeed striking. Despite the fact that Acadia was a strategically vital area and the wealth of the fisheries so important both to the French economy and to the development of a merchant marine, Colbert and Louis XIV allowed the province to stagnate, seemingly content to have regained title to the region. By the end of the century the pathetically small French population had barely doubled, scattered in farming settlements on the south shore of the Bay of Fundy, at a few fishing ports on the Atlantic shore of the peninsula, and at fur trade posts on the rivers flowing down from what are today Maine and New Brunswick.[10] The real rulers of Acadia were the Abenaquis, Micmac and Malecite. Out of necessity the French maintained good relations with these nations. Moreover, there were so few French they made no encroachments on the Indians' hunting grounds. Their main aim was to deny the area to the English, not to settle it themselves. The picture was very different on the English side of the line, where an expanding population, greedy for land, sought to dispossess the Indians by any means.[11] King Philip's War served as a savage warning to the Acadian tribes; thus for nearly a century it was they who, unwittingly, were to preserve French claims to sovereignty against English encroachment.

In Canada the situation was very different. The main threat was not the English, but the Five Nations Iroquois confederacy. Before any of Colbert's plans for the development of the colony's economy could be implemented, the continual assaults of these tribes on the settlements had to be halted. In 1665 the Carignan-Salières regiment, over a thousand strong, was sent out. In two rather fumbling campaigns, one recklessly undertaken in mid-

[10] See W. J. Eccles, *Canada under Louis XIV, 1663–1701* (Toronto, 1964), pp. 44–45, 127–130; Andrew Hill Clark, *Acadia: The Geography of Early Nova Scotia to 1760* (Univ. of Wisconsin Press, 1968), pp. 109–185.

[11] See Douglas Edward Leach, *The Northern Colonial Frontier, 1607–1763* (New York, 1966), pp. 33–61.

winter, the country of the Mohawks was invaded and their villages and food supplies destroyed, much to the perturbation of the Dutch residents of Orange, recently conquered by the English and renamed Albany. This action of the English, in turn, upset the French, who prophetically remarked that "the King of England did grasp at all America."[12] All the Five Nations then sent delegates to Quebec and agreed to keep the peace. Despite the fact that the French had inflicted little real damage on the enemy —had, in fact, suffered heavier losses during the two campaigns than they had inflicted—the Iroquois were sufficiently cowed by this display of might and the full panoply of a European campaign that they honoured the terms of the peace treaty for nearly two decades. This was just long enough for Colbert to implement his colonial policy.

With the external threat removed, Colbert was able to impose a new administrative framework on the colony, similar to that of a province in France, but with significant modifications. The state of virtual chaos that had endured in France during much of the first half and more of the century had engendered a reaction in favour of a strong centralized administration. The descriptive term "absolutism" — usually used in a pejorative sense — is really not appropriate, for the power of Louis XIV was by no means absolute. Poor communications, customs, and "privileges" — which in the seventeenth century meant the traditional liberties — circumscribed the power of the monarch. During his reign, however, the people came to hold the central government responsible for their well-being and to blame it when times became hard.[13] What was even more significant, the government of Louis XIV accepted this responsibility. Nowhere was this truer than in New France. The people of the colony were not consulted when the new administration was inaugurated, but it brought so many tangible benefits that all welcomed it. Moreover, they had previously displayed a marked inability to run their own affairs in a satisfactory manner, and the calibre of senior officials sent

[12] E. B. O'Callaghan (ed.), *Documents Relative to the Colonial History of the State of New York* (15 vols., Albany, 1853–87), III, pp. 118–119.

[13] See Robert Mandrou, *La France aux XVIIᵉ et XVIIIᵉ siècles* (Nouvelle Clio, Paris, 1967), p. 110; Marcel Giraud, "Tendances humanitaires à la fin du règne de Louis XIV," *Revue Historique*, CCIX (1953), pp. 217–237.

by the Crown to administer the colony was much higher than the colonists could have provided from among their own ranks. During the first decade, however, bitter conflicts among the senior officials required the intervention of Louis XIV and the eventual dismissal of the principal antagonists. But, as an attorney general later remarked, "the best laws usually emerge from the worst disorders."[14] As a result of these conflicts the Crown defined more clearly the spheres of authority of the officials, and thereby limited them.[15] From that point on, the administration discharged its responsibilities with commendable efficiency and, as a rule, equity.

The colonial administration was organized along military lines with a clear-cut chain of command. At the top was, of course, the King, to whom the minister of marine gave oral reports and received oral decisions on the more important matters. Assisting the minister was the *premier commis*, who enjoyed great power since it was he who read the colonial dispatches and had abstracts made for the minister. What he sent to the minister for a decision and the manner in which he represented things made all the difference.[16]

In the colonies the governors and intendants were the dominant officials. In New France, for example, there was a governor general, always a professional soldier, holding office during the King's pleasure, and beneath him the local governors in Acadia, and at Montreal and Trois Rivières. Their main responsibilities were military, and the maintenance of law and order. The governor general was also responsible for external relations with the Indian nations and for seeing to it that all the subordinate officials performed their duties in a satisfactory manner. He had, however, to have very good cause indeed before he dared interfere with these other officials, more particularly the officers of justice.

---

[14] Public Archives Canada, MG18G6, Mémoire Pour les gens tenans le Conseil souverain du Roy en la ville de Quebecq.

[15] See W. J. Eccles, *Frontenac: The Courtier Governor* (Toronto, 1959), pp. 31–50, for these disputes. For a succinct analysis of the government of New France see the essay by André Vachon in *The Dictionary of Canadian Biography* (Toronto, 1969), II, pp. xv–xxv.

[16] See Robert La Roque de Roquebrune, "La Direction de la Nouvelle-France par le Ministère de la Marine," *Revue d'Histoire de l'Amérique française*, VI, 4 (mars 1953); Guy Frégualt, *Le XVIIIe siècle canadien: Études* (Montreal, 1968), pp. 159–241.

The intendants of New France and the West Indies were responsible for justice, civil administration, and finance. They were also responsible for the ancillary services of the military — supply, pay, hospitalization. How well the intendants performed their duties affected the lives of the settlers at every turn; they were virtually *in loco parentis*. Whereas the governors were almost invariably members of the *noblesse d'épée*, the intendants were always of the *noblesse de robe*, the one a soldier, the other a lawyer, and this sometimes exacerbated differences between them. By the eighteenth century the intendants had subdelegates at the main towns to assist them, and beneath them, in turn, a number of minor officials: royal notaries, road surveyors, port and customs officials, down to lowly town criers. In short, the French colonial administration was a well-organized bureaucracy, a model for the other powers.

With the establishment of the Sovereign Council at Quebec, the Canadian settlers were granted some say in the government.[17] Modeled on the provincial *parlements*, its main functions were to serve as the judicial court of appeal from the lower courts and to register, with the right of remonstrance, all royal edicts. In the early years the council enacted a good deal of legislation, but by the eighteenth century this task was left to the intendant, and the council confined itself to its judicial function. With the exception of the governor general, the bishop, and the intendant, the members of the council — five councillors originally, increased to seven in 1675, and to twelve in 1703—were all colonial notables. The attorney general had to be trained in the law, a member of the bar at the Parlement de Paris, and the councillors relied upon him and the intendant for the interpretation of fine legal points. Although the emoluments of office were meagre, 500 livres a year for the senior councillor, 350 for the rest, in contrast to the 12,000-livre salary of the intendant, the prestige attached to the office was enough to ensure that the incumbents took their responsibilities seriously. Three thousand livres a year was considered an adequate income for a member of the nobility to live with modest dignity.[18]

---

[17] The best study of this important body is still Raymond Du Bois Cahall, *The Sovereign Council of New France* (New York, 1915).

[18] AN. C11A, vol. 105, ff 137–8. Vaudreuil au Ministre, Mtl. 30 juin 1760.

For the first few years the elected syndics from the three governmental districts made known the views of the people, but at Colbert's behest this institution withered on the vine. He declared that every man must speak for himself, not one for all. There was, however, a genuine need for an agency at the local level that could represent the civil government, pass on its orders, and inform it of anything untoward that occurred. This function came to be performed by the captains of militia.[19] In 1669 Louis XIV ordered the governor general to form the *habitants* between the ages of sixteen and sixty into militia companies. In every parish a company was formed. In the more populous parishes they had a captain, a lieutenant, an ensign, and a sergeant. In those more sparsely settled, a captain and a sergeant sufficed. In the three governmental districts a commandant of militia, a major, and an aide major had overall command under the local governors. The militia captains, with few exceptions, were *habitants* rather than seigneurs. The exceptions were a few *roturier* seigneurs in Montreal and Quebec. The menial civil duties these militia officers were required to perform placed the office far beneath the dignity of members of the nobility. They were required to muster the men periodically to ensure that they had serviceable muskets, knew how to use them, and acquired a rudimentary acquaintance with discipline. Neither officers nor men were paid; the former enjoyed an elevated social status which was highly prized, and the latter accepted militia service as a proper obligation. In time of war this militia system allowed the governor general to muster the entire armed strength of the colony within a very few days.

Apart from their military function, the captains of militia, although appointed by the governor general, served as the agents of the intendant and were a linchpin of the civil administration. They reported to him any untoward incidents in their parish, provided him with the local information he required from time to time, arrested fugitives, and promulgated ordonnances of the

[19] Regrettably, the role of the militia, and more particularly that of the *capitaines de milice*, has not yet been critically examined. The article by Benjamin Sulte, "The Captains of Militia," *Canadian Historical Review*, I (1920), pp. 241–245, is superficial. Fernand Ouellet, "Officiers de milice et structure sociale au Québec (1660–1815)," *Histoire Sociale/Social History*, vol. XII (No. 23) mai 1979, pp. 37–65, and Louise Dechêne, *Habitants et marchands de Montréal au XVIIᵉ siècle* (Paris et Montréal, 1974) pp. 358–9, sadly misconstrue the social origins and role of the militia officers during the French regime.

civil authorities. In this role the fact that they were mere *habitants* had far-reaching consequences. It meant that the seigneurs had been by-passed in the chain of civil command. There was far less likelihood of a *habitant* militia captain's becoming a petty, local tyrant, after the style of an English justice of the peace, than there would have been had the seigneurs served in that capacity.

In the three urban centres, issues frequently arose on which the intendant and the governor felt it advisable to obtain the people's views before taking legislative action. On such occasions an open assembly of all concerned was held and a record kept of the decisions arrived at.[20] There is no evidence of ''frontier democracy'' at work here. These ad hoc assemblies were not instituted at the behest of the people, but were imposed by the royal authorities with the full approval of Louis XIV. On certain major issues the King instructed the governor and intendant to call an assembly and report its recommendations to him. It rested, however, with these authorities to act upon or ignore the assembly's recommendations. Similarly, the intendant frequently ordered the *habitants* of a parish to hold an assembly to settle how they would deal with some local issue. Since the only taxes levied in the colony were an import duty on wines, spirits, and tobacco, an occasional tax for local improvements more easily agreed to than collected, and until 1717 an export duty on beaver pelts and moose hides, there was no need for an elective assembly on the British model. The government was certainly authoritarian, but it was both responsive and responsible, and far from being arbitrary. When the people complained, it was usually not against the system. The only serious protest occurred in 1717 when some habitants of Longueuil, across the St Lawrence from Montreal, refused to obey an order to work on the construction of a stone wall around the town. They took up arms in defiance but were swiftly reduced to obedience by Governor General Vaudreuil, who clapped ten of the ringleaders in gaol for two months.[21]

---

[20] See Allana G. Reid, ''Representative Assemblies in New France,'' *Canadian Historical Review*, XXVII (Mar. 1946); W. J. Eccles, *The Canadian Frontier, 1534–1760* (New York, 1969), pp. 80–82.

[21] AN C11A vol. 38, pp. 121–4. Vaudreuil au Conseil de la Marine, Qué. 17 oct. 1717.

Although the bishop was second in status in the Sovereign Council, his authority declined markedly under the royal regime. He was early deprived of his right to appoint and dismiss, jointly with the governor general, the members of the Sovereign Council, and his attendance at its meetings became less frequent. In fact, he was little more than an honourary member. Colbert instructed the intendant to do all that he could to discourage the bishop from attending. Colbert was, of course, markedly anticlerical and particularly suspicious of the Jesuits; he was convinced that they and the bishop already had too much power, were avid for more, and had to be rendered subservient to the royal authority.[22] On only one issue did Laval and the Jesuits openly oppose the royal officials, with the support of several of the leading colonists, and that was the trading of brandy to the Indians. This struggle they lost. The trade was sanctioned by the King, but with restrictions that the governor general, who had vigorously opposed them, was easily able to circumvent.[23] Succeeding governors general, however, from the end of the century to the Conquest, did make an honest effort to restrict the trade, and with some success.

When the tithe was first introduced in the colony in 1663, to provide for secular priests in the parishes and to help pay for the maintenance of the seminary that Laval had founded at Quebec to train a native priesthood, the bishop again failed to have his way. He asked for a tithe of one-thirteenth of the produce of the land, this being the usual tithe in France, but the *habitants* would agree to pay only half that amount, and on their cereal grains alone. They received the support of the seigneurs and the governor general, and Laval had to be satisfied with the lower rate. Although he devoted his own revenues and obtained some funds from private sources in France, the Canadian secular clergy were to a considerable degree dependent on annual subventions from

---

[22] Colbert's animosity toward Laval may have stemmed from the latter's connection with the Compagnie du Saint-Sacrement, which had fought Colbert tooth and nail in his savage campaign to destroy Fouquet. The Compagnie had also supported the Frondeurs against Mazarin, whose private secretary and creature Colbert had been. See E. R. Adair, "France and the Beginnings of New France," *Canadian Historical Review*, XXV (Sept. 1944), pp. 167-268.

[23] See W. B. Munro, "The Brandy Parliament of 1678," *Canadian Historical Review*, II (June 1921).

the Crown to make ends meet. By 1720 these subventions amounted to at least 120,000 livres a year, about one-third of the revenue of the Canadian Church.[24] This financial dependence inhibited the clergy's freedom of action not a little.

In any event there is no evidence that the clergy wanted to dominate the civil authorities, or to suborn their functions. Even had they so desired they were too divided among themselves; Sulpicians against Jesuits, both against the Cathedral chapter at Quebec; and in 1670 the Récollets were sent back to the colony by Louis XIV after an absence of forty-one years in a deliberate attempt to reduce the influence of the Jesuits. It also has to be borne in mind that the clergy, royal officials, and laity were all members of the same church; all desired the same main end, to attain access to heaven and avoid going to hell. They merely differed on occasion how best to achieve it. Only the fact that the colony enjoyed unity of religion allowed them to indulge their human frailty by squabbling among themselves. There is no viable evidence to support the contention that New France was a theocracy, torn by the power struggle between an ultramontane church and an absolutist state. After 1663 there was never any doubt that the clergy were subservient to the Crown.[25]

With the inauguration of royal government came a much more sophisticated judicial system. This was the intendant's responsibility. The code of law in use since 1640 was the *Coutume de Paris*, augmented by the King's *Ordonnance Civile* of 1667 and *La Grande Ordonnance Criminelle* of 1670.[26] There were, in all, three courts in the colony through which a case might progress. The lowest were the seigneurial courts, but only a few seigneurs went to the trouble and expense of dispensing *haute, moyenne, et basse justice*.[27] A case heard in a seigneurial court could be

---

[24] See Noël Baillargeon, *Le séminaire de Québec sous l'épiscopat de Mgr de Laval*, (Québec, 1972) pp. 135–144; Guy Frégault, *Le XVIIIᵉ siècle*, p. 293.

[25] W. J. Eccles, "The Role of the Church in New France," in *Essays on New France* (Toronto, 1987).

[26] See Isambert, Decrusy, Taillandier, *Recueil général des anciennes lois françaises depuis l'an 420 jusqu'à la révolution de 1789*, Vol. XVIII (Paris, 1829).

[27] It is frequently stated that these seigneurial courts heard civil cases involving not more than 5 livres and petty criminal cases meriting a fine of not more than 100 sols. This is erroneous. Fines of up to 500 livres were levied in criminal cases, and civil cases wherein amounts of more than 30 livres were involved were frequently adjudicated in one seigneurial court, Notre Dame des Anges. In 1755, apparently a normal year, thirty-eight cases were adjudicated in that court. It merits attention that these seigneurial courts also enacted legislation as the local need arose.

appealed to the royal courts of first instance at Montreal, Trois Rivières, or Quebec, and from those courts to the Sovereign Council. Although Colbert tried to put a stop to the practice, some cases were taken on appeal from the Sovereign Council to the Conseil des Parties in France, but this was hideously expensive and gave the rich an advantage. Petty civil cases involving not more than 100 livres could be adjudicated by the intendant without fee, with the consent of both parties, but there could be no appeal against his judgment. The intendant could also intervene in any case, take it out of the court, and render judgment himself if he thought that justice was not being done, and appeal against his decision could be had only at the Conseil des Parties. This action was, however, extremely rare. In 1717 an Admiralty Court was established at Quebec which, in addition to hearing all cases concerning maritime affairs, was responsible for the maintenance of law and order in the port.

Lawyers were not allowed to practise in the colonies. Their reputation was such in France that this was considered a major reform.[28] Notaries, with whom the colony was adequately supplied, served the same function as an English solicitor. During a trial each litigant presented his own case, or he could have someone represent him, but neither he nor his advocate had the right to interrogate or cross-examine, only to challenge the testimony presented by the witnesses.

Unlike in the British adversary system, where the accused cannot be made to testify against himself, under the inquisitorial system the accused was interrogated. But the incidence of crime in New France was not great, and the rights of an accused were carefully protected. No one in New France was condemned by the courts without a very thorough investigation, the interrogation of the accused and the witnesses under oath, confrontation of accused and witnesses where the testimony of the witnesses could be challenged by the accused and modified by the witnesses,

---

[28] Significantly, in sixteenth-century Mexico there were vociferous complaints about the venality (in the pejorative sense) of lawyers who encouraged lawsuits to the ruin of the settlers, and some towns pleaded with the King to bar them from New Spain. See François Chevalier, *Land and Society in Colonial Mexico* (Univ. of California Press, 1963), p. 29. The same abuse arose in Canada after the British Conquest with the introduction of English law, its attendant lawyers, and fee-taking officers of the courts. See Hilda Neatby, *Quebec: The Revolutionary Age, 1760-1791* (Toronto, 1966), pp. 45-55.

reexamination, then reconfrontation, until proof of guilt suffi-cient to convince the five judges required in criminal cases was produced, or in the opinion of the attorney general the case warranted dismissal. In serious crimes an accused against whom there was considerable evidence, but who persisted in denying his guilt or who refused to name his accomplices, could be sub-jected to a circumscribed degree of torture. In the majority of cases this resulted in a reduction of the sentence by the appeal court. Within limits, the judges could tailor the punishment to fit the crime, ranging from monetary fines or public ignominy for the well-to-do, to flogging, hanging, or being broken on the wheel. Members of the nobility condemned to death had, of course, the privilege of being beheaded rather than hanged. The total number executed in Canada during the French regime was eighty-five, six of them being broken on the wheel.[29]

Legal fees were strictly regulated by royal edict, yet notaries and court officials still managed to make quite a good thing out of drawing up deeds and contracts, taking evidence, and hearing civil suits. In cases heard before the Sovereign Council there were no fees, and Louis XIV insisted that no subject be denied justice because he lacked means. No evidence has come to light that would suggest the Canadians had cause to be dissatisfied with the administration of justice. In civil matters they sought to avoid the courts like the plague, owing to the expense involved. When companies were formed to exploit the fur trade at the western posts for limited periods it was customary to insert a clause in the notarized acts defining the responsibilities of the partners, declaring that in the event of a dispute recourse would not be had to the courts, instead it would be submitted to arbitration by two disinterested persons whose decision would be final and as bind-ing as a judgment by the Superior Council at Quebec.[30]

---

[29] See André Lachance, *Le bourreau au Canada sous le régime française* (Québec, 1966); *La justice criminelle du roi au Canada au XVIIIe siècle* (Québec, 1978); *Crimes et criminels en Nouvelle-France*, (Montréal, 1984); "Women and Crime in Canada in the early Eighteenth Century, 1712–1759," in Louis A. Knafla (ed.), *Crime and Criminal Justice in Europe and Canada* (Wilfrid Laurier Un. Press, 1981); John Alexander Dickinson, *Justice et justiciables. La procédure civile à la prévôté de Québec, 1667–1759* (Québec, 1982).

[30] See Jacques Mathieu, "Les causes devant la Prévôté de Québec en 1667," *Histoire Sociale History*, 3 (Apr. 1969) pp. 101–111. See also, Archives Nationales du Québec à Montréal, Greffe. Adhemar, Société fait entre les Sieurs Vidal et La Coste, 23e juillet 1729; one example among many.

The Canadians manifested a marked repugnance for the infliction of corporal punishment. The public hangman, occasionally a criminal who had escaped the scaffold himself by accepting the post, was universally reviled. Carpenters refused to construct gibbets or pillories; drovers refused to use their teams to draw the cadaver of an executed criminal through the streets on a plank as the court sometimes commanded, and the intendant had to resort to harsh measures to force them to comply. This attitude stands in marked contrast to that of the public in England and on the Continent, where hangings were spectacles greatly enjoyed by all. Why the Canadians differed in this respect can only be guessed at.

Perhaps the most significant feature of the entire colonial administration was that, unlike in France, none of the administrative or judicial posts were venal. All appointments, except that of naval commissary for a few years in the early eighteenth century, were awarded on merit and held during the King's pleasure, which meant as long as the incumbent performed his duties in a satisfactory manner. This ensured efficiency and went a long way toward avoiding the chicanery and hideous expense for which the French courts in the eighteenth century were notorious.

With the new administrative framework established in rudimentary form, and the Iroquois subdued, Colbert was able to begin implementing his plans for the development of the Canadian economy. He demanded, first of all, that the colony become self-sufficient in the essentials of life and be no longer at the mercy of maritime disasters. Agriculture and fishing had to be expanded and diversified, the forests exploited, and an intensive search made for mineral deposits, particularly copper. He was especially anxious to create a shipbuilding industry in Canada and to have the colony export to France the naval stores that were currently imported from the Baltic countries.[31] He wanted foodstuffs such as wheat and fish, and timber, exported to the French West Indies in exchange for sugar, and he even encouraged the export of these products to New England. What he was striving to do was to convert a subsistence economy, with furs its only export, into a diversified industrial economy capable of supporting a large

---

[31] See P.W. Bamford, *Forests and French Sea power* (Toronto, 1956).

population, and to do it almost overnight. Because no private agency had in the past, or showed any inclination then, to provide the massive infusion of capital, labour, and managerial ability that was required, the Crown had to do it.[32]

Every summer during the ensuing decade ships brought hundreds of indentured workers, settlers, and marriageable girls whose backgrounds had been investigated to ensure that they were morally healthy as well as physically fit.[33] Colbert refused to have recourse to the jails, declaring, "It is important in the establishment of a country to plant there good seed." The indentured labourers were required to work for the established settlers for a three- to five-year term at fair wages before being granted land of their own. This enabled them to gain experience to cope with the peculiar conditions in the colony and provided the settlers with the labour needed to clear their land. Not all of these colonists were French. In 1668 one ship brought Portuguese, Germans, and Hollanders, and the first woman in that shipment to find a husband was a Moor.[34] Horses, sheep, goats, and cattle were also shipped by the Crown and distributed by the intendant among the established settlers. Within a very few years there was an abundance of livestock, and by the end of the century there were more than a thousand horses in the colony. When the first horses to arrive at Quebec were ferried ashore the local Indians were astounded by the tractability of the French moose without antlers. The costs to the Crown for passage alone of immigrants and livestock exceeded 50,000 livres a year.

This subsidized immigration, however, was not sustained. The wars in Europe during the decade of the seventies drained the French exchequer and the country's manpower.[35] Colbert declared that he had no intention of depopulating France to populate the colonies. They now had to stand on their own. Thus the basic French population of Canada, those who came and stayed,

[32] As to why this was so see Eccles, *Canada under Louis XIV*, pp. 52–58.

[33] Silvio Dumas, *Les Filles du Roi en Nouvelle-France* (Québec, 1972).

[34] See *Word from New France: The Selected Letters of Marie de l'Incarnation.* trans. and ed. by Joyce Marshall (Toronto, 1967), p. 345.

[35] Between 1670 and 1679, the army numbered more than 160,000 men and expenses mounted from 77,209,879 to 128,235,300 livres while Crown revenues steadily declined. See Ernest Lavisse, *Histoire de France* (9 vols., Paris, 1903–11), VII-2, pp. 374–380; Frederick L. Nussbaum, *The Triumph of Science and Reason, 1660–1685* (New York, 1953), pp. 147–178.

numbered approximately ten thousand.[36] From the mid-seventies on, the increase in the colonial population was mainly by natural growth, and Colbert employed various devices to stimulate it. Royal dowries of twenty livres were offered to all men marrying at the age of twenty, or lower, and fines were ordered imposed on parents whose sons were not married at twenty or daughters at sixteen.[37] Had this directive been carried out, virtually the entire married population would have been fined. The average age at which girls married in Canada was twenty-two, compared to twenty-four to twenty-five in France. As for the pensions for large families, they were not a noticeable item in the colonial budget and were soon dropped. The number of surviving children per family in Canada averaged between five and six compared with four to five in France. In Canada the number surviving to the marriageable age was double that in France, where barely half the children survived beyond their teens. The intendant Jacques de Meulles commented that far more Canadian children perished by drowning than from natural causes. Thus, while the population of France rose but little in the eighteenth century, that of Canada doubled each generation.[38]

Given such a small base, roughly ten thousand in 1680, even the relatively high fecundity and survival rate in Canada was inadequate to people such a vast terrain. Colbert therefore urged very strongly that the native Indian population be Christianized, civilized, and constrained to settle and intermarry with the French. This Frenchification policy failed dismally.[39] The Indians showed no desire whatsoever to adopt European ways; in fact the trend was in the opposite direction among Canadian youths.

At the end of the seventeenth century it was proposed to relieve the labour shortage by the introduction of Negro slaves, but

---

[36] Jean Hamelin, *Économie et société en Nouvelle-France* (Québec, 1960), pp. 76–100, gives approximate figures of 3,500 soldiers, 1,100 girls, 3,900 indentured workers, 500 independent males, 1,000 condemned criminals. The last group were mostly salt smugglers, sent in the eighteenth century.

[37] Archives Nationales, Colonies, Paris, C11A, II, pp. 26–29, Arrêt du Conseil . . . du 3 avril 1669.

[38] For France see Fernand Braudel and Ernest Labrousse (eds.), *Histoire économique et sociale de la France* (4 vols., Paris, 1970), Vol. II, *1660–1789*, pp. 9–21. For Canada see Jacques Henripin, *La population canadienne au début du XVIIIᵉ siècle* (Travaux et documents cahier No. 22, Institut national d'études démographique, Paris, 1954).

[39] See Jean Delanglez, *Frontenac and the Jesuits* (Chicago, 1939), pp. 36 ff.

although some were brought in by the wealthier colonists they proved to be no answer to the problem. Similarly, Indian slaves, up to sixty a year by the mid-eighteenth century, were purchased from the Crees and Assiniboines at Michilimackinac.[40] Most of them were women and children of the Panis (Pawnee) nation. hence Panis became a generic term for slave, although many were of other tribes with whom the French allies warred, including the Sioux. Some of these slaves were purchased by the Crown for humanitarian purposes, to exchange for white prisoners captured by the French allies in raids on the English colonial settlements.[41]

Significantly, the second largest single group of immigrants who remained permanently in the colony was the military. After the successful completion of the Mohawk campaigns several of the officers and four hundred of the men of the Carignan-Salières regiment were induced to remain in the colony and take up land when their tour of duty was completed. The officers were granted seigneuries; the men became their *censitaires* and received discharge bounties of 100 to 150 livres according to rank. Six infantry captains in France, each with a company of fifty men, also contracted with the Crown to settle in Canada. They received full pay for eighteen months while they cleared their land and became self-supporting. The Carignan-Salières regiment had previously given a great fillip to the colony's economy, providing a sizable market for the growing surplus of grain and other produce. The cost to the Crown for the subsistence of the troops during the three years they remained substantive in the colony was 152,000 livres a year. The significance of this is made apparent by Colbert's order that the civil budget was not to exceed 36,000 livres a year. Mother Superior Marie de l'Incarnation commented: ''Money, which was rare in this country is now very common, these gentlemen having brought a great deal with them. They pay for everything they buy with money, both their food and their other necessities, which suits our habitants very well.''[42]

---

[40] See Marcel Trudel, *L'esclavage au Canada français* (Quebec, 1960).

[41] See Eccles, *The Canadian Frontier*, pp. 149–150.

[42] *Word from New France*, p. 314. On the continuing contribution of the military to the colonial economy and society see W. J. Eccles, ''The Social, Economic, and Political Significance of the Military Establishment in New France,'' in *Essays on New France*.

This great influx of military men also had far-reaching social effects. All told they numbered nearly eight hundred, a figure which must have exceeded the number of adult males resident in the colony in 1665.

Once in Canada, the immigrants were expected to remain permanently. In 1672 secret instructions were sent the governor general to allow only those who had a wife and family and a considerable establishment in the colony to cross to France on business.[43] Colbert was, however, careful to preserve the hierarchical structure of society. Girls of good family were shipped out to provide wives for the officers, and he instructed the intendant that any officer who could not find a suitable wife in the colony should be allowed to cross to France to marry there, provided that he could be relied on to return.

Under this economic stimulus most of the virgin forest land on both sides of the St. Lawrence from a few miles below Quebec up to Montreal was settled and cleared. With white bread the staple food, wheat was the principal crop grown. Yields 600, 750, even 1200 litres from 40 litres of seed grain were realized from the virgin soil. Ten litres of wheat was regarded as sufficient to provide enough bread to feed an adult for a month at the customary consumption of a one kilogram loaf a day. In normal times the colony provided enough grain for its own needs; in good years there was a surplus for export, but in Canada, as in France, a poor crop had to be anticipated every four or five years.[44] This required the intendant to forbid exports of grain in such times of shortage, frequently to import it from France, and to regulate the price to curb profiteering.[45]

The terms under which land was ceded were heavily weighted in favour of the humbler class. After 1663 the size of the concessions granted to seigneurs was considerably reduced, and edicts were issued from time to time to revoke grants that had not been cleared. The onus was placed on the seigneurs to bring their lands into production. The seigneurial dues they received from their

---

[43] Archives Nationales, Colonies, Paris, B, IV, pp. 66–67.

[44] See *Rapport de l'Archiviste de la Province de Québec, 1942–1943*, p. 408, Le Roi à Vaudreuil et Raudot, Versailles, 6 juillet 1709.

[45] See F. W. Burton, "The Wheat Supply of New France," *Proceedings and Transactions of the Royal Society of Canada*, Ser. 3, XXX (1936), pp. 137–150.

censitaires were very low, representing 10 percent of the produce of their concessions. Some seigneurs made no attempt to collect the *cens et rentes*, regarding them as not worth the trouble. Only when forty to fifty families were settled on a seigneury did a seigneur receive an annual revenue of approximately 1,500 livres. Meanwhile he had to make a living off his domain land. In addition he was required to build a mill to grind his *censitaires'* grain at a fixed charge, the *banalité*, of one-fourteenth of the grain ground. If he failed to construct a mill within a year of receiving his concession he sacrificed the *banal* right and it could be granted by the intendant to a *censitaire*. By 1688, of the forty-four grist mills in the colony only half showed even a marginal profit. Fifty years later all but a few of the hundred and twenty mills were profitable.[46]

Thus, with the availability of as much land as they could work on payment of very modest dues, a mill to grind their grain, a parish church, courts of law to regulate disputes at nominal fees, the right to hunt and fish on their land, and rights to graze their cattle on the seigneurial common for a modest fee, the Canadian *habitants* were much better off than the bulk of the rural population in Europe.[47] They were well-fed and could clothe themselves from their own wool, linen, and leather. Their homes, in the early years constructed of squared logs chinked with clay and roofed with bark or thatch,[48] were replaced by the early eighteenth century with frame and stone-filled structures, or by houses of masonry with white-washed walls two feet thick and steep-pitched roofs of thatch, boards, shingles, or tile. The problem of heating in winter dictated that houses could not be overly large, but the availability of firewood for the cutting ensured that the Canadian was warmer in winter than the majority of the citizens in northern France.[49]

---

[46] Richard Colebrook Harris. *The Seigneurial System in Early Canada* (Univ. of Wisconsin Press, 1966), pp. 71–73.

[47] On the condition of the lower class in France see Braudel and Labrousse, *Histoire économique et sociale*, pp. 529–552, 598–599, 672–678; Pierre Goubert, "The French Peasantry of the Seventeenth Century," *Past and Present*, X (1956), pp. 55–77.

[48] Thatch and elm bark roofs normally lasted for 50 years.

[49] This created a unique problem for the Compangie des Indes which, in the 1730s had the monopoly on the marketing of Canadian beaver pelts. In 1734 the directors complained to their Quebec agent that the bales of furs were arriving at La Rochelle in a shocking state, very poorly

The seigneur, on the other hand, in the seventeenth century had a hard time making ends meet, and his standard of living then was little better than that of his *censitaires*. The dues he could levy were closely regulated by the Crown. If his *censitaires* honoured their contractual commitments he could not throw them off the land and lease it to others at higher rates; the land was, in fact, more theirs than his. They owned the means of production and could not be separated from those means to form a pool of cheap exploitable labour. With labour always in short supply and the Crown insistent that concessions be brought into production, there was no possibility of a group of large landholders coming into existence, as occurred in Mexico and the English colonies. Nor could the Canadians, either seigneurs or *censitaires*, become rich through speculation in land. The availability of free land, the decree of the Coutume de Paris that a *quint* (a fifth of the price on all sales of seigneuries) be paid to the Crown, and the inheritance laws of the Coutume de Paris put land speculation out of the question.[50] The land-tenure system thus hampered the development of the colonial economy on traditional capitalist lines because it hindered the emergence of either a capitalist group or a proletariat.[51]

Fishing was another industry that Colbert was anxious to see developed, and the Crown provided quite generous subsidies to individuals who undertook to establish sedentary fishing stations along the shores of the Gulf, but again the success achieved did

baled, with no regard for the varying grades. The company's Quebec agent, Fleury de Lagorgendière, protested vigorously that the furs were properly sorted and baled before being loaded aboard the ship; he could not imagine what had transpired. He duly investigated and discovered that the ship's crew had craftily packed cords of firewood between the bales which, during the Atlantic crossing, frayed the cords, releasing the pelts. At La Rochelle, the sailors swiftly rebaled them, any which way, without regard for the different grades, merely for the weight of each bale, then they sold the firewood at a very handsome profit. See Paris, Achives Nationales, Série C 2, f 84. Paris, 11 mai 1734; Qué., 25 oct. 1734, f 84.

[50] See Harris, *The Seigneurial System*, pp. 56–62.

[51] In 1769, after the Conquest, Guy Carleton, governor of Quebec, and Chief Justice William Hey commented on this phenomenon: "The Rule of Inheritance of Lands en Roture established a perfect equality among the peasants, an equality, which excluding all Subordination became fatal to Manufactures and Industry of every kind, tho' at the same time, under the Regulations established here, it was highly productive of population and settlement, but tho' there was no civil subordination, the institution of the Militia produced a Military one, which was effectual for the restraining of disorder and licentiousness." W. P. M. Kennedy and Gustave Lanctot, *Reports on the Laws of Quebec, 1767–1770* (King's Printer, Ottawa, 1931), pp. 58–59.

On this very significant question see L. R. MacDonald, "France and New France: The Internal Contradiction," *Canadian Historical Review*, LII, 2 (June 1971).

not measure up to expectations. The difficulties were that although the Gulf teemed with all manner of fish, white whales (belugas), seals, and sea lions, the waters were very treacherous and the colony lacked a source of salt; this essential commodity had to be imported from France at considerable cost. In time of war, New England privateers frequently captured the fishing vessels and destroyed the shore stations. It was impossible for Canadian-based fishermen to compete successfully on the French market with the fishermen of northern France who could make a catch on the Banks and reach the Lenten market at home before the Canadians could put their boats in the ice-clogged river. As for the West Indies market, the Canadians could not compete successfully with the New England seamen. Fishing did become a modestly successful enterprise in the eighteenth century, but for the growing urban Canadian market, rather than for export.

Both mainland Acadia and Canada abounded with the forest resources needed to supply a maritime power with masts, ship timbers, and naval stores. Not until the turn of the century was an attempt made to obtain timber from Acadia, and only then because that supplied by Canada had been judged to be of poor quality by the officials in the French dockyards. Colbert had been extremely eager to obtain these supplies from New France, regardless of cost, to remove dependence on the Baltic timber that could too easily be blocked by the Dutch or English in time of war.[52] The trouble was that although these colonies abounded in the pine and oak required for shipbuilding, to convert the standing timber into dressed masts and balks and then transport them across the Atlantic required some skilled, and a lot of unskilled, labour and the right type of ships. All of this caused costs to soar far beyond the prices at which Baltic timber could be had in France from the Dutch merchants. One answer was to establish a shipbuilding industry close to the forests, at Quebec, but far more than wood went into ships. Sails, rigging, all the hardware, had to be transported from France, and so did the

---

[52] See Bamford, *Forests and French Sea Power;* A. R. Lower, "The Forest in New France: A Sketch of Lumbering in Canada before the English Conquest," *Canadian Historical Association Report, 1928;* R. G. Albion, *Forests and Sea Power* (Cambridge, Mass., 1926); Joseph J. Malone, *Pine Trees and Politics* (London, 1964).

skilled workmen who demanded much higher wages on short-term contracts than were customary in the French shipyards. The cost of building a ship in Canada was twice that in France. Moreover, Colbert was not satisfied to begin by building the normal 45 to 90 tonne ships. He, and his enterprising intendant at Quebec, Jean Talon, who had no maritime knowledge, embarked on a grandiose plan to build vessels of 135, 180, even 360 tonnes — veritable monsters at that period. Even had these larger vessels been built, they would have been very uneconomical. Some smaller ships were constructed, and they inaugurated trade between Quebec and the West Indies, but when two of them were lost at sea, requiring a write-off of 36,000 livres, enthusiasm for this sort of venture waned. In fact fewer than seventy-five cargoes were shipped between Quebec and the West Indies.[53] Ships continued to be built in the colony, but small ones for the river traffic and fishing in the Gulf. Not until well on in the eighteenth century did the government make another major effort to establish a large-scale shipbuilding industry.

In the 1680s Jean Bochart de Champigny, a very energetic and level-headed intendant, struggled to establish a naval stores and mast industry. The forests were surveyed for mast pines and oak, both of which were reserved for the Crown. Experts were brought from France, and in the midst of King William's War, a ship's carpenter captured in a raid on the New England frontier was put to work in the pine forests along the St Lawrence to get out the extremely valuable pines for masts, without which ships were helpless hulks. He enjoyed, however, scant success. The problem of transporting these commodities across the Atlantic proved to be almost insuperable, and what appeared to Champigny to be prejudice in the French shipyards against Canadian timber was another stumbling block. Some timber and masts were shipped out from time to time to France or the West Indies, but the industry required massive infusions of capital from the Crown which, although sometimes forthcoming, were never sustained long

---

[53] James Stewart Pritchard, "Ships, Men and Commerce: A Study of Maritime Activity in New France" (unpublished Ph.D. thesis, University of Toronto, 1971). But see Jacques Mathieu, *Le commerce entre la Nouvelle-France et les Antilles au XVIIIe siècle* (Montréal, 1981). Mathieu lists 893 voyages from Canada to the Antilles.

enough to allow the industry to be established on a firm footing.[54]
Perhaps the main drawback, however, was the lack of interest
shown by Canadian entrepreneurs in this industrial activity. Few
in number, they preferred to employ their talents and capital in
an enterprise that offered much greater and more immediate
profits.

That enterprise was, of course, the fur trade. More than anything else it frustrated Colbert's efforts to make Canada play the
same economic role in the French empire as the northern English
colonies played in that of England. Ironically, it was Colbert
himself who, in his attempts to prevent the fur trade from hind-
ering his plans for diversified economic development, inadvert-
ently assisted in its overexpansion to the eventual point of
collapse. Beaver fur, which was used in vast quantities by the
European hatmakers, was the staple.[55] As with the other furs,
there were two main stages in the trade: obtaining the furs in
barter from the Indians, then the marketing of them in Europe.
The Canadians demonstrated outstanding ability in the first stage,
but little competence in the second. Colbert had granted the
monopoly on the marketing of beaver pelts to his Compagnie de
l'Occident. At the same time, and with grave misgivings, he
allowed the Canadians freedom to trade with the Indians. They
had, however, to sell all the beaver and moose hides they obtained
to the company at fixed prices. Other furs they could dispose of
on a free market — in France. The trade of the vast area centred
at Tadoussac was reserved for the company. The prices paid for
beaver and moose hides were fixed initially at 4 livres 10 sols
the livre weight for beaver, 11 livres for moose hides, but from
these prices a sales tax of 25 percent on beaver and 10 percent
on moose hides was deducted. These taxes and a 10 percent
import tax on wine, spirits, and tobacco were the only imposts
the Canadians paid. When the Compagnie de l'Occident was

---

[54] Yet during the Napoleonic wars Canada was the main supplier of timber for British shipyards.
In 1811, 23,053 masts, 24,469 loads of oak, and 52,888 loads of pine, enough to fill 500 timber
ships, were shipped from Quebec. See Albion, *Forests and Sea Power*, p. 357.

[55] See Harold A. Innis, *The Fur Trade in Canada* (New Haven, 1930; rev. paperback ed.,
Toronto, 1962). This pioneering and seminal work has to be used with caution; the statistics cited
are too often incomplete or inaccurate, and the generalizations and conclusions drawn sometimes
take economic determinism to mind-boggling lengths. See W. J. Eccles, "A Belated Review of
Harold Adams Innis's *The Fur Trade in Canada*" in *Essays on New France*.

liquidated in 1674 Colbert farmed out the right to collect all duties and taxes in the West Indies and New France to a syndicate, the Domaine de l'Occident, for 350,000 livres a year. The Domaine, usually referred to as the Company of the Farm, immediately subleased the Canadian beaver trade to a Canadian entrepreneur, Aubert de la Chesnaye, for 119,000 livres.[56]

For the Canadians these transactions meant that they could sell all the beaver they could obtain at a net price of 3 livres, 7 sols, 6 deniers. Although not high, this price still allowed handsome profits, and the Canadians had no worries over marketing. They merely had to deliver their pelts to the company warehouses before the close of navigation, arbitrarily set at October 20. If demand fell off in Europe, it was the company's concern, not theirs. The law of supply and demand did not affect them.[57] This assured market, combined with the cessation of the Iroquois war, caused a tremendous expansion in the fur trade. Hundreds of young men, the most active segment of the population, now headed west in their three-man canoes with a load of trade goods.[58] With the population still small, this greatly reduced the supply of labour available to clear and work the land, and for the industries that Colbert so ardently desired established.

The minister sought to curb this labour drain by edict, forbidding the Canadians to leave the confines of the St Lawrence settlements. He ordered that the trade be confined to Montreal, Trois Rivières, and Quebec; that annual fur fairs be established, with the western Indians bringing the furs to the colony where all the Canadians would be free to barter with them. But it was all in vain. Despite the most severe penalties decreed to be imposed on the *coureurs de bois* when caught, very few were, and the courts were extremely reluctant to impose more than a

---

[56] See Frégault, *Le XVIIIᵉ siècle canadienne*, pp. 242-248, and the entry for de la Chesnaye in *The Dictionary of Canadian Biography*, II.

[57] For the mechanics of the trade see Eccles, *Frontenac*, pp. 75-77.

[58] Another significant factor that encouraged this development was the disproportion in numbers of the sexes. To establish a viable farm a wife was essential, but in the 1660s and 1670s more than half the male population was doomed to remain celibate because there were fewer than half as many women of marriageable age as men. See Hubert Charbonneau and Yolande Lavoie, "Introduction à la reconstitution de la population du Canada au XVIIᵉ siècle: Étude critique des sources de la période 1665-1668," *Revue d'Histoire de l'Amérique française*, XXIV, 4 (mars 1971), pp. 485-511.

modest fine. The intendant Jacques Duchesneau in the 1670s tried his best to carry out Colbert's orders but had to admit failure. He plaintively stated in 1679 that practically the entire colony con- nived to protect and supply the outlaws, who, he claimed, had come to number five to six hundred.[59]

Another of this poor benighted official's difficulties arose from the fact that the governor general, Louis de Buade de Frontenac, the flamboyant, bankrupt old courtier who tried to govern New France as though it were his private feudal domain of an earlier era, strongly espoused the establishment of French power throughout the whole interior of the continent. Like the Intendant Jean Talon before him, who had also been a strong advocate of expansion westward, Frontenac was chiefly concerned with short-term fur trade profits. Colbert saw the danger here very clearly. He strongly opposed this expansionist policy and demanded that the central colony in the St Lawrence Valley, from Montreal to below Quebec, be made secure before any thought be given to occupying territory in the West. With rare prescience he declared that French activities had to be concentrated in a region that could be defended against all foes, and not scattered thinly about a vast area which might well have to be abandoned one day with dire consequences.[60]

The Canadians, however, had no care for contingencies that might some day arise. They were concerned only with the quick profits that were within their grasp. The example of their gov- ernor, who allied himself with a succession of very dubious char- acters and in 1673 established Fort Frontenac on Lake Ontario, set up another fur trade post at Niagara, and sought to monopolize the fur trade of the continent, served as added incentive. Colbert unwittingly aided this process by granting Frontenac's protégé, Robert Cavelier de La Salle, the right to establish trading posts in the Mississippi Valley to further the exploration of this river to its mouth.[61] It took La Salle four years to get beyond the

---

[59] This number, of a surety, was a gross exaggeration. In 1679 the population was 9,400 of whom not more than 1,500 would have been males between the ages 18 to 50, hence physically capable of voyaging to the west. Had a third of the labour force absented itself from the settlements, the colony would have starved to death.

[60] Eccles, *Canada under Louis XIV*, pp. 63–65.

[61] See E. B. Osler, *La Salle* (Toronto, 1967).

Arkansas River, reached in 1673 by Louis Jolliet and Father Marquette, and be carried by the current to the Gulf of Mexico.

The Frontenac-La Salle monopoly of the southwestern fur trade would have been extended to the northern trade as well had they had the resources to do it. The Montreal fur traders, however, managed to hold their own in the west by establishing a base, Michilimackinac, at the strait between Lakes Huron and Michigan. Before long, the *coureurs de bois* were voyaging to the headwaters of the Mississippi, up the Missouri, and north and west of Lake Superior, bringing ever more distant nations into the French commercial orbit and incurring obligations to support these client tribes in their interminable wars. All of this occurred in spite of Colbert's edicts. Finally, in 1681, he admitted the impossibility of confining the Canadians to the St Lawrence Valley and tried merely to reduce their numbers by a licensing system which permitted twenty-five canoes to trade in the West each year. This did little or nothing to staunch the flood of Canadians to the Great Lakes and beyond, and of furs back to Montreal. The question that was not then asked, but soon would be, was: How long before the supply of fur exceeded the demand of the European market?

Before this point was reached westward expansion brought the colony face to face once again with the fearsome menace of a war with the Iroquois. While La Salle was establishing his posts on the Illinois River and down the Mississippi to the Ohio, the Iroquois confederacy was planning to seize this vast region, which they had once conquered from the Illinois but had had to relinquish owing to pressure from the Susquehannocks nation of the Susquehanna region. By 1675 the Susquehannocks, a tribe of Iroquoian stock, themselves under treacherous attack by the militiamen of Virginia and Maryland, had made their peace with the Iroquois. In 1680 the western Iroquois invaded the Illinois country only to find La Salle's men established among, and allied with, their foes. In the face of this threat Frontenac followed a pusillanimous policy, seeking to avoid an open rupture by appeasing the Iroquois. This merely encouraged them in their aggression until the entire Great Lakes basin was unsafe for the French. The Iroquois, the most formidable military power in North America, having defeated and scattered all their Indian foes, were now quite prepared to challenge the France of Louis XIV. In 1684, Father Jean de Lamberville, the missionary with the Onondagas, warned Le Febvre de La Barre, Governor General of New France, that the Onondagas, "say that the French have a great desire to be stript, roasted, and eaten; and that they will see if their flesh, which according to them, is saltish on account of the salt the French make use of, be as good as that of their other enemies whom they devour."[62]

Far to the north too a threat appeared. In 1668 an English ship had made its way into Hudson Bay and carried on a profitable trade. Two years later the Hudson's Bay Company received its charter and quickly established posts on the shores of the Bay that attracted the Cree tribes who had previously traded with the French. What made this threat appear so dangerous was that the costs of shipping goods from England to the Bay posts by sea was far less than from France to Quebec, then a thousand miles by canoe to Lake Superior and beyond. The threat was more apparent than real. The shipping season to the Bay posts lasted only a few weeks. Moreover, the main source of the better quality furs lay several hundred kilometres to the west of Hudson Bay; hence the Indian trappers preferred to trade at the French posts established in their midst, rather than undertake the long voyage to the Bay during the short summer season through a region with little game—"the starving country." Thus the French continued to garner the lion's share of the fur trade. These early events in Hudson Bay and the Great Lakes region did, however, mark the beginning of the Anglo-French struggle for the continent.[63]

In September 1683, Colbert died and was succeeded in office by his son Seignelay. That year marked the end of an era. During the preceding two decades Colbert had accomplished much in America, not as much as he had hoped, but more than anyone then living would have thought possible in 1663. The French hold on its islands in the West Indies was secure; the Dutch had been eliminated from their trade. In 1664 the Dutch had sent more

---

[62] NYCD IX, p. 253. Jean de Lamberville à M. de la Barre, Onondaga, 11 July 1684.

[63] On French westward expansion and the threat from Hudson Bay see Eccles, *Canada under Louis XIV*, pp. 99–118; Eccles, *Essays on New France*, pp. 67–68.

than a hundred ships to the French islands, the Compagnie de l'Occident some twenty-odd. In 1683 the French ports had more than two hundred ships in that trade, with sugar and tobacco the main staples. In 1663 France had had to import all its sugar. When Colbert died there were twenty-nine refineries in France, five in the islands, and France supplied much of Europe with this commodity.

In New France, however, Colbert's policies had not enjoyed equal success. Acadia was still very thinly populated; there were fewer than a thousand French settlers, and their main trade relations were with New England rather than with France or Canada. The settlements were still pathetically vulnerable to attack from the sea. It was, in fact, the Indian nations rather than the French who were sovereign in the region. In Newfoundland the picture was much the same. A few hundred French fishermen at Plaisance maintained themselves largely by trading their catch to New England ships. Although nominally under the authority of the governor general and intendant at Quebec, these officials were far too remote to exert any real control.[64]

Canada, which had burst out of its confines in the St Lawrence Valley, had conspicuously failed to fulfill the role intended for it by Colbert. Mainly as a result of his emigration policy, the population had grown from twenty-five hundred to more than ten thousand. Most of the land along the river between Montreal and Quebec had been cleared and brought into production, rendering the colony self-supporting in foodstuffs, but the attempts to export the surplus to the West Indies had failed. Similarly, Colbert's attempts to establish such industries as lumbering and shipbuilding had met, thus far, with scant success. The trade in furs still dominated the Canadian economy, drained its meagre labour supply, and provided profits for the Canadians. Very little of this money was invested in other economic endeavours, however; instead it provided the people with costly imported amenities of life.

Despite Colbert's attempts to curb expansion into the interior, geography and the fur trade had combined to draw the French

---

[64] See John Humphreys, "Plaisance," *Publications in History*, No. 3 (National Museums of Canada, Ottawa, 1970).

more than a thousand miles west through the Great Lakes, and south down the Mississippi until on April 9, 1682, Robert Cavelier de La Salle and Henri Tonti reached its mouth and claimed the vast region, predictably named Louisiana, for France. Once these regions, from Hudson Bay to the Gulf of Mexico, had been claimed for the French Crown, they could not be relinquished without defeat in war. France now had to be prepared to expend its blood and treasure to maintain its hold on half the continent without regard for the economic balance sheet.

Chapter 4

War and Trade, 1683–1713

While Colbert's life ebbed away in September 1683, so too did the years of peace for New France. From the time of his death until the end of the century, events in North America were dominated less by the European colonial powers, France, England, and Spain, than by the Five Nations Iroquois confederacy. These nations, with a fighting strength of 2,800 warriors, as well-armed as the Europeans, could put a larger force in the field than could the Canadians. In the previous Iroquois wars the French had been attacked only by the eastern tribes of the confederacy. Following on French expansion into the Illinois country, however, the Senecas, most numerous of the Iroquois nations, were determined to challenge the French presence on lands they claimed to be theirs by right of earlier conquest. Their aims were the same as they had been when they had destroyed the Huron confederacy at mid-century; they wanted hunting grounds, and all their ancient foes driven a safe distance away to provide security for their villages.[1]

It was at this juncture of events that New York received a new governor, Thomas Dongan, an aggressive Irish Catholic who had once served in the armies of Louis XIV. Dongan was eager to swell the coffers of his province by an increase in the fur trade,

---

[1] For the background to the struggle and the events of the ensuing Anglo-French-Iroquois hostilities see W. J. Eccles, *Frontenac: The Courtier Governor* (Toronto, 1959), *Canada under Louis XIV* (Toronto, 1964); Allen W. Trelease, *Indian Affairs in Colonial New York* (Cornell Univ. Press, 1960).

and he urged the Albany traders to adopt the French methods of voyaging to the Indian country to obtain furs rather than sit back and wait for the furs to be brought to them. Although he appears not to have incited the Iroquois to attack the French, he did refuse to accept French claims to sovereignty over the western territory, either north of the Great Lakes or in the Mississippi Valley, maintaining that the subjects of the King of England had as much right to trade there as a Frenchman. He also asserted that the Iroquois were British subjects, hence were the French to make war on them they thereby were at war with England.[2] He might have been more aggressive had it not been for instructions from Whitehall forbidding him to take any action that might give the French just cause for complaint. In London a joint Anglo-French committee was sitting to reconcile the differences between the two powers in North America and to establish territorial boundaries acceptable to both.[3] The Iroquois, however, if they knew of this committee's existence, certainly did not accept that they were in any way subject to its decisions. They regarded themselves as sovereign and the French as having invaded their lands. They were determined to drive them out, and were they to succeed then New York would be the gainer. Thus Dongan could hardly be expected to take effective steps to curb them by cutting off their supply of arms. Had he done so he would merely have alienated the confederacy, which would have been a dangerous thing to do, and harmed his province's interests.

New France also had received a new governor, Joseph-Antoine Le Febvre de La Barre, who in 1664 had taken Cayenne from the Dutch.[4] In the process, however, he had rendered himself

---

[2] Lawrence H. Leder (ed.), *The Livingston Indian Records, 1666–1723* (Gettysburg PA 1956). Propositions made by Tho. Dongan to the Five Nations, Schenectady, 14 July 1687. See also *Calendar State Papers Colonial, America and West Indies, 1681–1685*, pp 422–3, # 1059, April (?) 1683. Draft of a memorial in answer to Monsieur de la Barre, Governor of Canada; *ibid.*, 1685–1688, p 645, # 2091 (1683) Memorial for the French Ambassador.

[3] In seventeenth-century Europe, frontiers were ceasing to be ill-defined, broad areas. The sovereigns were striving to reduce them to lines, but the process was far from complete by the end of the century, and in North America was not completed until after the Conquest of New France. See G. N. Clark, *The Seventeenth Century* (2d ed., Oxford, 1947), pp. 140–152.

[4] For nearly seventy years the French had struggled to establish trading posts and a plantation colony on the Guiana coast, but to no avail. The Portuguese, hostile Indians, and disease defeated their every effort prior to 1664. See H. I. Priestley, *France Overseas Through the Old Regime: A Study of European Expansion* (New York, 1939), pp. 93–108.

suspect of serving his own interests rather than the King's. He had also on occasion displayed a lamentable lack of valour in action. Upon his arrival at Quebec in 1682 the leading Canadians and the Jesuits advised him that unless the Iroquois were curbed swiftly the French would be driven out of the West. They advised that the western Iroquois villages be destroyed, and at once. La Barre immediately sent an appeal to the minister of marine for six hundred regular troops and a supply of arms. With these he proposed to invade the Iroquois cantons, winter there, and break their fighting strength once and for all. At this stage there was no lack of confidence among the Canadians that such a campaign would be effective. Their only fear was that unless a campaign were waged the West would be lost by default. Nearly two decades had elapsed since the last Iroquois war, a majority of the colonists had come to Canada after peace had been made, and time appears to have dimmed the recollections of those who had endured the terror of the earlier Iroquois assaults on the settlements.

The military aid furnished by France was far less than La Barre had requested. His equivocal instructions from the Ministry of Marine advised him to avoid waging war if possible, but if it was unavoidable, then he was to crush the Iroquois swiftly and completely. La Barre now made his preparations. When word was received that the western Iroquois had laid siege to Fort Saint-Louis in the Illinois country, La Barre set off at the head of a force of 800 men, accompanied by 378 allied Indians. The campaign was a complete fiasco. La Barre's courage had begun to ebb even before he left Montreal. His supply system was inadequate, and Spanish influenza, brought with the troop ships, spread through the ranks of his motley army. By the time he reached Fort Frontenac at the eastern end of Lake Ontario he commanded a force that could barely stand, let alone engage the Iroquois. When the Iroquois proposed the settlement of their difficulties by negotiation he had no choice but to accept. Had he refused, very few of his men would have lived to see Montreal again. A haughty Onondaga chief dictated humiliating terms, and La Barre meekly had to accept them. The Iroquois spokesman declared the intention of the Five Nations to continue their drive in the West.

The French would not be harmed as long as they did not interfere.[5]

When this treaty was sent to France, Louis XIV recognized it for the humiliating defeat that it was; one that could not be tolerated. La Barre was recalled in disgrace, blamed for much more than he was really accountable for, and replaced by Jacques-Réné de Brisay, marquis de Denonville, brigadier of the Dragoons, a veteran soldier regarded as one of the better officers in the kingdom. With him went eight hundred Troupes de la Marine. Two years later another eight hundred were sent, and Denonville was given a free hand to curb the Iroquois by peaceful means or by war, as he deemed best.

When Denonville took stock of the situation he, to a far greater degree than his predecessors in office, grasped the strategic realities in North America. The Iroquois were the immediate threat that had to be dealt with swiftly, but behind them he saw New York. He therefore recommended to the minister that the threat to the security of New France and its control of the western fur trade could most easily be removed were Louis XIV to buy the province of New York from the perpetually hard-up James II. Failing that, the Iroquois would have to be crushed by force, and he was under no illusions as to the difficulty of the task. He was convinced that a much larger army than he had at his command would be needed, but were he to wait for more troops to be sent, which he doubted he would receive in time, the Iroquois would have subdued the western nations allied with the French and would be free to launch their full strength against the Canadian settlements. As though to drive the point home, in 1686 Dongan dispatched a party of Albany traders, escorted by Iroquois and guided by renegade Canadian *coureurs de bois*, to the Ottawas, where they drove a brisk trade.

To the north the Canadians had already taken up the challenge of the English Hudson's Bay Company by organizing, with Colbert's blessing, the Compagnie de la Baie du Nord,[6] but they enjoyed scant success. The English offered some goods to the

---

[5] For a detailed account of this campaign see Eccles, *Frontenac: The Courtier Governor*, pp. 157–172.

[6] See the unpublished M.A. thesis by Edward H. Borins, "La Compagnie du Nord, 1682–1700" (McGill University, 1968).

Indians at lower prices than did the French, but the latter's trade goods were of better quality and more suited to the Indian's needs.[7] Denonville decided that this competition could not be allowed to continue. The English were, after all, trespassing on territory claimed by France. In 1686 he sent 105 men under the command of an officer in the Troupes de la Marine north by canoe to James Bay. They exceeded their somewhat elastic instructions, captured three English posts at the foot of the Bay, and returned to Quebec with fifty thousand prime beaver pelts.[8] The success of the expedition, however, was dimmed by the fact that the overland route was found to be impractical for commercial purposes. In December a treaty of neutrality was ratified by Louis XIV and James II, but despite the outraged protests of the Hudson's Bay Company, the French refused to relinquish either the posts or the pelts they had seized. This success was undermined by the minister's ridiculous decision that all furs traded at the Bay had to be taken to Quebec and the export tax of 25 percent paid to the agent of the Domaine de l'Occident, before they were shipped to France, conditions which added immeasurably both to the hazards of navigation and to the company's costs and reduced profits to the vanishing point. Any hope that the Canadian company could compete successfully with the Hudson's Bay Company was thereby removed. They were able to hamper the English from time to time by outright aggression, but not to drive them out.

Farther south, the French had better success. In 1687 Denonville launched a well-organized campaign against the Senecas. He destroyed their village and their food supplies and inflicted some casualties but failed to make them stand and fight. After one brief skirmish they fled, and their material losses were easily replaced. However, the demonstration that the French could march an army, more than two thousand strong counting the Indian auxiliaries, into the country of the most distant and powerful of the Iroquois nations was not without effect on both them and the authorities of New York. Moreover, during the campaign

---

[7] See Eccles, *Essays on New France*, pp. 68–73.

[8] See I. Caron (ed.), *Journal de l'expédition du Chevalier de Troyes à la Baie d'Hudson* (Beauceville, 1918).

Denonville had succeeded in capturing the two parties of Albany traders sent by Dongan that year to break the French hold on the western fur trade. They spent a few weeks in prison at Quebec before being released. Albany was to make no more attempts to invade the western lands claimed by France. At least that dangerous threat had been eliminated.

Denonville now appealed to the minister for a much larger force to crush the Iroquois completely. He also suggested that they could be brought to heel far more easily were he allowed to invade New York and destroy Albany, their main supply base. He dispatched the governor of Montreal to Versailles with detailed proposals on how this could be accomplished. Failing adequate forces to accomplish either of these goals, he foresaw years of guerrilla warfare in which the Iroquois would inflict heavy losses on the Canadian settlements. He informed the minister that the choice was either a much greater military effort or the negotiation of a peace settlement with the Iroquois until such time as the King could provide the force needed to settle the issue. With a coalition of powers forming in Europe to wage war on France, more troops could not be spared. Denonville was, therefore, instructed to negotiate an honourable peace. This he succeeded in doing. In June 1688, the treaty was arranged, to be ratified the following year by all the Five Nations.

Events in Europe, however, intervened. In November 1688, William of Orange landed in England. Six weeks later James II fled to France and Parliament offered the throne to William and Mary. France was already at war with the Hapsburg empire, Spain, and the Netherlands. In May, England joined the coalition. When word reached the English colonies that hostilities between the two powers had begun, the Iroquois were immediately informed. Denonville knew nothing of this. The ships from France with badly needed supplies and the annual dispatches from the court were ominously delayed. So too were the Iroquois ambassadors, eagerly awaited to ratify the peace treaty. They were, in fact, preparing to go to Montreal, but not for that purpose. The "Protestant wind" that helped put William and Mary on the throne also blew for the Iroquois.

In France, Denonville's proposal for an assault by land and sea on New York had been accepted when England declared war, but radically modified. The execution was pathetically inadequate. Not until July 23 did the expedition sail from La Rochelle with the comte de Frontenac in command. He had been restored to favour through the influence of his courtier friends and relatives and reappointed as governor general, Denonville having requested his own recall on grounds of ill health. Encountering strong headwinds on the Atlantic, the convoy did not reach Quebec until mid-October. By then it was too late in the season for the invasion of New York to be launched. It was, in fact, three months too late. On the night of August 4, while the French convoy had been buffeted on the North Atlantic, some fifteen hundred Iroquois warriors had struck the Canadian settlements near Montreal. Surprise was complete. Fifty-six farms were destroyed, more than a hundred Canadians killed or captured. The savage ferocity of the attack struck terror in the colony. It was only the beginning. During the remainder of the summer small Iroquois war parties inflicted losses, then faded into the forest before a counterattack could be launched.

The Canadians, eager to strike back, wanted to attack Albany, the main Iroquois supply base. Had they done so they could have destroyed it, and both the Iroquois and the English colonials would have been thrown on the defensive. Frontenac, however, divided his forces. In the winter and spring of 1690, assaults were launched on the village of Schenectady and two isolated hamlets on the New England coast. These raids served no real strategic purpose, but they hurt enough to persuade the English colonies to combine their forces in a dual assault, by land and sea, to conquer Canada. The land assault, mustered at Albany to march on Montreal, collapsed as a result of the colonists' military ineptitude. In Acadia the New Englanders had better success. French privateers at Port Royal had captured several New England fishing vessels, and the Acadian Indians had killed some two hundred settlers on the frontier, even capturing Fort Pemaquid. Yet there the French were very vulnerable. Dissension was rife among the officials, the garrison strength was only ninety, some of them old and infirm with only forty serviceable muskets among them, and the civil population scattered and unbellicose. In the autumn of

1689 a New England expedition led by Sir William Phips captured
Port Royal without a fight, but promptly dishonoured the terms
of the capitulation, looting, pillaging, desecrating the churches.
No attempt was made to occupy the colony but the loot paid the
costs of the expedition and stimulated the General Court of Massachusetts to join the proposed English colonial assault on Canada
on a profit-sharing basis. The churches of Quebec and Montreal
were reliably reported to be crammed with gold and silver
ornaments.

It was to be a dual assault. The plan called for 855 militia from
New England, Maryland, and New York to join a large force of
Iroquois for an assault on Montreal, by way of Lake Champlain
and the Richelieu River. At the same time an armada was to
assemble at Boston, 2,000 men and 34 sail, under the command
of Phips, for an attack on Quebec. On 21 August, they set sail
for the St Lawrence. They did not arrive at Quebec until 15
October, frost already in the air. There they found themselves
facing almost the entire military might of Canada, more than
2,000 men, colonial regulars and militia, massed at the town on
its virtually impregnable site. The force intended for Montreal
had fallen apart before it even reached Lake Champlain; military
incompetence, chicanery, and an outbreak of smallpox saved
Canada. At Quebec, after a few days of skirmishing, which cost
them some thirty killed, the smallpox-ridden New England militia
had to admit that the task was beyond them. Without attempting
to launch an assault, on October 25 the motley fleet raised anchor
and slipped downriver, only to suffer heavy losses at sea. The
French casualties were six or seven killed and twelve wounded.[9]

The Canadians had earlier demonstrated their ability to carry
the war to the English settlements both winter and summer, but
they lacked the forces to conquer and hold the enemy territory.
The English colonials had failed miserably in their attempts to
conquer Canada; they were unable even to defend their own
frontiers from the raids by the Canadians and allied Indians. From
1690 on it was the Iroquois who bore the brunt of the fighting on
the Canadian frontier, and in Acadia it was the Abenaquis, Mic-

---

[9] For contemporary accounts of this Quebec campaign see 1690 *Sir William Phips devant Québec. Histoire d'un Siège* par Ernest Myrand (Québec, 1893).

macs and Malecites, allied with the French, who delayed the conquest of that neglected colony for another two decades.

In Canada the war became one of guerrilla tactics, what the French called *la petite guerre*. During the first two or three years the Iroquois had the best of it; they inflicted heavy casualties and ravaged the farms from Montreal to Trois Rivières. The *habitants* were forced to coop themselves up in stockades with their live-stock, going out to work their fields only in armed bands. In this type of warfare the Troupes de la Marine proved to be of little use, except to garrison forts in the exposed areas, and as a labour force. Most of the fighting was done by the Canadian militia in small war parties led by regular officers, many of them Canadian.[10]

Within two years they mastered the techniques of this savage forest warfare of swift raid and ambush, with no quarter asked or given. Canadian war parties waited for the Iroquois at river crossings, invaded their hunting grounds, and ravaged the frontier of New York, inflicting losses that gave the Iroquois pause. In addition the western nations allied to the French, the Hurons, Illinois, Miamis, and Ottawas, from time to time harassed the cantons of the western Iroquois, making it difficult for them to hunt and trap, cutting them off from the furs the Albany merchants demanded in exchange for the European weapons the Iroquois could not do without.

The French, on the other hand, suffered no interference in the fur trade. In fact, the war served as a device to expand it. Garrisoned trading posts were established throughout the basin of the Great Lakes, along the headwaters of the Mississippi, in the Sioux country, and in the Illinois territory. These posts, ostensibly to keep the Indian allies supplied with munitions to pursue the war, really served little more than a commercial purpose at the Crown's expense. The officers in command, with the connivance of the governor general, reaped rich harvests of beaver pelts. Throughout the war, convoys of canoes arrived at Montreal from the West bringing at least 140,000 livres' weight of beaver each year, this being three times what had been received prior to 1675.

---

[10] See "Military Organization in New France," in Eccles, *Frontenac*.

The minister's order to Frontenac to reduce the flow by reducing the number of men he allowed to voyage to the West went unheeded. By 1695 supply had risen to four times the annual demand of the French market, and the Company of the Farm, which had to accept all beaver at fixed prices, found itself with a surplus of 3.5 million livres' weight, with more flooding in. The Ministry of Marine was forced to take drastic action. The minister, Louis Phélypeaux de Pontchartrain, although a kinsman of Frontenac, on the advice of the intendant and other of the senior officials in the colony, became convinced that the governor general was dragging his feet in the conduct of the war, that an all-out campaign against the Iroquois would bring them to terms, and that the war merely served as a pretext for the Canadians, subsidized by the Crown, to add to the surplus of beaver.

Upon receipt of direct orders from the minister, Frontenac undertook a campaign against the Onondagas and Oneidas. Their villages and food supplies were destroyed. The Five Nations had borne the brunt of the war during the past seven years and had suffered very heavy casualties. The following year, 1697, hostilities ended in Europe. Any lingering hope the Iroquois might have had of receiving material support from the English colonies vanished. They had to sue for peace, but they still had not fallen so low that they would accept any terms. The negotiations were to drag on for four years before a definitive treaty between the Five Nations on the one side, and the French and their allies on the other, was finally concluded.[11]

The heartfelt joy of the Canadians at the end of hostilities was qualified by the economic disaster with which, in 1696, they had suddenly found themselves faced. The minister of marine, convinced that the glut of beaver resulted from the existence of military posts in the West that provided the excuse for the flood of trade goods in the guise of military supplies, ordered that all but one post in the Illinois country be abandoned and destroyed. All trading in beaver was at the same time suspended. This decision caused consternation in the colony, and a flood of memoirs

---

[11] See Anthony F. C. Wallace, "Origins of Iroquois Neutrality: The Grand Settlement of 1701," *Pennsylvania History*, XXIV (1957), pp. 223-235; Eccles, *Frontenac*, pp. 244-294, 328-333; Dale Miquelon, *New France 1701-1744 "A supplement to Europe"* (Toronto, 1987), pp. 20-25.

crossed the Atlantic to be added to those produced by the minister's advisers in France, who had been studying the plight of the Canadian beaver trade for the past three years. By 1698 the glut in the French warehouses had reached one million livres' weight, enough to manufacture half a million hats.[12] Despite this, the senior Canadian officials pointed out that it would be extremely dangerous to abandon the West. Peace had not yet been concluded with the Iroquois, and to withdraw precipitately, they feared, might lead the English to fill the vacuum. They pointed out that were control of the West once to be relinquished, it would be extremely difficult, likely impossible, to regain it. Economics dictated the abandonment of the West; politics dictated its retention.

Faced with this dilemma the minister dithered. The western posts were retained, the twenty-five annual trading congés were terminated, and the price paid for beaver was drastically reduced, but the Company of the Farm was still required to accept all the pelts that the Canadians brought in. Pontchartrain hoped that these measures would reduce the trade in furs sufficiently that the western posts would be abandoned, and with them the French commitment in the West. Fears were even expressed that the Crown might abandon the colony, leaving the colonials to resolve their problems by themselves, but this was really out of the question. After many months of cross-Atlantic bickering and bargaining, the Canadian fur trade community took over the marketing of beaver and formed a company for the purpose; but the terms of the agreement, and the huge glut of fur, virtually guaranteed failure. The Canadians, altogether too naïve in business transactions of this sort, had been overreached.[13]

Despite the economic debacle in Canada, the French in North America had had quite a good war. They had retained their hold on Acadia and had pushed back the English frontier to the Kennebec River. Yet the defense of Acadia still depended on their Indian allies, who had kept the New Englanders on the defensive by savage raids to within forty kilometres of Boston. In New-

---

[12] See A N Colonies, Série B, vol. XX, p 106, Ministre à Champigny, Versailles, 28 mai 1698.

[13] See Guy Frégault, "La compagnie de la colonie," in *Le XVIIIᵉ siècle canadien: Études* (Montréal, 1968), pp. 242–288; Miquelon, *New France*, pp. 57–64.

foundland, the great Canadian naval captain Pierre le Moyne d'Iberville had captured St John's, set it ablaze, then destroyed the fishing outposts all along the coast. Before he could capture the two remaining English outposts and consolidate his conquest, he was dispatched with a naval squadron to Hudson Bay. An English expedition with two thousand troops quickly reoccupied St John's. In Hudson Bay, Iberville won a brilliant victory against heavy odds, forced the English governor of the Bay to surrender, and occupied York Fort, leaving only the posts at the foot of James Bay in the possession of the Hudson's Bay Company.[14] Significantly, this assault on the Hudson Bay posts had been ordered by the Ministry of Marine, not because France hoped to reap any benefits therefrom; in fact, considering the glut of beaver, just the reverse. The assault was ordered for purely political reasons, giving a portent of future French policy for all of North America.

On the central front, the Canadians had also done very well. They had beaten back the direct attacks by the English colonies, carried the fighting to their frontier settlements, and forced the Iroquois to come to terms. What was more, they were farsighted enough to realize that the Iroquois should not be totally destroyed. The Five Nations served an extremely useful role as a barrier between New York and the western nations. Were they to be crushed, the English of the northern colonies might well surge into the northwest in force, threatening Canada on its western flank. The fighting strength of the Five Nations had been cut in half, whereas the population of Canada and New York was doubling every generation. The only viable policy now for the Five Nations was to play the one off against the other in order to retain some measure of sovereignty. Thus, during the protracted peace negotiations at Montreal, they accepted the French proposal that in any future war between France and England they would remain neutral.[15] Coming on the very eve of a renewed Anglo-French

---

[14] See Guy Frégault, *Iberville le conquérant* (Montréal, 1944), but see also the article by Bernard Pothier in *Dictionary of Canadian Biography*, Vol. II, *1701–1740* (Toronto, 1969), pp. 390–401.

[15] There has to date been no satisfactory history of the role played by the Iroquois in North America, only a few fairly good studies of aspects of the topic. When it is undertaken, the standard histories of the colonial period in North America will, I suspect, have to be completely rewritten. Meanwhile, see Francis Jennings et al (eds.), *The History and Culture of Iroquois Diplomacy* (Syracuse University Press, 1985).

war, this new turn held out a frightening prospect for the northern English colonies that had relied on the Iroquois for their defense,[16] while placing Canada in a much stronger position.

In Europe meanwhile, after five years of involved diplomatic manoeuvring, the great powers had blundered into war over the succession to the Spanish throne.[17] On 15 May 1702, England, the Netherlands, and the Hapsburg emperor declared war on France and its client state, Spain, now ruled by the first of the Bourbon dynasty, Philip V, grandson of Louis XIV. During the long-drawn-out negotiations that had failed to avert war, Louis XIV made a major decision on French policy in North America that resolved the colony's vexing economic problems by making them almost irrelevant and submerging them in a new and much larger context of imperialism.

In 1698 Louis XIV had made the opening moves to protect French interests in America, whichever way the Spanish question was resolved. Alarmed by reports from Canada that English traders were crossing the Alleghenies and establishing trade relations with Indian nations in the Mississippi Valley, as well as by other reports from England that William III planned to seize the mouth of the river and establish a colony peopled by refugee Huguenots, he dispatched an expedition commanded by Iberville to the mouth of the river to claim possession of the region for France. That mission successfully accomplished, Iberville returned to France only to be sent back to the Mississippi with secret orders to destroy by covert means any posts the English might try to establish between the Carolinas and the Mississippi.

This move was intended to serve one of two purposes: if the Spanish throne were to go to a Hapsburg, these new bases would serve as a staging area for an invasion of Mexico and other Spanish-held territory; if the throne went to a French prince, then

---

[16] On the effect the French threat had on settlement in New York see Sung Bok Kim, "A New Look at the Great Landlords of Eighteenth-Century New York," *The William and Mary Quarterly*, 3d Ser., XXVII, 4 (Oct., 1970), pp. 589–592.

[17] On the European background of this struggle see Ernest Lavisse (ed.), *Histoire de France* (9 vols., Paris, 1903–11), VIII-1; John B. Wolf, *The Emergence of the Great Powers, 1685–1715* (New York, 1951); M. A. Thompson, "Louis XIV and the Origins of the War of the Spanish Succession," *Transactions of the Royal Historical Society*, 5th Ser., IV (1954), pp. 111–134; J. S. Bromley (ed.), *The New Cambridge Modern History VI The Rise of Great Britain and Russia, 1688–1725* (Cambridge University Press, 1970), pp. 410–445.

they would serve to protect the Spanish colonies from a possible English thrust southwest from the existing southern colonies. On 9 October, 1700, Louis XIV accepted the offer of the Spanish throne for his grandson. The following May, in a dispatch to the governor general at Quebec he declared his intention to found a settlement at the mouth of the Mississippi to halt the advance of the English in that direction.[18] From Acadia on the north Atlantic coast, up the St Lawrence to Canada, then through the Great Lakes and down the Mississippi to the newly founded colony of Louisiana on the Gulf of Mexico, a cordon was to be drawn at the rear of the English colonies to hem them in between the Atlantic and the Appalachians. The existing French fur trading posts in the Mississippi Valley and the Great Lakes basin that the minister of marine had sought to abandon five years earlier now had to be maintained and new ones established. Missionaries had to be sent to the southwest to help weld all the Indian nations into an economic and military alliance. By these means a few French could hope to hold back the English colonials, whose population, already vastly greater than that of the Canadians, was doubling every generation.[19]

Ironically, news of this development caused consternation in Canada. The governor, the intendant, and the merchant fur traders saw it as a threat to the colony's interests. The officials feared that it would reduce Crown support for Canada, and the governor general pleaded, unsuccessfully, that the new colony be placed under his authority. The merchant fur traders feared that it would divert the western fur trade down the Mississippi, where a year-round port could be established. That their fears were not groundless was made plain when several *coureurs de bois* took the furs they had traded with goods obtained on credit at Montreal down the Mississippi and sold them to Iberville and his men.

They were also disturbed by the minister's decision to accept the proposal of La Mothe Cadillac, an officer in the Troupes de la Marine with a very persuasive pen but an unenviable reputation, to establish a settlement at Detroit and remove to it the

---

[18] On the founding of Louisiana see Marcel Giraud, *Histoire de la Louisiane française: Le règne de Louis XIV (1698–1715)* (Paris, 1953).

[19] So too was that of the Canadians, but on a much smaller base.

Ottawa and Huron tribes of Michilimackinac. Cadillac claimed that this new colony would serve as a barrier to English penetration of the west and restrain the Iroquois. The governor general, the intendant, and the Canadian merchants were strongly opposed to the scheme for political and economic reasons. They warned that were these western tribes to settle at Detroit they would be tempted to come to an agreement with the Iroquois to take their furs to Albany rather than to Montreal. The minister refused to

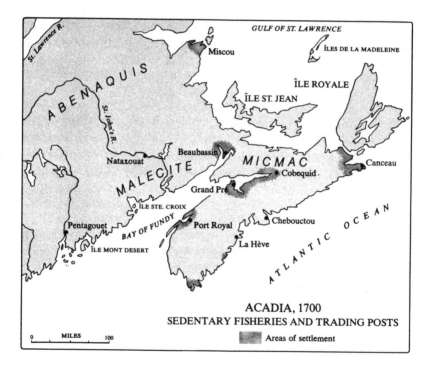

ACADIA, 1700
SEDENTARY FISHERIES AND TRADING POSTS
Areas of settlement

listen. Detroit was established and the fears of the Canadians were realized. It required all the considerable diplomatic skill of the governor general, Philippe de Rigaud de Vaudreuil, to prevent a wholesale defection of the western allies.[20]

---

[20] See Yves F. Zoltvany, "The Problem of Western Policy under Philippe de Rigaud de Vaudreuil (1703–1725)," *Canadian Historical Association Report, 1964;* "New France and the West (1701–1713)," *The Canadian Historical Review*, XLVI (Dec., 1965). p. 103 n 19; Yves F. Zoltvany, *Philippe de Rigaud de Vaudreuil Governor of New France 1703–1725* (Toronto, 1974), pp. 38–41. Particularly good on Cadillac's role is Miquelon, *New France 1701–1744*, pp. 33–46, 250.

These problems, however, faded into the background with the reopening of hostilities. The big question now was: Would the Iroquois honour the treaty they had just signed and remain neutral? This they did, and that negated any desire the colonials of New York might have had to attack Canada. The one thing the Canadians wished to avoid was a renewal of hostilities with the Iroquois, who made it known that they would not tolerate hostilities in their backyard. Fearful that Canadian attacks on New York would cause the Five Nations to abandon their neutral stance, Governor General Vaudreuil gave the Governor of New York to understand that, in the ongoing war, the Canadians would not be the first to strike. This covert understanding did not include New England, whose exposed settlements now bore the brunt of Canadian and Indian assaults.

Meanwhile, the understanding with New York led to a thriving clandestine economic alliance between the merchants of Montreal and Albany, much to the disgust of the Massachusetts authorities. The merchants of Albany paid higher prices for beaver than did the Canadian monopoly company; moreover, they paid cash whereas the Canadian company, like its predecessors, paid in postdated bills of exchange.[21] The Canadians also obtained plentiful supplies of goods at Albany, in particular the English woollen cloth, duffel and stroud, which at this time were much cheaper than French woollens. The Indians, who had been introduced to these goods by the Hudson's Bay Company, preferred them. Had it not been for the supplies obtained from Albany, the French

---

[21] It is doubtful if the difference between Montreal and Albany prices was as great as the Canadians claimed. They had a motive for exaggerating the price differential since it was their argument in their attempts to lower the prices charged by metropolitan merchants for goods, and to have the *quart*, the export duty on beaver, lowered or removed entirely. In any event, French trade goods were, with few exceptions, of higher quality and better suited for the Indian trade; this was particularly true of knives, axes, awls, gunpowder, muskets, and, of course, brandy, which the Indians much preferred to the rotgut dispensed by the Albany traders. Moreover, the price differential, such as it was, favoured the English only in beaver; the French paid higher prices for *menus pelleteries* — martin, fox, muskrat, etc. — and delivered the goods to the Indian at his village, sparing him the long journey to Montreal or Albany, if he had access to the latter town.

What is needed here is an exhaustive study of prices of all trade goods at Montreal, Albany, Hudson Bay, and the French western posts, at five- or ten-year intervals, along with a study of the Indians' scale of economic values, which were not always the same as those of the Europeans. A study of the latter question would, I suspect, find that the values of the French were closer to those of the Indian than were those of the English, which would help explain the former's dominance of the fur trade.

would have had a much harder time competing with the English traders at the Bay.[22] What was more, as long as the Albany merchants received adequate supplies of furs from the Canadians, delivered to their door, they had no incentive to contest French power in the Great Lakes basin.

On the Acadian frontier the situation was the reverse of that in Canada. In 1701 the French population was only 1,134; that of Massachusetts was expanding rapidly, and its frontier of settlement kept pushing northward onto lands that the Abenaquis regarded as theirs. Relations between these tribes and the Puritan settlers had never been good, but the New England traders frequently tempted them to desert the French and enter into a commercial alliance by offering them goods at very low prices. Canada was remote. The defense of Acadia therefore depended on the allied Indian tribes. Whenever they grew weary of fighting, or the French supply of trade goods was interrupted by losses at sea or other misadventures and they made overtures of peace to New England, the governor general at Quebec had to move swiftly to disrupt the negotiations lest they free the enemy for an assault on the French settlements in Acadia. This he did by sending war parties of Canadians to attack New England, and inducing the Abenaquis to join them. Throughout the war the English frontier settlements were ravaged by raids such as that on Deerfield in February, 1704.[23] Hundreds of prisoners were taken on these raids, and the French did their best to ransom those whom their Indian allies claimed as their slaves. More than a hundred of them, at the end of the war, chose to remain in Canada and were granted naturalization papers; how many others elected to stay without bothering about the legalities of citizenship is not known, but some certainly did.[24]

---

[22] See E. R. Adair, "Anglo-French Rivalry in the Fur Trade During the 18th Century," *Culture*, VIII (1947), pp. 434–435; Jean Lunn, "The Illegal Fur Trade Out of New France, 1713–1760," *Canadian Historical Association Report, 1939*.

[23] This border warfare is described graphically, but with righteous indignation, by Francis Parkman, *A Half Century of Conflict* (Boston, 1892), and in a more restrained fashion, but still from the New England side of the hill, by Douglas Edward Leach, *The Northern Colonial Frontier* (New York, 1966). Succinct explanations of Canadian policy in Acadia during the first quarter of the eighteenth century are contained in Zoltvany, *Philippe de Rigaud de Vaudreuil*, pp. 75–112 and Miquelon, *New France 1701–1744*, pp. 40–45.

[24] See W. J. Eccles, *The Canadian Frontier, 1534–1760* (New York, 1969), p. 198, n. 31.

In this type of guerrilla warfare the New England militia proved no match for the Canadians and Indians, but the New Englanders could strike back from the sea. In 1704 a maritime expedition ravaged the French settlements up the coast as far as Beaubassin at the head of the Bay of Fundy, but accomplished nothing of military significance. Five years later a much more ambitious campaign was undertaken; a land army moved against Canada by way of Lake Champlain, while a naval force invaded Acadia. It came to naught, but the following year a combined force of British regulars and colonial militia, more than nineteen hundred men in all, laid siege to Port Royal. With a garrison of only 258 officers and men the French held out for a week until their supplies were exhausted, then had to surrender.[25] The English, although they held only that one settlement, according to the terms of surrender now had a valid claim to the entire region. The Ministry of Marine made frantic efforts to regain Port Royal, and forces from Canada might well have done so, but they had to be retained for the defense of the colony when word was received of another land and sea assault directed at Quebec. The defenses of the town were hastily strengthened, at a cost of 150,000 livres. Part of the English fleet, commanded by a court favorite, Sir Hovenden Walker, ran aground on an island in the St Lawrence with a loss of more than seven hundred lives. The expedition was then abandoned.[26] When the land army, mustered for one more attempt to invade by way of Lake Champlain, received word of the maritime disaster it disbanded. All that had been accomplished was the prevention of a French counterattack to regain Acadia. Before the French could mount another campaign, negotiations for a peace settlement had begun in Europe.

At the close of hostilities Canada's frontiers remained secure. York Fort in Hudson Bay was held, but the English still occupied the posts at the foot of James Bay. They had been driven out of Newfoundland in a series of savage destructive raids on their fishing ports, but they had taken Port Royal in Acadia. In the

---

[25] See G. M. Waller, *Samuel Vetch: Colonial Enterpriser* (Chapel Hill, N.C., 1960), pp. 179–187.

[26] Gerald S. Graham, *The Walker Expedition to Quebec: 1711* (Champlain Society Publications, Toronto, 1953).

West, the French had retained their hold on the Great Lakes, established Detroit, consolidated their grip on the Mississippi Valley, and founded the new colony of Louisiana. Their only military loss had been in Acadia, and this more through their own negligence than from any display of military competence on the part of the British. Had even a fraction of the energy, manpower, and money subsequently devoted to vain attempts to regain Acadia been employed in its defense, France would not have had to surrender it in the first place.

In Europe, France secured the Bourbon dynasty for Spain and kept the fighting off French soil, but Louis XIV had to make concessions to obtain peace, as did the English and Dutch. France chose to make concessions in America, surrendering Hudson Bay, Acadia "with the ancient boundaries," and Newfoundland, recognizing British suzerainty over the Iroquois confederacy, and admitting that commerce with the western Indian nations would be open to English as well as French traders. These terms appeared to be disastrous for the French, but this was to prove more apparent than real. The French were able to contain the Hudson's Bay Company on the shores of the inland sea by building posts on rivers leading to the Bay, thereby taking the pick of the furs and allowing only what they did not want to go to the English. In Newfoundland, by the terms of the treaty, they retained fishing rights on the north coast, and this was all that really mattered at the time, for it allowed them to harvest the cod and thereby maintain a large fishing fleet. Because the fishery served as a training school for naval seamen, both powers considered it vital. Indeed, the French appear to have got the best of the arrangement.[27]

Acadia was a more contentious issue. The French interpreted the phrase "ancient boundaries" to imply only the peninsula of present-day Nova Scotia, thereby excluding the mainland between New England and the St Lawrence, Île Saint-Jean, and Cape Breton. The English protested vehemently, but to no avail. In fact, it was the Acadian Indian tribes, the Abenaquis, Male-

---

[27] On this point see the important article by Jean-François Brière, "Pêche et politique au XVIIIᵉ siècle: La France véritable gagnante du traité d'Utrecht" in *Canadian Historical Review* vol. LXIV No. 2, June 1985, pp. 95–187.

cites, and Micmacs, who retained their sovereignty over their old
hunting grounds and with French aid were able to keep the English out until well after the Conquest of Canada.

The real victims of the Treaty of Utrecht were the French
Acadians, numbering some five hundred families, estimated to
comprise five thousand persons in all. They were given the alternative of removing to French territory with their portable property within one year, or remaining where they were in possession
of their lands and property with free exercise of their religion,
but as British subjects. This last required them to swear an oath
of allegiance to the British Crown. The vast majority of them
could not bring themselves to take this oath, since it would have
required them to take up arms against the King's enemies, who
could only be the French. The problem was temporarily solved
by procrastination on all sides. The British did not force the issue
since the province would have had little value had the Acadian
settlers been driven out, and the New Englanders showed no
inclination to emigrate to the conquered territory in any numbers.
Moreover, were the Acadians to have removed to French territory
they would merely have provided reinforcements for a future
attempt to reconquer the lost territory. The French at first did try
to persuade the Acadians to remove to Cape Breton; a few did,
but the land there was rocky wilderness, a sad contrast to the rich
diked lands they held in Nova Scotia. The French did not force
the issue, deciding that to have the Acadians remain on British
territory might prove useful in the next war, when they could be
called upon to assist French forces come to liberate them. And
so the majority remained, their population more than doubling
with each generation. Priests were provided for them by the
bishop at Quebec, and some of them even continued to pay token
dues to their old French and Canadian seigneurs. The legalities
of the situation, the niceties of international law, were incompre-
hensible to them. They were merely simple farmers and fishermen. Yet they still had a very deep attachment to their religion
and to France. What they wanted above all was to be left alone,
but preferably under the French Crown.[28] For these simple loy-

[28] See J. B. Brebner, *New England's Outpost: Acadia Before the Conquest of Canada* (New
York, 1927); D. C. Harvey, *The French Regime in Prince Edward Island* (New Haven, 1926);
Andrew Hill Clark, *Acadia: The Geography of Early Nova Scotia to 1760* (Univ. of Wisconsin

alties those of them who were still alive some forty years hence, their children, and grandchildren yet unborn were to suffer cruelly.

Immediately after the cession of Acadia, France began the construction of a naval base on Cape Breton. Eventually, a garrisoned and fortified town, with facilities to service the Atlantic fleet, was constructed at Louisbourg.[29] It did not guard the entrance of the St Lawrence, as has been claimed, for it could guard nothing beyond the range of its guns, but a fleet operating out of this naval base could guard the entry to Canada, protect the French fisheries, and constitute a grave threat to New England shipping. Without the fleet it had little military value. In peacetime, however, it served as a very useful entrepôt for the North Atlantic maritime trade, between Canada, France, the West Indies, and New England.[30]

The threat posed to French control of the interior of the continent by the clause in the Treaty of Utrecht which granted the English commercial privileges did not become real for nearly forty years. The French merely tightened their hold on the Great Lakes basin. Detroit blocked one passage, and they quickly established trading posts at Niagara and on the south side of Lake Ontario from Irondequoit Bay to Cahaquhee, east of Oswego. They provided the Iroquois with the vital services of blacksmiths, spent 20,000 livres a year on presents, and gave some influential chiefs trips to France, where they were royally treated to impress them with the power and majesty of the French King.[31] But the main reason why the French were able to retain the allegiance of the western tribes was that the English made no real attempt to contest it. When in 1719 the governor of New York sought to

---

Press, 1968). Francis Parkman's treatment of the Acadian issue in *A Half Century of Conflict* is unblushingly partisan; so too is that of L. H. Gipson, *The British Empire Before the American Revolution* (14 vols., New York, 1936-69), V, pp. 167-205. The best treatment of the issue to date is Miquelon, *New France 1701-1744*, pp. 95-123.

[29] See J. S. McLennan, *Louisbourg from Its Foundation to Its Fall* (London, 1918); F. J. Thorpe, *Les remparts lointains* (Univ. of Ottawa Press, 1980).

[30] See John Robert McNeill, *Atlantic Empires of France and Spain*, (Chapel Hill, NC & London, 1985).

[31] See Peter Wraxall, *An Abridgement of the New York Indian Records*, ed. by C. H. McIlwain (Cambridge, Mass., 1915), pp. 116-131, 196, 207; W. R. Jacobs, *Indian Diplomacy and Indian Gifts: Anglo-French Rivalry Along the Ohio and Northwest Frontier, 1748-1763* (Stanford, 1950); W. J. Eccles "The Fur Trade and Eighteenth Century Imperialism", in *Essays on New France*, pp. 83-90.

seize the Niagara passage and erect a fort there he received little support from the assembly; but when the governor general at Quebec heard of the proposal he moved swiftly, and before the New York politicians knew it, the French had a fort built and garrisoned. The governor of New York did subsequently manage to establish a fortified trading post at Oswego, which caused the French considerable concern. In order to keep too many of the western Indians from crossing the lake, they had to subsidize the price of trade goods at Forts Frontenac and Niagara, and relax the stringent edict on the sale of liquor to the Indians, since at Oswego, they were given all the cheap rum and whiskey they could pay for. Oswego, however, proved useful to at least some of the French traders, who exchanged their furs there for English trade goods despite the efforts of both the Canadian and the New York officials to curb this contraband trade.[32] Farther south the mission posts at Kaskaskia and Cahokia in the Illinois country became important agricultural settlements and way stations on the route from Canada to Louisiana, providing food for the fur traders, missionaries, and western garrisons.[33] Thus, from Louisbourg on the north Atlantic coast to the mouth of the Mississippi the French still maintained their cordon sanitaire at the rear of the English colonies, blocking their future progress into the interior of the continent.

By this time New France had been mobilized for war for three decades. During twenty-five of those years there had been savage fighting. A whole generation of Canadians and Acadians had grown up in the midst of these hostilities. The effects on Canadian society, and the economy, were profound and enduring.[34] During those years the military establishment became the dominant element in the colony, and remained so down to the Conquest. This development had begun with the arrival of the first companies of Troupes de la Marine in 1683, sent to bolster the colony's defen-

---

[32] ANQM Documents judiciares 16 juillet 1736. Duplessis et Deniau, voyageurs, accusés d'avoir obtenu marchandise à Oswego.

[33] See Natalia Maree Belting, *Kaskaskia under the French Regime* (Univ. of Illinois Press, 1948); "The French Villages of the Illinois Country," *Canadian Historical Review*, XXIV, 1 (Mar., 1943), pp. 14–23.

[34] The hypothesis advanced in the following pages is that contained in my article "The Social, Economic, and Political Significance of the Military Establishment in New France," *Canadian Historical Review*, LII, 1 (Mar., 1971), pp. 1–22.

ses.[35] By 1685 they numbered more than sixteen hundred. The civilian population was then less than eleven thousand, only a quarter of which, about 2,750, would have been males between the ages of sixteen and sixty. The military thus dominated society by sheer weight of numbers, being by far the largest single cohesive group in the colony.

These colonial regulars were under the authority of the minister of marine, not the minister of war, and their framework of organization reflected the reforming zeal of Colbert. They were not comprised in regiments but in independent fifty-man companies, each commanded by a captain with a lieutenant, two ensigns, and two cadets. This obviated the serious problems that arose with regiments in the French and English armies that were the private property of their colonels, bought and sold at high prices.[36] Although in France commissions below the rank of captain were not strictly venal, a few thousand livres usually had to be forthcoming before a colonel could find an opening in his regiment for a junior officer. In the Troupes de la Marine, commissions were not purchased and promotion was based on merit.

The original officer corps of these troops in Canada all came from France, but many of them, if not most, remained permanently in the colony, married Canadian girls, acquired seigneuries, and became members of the colonial upper class. Governor General Denonville, in 1687, recommended to the minister that in the future Canadians be given commissions in these troops in preference to replacements sent from France. He gave two reasons for the proposal, first that the sons of the seigneurs were a wild, undisciplined lot, living like savages because the only occupation open to them, other than the hard, unrewarding labor of clearing their families' domain lands, was the much more profitable one of voyaging to the west to trade among the Indians. He proposed that they be given commissions in the Troupes de la Marine, and that those of noble families be sent to France to

---

[35] See the unpublished Ph.D. thesis, Jay Cassel, "The Troupes de la Marine in Canada, 1683–1760: Men and Materiel," (University of Toronto, 1988).

[36] The Marquis de Denonville, for example, in 1685 sold his regiment of Dragoons to Louis XIV for 60,000 livres. By the mid-eighteenth century a cavalry regiment cost 100,000 livres and the older infantry regiments were worth as much as 75,000. See Lee Kennett, *The French Armies in the Seven Years' War* (Duke Univ. Press, 1967), p. 55.

serve as cadets in the Guards. They would then cease to be a social problem but instead, he argued, would serve a useful function. Moreover, he gave it as his opinion that these young Canadians would make better officers than those sent from France, given the peculiar conditions of warfare in the North American wilderness. This recommendation was accepted by Louis XIV, and during the ensuing years the officer corps of the Troupes de la Marine became Canadian. In fact, by the mid-eighteenth century the corps, some two hundred strong, had become a virtual caste, commissions being reserved for the sons of Canadian serving officers.

This gave the governor general, who initially had the authority to grant commissions, not a little power. Only by pleasing him could a family hope to receive this coveted favour. Subsequently, in 1696, the King stripped the governor general of this authority. The incumbent, Frontenac, protested vigorously, declaring that without such patronage a governor could acquire little credit in the colony. Yet the fact that commissions given to Canadians, although granted by the King, were so granted on the joint recommendation of the governor general and the intendant still gave these two officials a powerful weapon to render the leading families, if not subservient, at least less likely to give trouble.

The political consequences of this system were very significant. Although the recommendation of the governor general and intendant, or of a powerful friend at the court, was essential to gain a commission and promotion, in the final analysis, both the commission and future promotion came from the King through the minister. Thus the seigneurs, the colonial elite or dominant class, looked to the metropolitan government in France, and to its creatures in the colony, the governor general and intendant, for the advancement of their careers and the careers of their sons. This was in marked contrast to the situation in the English colonies, where only the governors, a handful of royal officials, and, to a lesser degree, the appointed members of the provincial councils —usually twelve in number—had ties with the metropolitan government. Because this large, dominant, segment of the seigneurial class looked to France for the realization of its aspirations, the development of anything akin to Canadian nationalism, or even particularism, was out of the question. Because there were so many posts in the military, plus those in the judiciary, reserved for Canadians, the bitter resentment that many historians see in the Spanish colonies of the *creoles* against the *peninsulares* was conspicuously absent in Canada.

As for the mass of the Canadians—*habitants*, artisans, labourers, small shopkeepers — they had few direct ties with France. Their economic existence, their peculiar mores, virtually everything in their lives was firmly rooted in Canada, where, by the eighteenth century, the overwhelming majority had been born. The personal ties that their parents, or grandparents, had had with France had long since been severed. Although they regarded themselves as Canadians and were readily distinguishable as such, without grievances—either real or imagined—social friction, propaganda, and direction from above, the virus of nationalism could not take hold. Anything resembling the latent urge for independence that was remarked on by many observers in the English colonies as the century wore on was conspicuous by its absence in Canada.

With the accessibility of military careers to the Canadian seigneurs, the ethos of the nobility rather than of the bourgeoisie gained a much stronger hold on the upper strata of colonial society. A majority of the seigneurs and officers were nobles and those who were not aspired to be; meanwhile they lived as though they were. None of them could afford the prodigious lifestyle of the court nobles in France, rather they lived like the *hobereaux* that they were; that is, like the English squirearchy. In 1685 Louis XIV had decreed that nobles resident in Canada could engage in commerce and industry without sacrificing their noble status.[37] With a few notable exceptions such activities were forbidden the nobility in France. There a member of the third estate who aspired to gain entry to the nobility had somehow to amass a large fortune, then purchase a government office at a horrendous price that had, in due course, noble status attached. Entry into the *noblesse de*

---

[37] ANQ à Québec. Conseil Supérieur 1664–1711. Pièces détachées N.F. 14–1. In the West Indies a royal edict of 1669 had granted nobles resident there the right to engage in commerce without derogation. See Lilianne Chauleau, *La société à la Martinique au XVIIᵉ siècle (1635–1713)* (Caen, 1966), p. 99.

robe in this fashion usually required at least three generations whilst the aspirants endured the disdain of the *noblesse d'épée*. Once achieved, a further two generations were required for the stigma of bourgeois antecedents to wear off. In seventeenth-century Canada, entry into the privileged class for a select few was swifter. The edict of 1685 allowed an ambitious *roturier* to acquire capital and an adequate income in the fur trade, then a seigneury, then commissions for his sons in the Troupes de la Marine, who could then aspire to obtain *lettres de noblesse* for valorous service.[38]

Although noble status in Canada did not carry with it the economic privilege, exemption from the *taille*, the land tax, that it did in France, since there was no such tax in the colony, yet it was still avidly coveted by the leading colonial families. That many were called but very few chosen proved no deterrent. The quick profits that could be realized in the fur trade in the seventeenth century were the means to that end. In addition the fur trade had no menial, bourgeois, connotations. The qualities most needed for a successful military career—valour, hardihood, willingness to take great risks, adroitness, and the courtier's skills in dealing with both the Indians and the governor and intendant— were the same qualities required for success in the fur trade. Any lingering hope there might have been of breathing life into Colbert's original plans for diversifying the colony's economy, of having it develop along the same economic lines as the English colonies, was laid to rest by the prospect of military careers for the colony's leading families, and by the edict of 1685. Consequently the profits of the fur trade were spent more on conspicuous consumption, lavish hospitality after the manner of the nobility, than they were invested in other economic endeavours. Social life in New France among the military fur-trading elite was thereby rendered urbane and agreeable, but the economy remained fragile.

Wartime conditions also brought about economic innovations that were regarded at the time as both a blessing and a curse. In 1685 the ships bearing the colony's supplies and funds to pay the

---

[38] See, for example, the entries in *Dictionary of Canadian Biography*, vol. I, pp. 463–65: Charles le Moyne de Longueuil et de Châteauguay; vol. II, pp. 374–76 Jacques Le Ber.

troops did not leave France until late August and did not reach Quebec until late autumn. The intendant, Jacques de Meulles, found himself with no funds to pay the troops and also with a grave shortage of labour to bring in the harvest as a result of heavy losses from the epidemic that had brought La Barre's pathetic little army to its knees at Lake Ontario. De Meulles coped with both these problems by ingenious innovations that he regarded as merely temporary expedients. The lack of ready cash he overcame by the emission of paper money, made from packs of playing cards. He simply wrote the denomination on the cards, signed them, and issued an ordonnance declaring that these notes would be redeemed as soon as the ships arrived and meanwhile they had to be accepted in all transactions at face value.

There had always been a chronic shortage of specie in the colony; all manner of foreign coins circulated, but the supply of hard money was continually drained off to France. Beaver skins were commonly used as a medium of exchange, but the disadvantages of this device were great. Card money, therefore, removed a chronic want. It proved so useful a device that, although regarded by the orthodox minds of officials in the Ministry of Marine as highly dangerous, likely to result in all manner of intolerable abuses, de Meulles' successors had constant recourse to it. The minister of marine frequently demanded that it all be called in and no more issued, but no sooner would this be done than circumstances compelled the intendant to emit a new issue. The mere fact that the Canadians not only accepted this money so readily but that a sizable percentage disappeared for years from circulation indicates the degree of confidence they placed in it. Such confidence permitted the intendants to issue far more than the supply of goods warranted, since they knew they would not have to redeem it all at any given time.[39]

The other innovation of de Meulles' was the use of the rankers in the Troupes de la Marine to augment the colony's meagre supply of labour. Lacking funds to pay them, he gave them per-

---

[39] On card money and currency problems in general see Adam Shortt, (ed.), *Documents Relating to Canadian Currency, Exchange and Finance During the French Period* (2 vols., King's Printer, Ottawa, 1925–26), I, pp. xxxiii–lxxxix; Miquelon, *New France 1701–1744*, see Index, entry Money.

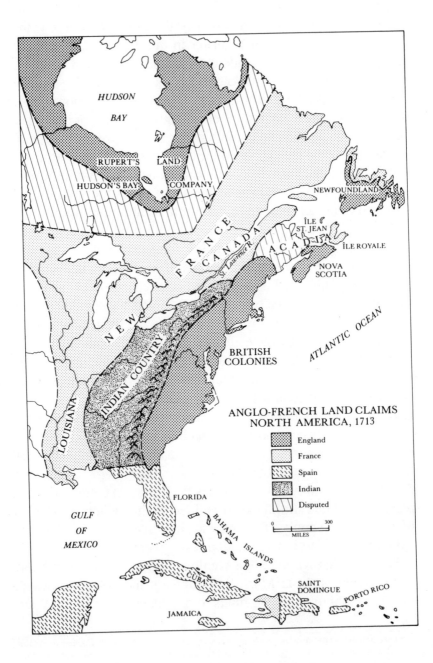

HUDSON

BAY

RUPERT'S LAND

HUDSON'S BAY

COMPANY

NEWFOUNDLAND

ÎLE
ST JEAN

ÎLE ROYALE

F R A N C E

C A N A D A

A C A D I A

St Lawrence R.

NOVA
SCOTIA

N E W

INDIAN COUNTRY

ATLANTIC OCEAN

BRITISH
COLONIES

LOUISIANA

**ANGLO-FRENCH LAND CLAIMS
NORTH AMERICA, 1713**

England

France

Spain

Indian

Disputed

FLORIDA

GULF

OF

MEXICO

BAHAMA ISLANDS

0   300
MILES

CUBA

SAINT
DOMINGUE

PORTO RICO

JAMAICA

mission to hire themselves out to the *habitants* at wages of not more than twelve livres a month and their keep; soldiers with a trade were allowed to work in the towns at a wage not to exceed fifteen sols a day, plus their board. The soldiers, who were billeted on the *habitants* in any event — except those on garrison duty in the forts — accepted this opportunity eagerly. Unfortunately, it led to a serious abuse. The captains of the companies refused to release their men to work for wages unless they relinquished their military pay, which the captains pocketed, and the men accepted this condition without protest. The outcome was that during the war when men were needed for war parties the troops frequently could not be mustered swiftly enough, and the Canadian militia, who in any event had proved themselves far better fighters against the Iroquois, went instead. Despite strong protests from the intendant, and the bishop's threat to bar from the sacraments officers who so defrauded their men, the abuse continued throughout the war. The governor general and the commandant of the troops who tolerated these practices were able to argue, quite persuasively, that the Troupes de la Marine were of little use in forest warfare and that the defense of the colony required them to make the best use possible of the colony's available manpower. Thus the regular troops performed noncombatant duties, and the civilian militia bore the brunt of the fighting in the *petite guerre*. The regular soldier billeted on an *habitant* family waved goodbye to the husband and sons going off to war, then settled down at the hearth with the womenfolk. Not a situation that endeared the regulars to the Canadians.[40]

At the upper end of the social scale, war and the military establishment had opened a badly needed career to the seigneurial class, one that they entered with alacrity and considerable success. At the lower end, the ordinary *habitants* in the militia, through necessity, became highly skilled guerrilla fighters, and by the end of the seventeenth century they were a match for the Iroquois. In 1715 a former attorney general of Canada, Ruette d'Auteuil, remarked that the Canadians from infancy were accustomed to hunt and fish, to undertake long voyages by canoe, and

---

[40] See Eccles, *Frontenac*, pp. 212–222.

this had made them tough. The Canadians, having defeated their enemies, the Iroquois and the English, and successfully defended what they now regarded as their homeland in two long wars, were understandably proud of their prowess as fighting men. Little wonder then that the military virtues, rather than those of the prudent bourgeois and husbandman, were the ones that commanded the greatest respect in the colony.

Chapter 5

The Long Peace, 1713–1744

Following the Treaty of Utrecht, both England and France desired peace to reconcile their particular internal problems. The Hanoverian succession in England, followed by the Jacobite uprising of 1715, and in France the death of Louis XIV with the ensuing danger of a struggle for the throne in the event of the demise of the sickly child Louis XV, meant that neither country could afford to follow an aggressive foreign policy. In addition, Europe was bankrupted by the preceding decade of warfare, waged on a world scale. By the time these dynastic and economic difficulties had been resolved two men had come to power in France and England, respectively, Cardinal Fleury and Robert Walpole, each convinced that peace was better than war for his country. These circumstances in Europe dictated peace for three decades, the span of one generation, between the colonies of France and England in North America.[1]

Not only was Europe bankrupted by the past war; so too was Canada. Maritime shipping costs had risen astronomically, and with them the price of everything in the colony. Wages had tripled, and military expenditures had resulted in the issuance by the intendant of a flood of bills that the government in France could not honour. The colonial budget, struck annually by the intendant and subsequently slashed by the minister, became an

[1] See Penfield Roberts, *The Quest for Security, 1715–1740* (New York, 1947); Paul Vaucher, *Robert Walpole et la politique de Fleury (1731–1742)* (Paris, 1924).

exercise in futility. Expenses exceeded the budget by a sum ranging from more than 100,000 to close to 200,000 livres a year, and by 1714 among a population of 19,315 more than 1,600,000 livres of paper money were in circulation. This meant that 83 livres per capita were available to purchase a limited store of goods. In France, later in the century, where goods were much more plentiful and wealth more concentrated, it was estimated that 75 livres per capita were in circulation. Thus with the French treasury empty and an accounting system that made it impossible to know the exact size of the deficit, or what revenues could be anticipated, devaluation was the only solution. Merchants, *habitants*, and labourers had compensated by raising their prices for goods and services. As always, those on fixed incomes became the real sufferers.[2]

Fortunately, after 1714 the beaver trade suddenly revived when it was discovered that the huge glut in warehouses in France, which had so depressed the market, no longer existed. Moths and vermin had effectively disposed of it. Prices rose accordingly. Politics, however, as much as economics, regulated the fur trade. A free market responding to supply and demand was out of the question. The French were determined to retain the Indian nations in the French alliance for present political purposes and possible future military needs. This required that they provide the allied tribes with the European manufactured goods that they craved. All that the Indian could offer in exchange was furs in peacetime, military support in war. For these reasons the French Crown had to subsidize the fur trade. Fort Frontenac, Fort Niagara, and Detroit were maintained as King's posts where goods were sold at prices lower than the merchants could profitably sell them, in

---

[2] In 1717, when New France was placed under the economic and financial direction of John Law's Compagnie des Indes and French government finances were being overhauled, the Canadian card money was called in at 50 percent of its face value, the export duties on beaver and moose hides were removed, the 25 percent premium on French currency in the colony was abolished, and copper coinage for circulation only in the colonies was minted. These reforms did not enjoy the success envisaged; the money supply and credit facilities in New France proved inadequate, which stimulated the contraband trade with the English colonies. In 1728 the home government authorized the emission of 400,000 livres of new card money as a temporary expedient. From then on, new issues were made as circumstances dictated. On this tangled question of colonial finance see Adam Shortt (ed.), *Documents Relating to Canadian Currency, Exchange and Finance During the French Period* (2 vols., King's Printer, Ottawa, 1925–26), I, pp. xxxiii–lxxxix and supporting documents; Guy Frégault, "Essai sur les finances canadiennes," in *Le XVIIIᵉ siècle canadien: Études* (Montreal, 1968); Miquelon, *New France 1701–1744*, pp. 77–94.

order to keep the northwestern Indians away from Oswego. At
Michilimackinac the trade was open to all licensed traders in the
hope that competition would keep prices down. The other more
remote posts were leased, first to private entrepreneurs and subsequently to officers in the Troupes de la Marine appointed to
command the garrisons and execute the King's orders in the vast
territories wherein the posts were located. The maintenance of
these posts cost the Crown large sums; by 1754, to be precise,
183,427 livres a year.

As furs became increasingly more scarce, the French traders
pushed farther and farther west. This movement was accelerated
by the vogue for science and the expansion of knowledge that
was so pronounced in eighteenth-century Europe. The regent,
the duc d'Orléans, was much interested in the discovery of a
route to the western ocean, and the fur trade was used as a means
to this end. This led to the wars with the Fox nation, who sought
to bar French progress westward. Four campaigns at a cost that
appalled the minister of marine were required before they were
finally crushed in 1734.[3] Beyond the Fox, however, were the
powerful Sioux. The barrier they presented forced the French,
with Pierre Gaultier de Varennes, sieur de La Vérendrye, his sons
and a nephew, to attempt to reach the western sea by the more
northerly route through Lake Winnipeg and along the Saskatchewan River until eventually the barrier of the Rockies was reached.[4]

Within the colony, as the population expanded from 19,315 in
1714 to 43,382 in 1739, more land was brought into production,
and there was frequently a sizable surplus of wheat. The land
under cultivation rose from 2.1 arpents per capita in 1721 to 4
arpents by 1738 and wheat production from 400 litres in 1720
to 800 litres per capita in 1734.[5] This expansion is also reflected
in the number of grist mills; 41 in 1685, 118 in 1734.[6] The

[3] See Louise Phelps Kellog, *The French Regime in Wisconsin and the Northwest* (Madison, Wisc., 1925). Richard Lortie, "La guerre des Renards, 1700-1740 ou quatre décennies de résistance à l'expansionisme française," (Unpublished Maitres d'Arts thesis Université Laval, 1988.)

[4] See Eccles, "La mer de l'ouest : outpost of empire", in *Essays on New France*, pp. 96-109.

[5] See A. J. E. Lunn, "Economic Development in New France, 1713-1760" (Unpublished Ph.D. thesis, McGill University, 1942). Translated by Brigitte Monel-Nish, *Développement de la Nouvelle-France 1713-1760* (Les Presses de l'Université de Montréal, 1986).

[6] Richard Colebrook Harris, *The Seigneurial System in Early Canada* (Univ. of Wisconsin Press, 1966), p. 112.

military base at Louisbourg provided an outlet for this and other agricultural products, but attempts to ship wheat, fish, and timber to the West Indies were not very successful. A voyage from France to Quebec took twice as long as to Cape Breton or the West Indies, with commensurate higher labour costs for crews' wages. Ships frequently had to spend several weeks in the Quebec roadstead while the captain sought a return cargo, and the waters of the St Lawrence were always dangerous; reefs, fog, and treacherous currents added to the difficulties of the short navigation season. To overcome this problem a school of navigation was established in the colony, operated by the Jesuits, and it produced excellent pilots. Early in the eighteenth century the Ministry of Marine undertook the careful charting of the river; and by mid-century very accurate charts were available and navigation markers were installed from Quebec to the Gulf. Colonial shipping, however, was dominated by ship owners in La Rochelle and, later, Bordeaux, but with some Canadian participation in joint ventures. Canadian merchants who did enjoy success frequently had a member of the family established at La Rochelle, and marriage alliances with Rochellois families were what held business partnerships together over long periods. Colonial commerce was really imperial trade, and it is doubtful if the Canadians engaged in it regarded themselves as colonials.[7]

As in the English colonies, agricultural practices, compared to those of Europe, appeared wasteful and inefficient. This, however, was more apparent than real. With an unlimited supply of land, and given the high productivity of virgin soil, there was no need to employ the intensive agriculture methods that European conditions demanded. Moreover, the American colonies were settled before the agricultural revolution in Europe had taken effect. In any event, the extensive agricultural system of New France likely produced yields as great *per worker*—perhaps even greater — as the intensive methods of northern Europe, and the

---

[7] The largest export items to Canada were wine and brandy, taking up nearly 70 percent of the cargo space. By 1700, with a population of 15,000 compared to 19 million in France, Canada imported 1 percent of Bordeaux's total wine production. See C. Huetz de Lemps, "Le commerce maritime des vins d'Aquitaine de 1698 à 1716," *Revue Historique de Bordeaux*, 1965, p. 32, and James S. Pritchard, "Ships, Men and Commerce: A Study of Maritime Activity in New France" (Unpublished Ph.D., thesis, University of Toronto, 1971).

chronic shortage of labour in the colony made yield per worker rather than per acre the vital issue.[8]

Although the climate of the St Lawrence Valley was unsuitable for it, wheat was the principal crop, grown simply because bread was the staple food. Normal consumption was a kilogram loaf per person per day. That bread, made from stone-milled wheat, was, of course, infinitely more nutritious than the denatured substance sold as bread in North America today. In the eighteenth century the colony frequently had a wheat surplus that was exported to Louisbourg and the West Indies. The intendant, however, had to ensure that adequate supplies were retained for the colony's own needs. To prevent profiteering he had, on occasion, to fix the price of wheat and flour and forbid exports. The same occurred with timber. In 1729 the intendant noted that the export of large shipments of boards and planks had sent the price of lumber in the colony up by more than 50 percent. Only for a few years was Canada able to export sizable quantities of these commodities, and only when the West Indies could not obtain supplies from France or the English colonies was that market profitable. Thus, with the colony largely self-sufficient in the essentials of life, the amount of maritime trade, compared with that to the French West Indies, was minimal: some twenty ships a year from France to Quebec compared with six hundred to the Antilles.

Yet the tendency, only very recently brought into question, to pass judgment on a country, colony, or society in purely economic terms, to regard expansion of the economy with a steady rise in exports exceeding, or at least keeping pace with, imports as the sole criterion of value, can lead to bizarre conclusions. In Canada, when wheat production fell off and food had to be imported, a sharp increase in shipping resulted. Conversely, crop failures in France caused an increase of shipping from Canada to the other colonies. Thus, had there been more frequent crop failures in the empire the volume of shipping would have been greater, and economic activity appeared more flourishing. Looked at another way, that the number of ships voyaging to Canada was infinitely less than to the West Indies could be interpreted as a sign of

---

[8] See Richard Colebrook Harris, *The Seigneurial System in Early Canada* (Univ. Wisconsin Press, Les Presses de l'Université Laval, 1968).

healthy economic self-sufficiency. In any event, these dubious economic statistics are a poor measure of the quality of life.

In the 1730s a very enterprising intendant, Gilles Hocquart, inaugurated a major shipbuilding program, and the King agreed to provide modest subsidies to encourage the industry. Once again, however, the program was overly ambitious. Instead of ships of 45 to 180 tonnes, such as were built in the English colonies, monsters of from 450 to 900 tonnes were laid down. The Canadian forest did not provide enough knee timbers of adequate size and the requisite soundness for such ships. A goodly number of smaller vessels were built, some for ship owners in France, but the naval shipbuilding program was a failure.[9] Moreover, by absorbing the scanty supply of skilled labour it hindered the building of smaller, more practical ships for colonial commerce. Much of the timber, and the mast pines for these ships, was obtained from the Lake Champlain region. In 1731 the French had forestalled the English of New York and backed up their territorial claim to the area by building Fort Saint-Frédéric at Crown Point where the lake narrowed almost to musket range. In the 1730s and 1740s most of the land down both sides of the lake was conceded as seigneuries to Crown officials and officers in the Troupes de la Marine. The land was not settled, and the recipients likely intended to hold the title for their children, but these concessions made plain that France regarded the territory on all the rivers and lakes flowing into Canada as hers. This was something the Mohawks denied, and in 1739 they belatedly protested this encroachment on land they had always assumed to be theirs, but to no avail.[10]

Apart from shipbuilding, the only other heavy industry in the colony was the iron forges on the Saint-Maurice, near Trois Rivières. Their history embodies all the difficulties that industrial development encountered in Canada: inefficiency, undercapital-

---

[9] See Jacques Mathieu, "L'échec de la construction navale royale à la fin du régime français," *Canadian Historical Association Historical Papers, 1968*, pp. 24–34.

[10] See Peter Wraxall, *An Abridgment of the New York Indian Records*, ed. by C. H. McIlwain (Cambridge, Mass., 1915), p. 213. The lieutenant governor of New York had intended to settle Scottish highlanders along Wood Creek, and there is no indication the Mohawks were consulted. They were hard pressed on both sides. In 1732 they had protested Mr Philip Livingston's claims, by very dubious means, to a large section of their land on the Mohawk River. See *ibid.*, p. 179. See also Eccles, "Sovereignty Association 1500–1783" in *Essays on New France*, pp. 174–5.

ization, lack of skilled labour, incompetent management under private enterprise, and a fair degree of success when taken over by the Crown. The bog iron at the site was of excellent quality, and in 1730 a wealthy Montreal merchant obtained the land and the right to build a forge. Two skilled foundry men, brought from France, were sent to study the methods employed at foundries in New England. By 1733, iron products as good as or better than those of Sweden, then regarded as the best in the world, were produced, but the company was continually in financial and technical difficulties and had to receive assistance from the royal treasury to the tune of 192,642 livres. In two years only as much iron had been manufactured as a forge in France could produce in two weeks. By 1741 the directors of the company declared themselves bankrupt, and two years later the forges were taken over by the Crown. From this point on things went better. Despite chronic labour troubles, sizable quantities of anvils, cannon and cannonballs, cooking pots and pans, stoves, cauldrons, bar iron, and hardware for ships were now produced, and by 1748 the forges even showed a modest profit.[11] It could not, however, be said that the Canadians had displayed much aptitude for the establishment and operation of industrial enterprises.

On a much more modest scale there was a goodly number of small industries catering to local needs, tanneries, sawmills, brick and tile works. In Quebec and Montreal a considerable number of skilled artisans operated on the apprentice system. Some of them, particularly the silversmiths, and the woodcarvers who produced very fine works for the churches, also ships' figureheads as well as domestic furnishings, were very skilled craftsmen, artists in fact.[12] Colonel Louis-Antoine de Bougainville, an officer serving under Montcalm in 1757, commented that the *habitants* were well-provided with silver platters, bowls, and

---

[11] The best work to date on the Forges de Saint-Maurice is Louise Trottier, *Les Forges. Historiographie des Forges de Saint-Maurice* (Montréal, 1980). See also Joseph-Noël Fauteux, *Essai sur l'Industrie au Canada sous le régime français* (2 vols., Québec, 1927), I, pp. 55-126, and the comments in *Peter Kalm's Travels in North America*, ed. by Adolph B. Benson (2 vols., paperback ed., New York, 1966), II, pp. 420-421. A sample of the iron produced by the forges was submitted to expert analysis and found to be, as was claimed in the eighteenth century, equal to the best produced in Sweden, England, or Spain. See Henry Miller, "Canada's First Iron Castings," *Mines Branch Information Circular IC 209* (Queen's Printer, Ottawa, Dec., 1968).

[12] See Jean Palardy, *The Early Furniture of French Canada*, trans. from the French by Eric McLean (Toronto, 1963); Ramsay Traquair, *The Old Silver of Quebec* (Toronto, 1940).

goblets which they had had made from melted-down silver coins. This indication of affluence is borne out by the comments of other visitors to the colony in the eighteenth century. A British officer, upon entering Montreal immediately after the capitulation in 1760, remarked that "from the number of silk robes, laced coats, and powdered heads of both sexes, and almost all ages, that are perambulating the streets from morning to night, a stranger would be induced to believe Montreal is entirely inhabited by people of independent and plentiful fortunes."[13] A quantitative study of considerable depth will have to be undertaken to determine the living standards of the Canadians, but all the surface evidence indicates that although the colony lacked a very wealthy element,[14] the dominant group, representing perhaps 1 to 2 percent of the population, the judiciary, merchant fur traders, and officers in the colonial regulars, were fairly well off, and relatively speaking, so appear to have been the *habitants* and artisans.

The problem is, given the struggling condition of the economy, how to account for this apparent affluence. The lack of taxation is a partial explanation; so too is the fur trade. But furs must not be overestimated. In 1715, Ruette d'Auteuil, onetime attorney general, estimated the beaver trade to be worth 500,000 to 600,000 livres a year. In addition there were hides for leather, and small furs. Of the latter, 250,000 to 300,000 livres' worth of martin pelts alone were exported. All told, upwards of a million

---

[13] Arthur G. Doughty (ed.), *An Historical Journal of the Campaigns in North America for the Years 1757, 1758, and 1759, by Captain John Knox* (3 vols., Champlain Society Publications, Toronto, 1914), III, p. 605. To confirm this estimate, shortly after the Conquest a letter appeared in the New York *Gazette and Post Boy*, stating: "A stranger would take Montreal to be a city inhabited by none but the rich and idle. They are all finely powdered, walk with their hats under their arms and wear long coats adorned with tinsel lace, buttoned down to the extremity. The ladies in general are handsome, extremely gay and well bred. . . ." Louis Des Cognets, Jr., *Amherst and Canada* (Princeton, 1962), p. 292.

[14] In the absence of exhaustive quantitative studies of the actual financial condition and living standards of the colonists, care has to be exercised in accepting at face value the subjective opinions of visitors to the colony. In France to be wealthy meant to enjoy an income of, at least, 100,000 livres a year, that being the salary of senior officials. Marriage dowries of 100,000 to 150,000 livres were the norm among the wealthier families of the *robe*, such as the Bégons. Thus when an intendant remarked that there were no rich families in Canada it should not be taken to mean that the people were poverty-stricken. There were no great fortunes, no huge châteaux of the Loire along the St Lawrence, but by the 1720s the seigneurial class, like the merchants and planters of the English colonies, appear to have lived well. Moreover, the gap between the incomes of the more well-to-do and the working class was far wider than today. The intendant's salary was 12,000 livres, his secretary's 1,200, their servants' 100 livres a year.

livres a year.[15] But from these sums the cost of trade goods, salaries, wages, commissions, freight, insurance, and storage had to be deducted. It has been asserted that between 1675 and 1760, 72 percent of the fur trade revenue went to France, 14 percent went to Canadian merchant traders, 9 percent was spread out about the colony, and 5 percent went to the Crown.[16] In other words, if these figures be accepted, then roughly 200,000 livres a year, at most, remained in the colony; about 140,000 livres of that amount being divided among perhaps twenty or thirty families.

There was, however, another major source of revenue: the military establishment. Every year the Crown spent large sums for the maintenance of the regular troops in the colony. The pay of the officer corps in the Troupes de la Marine alone mounted to 109,280 livres, and in wartime the amounts spent on fortifications and campaigns, for goods and services, were astronomical. In 1712, before military expenditures really soared, Ruette d'Auteuil stated that the cost of maintaining twenty-eight companies of Troupes de la Marine, reduced to thirty-five men per company, amounted to 150,000 livres, with another 150,000 livres going to the civil administration, and a modest 25,000 to fortifications. Prior to 1730, expenditures by the Crown amounted to about 500,000 livres a year, about 600,000 down to 1743, and in the millions from then on.[17] A large share of these amounts was spent on fortifications, providing employment and profits for *habitants*, artisans, contractors, and suppliers. In 1710, for example, 150,000 livres were spent on strengthening the colony's fortifications when an English assault was expected. In 1745 the extraordinary defense expenditures for Quebec and Louisiana, but mostly for Quebec, amounted — according to the minister of marine — to 681,408 livres, 14 sols, and the normal cost of maintaining Fort Saint-Frédéric alone for a year amounted

[15] *Rapport de l'Archiviste de la Province de Québec, 1922-1923*, pp. 59–60.

[16] Jean Hamelin, *Économie et société en Nouvelle France* (Québec, 1960), pp. 51–57.

[17] Unfortunately, French government accounting practice being what it was, reasonably accurate estimates on the proportion of the total budget devoted to military expenditures are extremely difficult, if not impossible, to ascertain. See Lee Kennet, *The French Armies in the Seven Years' War* (Duke Univ. Press, 1967), pp. 89–90; Guy Frégault, "Les finances canadiennes," in *Le XVIIIᵉ siècle canadien: Études* (Montréal, 1965); J. F. Bosher, *French Finances, 1770-1795: From Business to Bureaucracy* (Cambridge Univ. Press, 1970).

to 76,000 livres. The military in Canada, and the garrison at Louisbourg, offered a sizable market for the colony's surplus agricultural produce, mainly wheat, peas, and pork. In addition, there were the garrisoned posts in the West that provided employment for voyageurs and profits for the merchant suppliers of goods, but much of the latter likely went to French merchants who shipped goods to Quebec. Colonel Bougainville for once spoke the truth in 1757 when he remarked, "La guerre enrichit le Canada."

The relative affluence these military expenditures, the fur trade, and the absence of taxation engendered was a contributing factor to the very independent attitude of the *habitants*. The royal officials continually complained that the Canadians always pleased themselves and paid little attention to directives that did not suit their fancy. Visitors to the colony also commented on this proclivity, that the Canadians could be led but not driven. Bougainville remarked: "The ordinary *habitants* would be scandalized to be called peasants. In fact, they are of a better stuff, have more wit, more education, than those of France. This comes from their paying no taxes, that they have the right to hunt and fish, and that they live in a sort of independence."[18] One governor general, the Marquis de Beauharnois, had to have servants sent from France because the Canadians were too proud to put their children into service, and when the intendant Gilles Hocquart tried to persuade a Montreal merchant to take on the job of collecting the local tax for the construction of the town wall he was refused. Hocquart tried to impress on the merchant that it was his duty, offering him 10 percent of the tax collected, all to no avail. The proffer of an annual gratuity was likewise declined. The merchant would have none of it because he feared he would render himself odious. "This trait," wrote Hocquart, "is an example of the pride of the Canadians."[19]

Some observers blamed what they regarded as serious defects in the Canadian character, their indocility, lack of discipline, laziness, disobedience, want of respect for duly constituted

---

[18] *Rapport de l'Archiviste, 1923–1924*, p. 58.
[19] Paris, Archives Nationales, Colonies, C11A, LI, 290, Hocquart au Ministre, Québec, 23 oct. 1729.

authority, and self-indulgence—particularly with wines and spirits — on the influence of the Indians with whom they were in constant contact. There can be no doubt that the Canadians were influenced by the tribesmen, upon whom they were dependent to a considerable degree. On a superficial level they adopted many Indian articles of dress — Peter Kalm, the Swedish professor of botany who visited the colony in 1749, made frequent references to this. An eminent scientist, hence a keen observer, in his journal he several times mentioned, and not with distaste, the miniskirt, the hem well above the knees, as worn by Canadian women. This was a mode adopted from the dress of the Indian women, and far better suited to Canada's sultry summer climate than the floor-length dresses worn in northern Europe.[20] Indian modes of travel by canoe, toboggan, and snowshoe were early mastered, as was the Indian method of waging war. Yet the influence of the frontier should not be overemphasized. Several peculiarities that have been attributed to the frontier really had little or nothing to do with the environment, resulting rather from changes made by the Crown in the colony's institutional framework.[21]

The Canadians, like the French, tended to be a violent people in their personal relationships. All ranks in society, gentlemen, bourgeois, *habitants* — women as well as men — officers and other ranks, tended to take offence swiftly at a slight, real or imagined, and seek redress on the spot with sword, sabre, cane, cudgel, fists or stones.[22] Tavern brawls and duels were not infrequent. In the latter case the victor, if an officer, could usually count on receiving a royal pardon (*lettres de grace*), after having been tried, convicted for homicide, and sentenced to death. At

---

[20] Adolph B. Benson (ed.,) *The America of 1750. Peter Kalm's Travels in North America*, 2 vols. (Dover Edition, New York, 1966).

[21] An example of the environmentalist interpretation carried to extremes is A. L. Burt, "The Frontier in the History of New France," *Canadian Historical Association Report, 1940*. For a different view see W. J. Eccles, *The Canadian Frontier, 1534–1760* (New York, 1969), pp. 73, 81–82.

[22] On violence in French peasant society see T. Le Goff & D. M. G. Sutherland, "The Revolution and the Rural Community in 18-Century Brittany," *Past and Present*, vol. 62, 1974, pp. 96–119. The series Documents Judiciaires in the ANQM is rife with cases of assault and battery. One can safely assume that there were far more such cases than ever reached the courts. On verbal abuse see Peter N. Moogk, " 'Thieving Buggers' and 'Stupid Sluts': Insults and Popular Culture in New France," *William and Mary Quarterly*, 3d Series, Vol. XXXVI, October 1979, pp. 524–547.

Montreal, visiting and local Indians frequently became wildly intoxicated, committed mayhem and all too often manslaughter. The citizens protested vigorously to the authorities, claiming that the town too often resembled a charnel house. There was little that the Town Major could do save to have the bodies removed in the morning, and the offenders thrown into gaol to sober up. It proved next to impossible to make the Indians submit to French law; they claimed that they were not to blame, rather it was the alcohol they had consumed that was at fault. They would offer compensation, wergeld for manslaughter and payment for other damages, according to Indian custom, but that was all. Unable to hold the Indians accountable for civil disturbances of this sort, the authorities prosecuted the French subjects who had provided the Indians with the liquor that had led to the abuses.[23] Visiting Indians frequently became wildly intoxicated, caused trouble, and were thrown into jail to sober up, but it proved impossible to make them submit to French law, and the authorities had to give up trying.

As for popular uprisings, *jacqueries*, there were none. There were some instances of irate *habitants* gathering to protest one thing or another. Occasionally groups of town or country folk assembled to object to some action, or lack of it, by the authorities. Profiteering by the colony's merchants was a frequent cause of complaint, and on occasion resulted in what the authorities chose to regard as seditious assemblies, but they were easily dealt with. A stiff fine, or a few weeks in gaol for the ringleaders, and a stern warning that they could have been hanged, sufficed.[24] The authorities could always call out the Troupes de la Marine should serious trouble arise, and the people knew it. That the crime rate in Canada was much lower than in France can perhaps be attributed to the absence of dire poverty in the colony, but why it was less than half that of Massachusetts is puzzling.[25]

---

[23] For a succinct explanation of the dilemma facing the Canadian authorities over this issue see Paris, AN Série C11A vol. 34, ff 26–29, Vaudreuil et Bégon au Ministre, 15 nov. 1713.

[24] RAPQ 1938–1939, p. 109, Vaudreuil au Ministre, Qué. 28 avril, 1 & 4 nov. 1706; *ibid.*, pp. 112–113, MM de Vaudreuil et Raudot au Ministre, Qué. 30 avril 1706; p. 132 Le Roi à MM de Vaudreuil et Raudot, Versailles le 9 juin 1706.

[25] See André Lachance, *La justice criminelle du Roi au Canada au XVIIIᵉ siècle* (Québec, 1978); André Lachance, *Crimes et criminels en Nouvelle-France* (Montréal, 1984).

The colony did not have the problem of vagabonds that plagued England and Europe, yet poverty was inevitably a concern, albeit never a very serious one. The family, rather than the individual, was the nucleus of society; thus each family was required by custom and by law to care for its own. When this was not possible, the state shouldered the responsibility. The methods and institutions employed were those that had developed in France during the course of the seventeenth century, *bureaux des pauvres* and *hôpitaux*. The poor were divided into two groups: those who were unable to provide for themselves through no fault of their own, and those who preferred to live as mendicants rather than work for a living. The former were provided for, and care was taken that they were not exploited; the latter were obliged to accept the employment found for them by the *bureaux des pauvres*. Those too aged or decrepit to be gainfully employed or to care for themselves were placed in the *hôpital* at Montreal or Quebec, along with the chronically ill, the insane, and girls of loose morals who, hopefully, would be reformed. These institutions were staffed by nuns, les Soeurs Hospitalières, financed mainly by the Crown and by revenues derived from endowed properties in France, and only partly from colonial revenues. The latter derived from a portion of the funds received from the sale of fur-trading licenses, fines imposed by the courts of law, and the dowries of the sisters.[26] Thus the colonists received a valuable service at virtually no cost. Similarly, the Hôtels Dieu provided excellent treatment for the sick who could not be treated at home, and only those who could afford to pay were expected to.

These female institutions also performed another social function; they provided careers for girls, mainly of the upper class, who had a religious vocation or did not choose marriage, or perhaps had no expectation of it, and desired to do something useful without sacrificing their social status. The nuns of the Ursulines, Hôtels Dieu, and Hôpitaux Généraux were largely of the nobility, and all but a few of the rest belonged to well-to-do

---

[26] See W. J. Eccles, "Social Welfare Measures and Policies in New France" in *Essays on New France*, pp. 38–49. Jean de la Croix de Saint-Vallier, second bishop of New France, donated 244,080 livres to these institutions from his private estate, and some 600,000 livres in all to worthy causes in the colony. See Mgr. Henri Têtu, *Les éveques de Québec*, (Québec, 1889) p. 149.

commercial families, likely with social ambitions.[27] The requirement of a dowry of 3,000 livres, raised in 1722 to 5,000, but lowered to 3,000 ten years later, ensured that only the daughters of the relatively wealthy could join the orders.[28] These sisters led a very ladylike existence, devoting their time to prayer, needlework, general supervision, and periodic visits to the patients in the wards, whose physical needs were cared for by lay sisters of humbler background. When, however, epidemics struck the colony, as occurred frequently at the turn of the century owing mainly to foul conditions on the troopships, they worked themselves literally to death. Subsequently, stiff port regulations were imposed to check the importation of disease. Upon arrival at Quebec, ships were quarantined. No one could land, no cargo be put ashore, until the crew and passengers had been given a clean bill of health by a surgeon.

In the seventeenth century there had been a shortage of doctors and surgeons, but in the eighteenth century there appeared to be no shortage of the latter, who performed most of the services of today's general practitioner. In 1710 they were granted protection from the competition offered by surgeons on ships arriving at Quebec, or surgeons entering the colony to set up practice from no matter what country. Only surgeons who had established residence in the colony were now allowed to practise. In 1750, surgeons coming from abroad were permitted to practise after they had submitted to a rigorous examination by the King's Surgeon at Quebec, in the presence of the judge of the Prévôté. It was common for the more well-to-do families to subscribe to private medicare plans whereby they received treatment for all but certain specified ailments for an annual fee.[29] The main treat-

---

[27] See Micheline D'Allaire, "Origine sociale des religieuses de l'Hôpital-général de Québec," *Revue d'Histoire de l'Amérique française*, XXIII, (mars, 1970), 559–581.

[28] The Crown was very reluctant to allow any increase in the religious orders. The large dowry required, by royal edict, was intended to limit their numbers, but the 3,000-livre stipulation was rarely met, 2,500 being the rough average for the three women's orders in the colony. This has been construed as evidence of poverty in New France. In fact the opposite might be argued, for these dowries were considerably in excess of those customarily paid for entry into fashionable convents in France. See John McManners, *French Ecclesiastical Society Under the Ancien Regime* (Manchester, 1960), pp. 92–95.

[29] See Maude E. Abbot, *History of Medicine in the Province of Quebec* (Toronto, 1931); A. D. Kelly, "Health Insurance in New France," *Bulletin of the History of Medicine*, XXVIII, 6 (Nov.–Dec., 1954).

ment afforded by these surgeons consisted of bleeding, setting broken bones, dressing wounds, the occasional amputation, administering purges, emetics, plasters, and unguents. Given the nature of some of these remedies, particularly bleeding and purges, only the healthy and strong could hope to survive them.[30]

In the field of education the colony was also well provided for, but again largely because it was able to draw on outside funds of the Crown and the parent religious orders in France. The Crown alone provided 40 percent of the funds of the Canadian Church.[31] A main endeavour was to train a native secular clergy. The seminary at Quebec accepted seventy-five students, most of whom paid no fees and had everything provided, room, board, and clothing.[32] The Sulpicians at Montreal also operated a school for boys and the Hôpital Général trained orphan boys committed to its care for posts as schoolmasters in the rural districts at a salary of 375 livres a year, which was about two-thirds what a skilled carpenter earned.[33] The Ursulines provided the daughters of the well-to-do with an excellent education, one of their aims being to inculcate in their charges good manners, the ability to converse well in polite company, and to know how to please. In the rural areas the nonconventual Sisters of the Congrégation de Notre-Dame, founded in 1672 in Montreal, who numbered forty by 1707 and eighty by mid-century, maintained several schools for *habitant* girls. To maintain standards, in 1722 the intendant issued an ordonnance requiring that all lay persons who wished to teach had to have his authorization and that of the bishop or archdeacon, then submit to an examination of their qualifications; they also had to be married.

The Jesuits at their college at Quebec offered an excellent advanced secular education for the sons of the upper-class fam-

---

[30] Yet self-medication also had its perils as the opening of a plaintive letter by Michel-Jean-Hugues Péan testifies: "Mon cher oncle, Je ne vous écrie que deux mots parce que jay pris medicine aujourdhuy qui m'a mené 75 fois et que je suis tres abattue."

[31] Guy Frégault, "L'église et la société canadienne," *Le XVIIIe siècle canadien*, pp. 104–111.

[32] For the extremely rigorous, Spartan, regime these young boys had to endure, see Eccles "The Role of the Church in New France," in *Essays on New France*, p. 30."

[33] See the salary and wage scales in Cameron Nish, *Les bourgeois-gentilshommes de la Nouvelle-France, 1729-1748* (Montreal, 1968), pp. 39–43. A breakdown of wage rates and food allowances for carpenters and other tradesmen is to be found at Public Archives of Canada, Series MG18G6, Papiers Beauharnois, Lettres et mémoires du Canada.

ilies who could benefit from it. That a good education was valued is indicated by the decision of the sieur de Marin, commandant at Fort Duquesne, who, when informed by the governor general that a vacancy had been found for his youngest son as a cadet in the Troupes de la Marine, declined the offer because he wanted the boy to complete his studies before entering the army. The letters that have survived, written by Canadian officers, with a few notable exceptions,[34] indicate that most of them had received excellent schooling; as good as or better than, in fact, most of the French or English officers of that period. Many Canadians had sizable private libraries, and Peter Kalm claimed that the upper-class Canadians were more interested in the world of science and literature than were the citizens of the English colonies.[35] No literary tradition, however, was established. The journals, descriptions, and travel accounts describing life in New France were, with rare exceptions, written by Frenchmen, for a French audience. No newspapers were printed in Canada. There was not even a printing press, but this lack did not result from any desire on the part of the authorities, lay or clerical, to keep the people in ignorance. Cut off from Europe seven or eight months of the year, with ships arriving only during the summer months, there would have been little news to print. In 1748 Governor General La Galissonière proposed the establishment of a printing shop. The minister replied that the King would gladly grant a licence to a private printer but was unwilling to have the Crown bear the cost.[36]

That the colony produced no great men of letters, no large body

---

[34] The most glaring exception was the very able capitaine Claude-Pierre Pécaudy de Contrecoeur who spelled everything phonetically. See Fernand Grenier (ed.), *Papiers Contrecoeur et autres documents concernant le conflit anglo-français sur l'Ohio de 1745 à 1756*, (Québec, 1952).

[35] *Peter Kalm's Travels in North America*, II, pp. 374–376.

[36] Paris, Archives Nationales, Colonies, F3 Moreau de St. Méry, XI, pp. 311–312, Le Ministre à La Jonquière, 4 mai 1749. (I am indebted to Professor Peter N. Moogk for providing me with this reference.) Significantly, the West Indies had a printer in 1726, duly sanctioned by the Crown. There was, however, a far greater need for a printer in the islands than in Canada. The West Indies, with their huge volume of shipping, six hundred ships a year compared with Canada's twenty-odd, its slave market with fluctuating prices, and the desire to know the going price of the islands' varied produce in Europe, offered ample scope for a printer. On the scope, utility, and vicissitudes of the *Gazette de Saint-Domingue*, see Moreau de Saint-Méry, *Description topographique, physique, civile, politique, et historique de la partie française de l'Isle Saint-Domingue* (Nouvelle édition entièrement revue et complétée sur le manuscrit suivie d'un index des noms de personnes, par Blanche Maurel et Etiénne Taillemite) (3 vols., Paris, 1958), I, pp. 493–497.

of literature, should not occasion surprise. Neither did the English colonies. For that matter, neither did English Canada for well over a century. Had a Canadian with literary talent emerged he would indubitably have had to pursue his career in Paris, for in France, unlike in the British empire, all cultural life was concentrated at the capital; the rest of the kingdom was an intellectual wasteland. When, however, the comparison is made between New France and the English colonies in the field of politics, the difference is indeed striking. In the second half of the eighteenth century, in fact in one generation, the thirteen colonies with a population of a million and a half produced a number of exceptional politicians. It has to be noted, however, that the ensuing republic has never succeeded in repeating that performance. Those colonies had achieved a remarkable degree of independence before the Revolution, and an indigenous culture. Once the political tie with Britain was severed the Revolutionary leaders had ample scope for their considerable talents. By contrast, New France was merely an underpopulated province, a provincial backwater, separated from the rest of the kingdom by the Atlantic. Given the political structure, and the dependent nature of Canadian society at the upper level, ambitious men of ability were obliged to make their careers in the imperial forces or the administration in competition with men, much better advantaged, in France. A few did: Pierre le Moyne d'Iberville and his brother Bienville are early examples. In the closing years of the regime, Canadians were moving up the scale in the royal administration: Denis-Nicolas Foucault, who sparked the revolt in Louisiana against Spanish rule, is one such. He later rose to be intendant of a province in France. Another, Jacau de Fiedmont, became governor of Guiana. After the Conquest, François-Joseph Chaussegros de Léry, a son of a Canadian officer, was to become commander in chief of the engineers in the Grande Armée. His name is engraved on the Arc de Triomphe with those of Napoleon's other generals. These were the limits within which the King's subjects born in New France had to pursue their careers, the heights to which they could aspire.

Although Canada, with a population one-twentieth that of the English colonies, by comparison produced very few towering individuals, that is not the sole criterion that can be used to judge a country, or a colony. If civilization means anything, then the ambience of a society, rather than its level of economic prosperity or the development of particular political institutions, is the more valid criterion. Social values, such elusive qualities as refined manners, good taste, the appreciation of the finer things in life, *la douceur de vie*, all have to be taken into account. In these respects society in New France compared favourably with that of the English colonies and, at the lower end of the social scale, with that of France. Newcomers to Canada from France were much struck by the urbanity and sophistication of the upper class at Quebec and Montreal, and by the simple dignity and courteous manners of the *habitants*. Peter Kalm, who toured both the English colonies and Canada in 1748-1749, found Canadian society much the more agreeable of the two. He wrote: "The difference between the favour and politeness which is my lot here and that of the English provinces is like that between heaven and earth, between black and white." After leaving Canada he wrote: "The people there, even the common man, are much more polite than the people in the English provinces, and especially compared to the Dutch. . . . The difference was as great as if one had gone from the Court to a peasant's house."[37] That, of course, is merely one man's value judgment. He was, unfortunately, the only foreign observer to visit both regions and record his impressions.

The rise in educational standards among the upper class, and of the standard of living of all classes, was matched by a steady decline of the influence of the clergy, and also of moral standards among the laity at all social levels. By the 1730s the seventeenth-century vision of a New Jerusalem had long since faded, and some of the clergy depicted the colony as more akin to Sodom or Gomorrah. As early as 1707 the intendant Raudot had issued

---

[37] Martti Kerkkonen, *Peter Kalm's North American Journey* (Studia Historica, I, Finnish Historical Society, Helsinki, 1959), pp. 109-110. Kalm omitted the two sentences above from the published version of his journal, but other passages he included indicate his views on the subject. In this connection it may not be without significance that in 1698 and again in 1713, at the close of hostilities, many — if not the majority — of the English colonial prisoners taken by the French refused to return home, preferring to take up residence in New France. In 1713 they numbered well over a hundred; 134 requested letters of naturalization, and many more appear not to have bothered with this formality. See W. J. Eccles, *The Canadian Frontier, 1534-1760* (New York, 1969), pp. 82, 198.

an ordonnance forbidding the young men of Montreal to continue maintaining mistresses in the town. In 1749, when the curé of Montreal thundered from the pulpit against the balls, parties, and assemblies with which the citizens enlivened the long winter nights, claiming that they were the occasion of all manner of adulteries and fornication, the auditors were incensed and one seigneur who accepted the curé's dictum was labeled a "Tartuffe."[38]

Another indication of the decline of morals was the soaring illegitimacy rate. Foundlings were wards of the Crown, and great care was taken to ensure that they were well cared for until they were old enough for adoption, and subsequently apprenticed. At the end of the seventeenth century the expenses incurred for this humanitarian service had been a quite insignificant item on the colonial budget. By 1736, however, it assumed large proportions. In that year the intendant posted in his accounts under "Enfants Batards à Québec" 4,970 livres, 10 sols, 4 deniers; for Montréal, clearly in the lead, 7,956 livres; for Trois Rivières, with a much smaller population, 1,042 livres, 13 sols, 3 deniers. The following year the amount required for the sustenance of these illegitimate children went up by 5,000 livres, and the intendant reduced the monthly stipend for their sustenance from ten livres a month to seven.[39] Another indicator of a decline in morals is the increasing number of cases coming before the courts of seduction, and alleged rape.

During the eighteenth century the clergy in the colony came increasingly to be staffed by Canadians. This was particularly true of the mendicant Récollets, rather less so of the secular clergy, who were still recruited in France to serve the growing number of parishes. By 1721 there were eighty-two parishes in

[38] *Rapport de l'Archiviste de la Province de Québec, 1934–1935*, p. 81.

[39] Paris, Archives Nationales, Colonies, C11A, LXV, M. pp. 222, 248–253. It is not possible to break the figures down to arrive at the number of foundlings, since the amounts include items for such things as medical care for ailing wet nurses. Moreover, only abandoned infants were cared for by the Crown. Some families likely made their own arrangements for children born on the wrong side of the blanket. The higher incidence of foundlings at Montreal may be explained by the presence of the bulk of the Troupes de la Marine and that the voyageurs returning from the west were paid off there by their merchant employers. It is worthy of note that a great increase in the number of foundlings during the eighteenth century also occurred in Paris, from 2,000 to 6,000. See Fernand Braudel and Ernest Labrousse, *Histoire économique et sociale de la France* (4 vols., Paris, 1970), II, p. 73.

the colony, but several had no resident curé. Thirty-five years later, forty-four parishes were able to provide for their resident curés, another forty-four still received subventions from the Crown, and sixteen more sparsely populated were served by itinerant priests.[40] The senior clergy, almost all natives of France, were somewhat reluctant to accept Canadians into the priesthood because of their independent and allegedly flighty character. Bishop Saint-Vallier agreed with the intendant Michel Bégon that it would be better to have a dean for the cathedral sent from France rather than appoint a Canadian, owing to the Canadians' notorious reluctance to recognize and submit to the authority of their superiors either temporal or spiritual. At the same time, however, the Crown maintained a tight control over the Church in the colony, as well it might, since it held the purse strings. When, for example, the bishop threatened to bar from communion and absolution those colonists who refused to pay their tithe the minister sternly ordered him, "It is necessary, if you please, that you change that ordonnance." On the other hand, the intendant frequently intervened to oblige the Canadians to show more respect for the cloth, to meet their financial obligations to the Church, and to behave in a more seemly manner than too often was their wont at Mass and in religious processions. New France was far from being the priest-ridden ultramontanist theocracy it has been depicted as being by some latter-day historians. In fact the Canadian Church could hardly have been more Gallican, indeed, Erastian.

The increasingly secular spirit of colonial society is also indicated by the fading of what today would be regarded as superstition: namely, the belief in sorcery.[41] In 1660 the bishop granted an annulment of a marriage on the grounds that it had proved impossible for the couple to consummate the marriage because they had been placed under an evil spell by an unknown sorceror.

[40] See A. Gosselin, *L'Église du Canada depuis Mgr de Laval jusqu'à la conquête* (3 vols., Quebec, 1911-14), III, pp. 431-433. The boundaries of the parishes as they were in 1721 are stated in *Édits et ordonnances royaux, déclarations et arrêts du Conseil d'État du Roi concernant le Canada* (Québec, 1854), pp. 443-462.

[41] On the French background of this phenomenon see Robert Mandrou, *Magistrats et sorciers en France au XVIIᵉ siècle* (Paris, 1968). R.-L. Séguin, *La sorcellerie au Canada français du XVIIᵉ au XIXᵉ siècle* (Montréal, 1961), provides some information on its incidence in the colony. See also Raymond Boyer, *Les crimes et les châtiments au Canada français du XVIIᵉ au XXᵉ siècle* (Montréal, 1966), pp. 292-306.

Ten years later, when a woman was accused of practising sorcery, the Sovereign Council ordered that the investigation would be kept open for a year, and nothing more came of it. Witchcraft, however, was unknown, and there was never anything to equal the hysteria that swept through part of New England in the 1690s. No one was executed in New France for occult practices, and in the odd case in which an individual was convicted by the courts it was for practising deception on the gullible for material gain rather than for having had a liaison with Satan. Fortunately, in New France, unlike in New England, anyone suspect of sorcery or witchcraft was not left to the mercy of a credulous jury. Instead the charge had to be thoroughly investigated and convincing evidence produced before the courts could convict.

The mid-seventeenth century had been the great age of religious enthusiasm in Canada, exemplified by the Jesuit martyrs. In the eighteenth century the Jesuit missionaries in the West were as much agents of the Crown as of Rome, extending French influence over the Indian nations of the Mississippi Valley. Father Pierre-François-Xavier de Charlevoix, S.J., professor at the Collège de Québec from 1705 to 1709, in 1720, on orders of the Regent, Philippe, duc d'Orléans, set off from Paris for Quebec. From there he was to voyage to the Far West to seek the great inland sea that was purported to reach from the Pacific far into the interior of the continent.[42] Upon reaching the Mississippi, he decided that it was pointless to go further west. He turned south, proceeded to New Orleans and from there returned to France. He subsequently wrote a history of New France, utilizing original documents in the archives of the Ministry of Marine. A typical Jesuit of his day, he found the Canadians, on his later visit, to be better educated and more urbane than heretofore.[43] If not anti-clerical, they clearly showed that there were limits beyond which they felt the power of the clergy should not extend. Among the upper strata of society, those who maintained contact with events

---

[42] For this mythical inland sea, see *Historical Atlas of Canada* (Toronto, 1987), plate 36.

[43] Père P.-F.-X. de Charlevoix, S.J. *Histoire et description générale de la Nouvelle-France, avec le journal historique d'une voyage fait par ordre du roi dans l'Amérique septentrionale* (Paris, 1744), 3 vols. By the mid-eighteenth century almost 25 percent of the Canadian population resided in the three towns. In France less than 20 percent was urban. See Guy Frégault, *La civilisation de la Nouvelle-France* (Montréal, 1944), p. 217; Braudel and Labrousse, *Histoire économique et sociale de la France*, II, p. 29.

and the intellectual climate of France, a more sceptical spirit prevailed and the clergy were aware that a few of their flock were secretly Freemasons.[44]

It is, of course, virtually impossible to discover at this remove the depth of religious feeling among the people of that age who, if they did discuss the question among themselves — which appears unlikely—did not commit their thoughts to paper. Compared to the Puritans of New England, their religious observances were more a sensual than an intellectual experience. They appear to have taken their religion for granted as an accepted part of their way of life. Its ethical precepts were not challenged, merely evaded by all to some degree, and by a few to a degree that obliged the authorities to take action. But were there to have been no such departures from the prescribed code, there would have been no need for an established church. One important factor influencing the Canadian religious climate was unity of religion. Although in the mid-eighteenth century there were some few Huguenots in the colony, indeed the intendant François Bigot declared that they controlled the colony's trade, the Church did not appear threatened from internal, or external, sources; thus the people could afford to wear their religion lightly; comfortably, in fact.

What did this colony look like by the mid-eighteenth century? A visitor from Europe, after a sea voyage lasting weeks, or even months, would likely form his first impressions at Louisbourg. There he would find himself in a fortified garrison town guarding the anchorage in a sheltered bay large enough to hold a fleet. Built at the cost of 3.5 million livres, with a population of forty-two hundred in 1752, it dominated the fishing industry of the North Atlantic, harvesting some 150,000 quintals of fish a year, approximately half as much as the fishing fleets of all the British colonies.[45] On an average, 154 ships a year called in at the port, a number exceeded only at New York, Boston, and Philadelphia.

---

[44] *Rapport de l'Archiviste de la Province de Québec, 1947–1948*, pp. 89–90.

[45] See Charles de la Morandière, *Histoire de la pêche française de la morue dans l'Amérique septentrionale* (2 vols., Paris, 1962); Harold Adams Innis, *The Cod Fisheries: The History of an International Economy* (Toronto, 1940; rev. ed., Toronto, 1954); John Robert McNeill, *Atlantic Empires of France and Spain, Louisbourg and Havana 1700–1763* (Chapel Hill NC & London, 1985); F. J. Thorpe, *Les remparts lointains* (Univ. of Ottawa Press, 1980).

The Citadel, where resided the governor, and other buildings belonging to the Crown as well as the hospital and the convents of the Récollets and the Sisters of the Congrégation, all built of solid stone with the slender flèche-style steeples, were far more imposing than anything to be found in the English colonies. Most of the houses of the private residents were of wood on stone foundations, and some of them made obvious the prosperity of their owners. At the tables of the governor and other senior officials the guest might find the menu restricted to fish during much of the year, but he would eat it off porcelain and wash it down with a good dry white wine from the Loire valley. He might also find himself one of eighty guests, served by black servants, at the governor's residence; or more likely at a more intimate gathering of twenty-odd. Should the visitor have been accompanied by his wife or daughter, she could have availed herself of the services of two dressmakers, and perhaps patronized M. Simon Rondel, the dancing master. Despite the bleak winter climate, the officers of the garrison, the royal officials, and the wealthier merchants contrived to pass the time fairly agreeably with a round of dinners, garrison balls, tense hours at the gaming tables, and the occasional duel.[46]

Ships that went directly to Quebec late in the summer, after the annual flow of icebergs down the Atlantic coast of Labrador and Newfoundland had ceased, might take the northern entry into the Gulf of St Lawrence and call first at the fishing port in Baye Phélypeaux at the Strait of Belle Isle for wood and fresh water. On that bleak, desolate coast, despite the determined efforts of the Inuit to drive them off, more than a thousand French fishermen in up to twenty ships took some fifty thousand cod a year, and the Canadian officer commanding the Labrador region did well for himself from the trade in fur, fish, oil, and sealskins.[47] Farther east, on Anticosti Island, stone chimneys marked the oil-rendering plants of the Basque and Canadian whalers. With a good northeast wind another three days' sail brought a ship to

---

[46] See J. S. McLennan, *Louisbourg from Its Foundation to Its Fall* (London, 1918); Helen Sutermeister, "An Eighteenth-Century Urban Estate in New France," *Post-Medieval Archeology*, II (1968), pp. 83–118; Clark, *Acadia*, pp. 293–296.

[47] *Rapport de l'Archiviste de la Province de Québec, 1922–1923*, pp. 359–406.

Tadoussac. Here the St Lawrence is a mere twenty-five miles wide, the south shore low and flat but with the Notre Dame mountain range faintly visible on the horizon. Along the north shore the steep, rugged, spruce-covered cliffs of the Laurentian Shield, plunging straight down into the river, offered the viewer some of the most magnificent scenery to be found anywhere.

From this point on, signs of settlement could occasionally be discerned along the south shore, while on the north, at Malbaie, a lumbermill marked the eastern end of the commercial assault on the Canadian forest. As the river narrowed, navigation became more hazardous. Reefs, hidden at high tide, abounded. On the heights, navigation markers gave the ship's pilots the bearing, some islands had swaths cut through their forest cover for the same purpose, and buoys marked the channel that skirted close to the steep north shore, but a strong northeast wind was needed to bring a ship up against the powerful current and the ebb tide. At the Île d'Orléans, settlement became more dense on both sides of the river, with whitewashed stone farmhouses evenly spaced along the riverbanks and the spires of churches standing out every few leagues. Then, as the western tip of the island was rounded, the capital of New France came into view.

No city in North America had a site as magnificent as Quebec. Jutting out into the river stood the steep 100-metre promontory. On the heights were the imposing buildings of the Crown and the Church, surrounded by the residences of the wealthier citizens. Dominating all was the Château Saint-Louis, residence of the governor general, with a row of cannon on its terrace overlooking the wide river. Nearby were the cathedral, the seminary, the Jesuit college with a clock in its chapel steeple, the convent of the Ursulines, the Hôtel Dieu, the bishop's palace, and the unpretentious church of the Récollets. These steep-roofed buildings were of stone, walls several feet thick, with the clean, simple, but graceful proportions typical of northern France. Within, the decoration of the churches was ornate, much more so than in those of equivalent towns of eight thousand inhabitants in France. The cream-coloured walls and ceilings were embellished with delicate appliquéd gilded woodcarving in lieu of the moulded plaster customary in Europe.[48] The bishops, the royal family, and private donors had been lavish in their donations. In the rococo style, gold leaf abounded; silver vases, chalices, and chandeliers of excellent workmanship, were there for all to see.[49] Some, at least, of the churches had organs, and the town's master of the clavichord was kept busy training musicians.[50] When, on a Sunday, the bells of these churches rang out across the town, calling the citizens to Mass, not only were they given spiritual solace; their aesthetic senses were treated to the sound of choir and organ, the visual richness of gold and silver, the fine lace and embroidery of priestly vestments, the fragrance of incense as the host was elevated to the tinkling of a silver bell.

In Lower Town, on the narrow strand between the cliff and the river with its six-metre tide, were the docks, batteries of cannon, the warehouses of merchants, the small church of Notre-Dame des Victoires facing the marketplace, with the Bernini bust of Louis XIV in a niche over the door of one of the merchant's houses. At the rear of the town, on the St Charles River side, stood the imposing intendant's palace, with its gleaming metal roof. It served both as the intendant's official residence and as the *palais de justice*. Here the Quebec Prévôté and the Superior Council sat, the latter body seated about a long table in a spacious chamber, the walls covered with fleur-de-lis tapestry, a portrait

---

[48] Canada's sub-zero winter temperatures and intermittent thaws would surely have destroyed plaster mouldings.

[49] Archives du Séminaire de Québec, Lettres N, 101, p. 9, M. Tremblay à Mgr Laval, 10 mai 1695. In a marginal notation Mgr. Laval remarked that he had ordered "deux milliers d'or" for the seminary chapel. The intendant de Meulles, in 1684, commented that the seminary had cost 150,000 livres, and Frontenac stated that it would cost 400,000 livres before it was finished. The late E. R. Adair in his paper "French Canadian Art," *The Canadian Historical Association Report, 1929*, gives a good description of this artwork, and notes: "It is not an accident that the Puritans of New England, though they lived under no worse frontier conditions, possessed no such art as this. . . . Their churches, in their cold austerity, frowned upon all decoration made by hands, and in their bitter struggle with nature there was no time and no strength left for other inspiration." To take the argument one step further, Canadian ecclesiastical architecture and art appear almost stark when compared to the baroque and rococo of Latin America. In Peru and Mexico the Spanish were able to employ the skilled Indian craftsmen who blended their traditional motifs with those of the Spanish baroque. See Victor-L. Tapié, *Baroque et Classicisme* (Paris, 1957).

[50] *Annales des Religieuses Hospitalières de la Miséricorde de Jésus* (5 vols., Québec, 1870), I, p. 249.

of Louis XV hung conspicuously. In the cellars below were the dank cells occupied by prisoners held during trial.

The forty-four streets in the town were mostly unpaved and lined with houses, shops, taverns, and billiard halls that crowded the wooden sidewalks. All the buildings had steep-pitched roofs and low dormer windows. In Upper Town, there were extensive open spaces, squares, and gardens behind many of the homes. At the rear of the town the stone fortifications ran from the cliff on the St Lawrence across the promontory and down the slope to the flat land by the St Charles River. Two muddy roads struggled up to the heights, one from near the intendant's palace, the other from the docks on the St Lawrence shore up between the governor general's residence and the bishopric. Up these roads (easily blocked in the event of attack) in dry weather, when the wells and springs ran dry, came Upper Town's water supply on little wagons drawn by dogs.

The major event of the year in Quebec was the arrival of the ships from France in the summer. When the wind turned to the northeast, the river was eagerly scanned for the first sight of the white sails rounding the Île d'Orléans into the wide basin. No one was allowed to set foot on the ships before the captain had gone ashore with the post, which he took to a designated merchant's place of business for distribution. The postal service between Quebec and Montreal was better then, than it is today [1989]. Letters normally took four days between the two towns.[51] The ship's officers, royal officials, returning Canadians, the occasional distinguished visitor, were eagerly entreated to dine by the leading Quebec families, the ladies being particularly anxious to have word of the latest fashions at Paris and Versailles. The ships' captains disposed of their goods and sought a return cargo, all too often in vain.[52] The taverns did a roaring business, members of an ancient profession plied their trade, and the archers of the Prévôté had a busy time preserving order. The colony was once again in touch with the outside world.

---

[51] Pierre-George Roy (ed.), *Inventaire des ordonnances des intendants de la Nouvelle-France. . . .* (Beauceville, 1919) vol. II, p. 126; ANQM pièces judiciaires. M. Raudot à M. Raimbault, Qué., le 23 mai 1710.

[52] On Canada's adverse balance of trade see Miquelon, *New France 1701–1744*, pp. 124–144.

Those arriving on the ships who had not been to Canada before were usually much impressed by what they saw and by their contacts with the colonists. Some visitors thought the common people were too well off, and should have been taxed to make them work harder. In the streets, officers in the Troupes de la Marine in their oyster-white uniforms faced with blue, Jesuits and secular priests in black soutanes, Récollets in hooded brown soutanes, nuns in black and starched white, or grey robes, officials, merchants, and gentlemen in lace-trimmed surcoats, some with wigs, ladies in long cloaks, mingled with Indians in a miscellany of French clothing, buckskin, furs, or just a breechclout and the *habitants* in rough homespun, moccasins, a woollen toque covering their pigtailed hair, the inevitable clay pipe in their mouths.

What impressed visitors most was the decorum and liveliness of this urban society. Those who had entrée to the governor's circle were every bit as interested in the world of the intellect as were the affluent in France. Hospitality was lavish, regardless of expense. The governor general in particular was expected to entertain extravagantly, maintaining a private orchestra and a large retinue of servants. So too were the local governors at Trois Rivières and Montreal. After each sitting of the Superior Council, the senior councillor, in the absence of the intendant, was expected to dine them well.

When proceeding to Montreal, the most comfortable way to travel was by boat or canoe. A road had been constructed along the north shore, but travel on it was comfortable only on horseback or in winter by sleigh. After a heavy snowstorm the *habitants* were obliged to make it passable by driving their oxen along it and marking the road with coniferous trees planted in the snow every few feet. The traveller who went by river was able to view the greater part of the colony. It made a very impressive prospect, with the narrow fields running back from the riverbanks on both shores, whitewashed farmhouses and thatch-roofed barns spaced every few hundred metres, giving the colony the appearance of a straggling village stretching for more than 275 kilometres. Where large streams ran down to the river, massive stone mills could be seen. Every few kilometres the spire of a small parish church rose above the tree line, and periodically, the larger stone manor houses of the seigneurs.

When obliged to stop for the night, distinguished visitors, if not the guests of the local seigneur, were expected to stay with the *capitaine de milice*, this being one of the prerogatives of his office. The houses were usually comfortable enough, the stone walls 60 to 120 centimetres thick, with a steep-pitched plank roof, in appearance resembling the houses of northwestern France.[53] The furniture within was made by local artisans, usually of pine, frequently of excellent design and craftsmanship in the style of the Louis XIII era. The more well-to-do, of course, imported their furniture from France.[54] In any house, seigneur's or *habitant*'s, the guest could be assured of sleeping on a down-filled mattress.

Trois Rivières, although only a small market town with a population of 808 in 1754, was a seat of local government. In the late seventeenth century the baron de Lahontan had commented that it was noted for the martial qualities of its men and its fleas. In the mid-eighteenth it had a little more to boast about; nearby were the Saint-Maurice forges.[55] Here too was another major industry, canoe-making. Five- to eight-man birchbark canoes, up to ten metres long, were essential for the fur trade and some military operations. With a life expectancy of four to five years, they cost 300 livres, and a master canoemaker earned as much as 6,000 livres a year, ten times the earnings of a skilled carpenter. At Trois Rivières the tide became negligible. It may be significant that the majority of the voyageurs in the fur trade came from the region between Trois Rivières and Montreal, beyond the pull of the tide.

Montreal, located midway on the south side of the forty-eight-kilometre-long island, had a splendid site. The town itself, surrounded by a stone wall adequate only as a defense against musket

[53] See Ramsay Traquair, *The Old Architecture of Quebec* (Toronto, 1947); Peter N. Moogk, *Building a House in New France* (Toronto, 1977); P. Roy Wilson, *The Beautiful Old Houses of Quebec* (Toronto, 1975).

[54] See Antoine Roy, "Le coût et le goût des meubles au Canada sous le régime français," *Cahier des Dix, XVIII* (Montréal, 1953), pp. 228–239; Palardy, *The Early Furniture of French Canada*. It has to be noted, however, that the woodcarving that has survived in Canada from the French regime does not compare very favourably with that produced in the Spanish colonies.

[55] See Trottier, *Les Forges*.

fire, stood close by the St Lawrence with Mount Royal rising steeply behind it. Beyond the river, studded across the broad plain that stretched to the Appalachians, were similar volcanic mountains, spaced well apart. All around the town were tilled fields, gardens, and orchards. With the growth of population, houses had been built toward the mountain and at the west end of the town, beyond the walls. Within the town walls, the streets, ordered widened to 11 metres in 1685, with masonry sewers on the main thoroughfares, were laid out rectilineally. Despite this width, traffic presented a serious problem, for the citizens rarely walked; they insisted on using sleighs in winter, finely sprung calèches in summer, or sedan chairs. Spirited horses were an obsession with the Canadians, seigneurs and *habitants* alike, and their number was estimated to equal that of the adult males.

Montreal, like Quebec and Trois Rivières, had suffered severely from fires that had razed entire sections more than once. To prevent and curb such conflagrations, elaborate precautions were taken. Houses had to be of stone, and where they were separated by a common wall, that wall had to be extended a good metre above the roof line to make a fire break. The citizens were mobilized into fire-fighting brigades, and implements, such as buckets and axes, were maintained in handy locations about the towns. Chimneys had to be cleaned once a month, Savoyard boys being brought from France to perform this duty.[56] Roofs were required to be of slate, or failing that, the attic floor had to be of flagstones, again to prevent fires from spreading. Painted metal shutters on the windows and graceful wrought iron grilles provided security against robbers in a day when property insurance was not obtainable.

The ambience of Montreal was quite different from that of Quebec. The latter, a seaport, looked to Europe; as the administrative centre of the colony, it was dominated by the senior officials and their entourage. Montreal stood at the edge of the

---

[56] In 1729 the governor general and intendant informed the minister that the two Savoyards sent out some years earlier had grown too big to scramble inside chimneys. They asked that four more, aged twelve to fourteen, be sent and pointed out that they would earn more in the colony than anywhere in the kingdom, seven or eight livres a day, almost double the wages of masons and carpenters. Paris, Archives Nationales, Colonies, C11A, LI, p. 114, Beauharnois et Hocquart au Ministre, Que., 9 nov. 1729.

wilderness, a frontier garrison town, dominated by the soldiery and the men of the fur trade. Across the St Lawrence was the village of the Mission Iroquois at Sault Saint-Louis, and to the west of the island of Montreal, on the Lake of Two Mountains, was another village of Christian Iroquois and Algonquins. The men of these villages served as voyageurs, and in wartime were a great asset. They also served as intermediaries in the flourishing clandestine trade between Montreal and Albany, since the authorities could not forbid their traveling where they willed. During the summer months, Indians from the Far West and the Five Nations confederacy were frequent visitors, and they had to be extended many privileges. To prevent tribal feuds from erupting in the streets of the town, separate taverns for the different nations had to be established, and heavy penalties were inflicted on tavernkeepers who allowed their Indian customers to imbibe too much.

In the spring, after the great grinding floes of ice had been swept down the river and the spate of the runoff had subsided, the fur brigades made ready to depart for the West. The voyageurs, mostly Canadians, but some of them Indians, and some of the latter, girls — to the great concern of the clergy — signed on with the merchants or with the Crown to transport trade goods and military supplies to the western posts. Some of these contracts were drawn up by a notary, and are very revealing. Whether the voyageur would paddle bow, middle, or stern was specified. A *congé*, or permit, to go to the *pays d'en haut* had to be obtained from the governor general and registered with the local authorities before departure. This was the busy time of year for the town, as carts transported the goods to Lachine, above the turbulent rapids which barred navigation, even to canoes. The Sulpicians had tried valiantly to build a canal linking two small rivers to by-pass these rapids and allow canoes to depart from Montreal, but despite very heavy expenditures they had failed. In the summer and early fall the canoes returned with their loads of furs. Some of the posts were so far distant that the voyageurs formed two groups. Those who transported the goods in large *canots de maître* to Michilimackinac, or Kaministigoya at the western end of Lake Superior, were referred to with something approaching contempt, as *mangeurs de lard* (pork eaters) by the *hommes du nord* (men of the north) who took the goods from those points to the headwaters of the Mississippi and beyond, or to the posts of the Mer de l'Ouest in the basin of Lakes Winnipeg and Manitoba, and westward along the Assiniboine and Saskatchewan rivers. The *hommes du nord* spent a large part of their lives in the Northwest, living among the Indian nations, marrying Indian girls, more Indian than French in their way of life and their values. Out of this union sprang the Métis nation of the northwestern plains.[57]

Between these far distant posts and Montreal was Fort Frontenac at the eastern end of Lake Ontario. It served as a transshipment base for military supplies brought by canoe up the turbulent St Lawrence to be taken on by sailing barque to Fort Niagara. Farther west again was the military settlement at Detroit. Within its palisade, log houses lined its straight-ruled streets; the only buildings of any consequence were the military governor's residence and the parish church, serving its six hundred parishioners. Surrounding the townsite and across the strait were the cultivated fields. Across the strait too were the villages of the Hurons and one of the Ottawa nations. To the north, Michilimackinac, at the entrance to Lake Michigan and a main base for the trade of the Northwest, was little more than an entrepôt. From it, canoes voyaged to the posts on Lake Superior and the Mer de l'Ouest or south down Green Bay to the most profitable of the trading regions, La Baye, in present-day Wisconsin, or down the length of Lake Michigan, then over the low height of land to the Illinois and south to Cahokia, Kaskaskia, and New Orleans. The frequency with which the Canadians, both military and civilian, made this voyage between Quebec and the Gulf of Mexico and thought nothing of it was astonishing to visitors from France.[58]

---

[57] See Marcel Giraud, *Le Métis canadien: Son rôle dans l'histoire des provinces de l'Ouest* (2 vols., Paris, 1945).

[58] In April 1757, Colonel Bougainville was astonished to encounter a courier, just arrived from Louisiana, cooling his heels at the governor general's door. "No one paid him any more attention than one would a man arrived at Paris from Versailles." *Rapport de l'Archiviste . . . 1923-1924*, p. 258.

It was by means of these forts on the strategic waterways that the French had gained a degree of sovereignty over a large part of the continent.[59] New France was, in fact, a river empire. Its main bases, Canada and Louisiana, dominated the two great rivers giving access into the interior, where military trading posts — tiny enclaves in the wilderness manned by an officer, a chaplain, and a handful of men amid numerous powerful Indian nations that tolerated them only out of economic necessity tinged with mingled respect and fear — were maintained by the French Crown to hold back the Anglo-Americans who coveted the continent. The fur trade now served political and strategic aims as much as, if not more than, economic ends, and the military establishment dominated colonial society. In fact, by 1744, when the Anglo-French thirty years' peace came to a close, war and the threat of war had become as much a staple of the Canadian economy as furs.

[59] On the military advantages control of the rivers gave the French, see the contemporary observations of John Mitchell, *The Contest in America Between Great Britain and France* (London, 1757), pp. 118-19, 125. See also Eccles, "The Fur Trade and Eighteenth Century Imperialism," in *Essays on New France*, pp. 79-95.

Chapter 6

The Slave Colonies, 1683–1748

Standing in striking contrast to the economic and social development of Canada was that which emerged in the West Indies, based on the institution of black (Negro) slavery. Intermediate between the two, sharing features of both, was Louisiana.

Unlike the aborigines of Canada, who had something of economic value to offer — furs — and a political role to play as military allies, the Carib Indians of the West Indies had nothing; hence they were early eliminated.[1] What the main islands provided was fertile land and the climate needed to cultivate tropical produce not indigenous to Europe — tobacco, cotton, indigo, sugar, cocoa, and, after 1730, coffee. All that was needed was a plentiful supply of cheap, unskilled labour. Since the local Indians proved useless for this purpose, and Louis XIV would not permit the forcible transportation of his indigent subjects, recourse had to be had — as in Canada — first to the *engagé* system, then to the African slave trade. *Engagés* — indentured workers — were hired in France for a three-year term. In early years it proved far easier to persuade *engagés* to sign on for the West Indies than for Canada. The islands were widely proclaimed to be veritable utopias where life was easy, the climate soft, and food grew wild

---

[1] The remnants of these tribes on the French islands were removed to Dominica, and subsequently, in 1748 by the Treaty of Aix-la-Chapelle, France and England agreed that the Neutral Islands of the Lesser Antilles — Dominica, St Lucia, St Vincent, and Tobago — would be left to the original inhabitants forever. In the event, "forever" meant until 1759 when those islands were seized by Britain.

on trees. The wages offered, four to five times the normal rate in France, appeared to be much higher than those offered in Canada.[2] From La Rochelle alone between 1660 and 1715, 5,200 *engagés* were shipped to the Antilles and only 928 to Canada.[3]

How many *engagés* all told emigrated to the West Indies is not known, nor is it known how many survived their term of engagement. What is known is that their living and working conditions were ghastly and the casualty rate extremely high. In 1681 a royal official estimated that of six hundred *engagés* who had come in recent years, fewer than fifty had survived their three years' indenture. The hours of work were the same as in Europe, from sunrise to sunset. At the latitude of the islands this meant twelve hours a day all year round, with a two-hour break at noon. In a tropical climate hard physical labour for that span for Europeans was killing, particularly the tending of cane-crushing machines and refinery boiling vats. Moreover, the food rations — starchy cassava and, at most, three pounds of salt beef a week—provided a diet grossly inferior to that enjoyed by the Canadians. Those who fell ill from fever, exhaustion, or scurvy were flogged back to work. The *engagés* were treated worse than slaves for the simple reason that the planters benefited from their labour for only three years compared to the lifetime — albeit short — of the slaves.[4]

Again in contrast with the Canadian *habitant*, the *engagé* could not hope one day to own land of his own and become his own master. After 1663, land was not granted in seigneurial tenure, but conceded only by the Crown to the planters *en roture*, and by 1670 all the land fit for use had been taken up. The grantees were under no obligation, as in Canada, to grant a part of their concessions to anyone requesting it. In the seventeenth century most of the plantations were established by a partnership between a merchant in France, or someone with capital to invest, and a

---

[2] G. Debien, ''La société coloniale aux XVIIe et XVIIIe siècles: Les engagés pour les Antilles (1634-1715),'' *Revue d'Histoire des Colonies françaises*, XXXVIII, 1 and 2 (1951), pp. 141-142, 158, 165.

[3] M. Delafosse, ''Le trafic maritime Franco-Canadien (1695-1715): Navires et Marchands à La Rochelle'' (Paper read at International Conference on Colonial History, Ottawa, 1969).

[4] Debien, ''La Société coloniale,'' pp. 202-220; Liliane Chauleau, *La Société à la Martinique aux XVIIe siècle (1635-1713)* (Caen, 1966), pp. 179-186.

resident of the islands. These partnerships were for three, four, most often six years, and the planters were intent only on making their fortunes. That done, many of them returned to France.[5]

When sugar became the dominant crop the smaller proprietors were squeezed out; plantations became larger and were increasingly owned by nonresidents who employed salaried agents as overseers and stewards.[6] As this capitalist type of economic struc-

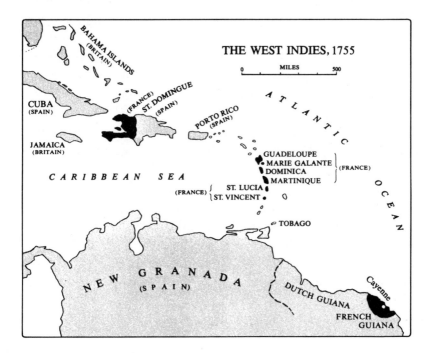

THE WEST INDIES, 1755

ture became more prevalent and the need for the more skilled labour that had been required for the raising of cotton, tobacco, and indigo declined, the *engagés* were replaced by black slaves. By the end of the seventeenth century hardly any were being transported from France. The few who survived their three years of indenture lacked the capital to buy land and slaves. At best they were reduced to working for minimal wages in the sugar

---

[5] Debien, "La société coloniale," p. 39.

[6] F. de Vaux de Foletier, "Les Minutes des Notaires de Saint-Domingue aux Archives du Ministère de la France d'Outre-Mer," *Revue d'Histoire des Colonies françaises*, XXXIX (1951), pp. 295–298.

refineries, as artisans, or in the retail shops in the ports. For these *petits blancs* there was now little hope of achieving the economic independence of the Canadian *habitant*, or of rising in the social scale.[7]

By 1687, when an official census was taken, the population of the French islands was 47,312. Of that number 18,888 were whites, approximately 27,000 slaves, and 1,484 freed blacks or mulattos.[8] Fifty years later the population was 20,000 whites, a few more than 20,000 free blacks and mulattos, and a quarter-million slaves. The white population remained stable but the slaves increased tenfold. During those intervening years 25,000 to 30,000 slaves a year were brought to the islands, more than one and a quarter million all told. Between 1763 and 1776 deaths exceeded births by 50,000. One-third of the blacks brought from the Guinea coast died during their first three years in the islands. The average working life of a slave was not more than fifteen years. It was not disease that decimated them but the whips of their masters who worked them beyond physical endurance.[9]

Some slaves managed to escape to the mountain jungles. Despite being hunted down by the militia and brutally executed when captured, these *marrons* continued to grow in numbers, and their mere presence was a constant menace to the white population. Given the ratio of ten slaves per white, the fear of a slave insurrection was very real. Some of the planters sought to keep their slaves subdued by cruel repressive measures that would have made an Iroquois warrior blanch.[10] This raised the fear that

---

[7] Gaston-Martin, *Histoire de l'Esclavage dans les Colonies françaises* (Paris, 1948), pp. 112–113; Leon Vignols, "Les Antilles françaises sous l'ancien régime: L'institution des engagés (1626–1774)," *Revue d'Histoire économique et sociale*, XVI (1928), pp. 12–45; Louis-Philippe May, *Histoire économique de la Martinique (1635–1763)* (Paris, 1930), pp. 40–41.

[8] Gaston-Martin, *Histoire de l'Esclavage*, pp. 24–26. The population of Canada was then approximately 10,000 with no slaves.

[9] *Ibid.*, pp. 103, 124–125. See also the appalling statistics and the specific cases cited in G. Debien, *Plantations et esclaves à Saint-Domingue* (Dakar, 1962), p. 50.

[10] See Antoine Gisler, C.S.S.P., *L'Esclavage aux Antilles françaises (XVIIe–XIXe siècle): Contribution au problème de l'esclavage* (Éditions Universitaires Fribourg Suisse, 1965), pp. 43–47. On the role of the militia see Chauleau, *La Société à la Martinique*, pp. 73–79. The problem of escaped slaves on Saint-Domingue was particularly acute. They fled to the Spanish part of the island, where they were given refuge and established villages, supported by the local freed slaves and mulattos. The French governor and intendant asked the minister to protest to the Spanish ambassador and demand that the practice be terminated, since it was "contre le droit des gens, et malgré notre union avec la couronne d'Espagne" (contrary to the rights of man and our union with the Spanish Crown). A.N. C9A, vol. 10, ff. 22–3, Blenac et Michou à Mgr, Saint-Domingue, 10 avril 1713.

such treatment would spark what it was intended to prevent. Moreover, not all the whites were devoid of human feeling. Although conceding the economic necessity of the institution, they also accepted the slaves as human beings who should be treated as such, net as beasts of burden.[11] Louis XIV and Colbert were in agreement, and in 1685, two years after his death, Colbert's Code Noir was promulgated, which placed slaves under the protection of a special law.[12] The main aim of the code was to prevent the all too frequent brutality, likely to cause the slaves to revolt. At the same time it clarified their legal status. They were still regarded as chattel whom their masters could dispose of by sale, but they had to be properly fed and families could not be broken up before the children had reached puberty. Although slaves could be lashed and put in chains by their masters, they could not be put to death, imprisoned, or mutilated without first being condemned by the normal courts of law. Moreover, a slave could have his master brought before the courts for a breach of the code, but the likelihood of this occurring was indeed slight. Slaves were to be instructed in the Christian faith, and although they could not marry without their master's permission, they could not be forced to marry against their will. The quantity and quality of food and clothing to be provided were laid down, as well as the hours of work — no longer than sunrise to sunset — and when old and sick, slaves had to be cared for. Although the main aim of the Code Noir was to protect the French settlers and their property, and its provisions were likely honoured in the breach rather than in the observance,[13] yet it does indicate a somewhat more humane attitude on the part of the Crown than was manifest in the other European colonies.[14]

One clause in the code was impossible to enforce, and no attempt was made to do so; this was the forbidding of whites to

---

[11] In 1672 the governor general of Martinique, Jean-Charles de Baas, pleaded with Colbert for more humane treatment of the slaves, and that the importation of Irish beef be allowed in order that they might receive adequate nourishment. See W. Adolphe Roberts, *The French in the West Indies* (New York, 1942), p. 151.

[12] See the analysis of the code in Antoine Gisler, *L'Esclavage aux Antilles françaises*.

[13] On this vital point see *ibid.*, pp. 34–74.

[14] Gaston-Martin, *Histoire de l'Esclavage*, pp. 27–29, will not admit that the Code Noir was introduced for humanitarian reasons, claiming that it derived purely from self-interest — to avoid slave insurrections. English and American historians, on the other hand, contrast the French attitude, as exemplified by the code, favourably with that of the English slave colonies.

take slaves as concubines. It was common practice for these concubines, and their children, to be granted manumission. This resulted in the emergence of a sizable mulatto class, equal in numbers to the whites and threatening to exceed them, thereby creating a dangerous social and economic problem. To curb it, a tax of three times the woman's value was imposed for manumission. This had some effect, but the problem remained serious as freed mulattos entered the labour force and competed with the *engagés* for work as artisans, shopkeepers, and plantation overseers. Once they had achieved their freedom, these mulattos sought economic independence and eventually full equality with whites. Many of the quadroons were barely distinguishable from whites and could easily have crossed the colour line. As the prosperity of the islands' economy grew so too did theirs, and they came to share the social values of the whites, contemptuous of the black slaves and at the same time resentful of their white superiors.

The government of the islands followed the same pattern as in the other colonies: governor general, local governors, intendants, superior councils, junior officials. Several companies of fever-ridden Troupes de la Marine were maintained for defense. Their main function, along with the militia, was to guard against slave insurrections and make periodic sweeps through the jungles in search of *marrons*. Justice was administered according to the Coutume de Paris and, as in Canada, and for the same reason, lawyers were not allowed to practise. Policy was laid down by the Ministry of Marine, and the colonists had only an indirect say in its formulation, but whenever it conflicted with their interests there was little hope of its being implemented. They were too independent, and unlike the seigneurs of Canada, too little beholden to the Crown to submit meekly to ordonnances that were not to their liking. In 1717, for example, the newly appointed governor general and intendant of Martinique sought to implement the reforms called for in their instructions, requiring them to stop the building of new sugar refineries and to tear down those then being built, a measure taken to protect the refineries in France from colonial competition. The instructions also dictated an embargo on Spanish ships calling at the island. The planters immediately rebelled, seized the two officials, and shipped them back to France. In Canada such an action would have been inconceivable. Oddly enough, the French government accepted this *fait accompli* and even issued an amnesty to those involved.[15] Significantly, the number of sugar refineries on Martinique continued to increase, from 338 in 1720 to 456 in 1742. The islands' interests had clearly won out over those of the metropolitan sugar refiners.[16]

The islands' budgets were derived from a poll tax of eight livres on each adult slave and five for each child, plus an export duty on raw produce that varied from year to year and was a continual source of conflict. Nine twenty-fourths of the tax revenue went to the local budgets, nine twenty-fourths to indemnify slave owners whose human property had been executed by judgment of the courts, and one-quarter to the Jesuits, Capucins, Jacobins, and Carmelites — each order to its own island — for their parochial duties and social services, the schools and hospitals. The salaries of the officials, the military establishment, and the costs of defense were paid for by the Crown. The colonists, having no responsibility for the administration, were free to devote all their energies to the running of their plantations. The land was productive enough and the demand for its produce so great that those of them who were not too incompetent, or too lazy, were assured of gaining enough one day to become rich. The plantations, however, did not run themselves; they were quite complex economic and social units. Plantation owners resident in France had early discovered that employing agents to take charge for them was not profitable; they therefore usually sent out a younger son or a relative who could be trusted. Whoever was in charge had to oversee the cultivation of the crops, the clearing of additional jungle land, the operation of mills and refineries, and the marketing of the produce. They could spend little time in towns, going there only on business, to dispose of their crops, buy slaves and supplies, arrange for credit, call on the governor, visit friends, and perhaps go to the theatre. Most of their lives had to be spent on their isolated plantations with

---

[15] See "Mémoire du Roy pour servir d'Instruction au Sr. de Ricouart, Intendant des Îles Françoises du Vent," *Revue de l'Histoire des Colonies françaises*, XVII (1924), pp. 85–106; Alfred Martineau and L.-Ph. May, *Trois Siècles d'Histoire antillaise: Martinique et Guadeloupe de 1636 à nos Jours* (Paris, 1935), pp. 80–93.

[16] Martineau and May, *Trois Siècles d'Histoire antillaise*, p. 138.

their large houses filled with servants to cater to every whim and between times intrigue among themselves; nearby were the mills for sugar and indigo, drying sheds for coffee, perhaps a refinery with its cloying, sickening stench, and the slave quarters. Persons running plantations had to be constantly on their guard, outnumbered as they were as much as ten to one by their slaves, employing resentful mulattos as overseers, and with bands of *marrons* in the mountains numbered in the thousands. They ruled by fear, and they had to endure it themselves: fear of sudden savage attack on life or property; and with disease rife, taking odd forms, there was the terrible fear of being slowly poisoned by the subtle, secret means believed to be widely employed by the blacks.[17]

By the mid-eighteenth century the islands' social hierarchy was well-defined and rigid. At the top were the senior officials sent from France — governors, intendants, officers of the garrisons. As elsewhere in the colonial empire these officials frequently engaged in controversy and bitter disputes that gravely affected the efficiency of the administration. Appointments in the islands were not greatly coveted, except by men who hoped to mend or make their fortunes. Among the lower-ranking salaried officials this was done by the usual bureaucratic method of requiring a sizable *pot de vin* before red tape would be untangled. At the top, marriage into a rich planter's family was the customary avenue. But the risks were great. The likelihood of living to enjoy an acquired fortune for many years was small. The festering climate combined with tropical diseases proved lethal to Europeans.[18]

---

[17] Just how prevalent and terrible was this fear of poison, and the fate of slaves suspected of the practice on their masters, their livestock, even their slaves, is vividly brought out in the correspondence cited in Debien, *Plantations et esclaves à Saint-Domingue:* e.g., p. 66: "Montaudoin n'a pas perdu comme nous 30 à 40 nègres sucriers sur l'habitation de sa femme par le poison. . . . "; p. 67: "J'ai appris que M. Collet que vous connaissez et qui est un digne magistrat, fort instruit, n'avait pas pour coutume de faire brûler ses nègres empoissonneurs, mais qu'il avait aussi un cachot affreux dans lequel il faisait périr le nègre ou négresse empoissonneur." See also Gaston-Martin, *Histoire de l'Esclavage*, pp. 106–116.

[18] In 1747 La Galissonière, governor general of Canada, besieged by Canadian families for commissions in the Troupes de la Marine for their sons and with promotion extremely slow, recommended that Canadian officers be given promotions and then posted to the Antilles, where the high death rate would quickly create fresh openings. (I am indebted to Professor D. Standen for this note. See Archives Nationales, Colonies, C11A, LXXXVII, p. 276.) Later in the eighteenth century a Canadian-born expatriate officer serving in Guadeloupe declared that the regular troops lost a third of their men every year, and that in one year the garrison at Tobago had lost more than half its officers. Officers serving in the West Indies received a 4,000 livre supplement to their salary. See "Lettres du vicomte François-Joseph Chaussegros de Léry à sa famille," *Rapport de l'Archiviste de la Province de Québec, 1933–1934.*

Most dread of all was leprosy. In 1721 the Conseil Superieur at Guadeloupe ordered lepers to be kept in isolation. Seven years later the census figures revealed there were 125 victims on the island, twenty-two whites, six mulattos, ninety-seven blacks.[19]

Of the creole families, those French born in the colonies, the owners of large plantations, *les grands blancs*, were at the top. As the eighteenth century wore on, the smaller planters, those owning no more than twenty slaves, were, owing to lack of capital to survive a bad year, forced to sell out and if lucky to obtain employment as an agent; if not, at some menial task in the ports. The *grands blancs* became richer, their establishments larger, their scale of living more opulent, and the gap between them and the *petits blancs* greater. Few of the *grands blancs* had noble antecedents, but unlike in Canada, where great wealth was unknown and status derived from a man's official post or his military reputation, in the islands wealth alone determined status. As in Canada, the landholders had to serve in the militia, but the wealthy monopolized the commissioned ranks. Captains received an exemption from the poll tax on twelve slaves — the same exemption enjoyed by the nobles — lieutenants on eight, and *enseignes* four. The *grands blancs* also monopolized the seats on the Superior Councils, intermarried, and became a caste. They became ultraconservative, ultraloyal to the Crown and to the colonial regime upon which their wealth and status depended. When these last were eventually threatened, their loyalty became questionable.[20]

The *petits blancs*, the poor whites, like the Canadian *habitants* but far fewer in numbers, had their roots in the islands because they lacked the economic means to move back to France. As their hopes of entering the ranks of the upper class declined, they clung to their badge of superiority, their colour. Although they had sired the bulk of the mulattos, they sought to keep them down because they competed with them for the few salaried posts available. Professor G. Debien describes the situation in the early years thus: "The population was in a perpetual state of flux, in

[19] Martineau and May, *Trois Siècles d'Histoire antillaise*, p. 192.

[20] Foletier, "Les Minutes des Notaires de Saint-Domingue"; Chauleau, *La Société à la Martinique*, pp. 73–79, 131–139.

its numbers, in its composition, in the degree of cohesion. The colonial milieu never ceased to receive, to assimilate, or to reject all types of men who came without cease. The milieu enforced its mores, its dress and its cuisine, also its distrust, its social reactions and its *filles de couleur.*"[21]

Yet the underlying basic economic and social assumption, slavery, was never questioned, not even by the clergy, who in contrast to the clergy in the Spanish colonies exercised little influence on public life. The clergy themselves employed slaves on their island estates and made little attempt to instruct them in the religion of their masters lest they should question the institution upon which the economy and the society it had produced squarely rested. In 1717 the Crown, persuaded that the Jesuits and Jacobins had grown rich, considered stopping their annual subvention and ordered that none of the orders could own more than a hundred slaves.[22] Fifty years later the overly enterprising superior of the Jesuits at Martinique, Father Lavalette, established a bank and commodity exchange which allowed the plantation owners to purchase their slaves with bills of exchange and avoid having to sell their crops to the Nantes slavers at heavy discounts. Unfortunately for himself and his order, Father Lavalette overextended his operations, and when in 1758 he was obliged to send a cargo worth several million livres to France to avoid nonpayment of his notes, the ships were captured by the English and his commercial venture was bankrupt. That incident provided the occasion for the suppression of the Society of Jesus in France by royal edict in 1764.[23]

The island economy, dependent as it was on the safety of the shipping lanes, was extremely vulnerable in time of war. From the Peace of Utrecht (1713) to the Seven Years' War, and again from 1763 to 1790, the French Islands flourished. The major crop, representing half the total exports, was sugar. In 1715, blight had destroyed the cocoa trees on Saint-Domingue and by 1718 had spread to Martinique and Guadeloupe. Tobacco, which

[21] "La société coloniale," p. 7.

[22] "Mémoire du Roy pour servir d'Instruction au Sr. de Ricouart," pp. 85–106. See note 15.

[23] Gaston-Martin, *L'Esclavage dans les colonies françaises*, pp. 150–151; Ernest Lavisse (ed.), *Histoire de France* (9 vols., Paris, 1903–11), VIII-2, pp. 319–332.

was important in the seventeenth century, was driven off the market by Virginia and Maryland. Indigo remained a significant item, as did cotton, but the most important crop, after sugar, became coffee. The original bushes were brought from the Jardin des Plantes in Paris in the 1720s and were found to flourish. Fifty years later coffee was almost as important as sugar. In those two products, France dominated the European market, displacing England as a major supplier. By 1740 the value of island exports to France was 100 million livres a year, and of imports, 75 million, the latter mainly slaves. Six hundred ships were employed in the transport of island produce, representing 60 percent of French external trade.[24] Canada, by comparison, rarely attracted more than a score.

Compared to the West Indies the economic balance sheet of Louisiana appears, to say the least, pathetic. Under the French regime it never succeeded in justifying its economic existence. However, this colony had not been established for economic reasons but to prevent the English, or Spanish, from gaining control of the mouth of the Mississippi. With their hold on the two great waterways, the St Lawrence and the Mississippi, the French could dominate the continent.[25] Canada and the West Indies had valuable staples, furs, and tropical produce, to form economic bases. Louisiana could supply the selfsame goods as these colonies, but not of the same quality or quantity, or at the same prices. Moreover, although in the beginning there was a flurry of missionary activity in Louisiana it quickly subsided. The French religious climate of the eighteenth century was very different from that of the first half of the sixteenth, thus the missionary drive that had sustained Canada until the Crown took over was lacking in Louisiana.[26] There was no attempt to create a New Jerusalem on the Gulf Coast.

At the outset the colony depended on the Crown for every-

---

[24] Gaston-Martin, *L'Esclavage*, pp. 81–105.

[25] See Richard W. Van Alstyne, "The Significance of the Mississippi Valley in American Diplomatic History, 1686–1890," *Mississippi Valley Historical Review*, XXXVI, 2 (Sept., 1949), pp. 215–238.

[26] See Charles Edwards O'Neill, *Church and State in French Colonial Louisiana* (Yale Univ. Press, 1966), p. 287.

thing,[27] and during the first thirteen years of its existence France was fully engaged in a war, aggravated by famine, that completely drained its resources. Very little could be spared for this new overseas venture. As Marcel Giraud put it: "No other French colony in America was born in such difficult circumstances, nor experienced such a painful growth because of a crisis in the homeland." There were hardly any funds available for the Ministry of Marine; sailors were up to eighteen months in arrears in their pay and forced to beg to keep from starving; officers went four years unpaid and had to sell their possessions to support their families. Ships were so rotten they sank on leaving harbor. Famine-engendered epidemics took a heavy toll in the seaports and hundreds fled inland. Brest alone lost more than five hundred families in four years. To find serviceable ships, supplies, and colonists was an almost insuperable task.[28] In 1707 Louis XIV seriously considered abandoning the colony. It was costing 80,000 livres a year, a sum the kingdom could ill afford. By 1711 the population was still less than two hundred, all being fed by the Crown. The few troops and settlers who were sent, for the most part, were so appalled by the terrible conditions they found on their arrival that they quickly deserted, either to the Spanish at Pensacola or to the English in Carolina. By 1710 the colony was on the verge of collapse, and in 1712 Louis XIV considered seeking an exchange of the province for the Spanish half of Saint-Domingue. But the minister of marine, Jérôme Phélypeaux de Pontchartrain, still subscribed to the philosophy of Colbert: that colonies were a source of raw materials that otherwise would have to be bought from foreigners with a consequent drain of bullion from the kingdom.[29]

Louisiana's major handicap was its geography. It did not possess a single good harbour; its coastline was low and screened

---

[27] In July 1713, the newly appointed *commissaire de la marine*, Jean-Baptiste au Bois Duclos, reported to Pontchartrain: "I have also found that in the first years there had been supplied to the inhabitants of this country as many as 36,000 rations for which they were to make payment in the future and for which they are still in debt. Several of them also have been given goods from the warehouse." *Louisiana Historical Quarterly*, XVI, 2 (Apr., 1933), p. 297.

[28] See Marcel Giraud, "France and Louisiana in the Early Eighteenth Century," *Mississippi Valley Historical Review*, XXXVI, 4 (Mar. 1950), pp. 657–674.

[29] See the very detailed study by Marcel Giraud, *Histoire de la Louisiane française: Le Regne de Louis XIV* (Paris, 1953).

by long, shifting sand bars, making access to the few sheltered bays dangerous. Access into the gulf itself through the screen of the West Indies was easily barred in wartime, and hurricanes were a menace. Losses from disease on the long voyage in tropical waters, usually taking three months, were heavy. To lose half the crew and passengers was not unusual, and one-third was the norm. Moreover, not only was it almost impossible to get a return cargo during the early years, it was even difficult to obtain food supplies for the return voyage, and the hulls of ships moored too long on that coast were soon riddled by worms. The mouth of the main artery of communication, the Mississippi, was blocked by the deltas with shifting channels, the deepest no more than three metres. Between the coast and the prairies to the north were kilometres of snake-filled swamps, then semitropical jungle that had to be cleared and drained before the land could be put to use. The climate was hot, humid, and unhealthy for Europeans. Food would not keep for long, nor would such produce as furs and hides. To cap it all, the clouds of mosquitoes made life almost unendurable.[30]

Yet Pierre le Moyne d'Iberville and his brother Jean-Baptiste le Moyne de Bienville had managed in 1699 to establish a base at Fort Biloxi on an unhealthy morass, manned by some eighty men. Several of the men and most of the officers were Canadians. The following year another detachment of Canadians arrived, recently returned from an expedition to Hudson Bay, raising the total to more than a hundred and twenty. Two years later a new settlement was established on the west side of the Mobile River some 80 kilometres from the sea, but it too proved to be a poor site and the settlers removed in 1711 to the river mouth. This new Mobile was to be the administrative center of the province until it was removed, in 1722, to New Orleans.[31] Farther north, in the Illinois country, settlements were established at the mission posts, Cahokia and Kaskaskia.

---

[30] *Ibid.*, pp. 135–137; Mrs. N. M. Miller Surrey, "The Development of Industries in Louisiana during the French Regime, 1673–1763," *Mississippi Valley Historical Review*, IX, 3 (Dec. 1922), pp. 227–235.

[31] See N. M. Miller Surrey, *The Commerce of Louisiana During the French Regime, 1699–1763* (New York, 1916), pp. 25, 404.

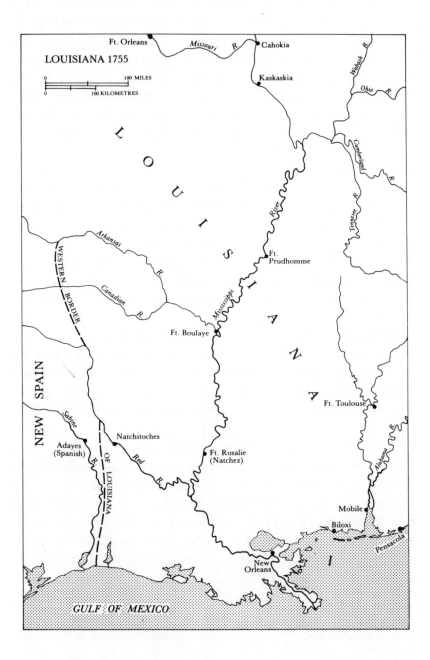

LOUISIANA 1755

Ft. Orleans

Missouri R.

Cahokia

Kaskaskia

Wabash R.

Ohio R.

L O U I S I A N A

River

Cumberland R.

Tennessee R.

Arkansas R.

Ft.
Prudhomme

WESTERN BORDER

Canadian R.

Mississippi

Ft. Boulaye

NEW SPAIN

Sabine R.

Natchitoches

Ft. Toulouse

R. OF LOUISIANA

Adayes
(Spanish)

Red R.

Ft. Rosalie
(Natchez)

Alabama R.

Mobile

Biloxi

Pensacola

New
Orleans

GULF OF MEXICO

During these early years French claims to this vast territory, sandwiched between the English colonies and Mexico, were purely nominal. As in the region north and west of the Great Lakes, it was the Indian nations that dominated throughout most of Louisiana. With traders from the Carolinas pushing over the mountains, amply supplied with cheap goods and eager to obtain Indian slaves as well as peltry, the French had to gain the allegiance of these tribes or see the hinterland between the Appalachians and the Mississippi fall to the English. Fortunately Bienville, who was in command during these war years, was very adroit in his dealings with the Indians, but with only a mere handful of troops, reduced to sixty-seven men by 1713 and ten of these too old or infirm to serve, and dependent on supplies from France, even of foodstuffs, which arrived very irregularly, the colony's survival was miraculous.[32]

Since the Crown could afford so little for colonial development, recourse was had to private enterprise, as with the first French endeavours in the Americas a century earlier, and with the same conspicuous lack of success. In 1712 the wealthy financier Antoine Crozat was persuaded to accept responsibility for the settlement of Louisiana in return for a fifteen-year monopoly on its trade. He was given title to any lands or mines that he developed; the goods he sent to the colony were to be free of export duty. In return he was required to send two ships a year, ten emigrants of either sex, and transport to the colony twenty-five tonnes of goods for the Crown. Land was not to be granted in seigneurial tenure, but directly by the Crown, and in small concessions. The King also appointed the governor and the *commissaire ordonnateur*, who performed the same function as the intendant of New France but with a lower rank. On paper both these officials were under the authority of the governor general and intendant at Quebec, but in fact they received their orders and instructions directly from the Ministry of Marine. A Superior Council was instituted in January 1714, to serve as the civil and criminal court of appeal, but the colony lacked men qualified to fill the posts, and in the early years its deliberations and decisions

---

[32] See Marcel Giraud, *Histoire de la Louisiane française: Années de Transition* (Paris, 1958), pp. 161–164.

were very dubious. But at least a viable administrative framework, modeled on that of the other colonies, had at last been established.

Unfortunately, Crozat concerned himself only in reaping swift and substantial profits with a minimum investment. He gambled 600,000 to 700,000 livres on the hope of finding rich mines — and lost. His monopoly prevented all other merchants from entering into trade with the colony — not that there was much likelihood of their doing so, since the colony had nothing to offer in exchange for goods transported except a few deerskins, buffalo hides, and some poor-quality pitch. In addition, on the goods he transported to the colony Crozat charged a markup of 100 to 300 percent, and at the same time he reduced the price he would pay for colonial produce by half. He also demanded cash for the goods sold at his storehouse, but paid for the produce offered by the settlers with merchandise at these inflated prices. If any profit was to be made from Louisiana produce, Crozat, not the colonists, was to reap it. The royal officials and the troops, on their meagre salaries, could barely subsist and had to resort to all manner of dubious expedients to make ends meet. As for the settlers, the few there gave up striving to produce for export. Merely to subsist was no mean feat.

Not only was the massive infusion of capital that was needed not forthcoming; neither was the equally necessary supply of labour, and particularly of girls to provide wives for the preponderance of males.[33] In Canada, the stationing of the Carignan-Salières regiment had given a great fillip to the economy, and later the permanent garrison of Troupes de la Marine had provided the necessary support when the fur trade faltered, but only a handful of regulars, swept up from the dregs of the French towns, were sent to Louisiana. They proved to be a greater menace to the security of the colony than a threat to any real or

---

[33] In 1713 Duclos, the *commissaire de la marine*, reported to Pontchartrain that twelve girls, selected by the bishop of Quebec, had arrived from France — "but so ugly and ill-made that the inhabitants of this country and especially the Canadians are not at all eager for them. . . ." He advised that more attention be paid to the appearance of the girls sent in the future, and less to their virtue. "The Canadians," he wrote, "of whom we have found a rather large number here who are all very well-made men, are not very scrupulous about the conduct that the girls have observed before they marry them and if they found some of them well-made and to their liking perhaps some of them would have remained here to marry them and to settle here, which would increase the colony, whereas they have all gone back asserting that they preferred the Indian women. . . ." *Louisiana Historical Quarterly*, XVI, 2 (Apr., 1933), p. 303.

potential enemy. During the war a few artisans had been sent out, but they were very difficult to recruit. Pontchartrain and Vauban both remarked that the poverty-stricken French preferred to emigrate to Spain rather than Louisiana, and the humanitarian philosophy of both the minister and Louis XIV forbade peopling its colonies by forcible emigration, using the colonies as a dumping ground for social undesirables.[34] For the type of crop—tobacco, cotton, sugar, indigo, rice—that Louisiana could produce, slave labour appeared to be the only answer; but Indian slaves, although some of the settlers obtained them, proved unsatisfactory. Those of them physically capable of hard manual labour made their escape to freedom too easily. Black slaves were what the colonists wanted, but they were priced out of reach.

By 1717 Crozat had given up all hope of realizing a profit from Louisiana, and he relinquished his privileges. Yet the Council of Regency still had faith in colonies as a means to strengthen the kingdom. Despite everything, the council still believed in Louisiana, whose vast spaces it hoped to see settled and whose mineral wealth it planned to exploit. After much study by committees, it was decided to place Louisiana under the charge of John Law, who had recently taken over the nation's finances and was enjoying great success with his bank and mushrooming financial schemes. To avoid arousing the suspicion and hostility of both Spain and England it was decided to establish a company, the Compagnie des Indes, to develop and expand French activities in the Mississippi Valley. To compensate for the heavy initial investment needed, the company was given the tobacco monopoly, the marketing monopoly of Canadian beaver, and also exclusive rights to the Guinea slave trade. This last was also intended to ensure a supply of slave labour for the West Indies and Louisiana. The company was required to transport six thousand settlers and three thousand blacks within twenty-five years.[35]

The company and the Crown quickly set about implementing their plans. A publicity campaign was launched depicting Louisiana in the most favourable terms. The old restrictions of

---

[34] Giraud, *Histoire de la Louisiane française: Le Regne de Louis XIV*, pp. 150–152.

[35] See Marcel Giraud, *Histoire de la Louisiane française: L'Époque de John Law (1717–1720)* (Paris, 1966); Penfield Roberts, *The Quest for Security, 1715–1740* (New York, 1947), pp. 86–98.

Louis XIV that had forbidden the peopling of the colonies by social undesirables, the forcing of his subjects to go against their will, were thrown into discard along with the edict forbidding all but members of the Roman Church to settle on French territory overseas. Between 1717 and 1720 more than eighteen hundred *engagés*, some of them accompanied by their families, were shipped to the colony. Settlers were recruited in Switzerland, and four thousand Germans, many of them Lutheran, in the Rhineland. Throughout France, the prisons, the workhouses, the back streets of the towns, the countryside, were combed for able-bodied vagrants, men sentenced to the galleys for dealing in contraband salt and tobacco, army deserters, common felons, and prostitutes. They were rounded up and marched to the Atlantic ports for shipment to Biloxi. Although these impressed migrants were far fewer than has been made out — 1,278, of whom only about 200 were women — they gave Louisiana the foul reputation of a penal colony. It then became almost impossible to persuade anyone to go of his own free will. When troops were ordered to the colony they deserted en masse. Sailors were loath to sign on for voyages there for fear they might be put ashore and forced to stay.

Louisiana, with its limited and barely developed resources, could not possibly have housed or nourished such a horde of humanity as the company was about to dump there. Had they arrived they would most likely have starved to death. As it was, few of them did. Many made good their escape while being herded to the ports, more perished en route owing to inadequate arrangements, then an epidemic struck those waiting for the long-delayed shipping. Most of the German settlers perished in the French ports; only some sixty families reached the colony. Most of the women swept from the streets went the same way. Of those who did sail, a large proportion perished during the crossing or upon arrival. Early in 1721 five hundred of them died at Biloxi alone. When word was brought back to France of these conditions, the reputation of Louisiana sank even lower, to that of a charnel house.[36]

---

[36] The best and most detailed account of the events of these years is Giraud, *Histoire de la Louisiane française: L'Époque de John Law (1717-1720)*.

Yet some settlers did manage to survive, and it was plain both to them and to the directors of the company that there was no hope of productive settlement along the littoral, and that slaves offered the only solution to the labour problem. The posts at Biloxi and Mobile were maintained, but the main axis of settlement now shifted from the coastal area to the Mississippi. In 1718 a settlement at New Orleans was begun, and despite floods, lack of drinking water, the mosquitoes, fever, and a host of other tribulations, it finally became firmly established. In 1722 it was made the seat of government. In 1719 the first shipment of 450 black slaves was brought in by the company; in 1720, 127 more were landed, and the following year 1,312. In all, the company imported more than 6,000 blacks during the ensuing decade. The company set the price at 650 livres for *pièces d'Inde* — males capable of hard labour. But supply never equaled demand; the price climbed as high as 2,500, but usually ran about 1,000 to 1,800 livres. In 1724 the Code Noir was introduced. By 1739 there were 4,000 blacks in the province, but two-thirds of them had been born there,[37] a figure indicative of the high mortality rate among the slave population.

With this less than adequate labour supply and the assurance that supply ships now would arrive from France every year, the colony began to produce enough food for its own needs, and tobacco, silk, indigo, some cotton, pitch and tar, furs and hides, and subsequently, rice, for export. But the value of the colony's produce never equaled what it cost the company. Twenty million livres had been invested by 1731 when Louisiana reverted to the Crown. By mid-century the Ministry of Marine was obliged to spend more than 800,000 livres a year to maintain the colony.[38] France, although always hopeful that the colony would one day be a source of profit to the kingdom, maintained its hold on the region for political rather than economic reasons.

After the death of Louis XIV in 1715, relations between Spain and France under the regency of the duc d'Orléans deteriorated

---

[37] See Surrey, *The Commerce of Louisiana*, pp. 154–168, 226–249.

[38] See Baron Marc de Villiers du Terrage, *Les dernières années de la Louisiane française* (Paris, 1904), p. 27; E. Wilson Lyon, *Louisiana in French Diplomacy, 1759–1804* (Univ. of Oklahoma Press, 1934), p. 29.

until in 1719 war was declared. One of the major bones of contention was Louisiana. The Spanish were resentful of its establishment on territory they regarded as part of their empire, but
during the short course of the war they proved incapable of
driving the French out. Instead, the French under Commandant
General Bienville and his brother Joseph Le Moyne de Serigny,
with a few companies of unreliable troops who deserted at the
first opportunity, captured Pensacola, but it was handed back
when hostilities ended. To the west the French were to expand
336 kilometres up the Rouge River to establish Fort Natchitoches.
The Spanish outpost of Adayes, some seven leagues beyond,
blocked further progress. Between those two posts the frontier
followed the Rouge, then turned north, but that whole region was
controlled by the plains Indians, and Europeans voyaged through
it only with their sanction.[39]

To the north, Fort Rosalie was established in 1717 near the
villages of the Natchez, and small settlements sprang up over
the years along the Mississippi to the Illinois country. There
the mission posts of Kaskaskia and Cahokia, established at the
beginning of the century, attracted a small number of Canadians
who lived mostly by hunting and trading furs. Their furs, however, went to Montreal rather than down the Mississippi. They
also began raising wheat, and when the Jesuits established their
mill the Illinois country was able to supply the lower colony with
fine-grade flour, in addition to meat.[40] Despite the rich prairie
land and the healthy climate, the remoteness of the Illinois settlements militated against rapid expansion. By 1752 the population numbered only 1,536 French, 890 blacks, and 147 Indian
slaves.[41]

To the east of the Mississippi, south of the Ohio, Fort Toulouse
was established on the upper reaches of the Alabama River in
1717 to block that route to Mobile to the English of Carolina.
Although relations between England and France were excellent
while Walpole and Fleury remained in power, the Carolinians

---

[39] See Henry Folmer, *Franco-Spanish Rivalry in North America, 1564–1763* (Glendale, Calif.,
1953).

[40] Surrey, *The Commerce of Louisiana*, pp. 288–303.

[41] See Guy Frégault, *Le Grand Marquis: Pierre de Rigaud de Vaudreuil et la Louisiane*
(Montréal, 1952), pp. 129–130.

exerted great pressure on the Indian nations in an effort to drive the French out and extend their control to the Mississippi. With their abundant supplies of trade goods, unlimited amounts of liquor, and eagerness to purchase slaves from the warring tribes, the English had great economic advantages in this struggle.[42] Only the diplomatic skill and experience in dealing with the Indian nations of Bienville and his Canadian officers, assisted by the greed and excesses of the Carolina traders, enabled the French to keep most of the tribes in the French alliance.[43] In 1723, Bienville was dismissed and recalled to France, not to return until ten years later. During his absence, relations with the allied tribes deteriorated. By 1729 the commandant at Fort Rosalie, in his attempt to deprive the resident Indians of some of their cultivated land, had precipitated an uprising of the Natchez and Yazous nations in which the garrison and settlers, numbering some 250, were massacred. It required a six-month campaign to quell the hostile tribes. The cost was so great that it forced the directors of the bankrupted company to request that it be discharged of its obligations, and to relinquish the charter to the Crown.[44] In 1736 a campaign had to be waged against the Chickasaws, commercial partners of the Carolina traders. It proved to be a disaster for the French. Their crushing defeat threatened the security of the entire province. Three years later another campaign was launched. This time a strong contingent of Canadian troops, militia, and allied Indians was combined with the Louisiana forces. It too came close to ending in the same fashion as the earlier campaign but finally succeeded in bringing the Chickasaws to terms without, however, reducing their fighting strength.[45] The cost of the campaign was 800,000 livres, at a time when the budget for Louisiana was set at 330,000.

---

[42] For the view of this contest from the English side of the hill, see Verner W. Crane, *The Southern Frontier, 1670–1732* (Univ. of Michigan Press, 1956 ed.), pp. 257–280.

[43] See Giraud, *Histoire de la Louisiane française: Années de Transition*, pp. 161–164. Marcel Giraud (Translation by George Woodcock) *The Métis in the Canadian West*, 2 vols. (Univ. of Nebraska Press, 1986).

[44] O'Neill, *Church and State in French Colonial Louisiana*, pp. 219–231; Villiers du Terrage, *Dernières années de la Louisiane française*, pp. 18–20.

[45] For Bienville's journal of the campaign and allied documents see *Rapport de l'Archiviste de la Province de Québec, 1922–1923*, pp. 156–190. For a brief account see Villiers du Terrage, *Dernières années de la Louisiane française*, pp. 21–23.

178 France in America

The inability of Louisiana to cope with the hostile Indian nations and the need to call on Canada for help indicate an essential difference between the two colonies. In Louisiana the military tradition that was so firmly entrenched in Canada never took hold. The twenty-one companies of Troupes de la Marine maintained in the province were always under strength, reduced by disease and desertion to about eight hundred men. Their morale, discipline, and character were of the lowest, and the officer corps came from France rather than from among the colonial gentry. Many, if not most, of the officers acquired plantations and were usually to be found on their estates rather than on duty. The noncommissioned officers ran taverns, where the troops spent their time and meagre pay.[46]

For the defense of the province, the governor had to depend on the Indian allies rather than on its own white population. From 1740 on, Bienville, who had returned as governor in 1732, and his successor, Pierre de Rigaud, marquis de Vaudreuil, managed to preserve peace between the Choctaws and the Chickasaws, despite the efforts of the Carolinians to foment war between them. Although intertribal wars, liquor, and European diseases greatly reduced the numbers of the southwest tribes, those allied to the French, the Cherokees, Choctaws, and Alibamous, still counted more than twelve thousand warriors at mid-century, and it was they who kept the English colonials from flooding over the mountains to seize the French-claimed territory.[47]

In one respect Louisiana surpassed all the French colonies: the constant bickering, intrigue, and open quarreling among the officials. Their dispatches to the directors of the company in Paris, or to the minister of marine, consisted largely of lengthy diatribes, accusations, and counteraccusations against each other. The colony was continually rife with dissension and cabals to a far greater degree than was the case in Canada.[48] Why this was so can only be guessed at. Perhaps officials of poorer character were sent to Louisiana than to Canada; perhaps the climate had

---

[46] Frégault, *Le Grand Marquis*, p. 140; Villiers du Terrage, *Dernières années de la Louisiane française*, p. 78.

[47] *Ibid.*, pp. 27, 108, 149.

[48] *Ibid.*, pp. 16, 122–128.

something to do with it. More likely the nature of the colonial society and its struggling economy were the main cause. The salaries of the officials were low, the cost of all imported goods high, and the supply uncertain. Governor Vaudreuil, whose salary was 12,000 a year, half that of the governor general at Quebec, remarked that if he exercised care he could get by on 40,000.[49] But then he lived quite extravagantly. These officials were obliged to make ends meet any way they could, usually by methods that were neither dignified nor honest. Such a situation constituted a fertile breeding ground for intrigue, jealousy, denunciations, and treachery. Unlike in Canada, whose seigneurial land tenure and the military establishment made status less dependent on wealth than on rank, function, and reputation, status in Louisiana, as in the West Indies, was based on wealth expressed in the size of a plantation and the number of slaves owned. Louisiana lacked the hard core of nobles that set the tone of society in Canada; it also lacked the wealth that produced the *grands blancs* of the islands. The shortage of women in the early years had led to a blurring of class lines as men of the higher social ranks were forced to take wives of humble birth, *faute de mieux*.[50] In Canada, where military careers were coveted and the fur trade was tightly controlled, the governor general and intendant disposed of enough patronage to keep the leading families quiescent by granting or withholding the military and civil posts they craved. The governor of Louisiana had very little such patronage at his disposal, and no effective means to curb intrigue and cabals among the officials and leading colonists. In fact the governor was usually the target.

The clergy too were not exempt from dissension, but much of it emanated from clerical intrigue among the senior clergy in France. At the outset the mission field was divided between the Jesuits and mission priests of the Quebec seminary. The Jesuits, who had long regarded the West as their particular province, put as good a face on this intrusion as they could, but disputes over jurisdiction inevitably arose and were magnified by senior clerics

---

[49] *Ibid.*, p. 79.

[50] On the gradations in Louisiana society during the early years see Giraud, *Histoire de la Louisiane française: Années de Transition*, pp. 121–124.

at the court. Eventually the seminary priests, unable to cope with conditions in lower Louisiana, withdrew and retained only a mission at Cahokia. They were replaced at the gulf posts in 1720 by Carmelites, and two years later members of the Capucin order were sent out to serve New Orleans and the posts along the Mississippi from the Wabash to Balize. In 1713 Duplessis de Mornay, the superior of the Capucins of Meudon, had been consecrated bishop of Eumenia *in partibus infidelium* and made coadjutor to Bishop Saint-Vallier of Quebec. He was given charge of Louisiana, but he never went to his province, preferring to run things from Paris.[51] On a technicality concerning the Gallican liberties, he had the Carmelites ousted from Louisiana in 1722. From this point on, the province was served by the Capucins and the Jesuits. In 1727 the first women's order appeared, the Ursulines, who established a school for girls and a badly needed hospital at New Orleans.

Apart from the clerical infighting and the lack of a senior cleric to maintain order and give proper support, the clergy in the province had to struggle with two almost insuperable difficulties: the indifference, and in some cases hostility, toward religion and the Church on the part of the bulk of the white population,[52] and the chronic lack of funds that made it extremely difficult for the clergy to carry on their work. The small white population, 4,100 in 1746, approximately 800 of whom were soldiers, could provide only a modest tithe, and the refusal by the Crown to grant seigneurial tenure precluded revenue from that source. The clergy were dependent on meagre grants from the chartered company and subsequently the Crown, grants that varied over the years between 400 and 600 livres a year for each priest, barely enough to keep body and soul together. The moral problem of concubinage between the whites and their black and Indian slaves was almost insuperable. The old policy of seeking to civilize and Christianize the Indians in order to assimilate them had long been

---

[51] When, in 1727, Bishop Saint-Vallier died, Mornay automatically succeeded, but although he made use of the revenues of the Quebec see he refused to cross the ocean. This situation became intolerable, and finally, in 1733, the minister of marine ordered him to go to New France on the next available ship. He thereupon resigned. See H. H. Walsh, *The Church in the New France Era* (Toronto, 1966), pp. 175–176, 181–182, 185–186.

[52] On this issue see O'Neill, *Church and State in French colonial Louisiana*, pp. 219–231.

abandoned, and marriage between whites and either Indians or blacks was now firmly opposed. It was, however, the mission of the Church to convert the pagan to Christianity, but if this were accomplished then the clergy were obliged to compel those Christians with Christian concubines to cease living in sin, and either abandon the concubines or marry them. The former proved impossible, the latter forbidden by the authorities. This particular moral dilemma, combined with a general lack of religious enthusiasm and a chronic shortage of both clergy and funds to support even the modest number there was, made it virtually impossible for the Church in Louisiana, even had it had the will, to wage the same sort of missionary drive that had been launched the preceding century in Canada.

Yet forces were building up in the world that made the retention of the Indian nations in the French alliance vital. The pressure exerted by the Carolina traders was a constant threat, and as the population of the English colonies increased, surpassing 900,000 by 1740,[53] the schemes of Anglo-American land speculators, covetously eyeing the lands beyond the Alleghenies, posed a grave new danger. To hold the allegiance of their Indian allies the French had to supply them with goods at prices competitive with those offered by the English colonials. This meant that, as at some of the Canadian posts, the Crown had to subsidize the trade. Were this not to be done, Governor Vaudreuil warned, the English would overrun the region.[54] From a strictly financial point of view this would have been no loss. Although the colony's budget was set at 330,000 livres a year, between 1731 and 1744 the Crown spent 10 million, most of it on defense,[55] and the value of goods exported from the colony, although rising steadily, was only a fraction of that sum.[56] But in this respect Louisiana was no different from Canada, which was also a drain on the French exchequer.

---

[53] *Historical Statistics of the United States, Colonial Times to 1957* (Dept. of Commerce, Washington, D.C., 1960).

[54] See Frégault, *Le Grand Marquis*, pp. 264-265.

[55] *Ibid.*, pp. 186-187.

[56] During the years 1743-1746 inclusive, the colony exported produce, mainly indigo, with some furs and tobacco, valued at 812,250 livres. See Surrey, *The Commerce of Louisiana*, p. 210.

French colonial trade and overseas commerce had increased greatly during the years of peace. In some parts of the world the French were depriving the English of their markets. The great expansion of French overseas trade came to be seen as a threat that could be stopped only by war. In the north Atlantic fisheries the French were taking the lion's share. The French sugar islands supplied continental Europe; 74 percent of the sugar shipped to Bordeaux was re-exported, and 80 to 100 percent of the coffee. More than half the goods exported from Cadiz to the Spanish colonies were French in origin, and in 1740 the French obtained commercial privileges in the Turkish empire. Between 1710 and 1741, French trade with her colonies rose from 25 million to 140 million livres a year, and by 1741 her total overseas trade was estimated to be worth 300 million livres. In contrast, during the decade of the 1730s, English overseas trade had remained almost stationary. It seemed that before too long France would overtake England as the leading commercial power, even that England might share the fate it had imposed on the Dutch and be reduced to the status of a third- or fourth-rate power, and by the same means. By the 1740s this had become an obsession. A pamphlet of 1745 could argue that ". . . our Commerce will, in general, flourish more under a vigorous and well-managed naval war, than under any peace which should allow an open intercourse with those two nations [France and Spain]."[57]

This situation was exacerbated by the Spanish, who began curbing the highly profitable contraband trade carried on by the English with their colonies. English ships were being boarded by Spanish *guarda costas*, who were none too gentle, as a certain Captain Jenkins was able to attest. The English mercantile community was highly incensed at the prospect of losing this rich smugglers' market. They insisted on the rigid implementation of England's Navigation Acts but demanded war to prevent the Spanish and French from protecting their own imperial markets.

---

[57] Quantitative studies of the French economy in the eighteenth century appear relentlessly. The most recent, at time of writing, and best survey is contained in Fernand Braudel and Ernest Labrousse, *Histoire économique et sociale de la France* (4 vols., Paris, 1970–   ), II, pp. 503–514. See also the pioneering work by Maurice Filion, *Maurepas, Ministre de Louis XV, 1715–1749* (Montréal, 1967), pp. 54–55, 137, 140; Paul Vaucher, *Robert Walpole et la politique de Fleury (1731–1742)* (Paris, 1924), pp. 243 ff.; Walter L. Dorn, *Competition for Empire, 1740–1763* (New York, 1965 ed.), pp. 251–291.

In October 1739, Walpole was forced to give way and the war with Spain began. Hostilities would also have commenced with France before the year was out had not the dynastic struggle over the Austrian succession intervened. France became embroiled in the continental war against Austria, and the war party in England forced Walpole to enter as the ally of the Empress Maria Theresa. Thus in 1744, after thirty years of peace, hostilities between England and France finally began.[58]

Fortunately for France the British army, after long years of disuse, was in a deplorable state and the navy little better off. Against the Maréchal de Saxe the British forces in the Netherlands made a poor showing. Then, in August 1745, Charles Stuart landed in Scotland, rallied the Highland clans, marched south on London, and was not turned back until he had reached Derby. In April of the following year the Scots were crushed at Culloden, but another six months were consumed in "pacifying the Highlands" by methods that boded ill for any other people conquered by British troops.[59] Thus the English were able to devote little attention to the American theatre.

In the West Indies neither France nor England made a serious attempt to conquer the other's possessions. The plantation and refinery owners on neither side desired to face increased competition from captured plantations and mills. The English in particular feared this, since the French produced sugar at lower cost. What they wanted was the destruction of French productive capacity in order to take over the European market dominated by France. For their part, the French would have been happy to see the plantations and refineries on the English islands destroyed. As Richard Pares succinctly put it: "These are the ambitions of the respectable tradesman who hopes to increase his custom, by hiring the racketeer to destroy his neighbor's shop."[60] In the event, neither side inflicted much damage on the other's possessions.

[58] See Vaucher, *Robert Walpole*; Dorn, *Competition for Empire*, pp. 129–147; Richard Pares, *War and Trade in the West Indies, 1739–1763* (Oxford, 1936); Roland Mousnier, Albert Labrousse, Marc Bouloiseau, *Histoire générale des civilizations, Tome V, Le XVIIIe siècle* (Paris, 1955), pp. 213–215.

[59] See John Prebble, *Culloden* (London, 1961); W.A. Speck, *The Butcher: The Duke of Cumberland and the Suppression of the 45* (Oxford, 1981).

[60] Pares, *War and Trade in the West Indies*, pp. 181–182.

The French islands, however, relied on imported food supplies and lumber that France had failed to provide in adequate quantity or competitive prices. Attempts to provide these necessities from Canada had not been very successful, and much that was imported from Cape Breton was in fact New England produce that had been "nationalized" by the deft manipulation of the ships' papers with the connivance of complaisant officials at Louisbourg.[61]

The economies of the islands and the Engish colonies complemented each other nicely, the French islands providing sugar and molasses, the latter commodity being distilled into rum in New England for the western fur trade and the African slave trade, while the English mainland colonies provided the flour, meat, fish, and lumber that the French West Indies needed. Throughout the war the trade continued to flourish. This trading with the enemy was defended by the English participants on the grounds of expediency. They claimed that were it to be broken off, the Dutch would merely step in, and once they had taken over the trade it would not be easy to get it back. This argument even extended to maritime insurance. Throughout the war, French ships, while hunted relentlessly by the Royal Navy, were insured against loss by London insurance agents, whose rates were lower than those of the French owing to their greater volume of business. They were also able, on occasion, to furnish their French clients with information on the disposition of the Royal Navy, thus enabling them to evade capture. Since the war was being fought for commercial supremacy, to seize the enemy's trade and markets, it was argued that it made no sense to abandon that part of the war aims already achieved.[62]

To the north, French privateers operating out of Louisbourg against New England shipping proved to be too successful for their own good. Determined to put a stop to this, and to end French supremacy in the fisheries, New England forces, aided by the Royal Navy, laid siege to the port in 1745. Louisbourg was in no condition to hold out for long. The fortifications were

---

[61] See Clarence P. Gould, "Trade Between the Windward Islands and the Continental Colonies of the French, 1683–1763," *Mississippi Valley Historical Review*, XXV, 4 (Mar., 1939), pp. 473–490.

[62] On the contemporary debate see Pares, *War and Trade in the West Indies*, pp. 395–470.

in a poor state; a few months before, the garrison had mutinied and had returned to duty only upon being promised redress of their grievances. After a siege and a bombardment lasting seven weeks the governor negotiated honourable terms — which were not kept — and surrendered the fortress. The following year a 5,000-man expedition sent to recapture Louisbourg and restore Nova Scotia to French rule ended in disaster. Storms and disease forced the sad remnants of that French fleet to return to France without firing a shot.[63]

On the Canadian front proper there was little action throughout the war. The Canadians, by destroying Saratoga and the frontier settlements of Massachusetts, demonstrated that they had not lost their old military ardour. The Mohawks were induced by the authorities of New York to destroy some of the outlying Canadian settlements south of Montreal, but the rest of the Five Nations confederacy and the Mission Iroquois of Canada forced them to desist. The Iroquois, although the British claimed suzerainty, if not sovereignty, over them, continued their old policy of neutrality, and they were still powerful enough to oblige both Canada and New York to abandon their plans to contest control of Lake Ontario. Neither side appeared distressed.

The worst threat that the French in Canada had to face during this war was the defection of their western allies in 1747. The fall of Louisbourg had disrupted normal trade between France and Quebec, and the flow of contraband between Albany and Montreal had been blocked by the Mohawks. Consequently, the supply of trade goods for the western fur trade was almost nonexistent, and for what little there was the prices charged by the Canadian merchants were exorbitant. Thus the western tribes, resentful of their dependence on French supplies and the subordinate position in which it placed them, were very susceptible to the urging of Anglo-American traders that they drive the French out. An assault by all the tribes to destroy the French posts throughout the West was planned, but the commandants of the western posts, unlike the British, during Pontiac's so-called

[63] See Guy Frégault, *François Bigot: Administrateur français* (2 vols., Montréal, 1948), I, pp. 187-272; J. S. McLellan, *Louisbourg from Its Foundations to Its Fall, 1713-1758* (Sydney, Nova Scotia, 1957), pp. 123-176.

"uprising" sixteen years later, were able to master the situation without much difficulty. The end of hostilities the following year, bringing the restoration of the flow of French trade goods at normal prices, doused the incipient insurrection.[64] South of the Illinois country, in lower Louisiana, there had been little activity. The French retained the loyalty of the Cherokees, Choctaws, and Alibamous nations, who numbered more than 12,000 warriors. The southern English colonies dared not risk an invasion of French territory when it would have meant bringing tribesmen swarming over their own frontier.

Despite the success against Louisbourg and the ensuing destruction of a French fleet, it was not until 1747 that the Royal Navy finally gained mastery in the Atlantic, swept French ships from the sea lanes, and blockaded the French Atlantic ports. In the West Indies, as in the Canadian West, the consequences were drastic. The French islands were then completely cut off, the Nantes slavers dared not put to sea, and the islands' produce rotted in the fields. At home, French industry, deprived of its overseas supplies of raw materials, suffered harshly. Bankruptcies multiplied, tax receipts declined severely, hunger stalked the western provinces.[65] For the French, peace was essential before the situation became a national disaster; peace during which to rebuild the shattered navy and merchant fleet, and recapture the lost overseas markets and supplies. Fortunately for France, England was also feeling the pinch of war. Her national debt appeared staggering, bankruptcy seemed imminent, and the war on the continent, far from glorious, was anything but popular. Both sides, therefore, were willing to make concessions.

In America the only territory that had changed hands had been Louisbourg. Maurepas, the minister of marine, was determined to have it back. He regarded that fortified harbour as essential to maintaining French dominance in the fisheries, which was the great training ground for seamen, upon whom maritime supremacy depended. He therefore gave up the French conquests in the Netherlands and Madras for Louisbourg. The disgust of the

---

[64] See W. J. Eccles, *The Canadian Frontier, 1534–1760* (New York, 1969), pp. 150–154.

[65] Gaston-Martin, *Nantes au XVIIIe Siècle: L'Ère des Négriers (1714–1774)* (Paris, 1931), p. 226.

French at this transaction was matched by that of the English colonials, who regarded their lonely conquest as vital to their interests. The Peace of Aix-la-Chapelle did little more than restore the colonial situation to what it had been at the Peace of Utrecht, thirty-five years before. It was, however, a truce rather than a peace, and both maritime powers now began making preparations for a renewal of the contest.

The prosperity of France depended on her overseas trade, of which the West Indies possessions constituted the single most valuable segment. To protect it against English aggression a much more powerful navy was required. To protect the French fisheries Louisbourg had to be strengthened. As for Canada, it had demonstrated that it could more than hold its own against the English colonies. Louisiana appeared to be in little danger, and it might in some measure aid Canada in a diversionary threat at the rear of those colonies. It was their sugar islands and the ancillary slave trade that the French feared for rather than their northern possessions, Canada and Cape Breton.

Chapter 7

The Preemptive Conquest, 1749–1763

In the Americas, the War of the Austrian Succession had changed nothing and settled nothing. After 1748 France wanted an enduring peace to rebuild and restore, but the British commercial community wanted a renewal of the war at the earliest opportunity. The latter powerful group, with Newcastle, Halifax, and Pitt as its political agents, was convinced that peace was good for France, but bad for England. The struggle just ended had achieved sufficient success to demonstrate that were Britain to concentrate her resources on a commercial war, France as a competitor in world markets could be destroyed and British merchants could then pick up the pieces.[1] This aggressive policy found a counterpart in North America where the planters and land speculators of Virginia and Pennsylvania were now eyeing the rich lands of the Ohio Valley. Land companies were formed in both provinces to seize and parcel out these lands for settlement. That these were the lands of the resident Indian nations, and had been for millenia, meant nothing to these men. They coveted the land, and the Indian peoples who had failed to cultivate them by husbandry, European fashion, had thereby forfeited their title. They had to be dispossessed by one means or

---

[1] See Paul Vaucher, *Robert Walpole et la Politique de Fleury (1731–1742)* (Paris, 1924), pp. 298–302; Sir Julian S. Corbett, *England in the Seven Year's War* (2 vols., London, 1918), I, pp. 23–29; E. E. Rich (ed.), *The Cambridge Economic History of Europe* (Cambridge Univ. Press, 1967), IV, pp. 536–537; Patrice-Louis-René Higonnet, ''The Origins of the Seven Years' War,'' *Journal of Modern History*, vol. XL, 1968, pp. 57–90.

another to make way for those who could make proper use of the land according to God's precepts.[2] Meanwhile, fur traders, who in some instances were also agents of the land companies, had established trading posts in the region and drawn the local tribes into a commercial alliance.[3]

The French in Canada were acutely aware of the danger posed by this encroachment on lands they claimed to be under the suzerainty of the French crown, this not to usurp the lands from the Indians, but to deny them to the Anglo-Americans for purely French imperial ends. Were it to go unchallenged, the English colonials would not only threaten the Canadian hold on the northwest fur trade but, by expanding down the Ohio to the Mississippi, would eventually sever communications between Canada and Louisiana. Looking even further ahead, were the English to seize and settle the lands between the Alleghenies and the Mississippi their rapidly expanding population would grow immeasurably in numbers and wealth, and with that, England's commerce. Since military power was determined to a considerable degree by the size of a country's population, by the number of trained men with muskets that could be put in the field, the much larger population of France compared to England's would eventually be offset by that of the English colonies. In America, therefore, English expansion had to be checked.

At Quebec the governor general, the comte de La Galissonière, took note of these dangers and recommended measures to circumvent them. He proposed that garrisoned forts be established in the Ohio Valley and the Indian tribes brought into the French alliance. In this way English expansion would be blocked. But more than that, from Canada and the proposed Ohio bases, the English colonies could be threatened by Canadian and Indian war parties. All that would be needed was a small force of French regulars to garrison the bases. In the previous wars the Canadians

---

[2] See Robert F. Berkhofer, Jr., *The White Man's Indian*, (New York, 1978), pp. 120–121, 131; Francis Jennings, *The Invasion of America* (Chapel Hill NC, 1975), pp. 15–16, 60–84.

[3] It is not without significance that the furs of the Ohio Valley were considered by the Canadians to be of very little value. See the informed comments by d'Aigremont; Paris, Archives Nationales, Colonies, C11A, vol. 29, p. 61. On Anglo-American aims and activities in the Ohio Valley see John Mitchell, *The Contest in America Between Great Britain and France with Its Consequences and Importance* (London, 1757), pp. iii–xlix, 17–38; Alfred P. James, *The Ohio Company: Its Inner History* (Univ. of Pittsburgh Press, 1959).

had more than held their own against the English colonials. In Britain's balance of trade those colonies were such an important item the English would have to respond to such a threat. They would have to send troops to aid the ineffectual colonial militia, and this would require the support of sizable elements of the Royal Navy which would then not be available for attacks on the French West Indies, or French maritime commerce, or to blockade the French ports as they had done so successfully in the past war. In other words, the role of the French in North America was to be that of a fortress, with a small garrison to tie down a much larger force of the enemy.[4]

With the approval of the Ministry of Marine, La Galissonière lost no time initiating this policy. In 1749 he dispatched an expedition, led by the veteran western commander Pierre-Joseph de Céloron de Blainville, to the Ohio to show the flag, claim the region for France, and drive out the Anglo-American traders. Céloron discovered that British infiltration of the region and influence over the Indian nations was far more serious than had been imagined. La Galissonière's successor, Pierre-Jacques de Taffanel, marquis de la Jonquière, strengthened the French forts in the Great Lakes area, but did little more. The governor of Louisiana, Canadian-born Pierre de Rigaud, marquis de Vaudreuil, showed a greater awareness of the need for action. He strengthened the garrisons at the posts in the Illinois country and began the construction of Fort Chartres, near Kaskaskia; but even after receiving reinforcements in 1751, he had only some two thousand indifferent regulars to hold the Mississippi Valley from New Orleans to the Illinois River. The French hold on this region had to depend on retaining the active allegiance of the Indian nations.[5]

On the Atlantic coast the French greatly strengthened the defenses of Louisbourg and sent out fifteen hundred garrison troops under officers who this time maintained discipline. Some of the Acadians of Nova Scotia were enticed to remove to Île

---

[4] See W. J. Eccles, *The Canadian Frontier, 1534–1760* (New York, 1969), pp. 157–160. Galissonière's pregnant memoire, Galissonière au Ministre, Qué., 1 sept. 1748, is in Paris AN Série C11A vol. 91, ff 116–123.

[5] Guy Frégault, *Le Grand Marquis: Pierre de Rigaud de Vaudreuil et la Louisiane* (Montréal, 1952), pp. 163–177.

Royale (Cape Breton); merchants and fishermen, with their families, reestablished themselves there until by 1752 the population stood at 5,845.[6] Other Acadians were persuaded to settle on Île Saint-Jean (Prince Edward Island), and at Beaubassin where the French had a fort. The swift economic recovery of Louisbourg fully justified the sacrifices made to regain it at the peace table. The fishery expanded rapidly, and the old trade with Canada, the West Indies, and New England throve. Yet in this region too the French had to count on the Indian tribes, the Micmacs and Abenaquis, and, hopefully, on the Acadians still resident in Nova Scotia. The English, however, were fully conscious of this revival of French power that threatened their North Atlantic trade. In 1749 they began the construction of a naval base and fortress at Halifax, which not only countered the menace to English shipping but precluded the possibility of the Acadians regaining control of their homeland for France.

In the West, the French seized the initiative.[7] Unlike the Anglo-Americans, the governor general of New France was able to mobilize the colony's entire military resources with no regard for cost. In 1753 he dispatched two thousand men to Lake Erie to construct a road from southeast of that lake to the headwaters of the Ohio and build a chain of forts at strategic points. The Indian nations, impressed by this show of strength, began to sever their trade connections with the Anglo-Americans. All that the latter could do to counter this erosion of their position was to send a major of militia, George Washington, with an escort of seven men and a letter from Governor Robert Dinwiddie of Virginia, protesting the French invasion of lands claimed by Great Britain and demanding their immediate withdrawal. Jacques Legardeur de Saint-Pierre, commandant at Fort Le Boeuf, a tough veteran of the west, received Washington politely, but contemptuously rejected Dinwiddie's blustering ultimatum.

The following year a small force of Virginia militia attempted

---

[6] George F. G. Stanley, *New France: The Last Phase, 1744–1760* (Toronto, 1968), p. 60.

[7] On the events, strategy, and tactics of the war see Stanley, *New France: The Last Phase*; Eccles, *The Canadian Frontier*, pp. 157–185; Guy Frégault, *Canada: The War of the Conquest* (Toronto, 1969); Corbett, *England in the Seven Years' War*; Lawrence Henry Gipson, *The British Empire Before the American Revolution*, Vols. IV–VIII (New York, 1939–54); Gerald S. Graham, *Empire of the North Atlantic: The Maritime Struggle for North America* (Toronto, 1950).

to establish a fort at the junction of the Ohio and the Monongahela. Before they were well begun, a French force, five hundred strong, swept down the upper Ohio and forced them to retire over the crest of the Alleghenies, which the French claimed to be the border between their territory and that of the English colonies. The French now built Fort Duquesne on the site and thereby dominated the whole region. The Anglo-American response was to send George Washington back, at the head of a motley collection of militia, to drive the French out. Contrary to all the norms of civilized conduct of that age, Washington's force ambushed the small French party sent on a mission, similar to that undertaken by Washington himself the previous year, to demand that the Anglo-Americans retire from the region that the French claimed to be under their suzerainty. The officer in command, Ensign Joseph Coulon de Villiers de Jumonville, and nine of his men were killed, twenty-one taken prisoner. This was the first clash of arms in what was to become a global war. Significantly, it began while both powers were at peace. It also began under very dubious circumstances.[8]

The French reacted swiftly. Washington, with some 350 undisciplined colonial militia, made a stand at Great Meadows, where 500 French and 100-odd Indian allies, after a combat of a few hours, compelled them to accept the surprisingly generous French terms, and surrender. Washington signed the capitulation terms without taking the trouble to inquire too closely into their meaning and subsequently dishonoured them, then fled precipitately with his men back to Virginia. In his haste he abandoned his baggage containing his journal. The contents of that journal were to be used by the French government to brand the English as perfidious throughout Europe.[9] Washington's ignominious defeat brought

---

[8] This incident has long been a subject of controversy, American historians seeking to excuse Washington, while French and French-Canadian historians, for the most part, declare his act to have been that of a common assassin. The evidence is incontrovertible. Washington's conduct was inexcusable. He was to show a similar disregard for the accepted military conventions two decades later.

[9] The journal was sent to Governor General Duquesne at Quebec, who predictably commented: "Rien de plus indigne et de plus bas Et meme de plus noir que les sentiments Et la facon de penser de ce Washington, Il y auroit eu plaisir de luy Lire Sous le nez Son outrageant journal." He had a translation made, a copy of which is in the Archives du Séminaire de Québec. See Fernand Grenier (ed.), *Papiers Contrecoeur et autres documents concernant le conflit anglo-français sur l'Ohio de 1745 a 1756* (Québec, 1952), pp. 133–181, 251.

the last of the wavering Indian nations to the French cause. From that point on, the English had not a single Indian ally in the West, while the strength of the French was enhanced immeasurably. At every turn of events the French had overreached the Anglo-Americans. They were securely in possession of the Ohio country, from its upper reaches to the Mississippi, and from their advanced forts war parties could fall on the rear of the English colonies at any time. For the time being, however, they kept their Indian allies securely on leash, determined on no account to give the enemy an excuse to attack.

The English colonies, with the exception of New York, which had no desire to have its profitable contraband trade with the French colonies disrupted, clamoured for war to drive the French out of North America once and for all. In the previous wars England had furnished scant aid to her American subjects. This time the war party, led by Cumberland, Henry Fox, William Pitt, and Halifax, forced Newcastle to agree to campaigns in America to drive the French out of Acadia, the Lake Champlain region, Niagara, and the Ohio valley. Were this to lead to open war, then so be it.[10] The London mob, whipped up by the warhawks, was clamouring for war.[11]

In October 1754, Major General Edward Braddock, commanding two battalions, eight hundred men, was ordered to North America with orders to capture Fort Duquesne, while the colonial forces attacked Fort Niagara, the French forts on Lake Champlain, and those on the Nova Scotia border. This force could not sail until the following April, and on the eve of its departure the French obtained a copy of Braddock's orders. Immediately, they raised six battalions, three thousand men from the better regiments of the *troupes de terre*.[12] In April they too were ready to sail. When the British cabinet learned of this they issued secret orders to Admiral Edward Boscawen with two squadrons com-

---

[10] Walter L. Dorn, *Competition for Empire, 1740–1763* (New York, 1963), pp. 287–289; Higonnet, "The Origins of the Seven Years' War."

[11] Vincennes, Service Hist. de l'Armée, Série A1, vol. 3405, f 181. Le Chev. de Warren, Colonel d'Infanterie à Dunkerque, à Calais, 27 nov. 1755.

[12] *Troupes de terre* were the regiments of the regular army, so designated because many of them took their nomenclature from the provinces where they were raised, e.g., Régiment de Languedoc, Régiment de Béarn.

posed of nineteen ships of the line and two frigates to intercept the French convoy, seize the ships, and if resistance were offered, give battle. A few days after he sailed, on April 27, the French ambassador to the Court of St. James's received word that Boscawen had orders to attack the French squadron. On May 10, however, two cabinet ministers dined at his house and cheerfully reassured him that such rumours were completely false, that no such orders had been issued.[13]

Off Newfoundland, Boscawen succeeded in intercepting only three ships of the French convoy. When Captain Toussaint Hocquart hailed Captain Richard Howe, asking if they were at peace or war, the reply came, "At peace, at peace," followed by shattering broadsides.[14] Two of the French ships were captured; the third escaped to Louisbourg. The rest of the convoy, with all but eight companies of troops, and with the newly appointed governor general of New France, Pierre de Rigaud, marquis de Vaudreuil, on board, reached Louisbourg and Quebec safely.[15] Elsewhere the Royal Navy had better luck. More than three hundred French ships and eight thousand sailors were seized in English ports or on the high seas.[16] This was a serious blow to French maritime strength. Needless to say, the French lost no time proclaiming the English to have been guilty of the blackest treachery.[17]

On land in North America, now that hostilities had begun in earnest, but still without a declaration of war, the British did not fare so well. Braddock, at the head of 2,200 men, two battalions of British regulars from the Irish establishment, the rest hastily

---

[13] See Corbett, *England in the Seven Years' War*, I, pp. 45–46: Richard Waddington, *Louis XV et le renversement des alliances* (Paris, 1896), pp. 96–97.

[14] Waddington, *Louis XV et le renversement des alliances*, pp. 104–110.

[15] The strength of the four battalions sent to Quebec, on arrival, was 108 officers, 1,693 other ranks. See Paris, Archives Nationales, Colonies, D2C, XLVI, p. 254.

[16] See A. T. Mahan, *The Influence of Seapower upon History* (New York, 1890; paperback ed., New York, 1957), 1957 ed., p. 251. The strength of the French navy was depleted further by an epidemic of typhus that swept through the fleet and naval ports in 1757. It was this, rather than the greater strength or efficiency of the Royal Navy, that allowed the latter eventually to blockade the French ports and dominate the Atlantic. Seamen and dockyard workers fled the ports; ships could not be manned for lack of crews and sometimes had to go into action with a handful of seamen amid impressed landsmen. See Ruddock F. Mackay, *Admiral Hawke* (Oxford, 1965), pp. 204, 213, 227, 234, 249.

[17] For an example of the use made of these incidents by French diplomats abroad on instructions of the foreign minister see *Rapport de l'Archiviste de la Province de Québec, 1949–1951*, p. 5; M. Durand d'Aubigny, Résident du Roi à Liège, au Ministre, Liège, 27 juillet 1755; *ibid.*, p. 9, D'Aubigny au Ministre, à Liège le 11 oct. 1755.

recruited colonials and untrained, ill-disciplined provincials, set off, struggled over the mountains with a large artillery siege train and got within a few kilometres of Fort Duquesne. In an almost forlorn hope, Captain Daniel de Beaujeu led 108 Troupes de la Marine, 146 Canadian militia, and 600 Indians to oppose him. The ensuing clash was a disaster for the British. The Canadian and Indian forces took cover on the flank of the enemy, encumbered by siege artillery and a vast wagon train. The measured British volleys had little effect against the concealed foe. The Canadians and Indians advanced close. Noting that the British ranks reloaded to ordered drumbeats, they picked off the officers and drummers.[18] Confusion, then panic, spread through the British ranks. The battle became a slaughter. The troops broke and fled. More than two-thirds of the British force were killed or captured, along with the cannon and a vast store of supplies. This, at a cost to the French and their allies of twenty-three killed and twenty wounded.[19]

In the mortally wounded Braddock's captured baggage the plans for the attacks on the other fronts were found. Thus, by the time the ill-organized colonial forces had mustered for an attack on Niagara, the French had moved reinforcements to oppose them. The acting commander in chief of the Anglo-Americans, William Shirley, governor of Massachusetts, after his 2,400 colonial troops had been reduced to 1,400 by sickness and desertion, abandoned the campaign. On the Lake Champlain front the Anglo-Americans failed to reach the lake, being forestalled by the French, led by the commander of the regular troops Jean-Armand, baron de Dieskau, who had the misfortune to be wounded and captured in the brief and inconclusive engagement that neither side could claim as a victory. The Canadians, however, convinced that with better generalship they would have

---

[18] See *Rapport de l'Archiviste de la Province de Québec, 1931–1932*, p. 19, Mémoire du Chevalier de la Pause.

[19] The most detailed and frequently cited study of this action is Stanley M. Pargellis, "Braddock's Defeat," *American Historical Review*, XLI (1936), pp. 253–269. It is, however, dated; the limitations of the musket were not taken sufficiently into account, and the effectiveness of guerrilla tactics against regular troops untrained for such warfare had not been as clearly demonstrated in 1936 as it was to be in subsequent years. See also Paul E. Kopperman, *Braddock at the Monongahela*, (Pittsburg, 1977). Unfortunately the latter work failed to take account of the la Pause mémoire and displays a marked chauvinist bias. For the French casualties see Paris, AN Colonies Série D2C, vol. 48, f 255. Joint à la lettre de M. Bréard du 13 aoust 1755.

utterly routed the Anglo-Americans under Sir William Johnson, regarded the outcome as having been a defeat despite the fact that the American attempt to gain control of the invasion route to Canada had been foiled. The Canadian officers contrasted their victory over Braddock with the ineptitude displayed by their French counterparts.[20] Relations between the French army contingent and the Canadian regulars, poor from the start, continued to deteriorate.

Only on the Acadian frontier did the British enjoy any success. Fort Beauséjour, at the foot of the Bay of Fundy, was captured and the threat to the English in Nova Scotia effectively removed. Then followed one of the most controversial acts of the war, the explusion of the Acadians.[21] Not only were the Acadians, both those captured in arms and those who had sworn the oath to His Britannic Majesty, expelled in brutal fashion, but the Indians were likewise driven off their land to make way for New England settlers. Many of the Acadians managed to elude the New England troops sent to seize them, and made their way to Quebec. They constituted a warning to the Canadians of what they could expect should they be conquered. Nothing could have been better calculated to make them fight with a ferocity born of despair. The French authorities at Quebec made the most of this.

Although war had not been declared, and would not be until May 1756, the British assaults on New France permitted Vaudreuil to take the offensive. Indian war parties led by Canadian officers ravaged the frontiers of Virginia and Pennsylvania; but Vaudreuil's strategy was defensive. His purpose was to use the advanced French bases in the West to hold the Indian nations in the French alliance, thereby offsetting the Anglo-American superiority in numbers. Thus small Canadian and Indian guerrilla

---

[20] Vincennes. Service Historique de l'Armée, Série A1, vol. 3405, No. 136. Lotbinière au Ministre, Carillon 24 8bre 1755; ibid., No. 147. Vaudreuil au Ministre, Mtl., 30 8bre 1755.

[21] On this issue many historians have allowed national sentiment to weight their judgment. This is particularly true of Francis Parkman, Montcalm and Wolfe (London, 1964 ed.), pp. 175–208, and Gipson, The British Empire Before the American Revolution, VI, pp. 212–344. Waddington, Louis XV et le renversement des alliances, pp. 372–417, gives a detailed account of events and roundly condemns the British. For a judicious view see Guy Frégault, Canada: The War of the Conquest, pp. 164–200; "La déportation des Acadiens," Revue d'Histoire de l'Amérique Française, VIII, 3 (1954–55), pp. 309–358. Regrettably, the history of Acadia and its peoples still remains to be written.

detachments could force the British to maintain large defensive forces on their frontier. To take the offensive against these bases the British would require an army, have to build roads through the wilderness to move and supply it, and employ large bodies of men to maintain their supply lines. With their command of the rivers the French could move men and supplies much more easily than could the British. Moreover, the Anglo-American militia usually fled at the mere rumoured approach of the enemy.[22]

On the New York frontier Vaudreuil's strategy was to block the Lake Champlain invasion route by maintaining a strong garrison at Fort Saint-Frédéric and by building an advanced fort at the head of the lake, Fort Carillon, later known as Ticonderoga. When the enemy attempted to attack Canada by this route, a relatively small force could delay them at Carillon and hold them at the narrows by Fort Saint-Frédéric while the Canadians and Indians harassed their supply lines. Carillon would also serve as an advance base to threaten Albany and the American frontier settlements, thereby containing sizable enemy forces. The main dangers to Canada were the threat of invasion from Lake Champlain, from Lake Ontario down the St Lawrence, and a maritime assault up the river against Quebec. On the Lake Ontario front, the English fort at Oswego was the major threat, and Vaudreuil made plans in 1755 to destroy it. As for an assault on Quebec, the best that could be done there was to harass an invading fleet

---

[22] A contemporary American observer put the situation very succinctly: "Our colonies are all open and exposed, without any manner of security or defense. Theirs are protected and secured by numbers of forts and fortresses. Our men in America are scattered up and down the woods, upon their plantations, in remote and distant provinces. Theirs are collected together in forts and garrisons. Our people are nothing but a set of farmers and planters, used only to the axe or hoe. Theirs are not only well-trained and disciplined but they are used to arms from their infancy among the Indians; and are reckoned equal, if not superior in that part of the world to veteran troops. Our people are not to be drawn together from so many different governments, views, and interests; are unable, unwilling, or remiss to march against an enemy, or dare not stir, for fear of being attacked at home. They are all under one government, subject to command like a military people. While we mind nothing but trade and planting. With these the French maintain numbers of Indians — We have none, — These are troops that fight without pay — maintain themselves in the woods without charges—march without baggage—and support themselves without stores and magazines — we are at immense charges for those purposes. By these means a few Indians do more execution, as we see, than four or five times their number of our men, and they have almost all the Indians of that continent to join them." Mitchell, *The Contest in America Between Great Britain and France*, pp. 137–138. See also *ibid.*, pp. 118–119, 125–126, and Charles Henry Lincoln (ed.), *The Correspondence of William Shirley* (2 vols., New York, 1912), II, pp. 133–134, Shirley to James Delancey, Boston, Feb. 24, 1755; Fred Anderson, *A People's Army. Massachusetts Soldiers and Society in the Seven Years' War*, (Chapel Hill, NC, 1984).

as it came up the treacherous St Lawrence, then rely on the natural defenses of the town to prevent its capture.

If necessary, the extended defense lines could be pulled back to Niagara, Fort Frontenac, and Fort Saint-Frédéric. The enemy's communications and supply lines would then be lengthened and more vulnerable to attack by the French irregulars. Thus the British would have to employ vastly superior forces, and their need to build roads through the forest to supply their armies on the periphery of New France, growing ever longer, would limit the number of troops they could bring into action.[23] The British could, of course, transport whole armies to America without much danger of attack from the smaller French fleet.[24] Moreover, Britain could use ports from Halifax to Charleston; Canada had only one. An English fleet in the St Lawrence could isolate Canada completely. Without reinforcements and supplies from France, the colony could have been starved into surrender. Yet, not until 1760 did the Royal Navy succeed in blocking the St Lawrence. French supply ships reached Quebec every year until the city fell. Much, however, depended on the food the colony could itself provide, and this became crucial with all the additional mouths to feed, the army, the Acadians, and the allied Indians who had to be fed and provided with military supplies before they would take the field. When the crops failed in 1758, famine threatened, and inadequate food supplies, to some degree, dictated military tactics; yet food was never the major factor that it has sometimes been claimed. The people went hungry at times,

---

[23] See Henri-Raymond Casgrain (ed.), *Collection des manuscrits du maréchal de Lévis* (12 vols., Montréal and Québec, 1889–95), Vol. IV, *Lettres et pièces militaires, instructions, ordres, mémoires, plans de campagne et de défense, 1756–1760* (Québec, 1891), p. 153.

[24] In 1756 France had 45 ships of the line ready for sea, 15 in dock being readied, several under construction (Waddington, *Louis XV et le renversement des alliances*, p. 246). England had 130 ships of the line, but they were inferior to the French; the reverse was true of the officers of the two navies. (Dorn, *Competition for Empire*, pp. 105–121). In 1756, with war declared, the French government decided on an invasion of England. The American theatre tied down a sizable part of the Royal Navy; a diversionary assault on Minorca would tie down more. Diversionary assaults were to be made on Scotland and Ireland, then the main invasion launched against England. It was anticipated that all the ships and troops in the latter assault would be lost, but not before they had caused worse panic than the Jacobite march on London in 1745, the collapse of the country's financial structure, and a consequent willingness of the ruling class to accept reasonable peace terms to avert worse losses. See Corbett, *England in the Seven Years' War*, I, pp. 83–95; Dorn, *Competition for Empire*, p. 355.

but they did not starve. It was not a food shortage that caused the eventual fall of New France.[25]

In 1756 a replacement for Dieskau arrived in the person of Louis-Joseph, marquis de Montcalm-Gozon de Saint-Véran, a battle-tried regimental commander. He had the rank of *maréchal de camp*, equivalent to major-general, and command over the *troupes de terre* only. He was subordinate to the governor general, Vaudreuil, who had overall command of all the military forces, *troupes de terre*, Troupes de la Marine, the naval detachments, and the Canadian militia; all told, some 16,000 men. In addition there were the Indian allies. One reason for Vaudreuil's appointment as governor general was his intimate knowledge of, and ability to sway, these proud, independent, and unpredictable warriors. Although he had served in the Troupes de la Marine from childhood and in 1738 had been recommended by Governor General Beauharnois for the post of commander of the companies stationed in Canada, he had served only briefly in one campaign in the West. Most of his experience had been administrative, lately as governor of Louisiana, where he had performed very creditably.[26]

Unfortunately, Montcalm and Vaudreuil quickly came to detest each other. Both were vain, each very jealous of his authority, each convinced of the other's incompetence and his own superior judgment. Vaudreuil did, however, know the country and what warfare in it entailed. He could, as much as anyone could, handle the Indians; and he was respected by both the Canadian militia and the Troupes de la Marine. He had contrived the strategy of extended defense lines and wanted to take full advantage of the differing capabilities of his motley forces. Montcalm rejected this strategic concept. He recommended that the French abandon the Ohio Valley and Lake Champlain, then concentrate the forces at the colony's inner defense line.[27] He wished the war to be con-

---

[25] On this vital logistical problem, on which so much undocumented nonsense has been written, see the salutary correctives, the recent unpublished Ph.D., theses André Coté, "Joseph-Michel Cadet (1719–1781), munitionnaire du roi en Nouvelle-France," (Université Laval, 1984); Jay Cassel, "The Troupes de la Marine in Canada, 1683–1760: Men and Materiel." (Toronto, 1988).

[26] See Frégault, *Le grand marquis.*

[27] See Frégault, *Canada: The War of the Conquest*, pp. 241–243.

ducted on European lines, sieges and set battles, in which superior
discipline, training, and his leadership would bring victory. The
sort of warfare that the Canadians excelled at he regarded with
contempt, as accomplishing no worthwhile purpose. As for the
Indian allies, he had no use for them at all.[28] But his greatest
weakness was his confirmed defeatism. He quickly convinced
himself that the French position was hopeless and devoted much
of his time and energy to casting blame on Vaudreuil for the
disasters he was sure would ensue. Nor did he make any attempt
to hide his opinion of the governor general. He criticized Vaudreuil and all things Canadian before his officers, thereby fanning
the latent hostility between the Canadian officers of the Troupes
de la Marine and those newly come from France with the *troupes
de terre* who looked down on the colonials. Naturally, the Canadian officers, with their much greater experience in forest warfare
and their unblemished record of victory, resented the attitude of
Montcalm and his staff. Montcalm's defeatism, and his attitude
toward the Canadians, could not but have failed to sap the morale
of both troops and militia.

Another major factor was logistics. The influx of troops from
France and the exorbitant demand of the Indian allies for arms,
munitions, food supplies for themselves and their families, were
far beyond the capacity of the colony to provide.[29] The supplies
had to be shipped from France, slipping through the Royal Navy's
blockade of the French ports, then running the Atlantic gauntlet.
Many ships were taken, but the majority got through to Louisbourg until its fall in 1758, and to Quebec every year until 1760.
Much, indeed far too much, has been made of the alleged mal-
versations of the intendant François Bigot and *munitionnaire du
Roi* Joseph-Michel Cadet. Recent research has revealed that, far
from being the villains previously portrayed, they actually performed prodigies to keep the French armies in the field. Without
their efforts the French war effort in New France would have
collapsed long before it did. Bigot and Cadet were, in fact, the

---

[28] His attitude is revealed by a comment in his journal: "À quoi donc sont bons les sauvages?
À ne pas les avoir contre soi." Casgrain, *Collection des manuscrits*, VII, p. 591.

[29] On this important point see Paris AN Série C11A vol. 101, ff 117–119, Vaudreuil au Ministre
Mtl. 13 8bre 1756; Grenier (ed.), *Papiers Contrecoeur*, p. 211, Péan à Contrecoeur, Chatacoin,
11 juin 1754.

victims of a pernicious system and used as scapegoats by inadequate ministers and the King to cover up their own utter incompetence.[30] Despite these internal problems, the French forces won a succession of victories during the first two years of hostilities. Before Montcalm's arrival, Vaudreuil had made plans to destroy Oswego and remove that threat to French communications with the West. In February 1756, he sent a war party that destroyed Fort Bull, a supply depot between Schenectady and Oswego. Other detachments hovered about Oswego, cutting down the supply columns, keeping it blockaded. In July, Montcalm, with many misgivings, took command of a three-thousand-man assault force which captured Oswego after a four-day siege.[31] Thirty Americans were killed, seventeen hundred taken prisoners, and a vast store of boats, cannon, and supplies captured, with only thirty casualties among the French. This was a stunning blow to the Anglo-Americans, opening up the northwest frontier of New York to invasion. The entire western frontier of the English colonies was now ravaged by Canadian and Indian war parties. The early confidence that Canada would quickly be destroyed was replaced by fear that the French would soon invade the English colonies in force. Pleas for aid, recriminations, fears of conquest, were voiced in the middle colonies. Far from winning the war, they were losing it.

The following year Vaudreuil continued this strategy of forcing the Anglo-Americans onto the defensive in the West with his raiding parties, supplied and sent out from Fort Duquesne.[32] On

---

[30] For the importance of logistics in warfare see Marin Van Creveld, *Supplying War. Logistics from Wallenstein to Patton*, (Cambridge, 1977). For Canadian logistics during the Seven Years' War see Cassel and Coté, note 25 above. See also the glowing tribute to the work of the munitionnaire Cadet by the chevalier de Lévis, who had succeeded to command of the French army upon the death of Montcalm: Henri-Raymond Casgrain (ed.), *Collection des manuscrits du maréchal de Lévis*, vol. II, *Lettres du chevalier de Lévis concernant la guerre du Canada (1756–1760)*, (Montréal, 1889), pp. 262–3, Lévis à M. Berryer, 10 nov. 1759. It is worth noting the difference in contemporary attitudes towards the alleged corruption in Canada, and the bland acceptance in England of Henry Fox's amassing of a fortune while serving as paymaster general. See Lucy S. Sutherland and J. Binney, "Henry Fox as Paymaster-General of the Forces," *English Historical Review* LXX (April, 1955). See also André Coté, "Joseph Michel Cadet (1719–1781), munitionnaire du roi en Nouvelle-France," (Unpublished Ph.D. thesis, Université Laval, 1984).

[31] D. Peter MacLeod, "The Canadians against the French: The Struggle for Control of the Expedition to Oswego in 1756," *Ontario History*, LXXX, No. 2, June 1988, pp. 143–158.

[32] For a brief contemporary desciption of the nature of this guerrilla warfare see *Rapport de l'Archiviste de la Province de Québec, 1931–1932*, Mémoire et observations sur mon voyage en Canada, Chevalier de la Pause, p. 43.

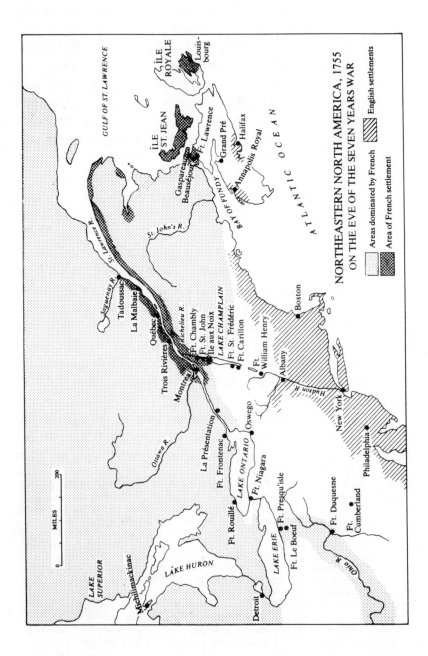

NORTHEASTERN NORTH AMERICA, 1755
ON THE EVE OF THE SEVEN YEARS WAR

English settlements

Areas dominated by French

Area of French settlement

the central front Vaudreuil had to expect the British to mass their forces for an assault on Lake Champlain to drive the French back and open the invasion route into Canada. To forfend this he sent Montcalm with 3,600 men and 1,500 Indian allies to destroy the advanced British fort, William Henry, and then press south to threaten Albany. Arriving at the fort on August 3, Montcalm went through all the motions of a siege in the accepted European style and mounted his batteries. On the ninth, the garrison commander, Colonel George Monro, asked for terms. He, with his 2,331-man garrison, was granted the honours of war and freedom to withdraw on condition they did not serve in operations against the French for eighteen months. After they had surrendered and were marching off, Montcalm's Indian allies, enraged at seeing their hated foe walk away unharmed, and inflamed by the liquor with which the Americans had foolishly tried to appease them, fell on the straggling columns. The French then did everything they could to stop the massacre, but twenty-nine were killed, over a hundred taken prisoner.

Regardless of this nasty episode, which afforded the British an opportunity to brand the French as war criminals, Montcalm had dealt the Anglo-Americans a severe blow. Their forward base was destroyed, they were deprived of a large body of troops and large stores of arms and cannon, and some three thousand barrels of pork and other valuable food supplies were added to the French stores. All this at a cost of thirteen killed and forty wounded. The Anglo-American troops defending the northern front were completely demoralized; Montcalm's were ready for anything. At New York the Provincial Council waited to hear that the French had taken the next strongpoint, Fort Edward, and fully expected Albany to fall. They wrote to Lord Loudoun, the commander in chief, who was at Halifax, "We may fear New York also."[33] Yet although Montcalm knew the dispirited and disorganized state of the enemy, that Fort Edward was only sixteen miles away, that its capture would have created panic in Albany and further reduced the offensive spirit of the Anglo-Americans, he refused to follow up his victory. He claimed the road was bad, his men

---

[33] New York State Archives, Albany, Colonial Documents, LXXXIV, p. 149.

worn out, and the militia needed back on their farms for the harvest. Since the harvest in Canada did not usually begin until September, even if the militia could not have been kept in the field beyond the first week of that month, it still allowed the French more than a fortnight to take Fort Edward, and that would have been enough time as things stood. Montcalm here betrayed his grave weakness as a commander. He was not aggressive; he could not seize the initiative when the opportunity presented itself. He preferred to react to the enemy's moves rather than make the enemy react to his.

Vaudreuil, of course, was infuriated by Montcalm's failure to execute his orders to march on Fort Edward. Their latent animosity now surfaced, and they quarreled openly. Their dispatches to the minister made their attitude all too plain. For his part, Vaudreuil infuriated Montcalm by taking credit for the victories; first at Oswego, then at Fort William Henry, as though he had commanded the troops during the actions, from his desk at Quebec.

Despite these victories, Canada had to have continued support from France to withstand the assaults that had been delayed but were sure to come.[34] Vaudreuil sent one of his Canadian officers to Versailles to explain the strategic and tactical situation and outline the additional forces needed to defend New France. He also allowed Montcalm to send two of his officers, Colonel Louis-Antoine de Bougainville and the commissary Doreil, to add their pleas. They were listened to much more attentively than was Vaudreuil's emissary. The dispute between the governor general and Montcalm was resolved in the latter's favour. Montcalm was promoted to lieutenant general and given overall command of all the military forces in the colony. Vaudreuil now had to defer to Montcalm's decisions in all military matters. In addition, the government ordered that Vaudreuil's extended lines defensive strategy be abandoned and Montcalm's instituted. The French forces were to fall back on the settlements in the St Lawrence

---

[34] Historians who accept — usually as an unstated, and likely unconscious premise — that what happened had to happen, and therefore regard the conquest of New France as inevitable, always advance as a main argument the dependence of Canada on France for support. They thereby ignore that the English colonies were more dependent on England for military aid than Canada was on France.

Valley as the enemy advanced and strive only to hold them on the doorstep of the colony proper. This meant that the enemy would be allowed to advance almost unopposed through the wilderness and consolidate their supply lines for a massed assault. Everything, therefore, would depend on the ability of the French forces to hold Quebec and defeat much larger enemy armies south and west of Montreal. The French were, in short, to conduct the war in Canada on European lines and strive to hold the rump of New France in the hope that some part of the territory could be retained until hostilities ceased. If France still had a foothold in North America it would be in a much stronger position when the bargaining began at the peace table. Montcalm, through his emissaries, had painted such a bleak picture of the military position that the King's council apparently decided it would be folly to commit large forces in a forlorn hope. Thus fewer than five hundred replacements for the army in Canada accompanied Bougainville on his return to Quebec, raising the effective strength of the regular troops to less than six thousand.

Ironically, the French government, although its armies in the field had won startling victories, reducing the authorities in some of the English colonies to plead for peace on any terms before further defeats rendered even those terms unobtainable, had adopted the defeatist attitude of Montcalm, whereas the British government, now dominated by Pitt, took determined measures to drive the French, not just out of the territory claimed by Britain, but out of North America. More British regiments were shipped to the colonies until more than 20,000 regulars of an army now totalling 140,000 soldiers and marines were in the theatre, and one-quarter of the Royal Navy, in addition to 22,000 colonial troops and militia. The French army, on the other hand, had only twelve of its 395 battalions serving in Canada and Louisbourg plus 2,000 Troupes de la Marine.[35] To that degree, fortress Canada was fulfilling its intended role in French imperial strategy; with a handful of troops it was tying down a much larger enemy force, preventing its being employed in some other theatre.

---

[35] In 1758 the British army and marines numbered 140,000. Rex Whitworth, *Field Marshall Lord Ligonier: A Study of the British Army, 1702–1770* (Oxford, 1958), pp. 208, 246. The French army at maximum strength, 1757–1762, was slightly under 330,000 men in line units. Lee Kennet, *The French Armies in the Seven Years' War* (Duke Univ. Press, 1967), pp. 75–78.

In 1758, Pitt, who dictated military strategy, planned three concerted campaigns against Louisbourg, Quebec, and Fort Duquesne. Louisbourg, without a strong naval detachment, withstood a sixty-day siege by 8,000 troops under Jeffery Amherst, but under fierce bombardment had finally to capitulate. It had, however, held out long enough to force the abandonment of the intended maritime assault on Quebec for that year. Brigadier James Wolfe acidly commented: "If this force had been properly manag'd, there was an end of the French colony in North America in one Campaign."[36] The fall of Louisbourg, by removing that potential threat to British shipping in the North Atlantic, allowed Pitt to transfer a large naval force to the West Indies. The object there was to capture Martinique to exchange at the peace table for Minorca, taken by the French in June 1756, and so avoid the necessity to give back Louisbourg. The French defenses of Martinique proving too strong, the assault was transferred to Guadeloupe. Not, however, until May 1, 1759, were that island's defenders forced to capitulate, but Pitt now had the gage his strategy required. The war had taken a new direction. Previously it had been waged for commercial aims. Now territorial conquest was the chief end.[37]

On the central Canadian front, Major General James Abercromby massed an army of 15,000, 6,000 of them British regulars, to drive down Lake Champlain to the Richelieu and the heart of Canada. He got no farther than Carillon, where Montcalm and 3,500 regulars and militia had hastily entrenched themselves behind a wall of logs and abatis of felled trees. Cannon would have blasted this breastwork asunder. Abercromby, however, chose to send his regulars against it in a frontal column attack. They suffered heavy losses, but returned again and again until even these disciplined troops could take no more. The British withdrew to Fort William Henry, their losses nearly 2,000 men. The French had lost only 380 killed and wounded. The demoralized British had suffered another stunning defeat. Their retreat

---

[36] McCord Museum, McGill University, Wolfe Papers, No. 1288.

[37] On the West Indies campaign and Pitt's strategy see Corbett, *England in the Seven Years' War*, I, pp. 371–395; Gipson, *The British Empire Before the American Revolution*, Vols. V and VIII.

was almost a rout. They abandoned boats, arms, and supplies, as though the devil had been after them. Although a large contingent of Canadians reached Montcalm immediately after his victory, he made no attempt to follow it up by pursuing the beaten foe. Vaudreuil pleaded with him to send raiding parties to harass the enemy and their supply lines, and hammer it home to them that the route to Canada was impregnable. Montcalm, however, appeared satisfied with what he had already accomplished. And certainly, he had put a stop to the drive on the colony for that year. But that was not enough.

In the West, the British had better success. In August, Lieutenant Colonel Bradstreet with nearly 3,000 men caught the French at Fort Frontenac off guard.[38] Although the fort was very poorly sited, its walls no protection against cannon fire, the commandant, Pierre-Jacques Payen de Noyan, conducted the defense very ineptly. With his armed sloops he could have intercepted the attackers in their bateaux and shot them out of the water. Instead they were allowed to land and bring up their cannon. Three days later the fort surrendered. After destroying the store of provisions, the small French fleet, and the fort itself, Bradstreet swiftly returned across the lake. It was not the destruction of the fort but the loss of the stores, and the boats to transport them to Niagara and the Ohio, that hurt the French.

Farther west the British slowly mounted a campaign to drive the French out of the Ohio Valley. Montcalm convinced himself that this was merely a feint to draw troops away from Lake Champlain. Unfortunately for the French, they were now deprived of their Indian allies in the midwest. In October the authorities of Pennsylvania had met with delegates of the war-weary Ohio tribes at Easton and there negotiated a peace, a principal condition of which was a renunciation by Pennsylvania of all claims to lands beyond the crest of the mountains. The

---

[38] The French appear to have suffered a breakdown in the intelligence service provided them by the Iroquois confederacy. Previously the Iroquois had kept Vaudreuil well informed of English plans and preparations. On this occasion they conspicuously did not. It may be that they regarded it as in their interests to have the British destroy Fort Frontenac, located as it was on lands they claimed as theirs. When the French destroyed Oswego in 1756 the Iroquois pointedly thanked Vaudreuil for having thus "reestablished the Five Nations in possession of lands that belonged to them." See *Rapport de l'Archiviste de la Province de Québec, 1932–1933*, p. 327.

Indians guilelessly assumed that the Americans would honour the treaty; thus having achieved their main objective, they withdrew from the war. When Brigadier-General John Forbes, whose forces had been badly mauled by small Canadian war parties, learned from a French prisoner that the garrison at Fort Duquesne was far less than the reputed thousand, and with the Indian menace removed, he pressed on against the fort. The commandant, François Le Marchand de Ligneris, his supplies almost exhausted, his men in like condition, stripped the fort of its cannon, blew it up, and retreated to Fort Machault, there to await reinforcements and supplies from Montreal. He fully intended, when they were received, to counterattack and drive the Anglo-Americans back over the mountains.

In Canada, that winter of 1758–59, food supplies in the three towns were again in short supply. The *habitants* suffered when they were pillaged by the French troops, but there was no real shortage of food; it was badly distributed. The *habitants* refused to accept the rapidly depreciating paper money drawn on the Ministry of Marine and kept their produce off the market until they were paid in specie.[39] Montcalm and his entourage complained bitterly of the hardship inflicted on the officer corps by rampant inflation. It was calculated that in France there was 75 livres per capita in circulation and in Canada 400 livres.[40] The officers were paid with postdated letters of exchange, which the colony's merchants would accept at only a quarter of their face value. They claimed that it cost them five times their pay to live.[41] Yet Montcalm somehow managed to amass a small fortune whilst in the colony; how he contrived it is a mystery.[42] The ordinary soldiers, who were billeted on the *habitants* when not on campaign, did not suffer unduly. They received their rations and worked for inflated wages, earning up to eleven livres a day

---

[39] Vincennes, Service Hist. de l'Armée, Série A1, vol. 3374 #29 M. Bernier à M. de Cremille, Trois Rivières, 15-iv-60.

[40] *ibid.*, vol. 3540 #47 Dépense Par mois en Canada d'un officier qui veut vivre décemment dans les temps présent.

[41] *ibid.*, vol. 3540 ff. 91–98, 102.

[42] Paris AN Colonies, série B, vol. 111, f. 165. A Mrs de Vaudreuil et Bigot, à Versailles le 22 fév 1760; C11A vol. 105 f. 4, Vaudreuil et Bigot au Ministre, Mtl. 28 juin 1760; vol. 105, f. 6, Canada Exercise 1759. Joint à la lettre de M de Vaudreuil du 28 juin 1760.

sawing firewood. Some of them married Canadian girls and were determined to remain in Canada when hostilities ended.[43] That to the contrary, relations between the French troops and the Canadians steadily deteriorated as the war dragged on. Bigot's subordinates complained bitterly that the French officers drew rations for far more men than they had on strength. They also failed to discipline their troops who, in general, behaved as they were wont to do in Europe when occupying enemy territory. They were then accustomed to live off the land and take whatever seized their fancy, and so they behaved in Canada.[44]

With the regular troops dispersed among the civilian population in this fashion, discipline suffered and training proved impossible. The battalion commanders did not know how many men they had on strength, except at the beginning of the campaigns in the spring and again in the autumn when muster parades were held. The lack of regular training exercises was to prove fatal. The reinforcements sent from France in 1757 had been a particularly poor lot; as casualties thinned the ranks of the regulars, Montcalm pressed Canadian militia into the battalions to maintain them at full strength. For the type of set battle that he wished to fight, it required eighteen months of training on the drill ground to turn a civilian into a soldier, capable of manoeuvring en masse, marching up to the enemy and firing in volleys on command, and standing fast in the face of the enemy's volley or bayonet charge. By 1759 Montcalm's troops were no longer capable of that style of warfare. Although he and his staff officers in their letters and dispatches expressed nothing but defeatism and the belief that the colony was doomed — indeed, Montcalm eventually proposed retiring to Louisiana with the army should the British break through his lines — yet his second in command, the Chevalier de Lévis, and some at least of the junior officers were more sanguine about the outcome.[45]

Fortunately for the French, twenty-two supply ships reached

---

[43] Vincennes, Service Hist. de l'Armée, Série A1, vol. 3457, #60, Montcalm au Ministre, Mtl. 24 avril 1757.

[44] *ibid.*, Série A1, vol. 3417, #137, Montcalm au Ministre, Mtl. 12 juin 1756; vol. 3574, #86, Lévis au Mal. de Belleisle, Mtl. 14 juillet 1760.

[45] See Archives de la Guerre, Series A1, Vol. 3540, pt. 1, pp. 115, 138–139.

Quebec in May 1759, bringing enough food to keep the army in the field until the harvest. Hard on their heels, however, came the Royal Navy, bringing an army of 8,000 seasoned troops commanded by Major General James Wolfe, for an assault on the bastion of New France. On the Lake Champlain front, Jeffery Amherst, the commander in chief of the British forces in America, had massed an army of 6,236 regulars and provincials to dislodge the French from their forts. It took him a month to get his army in motion. The French officers had orders to fight delaying actions only at Carillon and Saint-Frédéric, then retire on Fort Île-aux-Noix to make a stand. After Amherst had spent several days preparing trenches and gun emplacements at Carillon, the French mined the fort, lighted the fuses, and slipped away. They did the same at Fort Saint-Frédéric, but Amherst made no move to pursue them. Instead he devoted the remainder of the summer to repairing the fort at Ticonderoga and building a massive new fort near where Fort Saint-Frédéric had stood. The only purpose these forts could serve was to block an army advancing south from Canada. Were Quebec to be taken there was no danger whatsoever of that. Obviously, Amherst did not expect Quebec to fall. This was a view shared by others in the British forces.

In the West, de Ligneris renewed his raids on the British supply lines to Fort Pitt, constructed near the ruins of Fort Duquesne. He was, however, forced to desist and rush to the aid of the small garrison at Niagara, under siege by a combined force of British regulars, American provincial troops and 900 Iroquois, 3,200 in all. De Ligneris with his 600 men never arrived. His force was ambushed and the Iroquois, their blood up, gave no quarter. Only a hundred survived. Two days later, on 26 July, Fort Niagara with its 490 defenders capitulated. The Anglo-Americans had finally achieved their war aims. Their hold on the Great Lakes and the Ohio Valley was secure. Moreover, the St Lawrence was at last open for a descent on Montreal.

At Quebec, however, things were not going so well for the British. Although a French army engineer had proposed siting batteries downriver at three spots which dominated the river channel and could have made the passage very costly for a fleet at the mercy of wind, current, and tide, nothing had been done.

The French command believed that the Royal Navy could never get up the treacherous river without pilots, once all the navigation markers had been removed. They had not anticipated that the British would make use of captured Canadian pilots who, willy-nilly, brought the fleet to Quebec.[46] Thus Vice-Admiral Charles Saunders was able to bring up the army and land it, unopposed, on the Île d'Orléans on 27 June. Only when the British fleet was well up the river were panic-stricken measures taken to fortify the immediate approaches to Quebec.[47] Entrenchments were dug on the Beauport flats, across the St Charles River from Quebec. On the insistence of the Chevalier de Lévis they were extended to the Montmorency River, but, incredibly, Montcalm made no attempt to fortify the cliffs across the river from Quebec. To oppose the British, Montcalm had a total of nearly 16,000 men, regulars, militia, and Indians at his disposal, double the number that Wolfe commanded.

The French had prepared a flotilla of fire ships. On the night of 28 June, with Bougainville in command, they were sent down on the British fleet. The operation was a fiasco. Set alight too soon, British sailors in longboats were able to tow all seven clear before they reached their objective. The next day, on the insistence of Admiral Saunders, the British occupied Point Lévis and French attempts to drive them out failed miserably. The British were now able to mount heavy mortars to bombard the town across the river. They were also able to get their ships upriver above Quebec and to threaten a landing on either side of the town. A landing above Quebec was particularly to be feared since Montcalm had established his main supply depot at Batiscan, some 100 kilometres upriver. Wolfe, however, stuck resolutely to his original plan to break the Beauport lines, but every assault was beaten back.[48]

---

[46] *Bulletin des recherches historiques*, XV, p. 190, James Murray to the Earl of Egremont, Sec. of State, Que. 7 June 1762; Arch. Sem. Qué. Documents Faribault, Certificat de Quittance de Bazille tremblé (sic) Pilote de la Rivière du Canada. RAPQ 1928–1929, p. 47, Journal militaire tenu par Nicolas Renaud d'Avène des Meloizes 16 juillet 1759; Archives Université de Montréal, Col. Baby, 156, S. Jaug à M. Baby, Bordeau, 15 mars 1759.

[47] The extent of the panic and disorder in the French high command is made graphically plain in Arch. Sem. Qué. Ms 18, Journal du siège du Québec 1759.

[48] On August 11 he wryly remarked: "We had a lively skirmish this morning—we are as usual victorious and yet I am afraid we lost more than the enemy owing to our original disposition and partly to the irregularity and folly of our men. . . ." Public Archives of Canada, James Murray Papers, Wolfe to Brig.-Gen. Murray, Aboard *Sterling Castle*, 11 Aug. 1759.

Still convinced that if he could only force Montcalm to give battle on open ground he could defeat his foe, Wolfe, in his last letter to his mother, remarked, "The Marquis de Montcalm is at the head of a great number of bad soldiers, and I am at the head of a small number of good ones, that wish for nothing so much as to fight him—but the wary old fellow avoids an action doubtful of the behaviour of his army." There was more than a little truth in his judgment, as events were to prove. Although Wolfe was a poor strategist, he had always been an excellent regimental officer, a great admirer of Prussian military methods.[49] The training, discipline, and morale of his troops was now vastly superior to that of Montcalm's regulars. The Canadians, however, could be counted on to fight with savage desperation to protect their homeland and avoid the fate meted out earlier to the Acadians.

As July became August, Wolfe, frustrated at every turn and suffering from poor health, quarreled with his brigadiers. They regarded his tactics to date inept and resented his secretive, arrogant manner. Unable to force the enemy to come out of his lines, Wolfe gave orders for the systematic destruction of the colony. The Canadian settlements were to receive the same treatment as had the Scottish Highlands after Culloden, in which Wolfe had played an active part. Upon first landing on the Île d'Orléans he had issued a manifesto ordering the Canadian people not to assist the "enemy," warning them that if they took up arms in defense of their homeland they would be punished with fire and sword, treated as Indians, who Wolfe had earlier declared merited extermination.[50] He took no account of the fact that every Canadian male between fifteen and sixty was a member of the militia, and thus had to obey the orders of his officers and fight the invader. To Wolfe, war was the prerogative of regular uniformed troops; the civilian population had to stand aside and accept the outcome,

---

[49] See Wolfe to Captain Maitland, August 5, 1757: "I have ever entertained a profound admiration for the King of Prussia as the first soldier of this Age and our Master in the Art of War. . . . Some of H.M.'s manoeuvres are curious and the Deployments display uncommon ingenuity. They doubtless will be adopted by us if Occasion arises." McCord Museum, McGill University, Wolfe Papers, M1385. On Wolfe's generalship see E. R. Adair, "The Military Reputation of Major-General James Wolfe," *Canadian Historical Association Report, 1936*; C. P. Stacey, *Quebec, 1759* (Toronto, 1959), pp. 170–178.

[50] For Wolfe's views on the Indians, see McCord Museum, McGill University, Wolfe Papers, No. 1288. His manifesto is printed in Casgrain, *Collection des manuscrits*, IV, pp. 273–276.

regardless of its consequences for their lives and the lives of their descendants. At the end of July, Wolfe repeated his proclamation, then turned loose the American Rangers, whom he had labelled "the worst soldiers in the universe," to burn the houses, buildings, and crops in all the parishes up and down the river. When any resistance was met, and prisoners taken, they were shot and scalped. At least fourteen hundred farms were destroyed, most of them fine stone buildings in the earlier-settled and more prosperous part of the colony. Bigot tersely commented: "M. Wolfe est cruel."

Wolfe claimed that this devastation was intended to force Montcalm to emerge and give battle. In this it failed. At the same time he increased the number of cannon bombarding Quebec from the Lévis side to forty pieces. Hardly a building in the city was left undamaged; 80 percent of Quebec was destroyed. It was the civilian population, not the army, that suffered. The bombardment served no useful military purpose. This whole policy of calculated destruction of Quebec and of the seigneuries about it made no military sense whatsoever, unless it had been concluded that Quebec could not be taken, and Canada not conquered. In his journal, under date of August 13, Major Patrick Mackellar noted that the bombardment of Quebec had been stepped up, and commented, "This was thought to be done either to favour a storm by water, or to do the town all possible damage if it could not be taken, which was now becoming doubtful, as there was little or no appearance of making good a landing upon that coast, it being so well fortified and defended by such Superior Numbers."[51] Wolfe himself, in his dispatch of September 2 to Pitt, in which he reviewed the course of the campaign, expressed profound pessimism as to the outcome, declaring: "In this situation, there is such a choice of difficulties, that I own myself at the loss how to determine." At that late date only a few weeks remained before the fleet would be forced to withdraw, taking the army with it. Of his original troop strength of 8,500 barely half were fit for duty. Casualties had been heavy, more and more dispirited men deserted to the French. Over a thousand men were in sick

---

[51] Public Archives of Canada, MG23, GII-1, Series 2-7, P. Mackellar's short account of the expedition against Quebec, p. 20.

bay. The men were now on short rations and reduced to eating horse flesh. Dysentery and scurvy were taking a heavy toll. At the end of August, in a letter to Admiral Saunders, Wolfe stated, "Beyond the month of September I conclude our operations cannot go." He then made the revealing comment that Barré had prepared a list of where the troops would be quartered, "supposing (as I have very little hope of) they do not quarter here."[52] But Wolfe could not give up without making one last attempt to conquer Quebec.

He wanted to launch another attack on the Beauport lines below Quebec, but when he proposed three variants of this plan to his brigadiers they rejected the concept of any attack there. Instead they proposed a landing above Quebec between the city and the supply depot at Batiscan. Such a landing would, they pointed out, cut the road to Montreal. The brigadiers argued that there a landing in strength would force Montcalm to emerge from behind his defense works and give battle in the open. Ever since the fleet had forced a passage above Quebec, British raiding parties had landed above the town periodically. This had forced Montcalm to detach 3,000 of his better troops under Bougainville to march up and down abreast of the British ships to counter the threat.

Wolfe accepted the brigadiers' suggestion for a landing above Quebec; but whereas they had intended the landing to be made well above the city, he chose the Anse au Foulon, at the foot of the 53-metre cliff, less than four kilometres from Quebec. The operation required the troops to be transported above the city by the fleet, then, during the night, to embark in the landing craft, drift down with the tide, land, make their way up the steep path to the top of the cliff, overpower the French outpost stationed there, then assemble on the heights before the city walls, and wait for the French reaction. It was a most desperate gamble, requiring the complete cooperation of the elements—and also of the French. Rear Admiral Charles Holmes, who was in charge of the operation, afterward described it: "The most hazardous and difficult task I was ever engaged in: For the distance of the landing place; the darkness of the night; and the chance of exactly

---

[52] Christopher Hibbert, *Wolfe at Quebec* (London, 1959), p. 165; Stacey, *Quebec, 1759*, p. 102.

hitting the very spot intended, without discovery or alarm; made the whole extremely difficult."[53]

Everything depended on surprise. Were the French to have had a battalion of troops on the heights above the Anse au Foulon, the landing could never have succeeded. Montcalm was convinced that Wolfe would not lift the siege without one last assault, and reading his adversary's mind, he anticipated an attack on the right of the Beauport lines.[54] The fleet movements above Quebec he regarded as a diversion. He had moved a battalion to the heights near the Anse au Foulon on September 5 but recalled it the following day to the Beauport lines.[55] As it was, the small French detachment on top of the cliff was taken completely by surprise, routed by the first British troops to scale the heights. The way was open for the army to follow. When Wolfe himself landed, the situation still looked desperate. His comment reveals that he regarded the enterprise as a forlorn hope: "I don't think we can by any possible means get up here; but, however, we must use our best endeavour."[56] This they did, and the surprise of the French was complete. By daybreak Wolfe had more than 4,400 men on the Plains of Abraham, a thousand yards from the city walls. But they were in an extremely vulnerable position. Wolfe, incredibly, failed to take the high ground. Before his troops lined up on a reverse slope, in two sparse lines, stretched a ridge, the Buttes de Neveu that screened Quebec from their sight and their guns. From that ridge French cannon could have decimated Wolfe's army. Behind it was Quebec, poorly fortified, but protected by a wall that would have to be breached by heavy artillery before an assault could be launched. Between the ridge and the British lines, stretching down the slope, were cornfields

---

[53] Stacey, *Quebec, 1759*, pp. 132-133.

[54] C. P. Stacey, *Quebec, 1759*, pp. 111-112, 168, opines that Montcalm lacked one essential quality of a good general, the ability to divine his antagonist's intentions, citing his failure to anticipate the landing above Quebec as an example. Montcalm gave abundant evidence of poor generalship, but in this particular case he cannot be faulted, for he had read Wolfe's mind very accurately. What he failed to divine was that Wolfe would defer to the tactics proposed by his brigadiers. He could not have been expected to know that this had transpired.

[55] For the confusion that this incident occasioned in the minds of Canadian historians see the intriguing critique by C. P. Stacey, "The Anse au Foulon, 1759: Montcalm and Vaudreuil," *Canadian Historical Review*, XL, 4 (Mar. 1959), pp. 27-37.

[56] See C. P. Stacey, "Quebec, 1759: Some New Documents," *Canadian Historical Review*, XLVII, 4 (Dec. 1966), pp. 344-355; Frégault, *Canada: The War of the Conquest*, p. 253.

and clumps of bushes, providing excellent cover for the Canadian and Indian skirmishers who soon began to take a heavy toll of the enemy.

In Quebec and the Beauport lines Montcalm had some 6,000 troops, and a few kilometres above Quebec was Bougainville with 3,000 more. Wolfe's army was between the two. Moreover, he had to win a total victory. His men had had no sleep for some 24 hours, they had only dry rations in their haversacks, their only water what was in their canteens, they had no shelter from the elements and a gale was approaching from the west.[57] There was, apparently, not even a surgeon with them.[58]

Few generals have burnt their bridges as successfully as did Wolfe. Retreat was virtually impossible. The army would have had to withdraw down the steep cliff path, then wait for the tide to be taken off the narrow beach by the ships' long boats. Such an operation would have invited mass slaughter. The alternatives for the British would have been: be shot, drown, or surrender. It is doubtful that many would have escaped. The army most likely would have been destroyed. The fleet would have had to sail back with the shattered remnants. Wolfe had dug a grave for his army. But none of that happened, for Montcalm obligingly marched his army into the waiting grave. Yet the possibility must have been in the minds of the soldiers as they climbed the cliff. It speaks volumes for their morale and discipline.

Upon belatedly discovering that Wolfe's army had landed and was mustered on the Plains of Abraham, Montcalm had several courses of action open to him, and ample time to carry them out. He could have sent word immediately to Bougainville, 25 kilometres away, to bring his forces up to attack the British in the rear while he launched a frontal assault. He could have marched his army around the British and joined up with Bougainville for

---

[57] See William Wood (ed.), *The Logs of the Conquest of Canada* (Champlain Society, Toronto 1909), Logs of ships of the Royal Navy at Quebec 1759.

[58] When the French learned that Wolfe had been wounded Bougainville apparently suggested sending a surgeon to attend to him. Vaudreuil replied that he believed Ramezay, commandant of the Quebec garrison had "already sent two surgeons to the English general." This would have been perfectly in accord with eighteenth-century military protocol. It also reveals that the famous painting by Benjamin West, "The Death of General Wolfe" was a figment of his imagination. See A. G. Doughty with G. W. Parmelee, *The Siege of Quebec and the Battle of the Plains of Abraham*, vol. IV, p. 127, Vaudreuil à Bougainville, 13 sept. 1759.

a consolidated attack. He could have withdrawn his main force into the city and forced Wolfe to launch an assault while Bougainville and the Canadian militia harassed the British rear. Montcalm could afford to wait; Wolfe could not. Bringing up supplies for his army from the fleet would have been difficult, to say the least. A siege was out of the question. The British had only two or three weeks left in which to take Quebec or be forced to withdraw. In short, Montcalm could have forced Wolfe to fight on his terms. Instead, he chose to throw away all these advantages and fight on the ground and at the time chosen by the British, employing only half his available forces.

By nine o'clock he had some 4,500 men mustered on the heights in front of the fortified city, facing the British. The Canadian militia and Indians, sniping from cover on the flanks and the cornfields on the British front, were inflicting casualties. The red-coated army was forced to kneel. When the last of the French regiments, after their forced march from the Beauport flats, reached the heights, hardly letting them catch their breath, not waiting to bring up the guns, Montcalm gave the order to attack. In three massive columns, the French regiments, bolstered by Canadian militia, charged down the slope. The centre column veered to the right, leaving the British centre unscathed. At fifty paces they paused, fired ragged volleys, then advanced.

The British, in two thin lines, held their fire. At thirty paces, they stood up and fired volleys platoon by platoon, advanced through the gunsmoke, reloaded and fired again. That checked the French charge. Then came general volleys from the length of the British lines. The French fell back in shattered disarray, then turned and fled, the British in hot pursuit with bayonet and claymore. All that saved the French regulars from total destruction was the withering fire of the Canadian militia on the flanks that brought the British to a halt. That alone allowed the French troops to reach safety within the city walls. For that the Canadians paid a heavy price. It was at this point, just as he was about to pass through the St John gate that Montcalm received his mortal wound. By noon the British, almost as disorganized by victory as the French were by defeat, were in command of the field but of little else. The battle had lasted half an hour. As future events were to prove, in that short engagement most of North America was lost, and won.

When it was over, Vaudreuil, who had never thought Montcalm would attack so precipitately, arrived on the field with reinforcements. Bougainville appeared later still, then swiftly retired at first sight of the foe. The British still held only the Plains of Abraham.[59] The French had more than twice as many effectives and held the town. Casualties on both sides had been heavy: 658 for the British,[60] 644 for the French. Among the killed was Wolfe, and among the dying, Montcalm. For the generals on both sides to be killed in a battle was indeed remarkable. True to form, Montcalm's last action before expiring was to address a letter to Brigadier General George Townshend, who had succeeded Wolfe in command, yielding up Quebec.

Vaudreuil, meanwhile, was struggling to rally the French forces to attack the British the following day, but the colonels of the French regulars had no stomach for it. Vaudreuil therefore gathered up all the troops and militia and withdrew them around the British to join Bougainville's force above the Jacques Cartier River, 50 kilometres from the city. In Quebec he had left the Chevalier de Ramezay with a token force and ill-conceived instructions to hold out as long as possible but not necessarily to wait for a British assault before surrendering. The Chevalier de Lévis, come posthaste from Montreal, now took command of the French army and prepared to counterattack. Before he could do so Ramezay precipitately surrendered Quebec. The French then fell back and established their forward outpost at Jacques Cartier, while the main forces retired to Montreal.

In Quebec, when the fleet finally sailed in October, Brigadier James Murray was left in command with the bulk of the army.

---

[59] In 1711 Governor General Philippe de Rigaud de Vaudreuil, father of the governor general of 1759, had prepared to repel an English seaborne assault on Quebec. He had entrenchments made and cut all the roads everywhere the enemy could effect a landing on both sides of the city, from Beauport to Cap Rouge. He stated that even should the enemy break through these defenses, which they could not do without suffering heavy losses, "they would still hold nothing." *Rapport de l'Archiviste de la Province de Québec, 1946-1947*, pp. 433-434.

[60] The total British casualties in the Quebec campaign were 21 officers killed, 93 wounded, 1,384 other ranks killed, wounded, and missing. McCord Museum, McGill University, No. 824, A Return of the Kill'd & Wounded etc. of H.M. Forces up the River St. Lawrence from the 27th June to the Reduction of Quebec 10 [*sic*] Sept. 1759.

He likely did not receive a letter until the following year written by Thomas Ainslie at Louisbourg and dated October 28: "I now congratulate you on your success at Quebec a thing little expected by any here, and posterity will hardly give credit to it, that such a handful of men should carry a point against such numbers, and with such advantages, thank God you have escaped, it is a miracle that you have."[61] After the British ships had sailed, the French got some of their ships past Quebec with dispatches for France pleading for a strong naval squadron to be sent early to block the St Lawrence and prevent the British garrison at Quebec from being reinforced. Ten thousand troops, artillery, and supplies were also demanded to repel the British assaults that were sure to come the following year.

Murray's troops suffered cruelly during that winter in the city they had shattered. Sentries froze to death. Wood-cutting parties were savaged by the Canadians. Scurvy took a heavy toll.[62] In April, Lévis gathered up his forces, 7,000 men, and marched back to try to retake Quebec. On the twenty-seventh he was at Sainte-Foy, eight kilometres from the city. Ironically, Murray committed the same tactical error as Montcalm had done. He marched his troops out, 3,866 strong, to give battle.[63] Lévis had 3,928 on the battlefield. Again the armies were evenly matched. But this time the British were routed. Abandoning their guns, they were pursued right to the city gates. Lévis then laid siege to the town while awaiting the relief ships from France. Those ships never came. Versailles had decided that Canada was irretrievably lost. The duc de Choiseul sagely concluded that the British, by conquering New France, would merely strengthen their American colonies and their latent urge to strike out for independence. There was, therefore, no point in risking France's remaining naval strength, thousands of troops, and adding to the nation's

---

[61] Public Archives of Canada, James Murray Papers, Vol. (1), 3, pp. 8–9.

[62] Vaudreuil proposed to detach 1,500 to 1,800 men to harass the British garrison continually and by preventing their obtaining firewood force Murray to surrender. The proposal was rejected owing to the shortage of food supplies for such a detachment and also because the French were sure that Murray would retaliate by burning the homes of all the Canadians within his reach. This might indicate that the British policy of *schrechlichkeit* had served a purpose. See *Rapport de l'Archiviste de la Province de Québec, 1938–1939*, p. 2.

[63] The best means to see how this battle was conducted is the *Historical Atlas of Canada*, (Toronto, 1987), plate 43.

hideous load of debt to achieve an end that the loss of Canada would achieve in due course at no cost to France. A token force was sent to Canada—five ships escorted by one frigate, bearing four hundred soldiers and some supplies. They sailed late. When they arrived in the Gulf of St Lawrence a powerful British fleet was already in the Gulf. After putting up a gallant fight the French ships were sunk in Restigouche Bay.

By mid-May the British ships of the line were at Quebec. Lévis had to raise the siege and retire on Montreal, where he intended to make a last stand—not to save the colony, for that was clearly impossible, but to save the honour of the French army and his own reputation. Three British armies now moved in to crush what remained of Canada. Murray moved upriver, by-passing the French defense points, and pressed on toward Montreal. To quell the resistance of the Canadians, the homes at Sorel along a four-mile stretch were put to the torch. Even though their situation was hopeless, the consequences of further resistance cruel, many of the Canadians kept on fighting. Many, however, gave up.

On the Lake Champlain front the French had to fall back before Brigadier William Haviland's army, abandoning the chain of forts on the Richelieu after a heavy artillery bombardment. To the west, Amherst at long last put in an appearance, moving down the St Lawrence from Oswego. On September 6 he landed at Lachine. Seventeen thousand British troops now confronted Lévis. His forces had shrunk to fewer than two thousand. More than fifteen hundred of his regulars had deserted.[64] On the seventh, Vaudreuil asked Amherst for terms. With a conspicuous lack of gallantry Amherst refused to grant the honours of war. Lévis protested violently. He demanded that the regulars be allowed to make a final stand rather than accept such shameful conditions. Vaudreuil, fearing savage reprisals on the Canadian people and recognizing the futility of further resistance, ordered that Amherst's terms be accepted. That night Lévis ordered his

---

[64] Their officers reported that the majority of the regulars were resolved not to return to France. Some of them had married Canadian girls, with the consent of Montcalm, who had promised them that they would take their discharge and remain in the colony at the war's end. See Eccles, *The Canadian Frontier*, pp. 176, 184. For a graphic contemporary account of the collapse of French resistance see *Rapport de l'Archiviste de la Province de Québec, 1931–1932*, p. 120, Relation de M. Poularies.

regiments to burn their colours to avoid the dishonour and anguish of spirit of handing them over to Amherst. On September 9 the British marched into Montreal. What remained of the French and Canadian regulars stacked their arms on the Champ de Mars. Before the month was out, they and the administrative officials were transported to France.[65] According to the terms of the capitulation the troops could not serve again during the continuance of the war.

Canada had finally been conquered. Yet that conquest had, by no means, been inevitable. Had no regular troops been involved on either side it is highly unlikely that the Anglo-Americans could have conquered New France. Fifteen years later, on the eve of the American Revolution, Chief Justice Hey at Quebec remarked: "I believe it to be as true as anything can be that has not been reduced to absolute proof that the Colonies without the assistance of England, would have been reduced from North to south by this province in the last war. They thought so themselves . . ."[66] And against Louisiana, where no British troops were engaged, the Indian allies of the French punished the American frontier so severely that no attempts were made to invade that province. Had Montcalm not employed such disastrous tactics at Quebec on September 13, 1759, the fortress city would not have fallen; instead the British army might well have been destroyed. Then, the wavering, war-weary British government would have been more inclined to seek an end to the war. Ineptitude in the French military command and government at home, and the fortunes of war, gave Britain dominion over the vast French territory. But what might have been was now of no account. All that mattered to the conquered Canadians was to restore their destroyed homes before the onset of winter. Beyond that their main concern was what their ultimate fate would be. They were all disarmed and

---

[65] A handful of officers in the Troupes de la Marine, six captains, three lieutenants, four *enseignes*, were granted permission in 1760 to remain in the colony either to recuperate from serious wounds or to attend to urgent family affairs. Three Canadian merchants are known to have returned to France at the capitulation, Guillaume-Michel Perrault, Étienne Charest, Louis Charly de Saint-Ange. See Claude Bonneault de Méry, "Les Canadiens en France et aux colonies après la cession (1760-1815)," *Revue de l'Histoire des Colonies françaises*, XVII (1924), pp. 495-550.

[66] Shortt and Doughty, *Documents Relating to the Constitutional History of Canada, 1759-1791*, II, p. 669.

obliged to swear an oath of allegiance to the British monarch.[67] Over them all hung the terrible fear of deportation, not to be dispelled for three generations. Yet the war still raged in Europe. They could still hope that France might win victories elsewhere with which to purchase their liberation. Meanwhile they had to make the best they could of life under the military rule of their conquerors.

---

[67] The imposition of that oath of allegiance raises a vexing legal question. The war was not over, Canada had not been ceded to Great Britain, thus the Canadians remained subjects of His Most Christian Majesty. Amherst therefore forced them to commit an act of treason. Had Canada been returned to France they could only have pleaded that they had taken the oath under duress.

Chapter 8

Aftermath, 1760–1783

In Europe fumbling attempts were being made to end the war before bankruptcy engulfed the belligerents. After the loss of Guadeloupe in May 1759 and the capitulation of Canada the following year, France once again pinned its hopes of forcing the British government to accept reasonable peace terms on its well-conceived but ill-starred plan for the invasion of the British Isles. The Royal Navy's victories at Lagos and Quiberon Bay, coupled with, and to no small degree caused by, the crippling shortage of crews for the French ships, put an end to that.[1] The longer the war lasted, now that Britain had complete command of the seas, the worse the French position would inevitably become. The duc de Choiseul, the French foreign minister, realized that peace was essential but France was not brought so low that she had to accept any terms that Britain cared to dictate. Choiseul was quite willing to relinquish Canada, indeed anxious to do so, but not the Antilles sugar islands, the Guinea slave trade, or the fisheries of the Grand Banks and the Gulf of Saint Lawrence. Those fisheries employed 3,000 French ships and 15,000 men, double the number of British seamen.[2] Pitt, however, was determined to exclude the French

---

[1] See above, p. 194, n. 16.

[2] "See Gaston-Martin, *Nantes au XVIIIe siècle: L'Ère des Négriers* (Paris, 1931), pp. 278–283: Walter L. Dorn, *Competition for Empire, 1740–1763* (Torchbook ed., New York, 1963), p. 373; Paris, Archives affaires étrangères, Série Angleterre, vol. 445, pp. 21–24, Choiseul à de Bussy, Versailles, 4 juillet 1761, ''sans cette condition nous sommes déterminés a continuer la guerre, l'abandon de la pêche étant regardé comme une perte immense et irréparable pour le Royaume, Le Roy ne peut faire cet abandon que lorsque la France ne sera plus absolument en état de faire la guerre.''

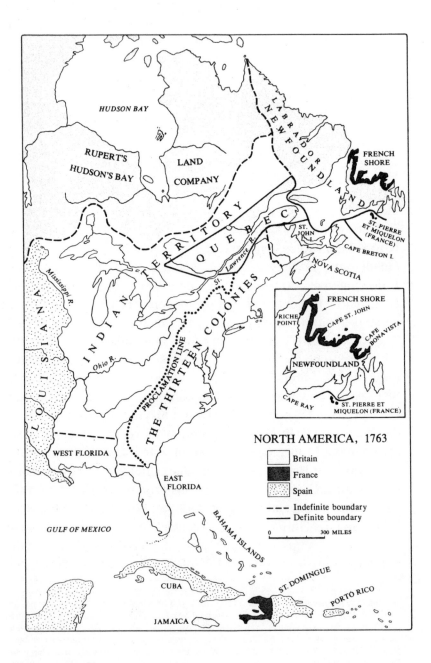

NORTH AMERICA, 1763

Britain

France

Spain

--- Indefinite boundary
— Definite boundary

0   300 MILES

from those fishing grounds. With a fury bordering on paranoia he was bent on crushing France, stripping her of all her colonial possessions and overseas commerce. If that policy led to ruin, he declared, at least the ruin of France would be greater than that of Britain.[3]

To force England to moderate its stand, Choiseul began negotiating in earnest to bring Spain into the war, should the British remain adamant.[4] His Most Catholic Majesty, Charles III, was acutely aware of the threat posed to his American empire by the British conquests in the Caribbean. On August 15, 1761, the Family Compact, an offensive and defensive Franco-Spanish alliance, was signed. When his cabinet colleagues refused to sanction hostilities against Spain, Pitt resigned. Three months later, in January 1762, Spain commenced hostilities. The consequences were disastrous for the Bourbon powers. The Spanish army and navy were far weaker than either government had realized; ships and regiments were found to exist only on paper. In February, Martinique was conquered, then, in May, Russia withdrew from the war, relieving the pressure on Britain's ally, Prussia.

Choiseul now had to seek peace on almost any terms before the situation became hopeless and Pitt regained power. In August, Havana fell to the foe, but Spain proudly and stupidly refused to treat for peace without compensation for her losses. To bring his stubborn ally to the peace table, Choiseul reluctantly agreed that France would cede Louisiana to Spain,[5] being fearful lest the British should seize it, but with the precondition that Spain accede to the British demand that Florida be ceded in exchange for Havana. Choiseul negotiated very shrewdly; he strove to obtain the return of Cape Breton, but had to settle for the retention of

---

[3] Zenab Esmat Rashed, *The Peace of Paris, 1763* (Liverpool, 1951), p. 30.

[4] For a lengthy, critical, and illuminating analysis of Choiseul's policy, written by an official of the Ministry of Foreign Affairs in the year VIII of the revolutionary calendar, see Paris, Archives Affaires étrangères, Mémoires et Documents, Espagne 1748 à 1797. Fonds divers, vol. 189, Analyse des négociations entre la France et les autres Puissances de l'Europe depuis le Traité d'Aix-la-Chapelle, en 1748, Jusqu'à la Révolution 1788.

[5] In July 1760 Charles III had informed the French ambassador that Spain wished to acquire Louisiana. See Arthur S. Aiton, "The Diplomacy of the Louisiana Cession," *American Historical Review*, XXXVI, 4 (July 1931), pp. 701-720; Pierre H. Boule, "Some Eighteenth Century French Views on Louisiana," in John Francis McDermot (ed.), *Frenchmen and French Ways in the Mississippi Valley* (Univ. Illinois Press, 1969).

fishing rights on the French shore of Newfoundland and the islands of St Pierre and Miquelon off the southern tip of Newfoundland. The Windward islands of Guadeloupe, Martinique and Saint-Lucia he also demanded back.[6] To obtain Saint-Lucia, he agreed to cede to Britain the territory to the east of the Mississippi, over which the French had never been able to exercise sovereignty, and the free right of navigation along that river to the Gulf. This cession took no account of the rights of the Indian nations whose lands these were. Ironically, it was they rather than the French who had prevented the Anglo-Americans from seizing the territory long before. When they got wind of it, they angrily declared that the French had no right to cede lands that were not theirs. The war axe quickly passed from tribe to tribe. They were determined not to sit passively by and be stripped of their ancestral territories.[7]

Choiseul had one main idea: to end hostilities, strengthen the Family Compact, which he declared to be a thousand times more valuable than the retention of Canada, rebuild the French and Spanish navies, then renew the war with Britain in five years' time. To Louis XV and his Court, far worse than the loss of colonial territory was the humiliation of such a catastrophic defeat. French pride, honour, *la gloire*, demanded that the shame of it be expunged. Britain, now suffering from a terminal case of hubris, had to be abased and the balance of power in the western world restored. Choiseul declared that he had "only one foreign policy, a fraternal union with Spain; only one policy for war and that is England".[8] Before the ink was dry on the Treaty of Paris, Louis XV ordered the duc de Broglie to have a new survey made of the English coasts, to revise the existing plans for an invasion of England. Choiseul had already set about rebuilding the navy; by 1770 there were 64 ships of the line and 50 frigates in service.

---

[6] On the debate in England whether to retain Canada or Guadeloupe, Guy Frégault, *Canada: The War of the Conquest* (Toronto, 1969), pp. 296–318; Sir Lewis Namier, *England in the Age of the American Revolution* (2nd ed., London, 1961), pp. 273–282; W.L. Grant, "Canada Versus Guadeloupe: An Episode of the Seven Years' War," *American Historical Review*, XVII (1912), pp. 735–743.

[7] See W.J. Eccles, "Sovereignty Association 1500–1783," in *Essays on New France* (Toronto, 1987), pp. 176–181.

[8] Paris. Ministère des Affaires Etrangères, Mémoires et documents, Espagne, vol. 574, f 132. Choiseul à d'Ossun, Paris, 23 fév. 1762.

Major and long overdue reforms were made in the army, particularly in the artillery.[9] As he put it, the policy was decided; the details could be left to the clerks.

In Britain, Lords Bute — who had replaced Pitt — and Newcastle, horrified by the mounting national debt that appeared to signal imminent national bankruptcy,[10] were almost as eager for peace as was Choiseul, despite the clamour of the mercantile hawks who wanted more conquests. The Treaty of Paris was therefore concluded on February 10, 1763.

During the ensuing decade the economic resurgence of France was little short of miraculous. Its overseas trade was soon more prosperous than ever. The Guinea slave trade was regained by the Nantes slavers. With great audacity French seamen and entrepreneurs recaptured their old foreign markets and French industry quickly revived. Choiseul was determined to rebuild the colonial empire and in 1762 he began preparing an expedition to conquer Brazil, but the peace intervened.[11] He then embarked on a massive development of Guiana and Cayenne. Some 9,000 colonists, including over 100 families of Acadians and Canadians, were shipped there in 1763 and 1764. Most of them quickly succumbed, victims of disease and bad management. By 1767 the enterprise had cost more than 14,000 lives and thirty million livres. The end result was some thirty plantations on Cayenne, a few on the mainland, a future penal colony, and a staggering debt.[12]

---

[9] See A. Goodwin (ed.), *The New Cambridge Modern History*, VIII, (Cambridge, 1971), pp. 190-217.

[10] By War's end the debt amounted to £137 million, the interest ran to nearly £5 million, while Crown revenue was not more than £8 million. See Robert J. Chaffin, "The Townshend Acts of 1767," *William and Mary Quarterly* 3rd Series XXVII, 1 (Jan. 1970), p. 91.

[11] G. Lacour-Gayet, *La marine militaire de la France sous le regne de Louis XV* (Paris, 1902), pp. 369-370.

[12] H.I. Priestley, *France Overseas Through the Old Regime: A Study of European Expansion* (New York, 1939), pp. 93-108. Of these colonists, thirty families were Acadian, fifty were from Louisbourg, eleven from Île Saint-Jean, eighteen from Canada. The Canadians were nearly all quondam officers in the Troupes de la Marine. The governor of the colony, Jacau de Fiedmont, was the valiant Canadian gunner captain who, at Quebec after the battle of 13 September, 1759, at the council of war called by the commandant Ramezay, alone voted against the surrender of the city before the ammunition was exhausted. He had the reputation of being honest, brave, and not too bright. The label could, of course, have been attached to the vast majority of the officers in Europe's old regime armies. See Claude Bonnault de Méry, "Les Canadiens en France et aux colonies après la cession (1760-1815)," *Revue de l'histoire des colonies françaises*, XVII (1964), pp. 518-9.

On the mainland of North America the vast French empire was no more. In reality it had been merely a paper empire. The great stretch of territory from the crest of the Appalachians to the Mississippi, and from the Gulf of St Lawrence north of the Great Lakes to the western and Arctic oceans was now blithely assumed to be under British sovereignty. Only Mexico and Louisiana remained apart, the latter territory still administered by French officials. New France had ceased to exist. The Canadians now became British subjects with some of the rights and privileges of Englishmen, and the disabilities of Roman Catholics, including the inability to hold any office under the Crown. When the news was received that Canada had, in fact, been ceded to Great Britain, the British officers were chagrined to see that the great majority of the Canadians could not bring themselves to believe that it had really happened. The Canadians had pinned all their hopes on a return to the French Crown and the removal of their conquerors. Their worst fears had now been realized. Those not wishing to change their allegiance were free to return to France, but for the mass of the people that was out of the question. Only 270 left the colony.[13]

In marked contrast to the Canadian experience and attitude was that of the French planters on Guadeloupe, seized by the British in May 1759. As in Canada during the military regime, when the British took over the administration they did not disturb the local arrangements and they kept the Conseil Supérieur in being. They did introduce representative institutions, and the colonists were allowed to send an agent to London to represent their interests. What was more important, unlike in Canada, there was no influx of British merchants, no exodus of French planters. Moreover, the British kept the island well supplied with merchandise and ships for island produce. The Liverpool slavers brought in 30,000 slaves at lower prices than the Nantes slavers had charged. Prior to the conquest, the island had lacked all these things; few ships

---

[13] The passenger fare charged on British ships for the Atlantic crossing was 15 guineas — 377 livres tournois — five times what the fare had been on French ships. This was considered to be exorbitant by all but the ships' captains, but the British authorities declined to intervene. Hence the option of removing to France, had they so desired, was effectively placed out of reach of most of the Canadians. See Marcel Trudel, Le régime militaire dans le Gouvernement des Trois Rivières, 1760–1764 (Trois Rivières, 1952), p. 166.

had slipped past the Royal Navy. Trade with London and the mainland colonies brought prosperity to the island and within two years it surpassed Martinique in wealth. A number of the colonists found the British regime, with its freer trade and attendant prosperity, more to their liking than the former restrictive rule by French metropolitan officials.[14] They, perhaps, like the Canadians but for the opposite reason and likely not to the same degree, were not overjoyed by the Treaty of Paris as it affected them.

Spain too had its colonial problem. Louisiana had been ceded to Spain by France in November 1762. This had been kept quiet until after the Treaty of Paris was signed. Not until September 1764 did the colonists learn of their fate. If anything, they regarded their forcible transfer of allegiance with less favour than the Canadians did theirs. Thus, when Spain made no immediate move to take over the colony, they began to hope that the cession was not going to take place after all. French ships, rather than Spanish, came to New Orleans and French merchant houses kept the colony supplied with goods for a time but, as in Canada, the French government's refusal to honour the bills of exchange drawn on it left the colonists with little but worthless paper. There were no funds to pay the troops or the officials, and the La Rochelle merchants, owed 320,000 livres for goods supplied in the past, cut off all credit.

Then, in March 1766, the colonists' hopes were shattered when a Spanish Governor, Don Antonio de Ulloa, arrived with a small coterie of officials and 100 soldiers. They were inadequate, in all respects, to cope with the governance of the vast extent of the colony. Thus the French administrators remained in place, faute de mieux, and Ulloa had to accept this surrogate government. A trickle of trade with France kept the colony alive, but barely. Then, in October 1768, a decree of the Spanish government appeared to squelch that last faint hope. By decree, only Spanish ships, sailing from Spanish ports, could trade with the colony. Since no Spanish ships had ever called at New Orleans, the colonists feared that they had been abandoned.

---

[14] See Gaston-Martin, *Histoire de l'Esclavage dans les Colonies françaises* (Paris, 1948), pp. 132–5; Alfred Martineau et L.-Ph. May, *Trois siècles d'histoire antillaise, Martinique et Guadeloupe de 1635 à nos jours* (Paris, 1935), pp. 194–5.

On 29 October, backed by the Canadian-born *commissaire ordonnateur*, Denis-Nicolas Foucault, and the leading colonists, the Superior Council declared Ulloa to be a usurper. He and his retinue were forcibly and ignominiously shipped off to Havana. That act of rebellion successfully accomplished, the members of the Council petitioned Louis XV to repeal the cession of 1762 and restore the colony to French rule.[15] Meanwhile, Anglo-American traders, taking advantage of their right of free navigation on the Mississippi, had stepped into the commercial vacuum and quickly came to dominate the colony's economy.[16]

The reaction in France to these events proved very revealing.[17] Lieutenant General the comte d'Estaing and the comte de Châtelet, French ambassador to the Court of St James's, strongly recommended a daring plan to block any attempt by Britain to seize Louisiana, and at the same time to foment rebellion in her colonies. They proposed that Louisiana be converted into a semi-independent republic, its security guaranteed by France and Spain, enjoying free access to French and Spanish markets, with New Orleans a free port. Thus it would remain as a buffer between the British colonies and Mexico, while sparing either France or Spain the costs of its administration. Beyond that, by granting independence on such favourable terms to Louisiana, the English colonies would be incited to demand the same from Britain, which would surely be refused. That, the French anticipated, would spur the Americans on to take up arms for their independence. Were they to succeed, it was fondly believed that the loss of the major market for Britain's manufactures would deal her economy a crippling blow. The loss of New France would be as nothing compared to Britain's loss of her original American colonies. Moreover, the British would then be saddled, for generations to come, with the expensive and onerous task of de-

---

[15] For a detailed account of the insurrection, see Marc de Villiers du Terrage, *Les dernières années de la Louisiane française* (Paris, 1903).

[16] John G. Clark, *New Orleans 1718–1812. An Economic History* (Baton Rouge, 1970), pp. 159–163.

[17] See the article by Pierre H. Boule, "French Reactions to the Louisiana Revolution of 1768," in John Francis McDermott (ed.), *The French in the Mississippi Valley* (Univ. of Illinois Press, 1965).

fending Canada and Nova Scotia against the constant threat of American aggression.[18]

Choiseul was greatly tempted by the Louisiana scheme but when the Spanish government displayed its determination to crush the revolt, reassert its rule, and incorporate the colony fully into the empire, he drew back. The preservation of the Spanish alliance was too important in his long-range plan for a war of revenge with Britain to allow of any such adventures. In August 1769, Lieutenant General Don Alexandro O'Reilly arrived at New Orleans with 3,000 troops. Swiftly and without opposition he took over the administration. Eleven ringleaders of the revolt were arrested and, after a summary trial, five were executed.[19]

In Canada no such rebellion against foreign domination occurred, and the reasons are not hard to find. Unlike in Louisiana, the Canadian dominant class had been eliminated, replaced by British administrators, backed up by some fifteen hundred regular troops. Moreover, the mass of the Canadians had lost their respect for the seigneurs and ex-officers in the colonial regular troops who had lost the war and delivered the people into servitude, but of whom many were now actively collaborating with the conquerors, in the hopes of regaining their dominant position in society.[20] Without arms, without leadership and support from outside, there was no possibility of a resistance movement emerging to stage a general uprising and throw off the British yoke.[21]

---

[18] On this aspect of French foreign policy see W.J. Eccles, "The French Alliance and the American Victory," in *The World Turned Upside Down: The American Victory in the War of Independence* (Westport Connecticut, 1988), pp. 147–163; Lawrence Henry Gipson, *The Coming of the Revolution 1763–1775* (New York, 1954), p. 215: Marcel Trudel, *Louis XVI, le congrès américain et le Canada*, pp. 1–12.

[19] David Ker Texada, *Alejandro O'Reilly and the New Orleans Rebels* (Lafayette, Louisiana, 1970).

[20] See Michael Brunet, *Les Canadiens après la Conquete, 1759–1775* (Québec, 1969), pp. 111–140.

[21] A French engineering officer who had served in Canada with the *troupes de terre* under Montcalm, in advocating in 1778 the reconquest of the colony, stated that the Canadians would rise in support of a French invasion to liberate the colony only if they were convinced it would succeed; thus a force at least half as large again as the British garrison would be required. Significantly, he suggested that, once retaken, Canada should be held by France as a gage to prevent the Americans making a separate peace or one having terms prejudicial to France; or it could be exchanged with the Americans for something of greater value. Vincennes, Service historique de l'armée, Génie, Article 14, Liasse 1.

Meanwhile the British suddenly found that their shattering victory and its attendant vast overseas territorial gains had brought in their wake problems that were beyond the capacity of their political leaders to resolve. Under Pitt, Britain had had a simple, clear-cut policy for war, the destruction of the French navy, the French colonial empire, and the capture of France's overseas markets. With the advent of peace Britain had no viable policy; it lurched from one crisis to another. The magnitude of the national debt dictated retrenchment in government spending. The easiest place to reduce expenditures was the Navy, thus new ships were not laid down, old ones were inadequately maintained, stocks of masts, spars, and naval stores were not replenished; this at a time when France and Spain were rapidly rebuilding their navies.[22]

The vexing problems in Britain's recently acquired territories, Bengal, Canada, and particularly in its old American colonies, appeared insuperable and would have taxed the genius of political giants, but the politicians of the day were incompetent, mediocrities at best. Ministers and ministries changed in rapid succession, and the opposition factions would go to any length to bring down the government of the day.[23]

In America, in an honest but vain attempt to curb the abuses of the hordes of Anglo-American traders, land speculators, and would-be settlers who, in defiance of Royal directives, were pouring onto the lands of the Indian nations between the Appalachians and the Mississippi, the British government issued the Royal Proclamation of 1763. It sought to avert the outbreak of hostilities between the Indians and the Americans bent on driving them off their lands by any means. Unfortunately, it came too late. The Indian nations, outraged beyond endurance, struck out against their despoilers.[24] Once again, to the disgust of the British,

---

[22] A.T. Mahan, *The Influence of Seapower upon History* (New York, 1957), pp. 296–301; R.G. Albion, *Forests and Seapower* (Cambridge, Mass., 1926), pp. 274–315.

[23] Vincent T. Harlow, *The Founding of the Second British Empire*, Vol. I *Discovery and Revolution* (London, 1952), pp. 146–162; Sir Lewis Namier, *England in the Age of the American Revolution*, 2nd. ed. (London, 1961), pp. 171–228.

[24] This episode in American history has not received the attention it deserves by historians. There have been two studies to date, both dated, both shoddy, both prize examples of the enduring American Whig version of history: Francis Parkman, *The Conspiracy of Pontiac* (Boston, 1851); Howard H. Peckham, *Pontiac and the Indian Uprising* (Chicago, 1947). The role of Pontiac was

the American colonists who were mainly responsible for the hostilities proved unwilling and incapable of defending their frontier settlements. Some 2,000 of them and 400 British troops were slaughtered; the survivors fled back over the mountains. British-held forts were attacked and several taken, supply convoys were captured. The Indian nations, lacking the logistical support provided in previous wars by the French, could not sustain a lengthy campaign. British regular troops, employing bacteriological warfare on the direct orders of the commander in chief, Jeffery Amherst, finally quelled the hostile nations, and the British taxpayer had to foot the bill.[25]

The British government's stubborn determination to make the Americans pay their fair share for their own defense enraged the colonials.[26] Moreover, an influential group of land speculators, including such notables as George Washington, his kinsmen the Lees, Benjamin Franklin, Thomas Walker, William Crawford, and Phineas Lyman, had long eyed the lands of the Ohio Valley. Washington, Walker, and Crawford had even secretly marked out the lands they intended to claim.[27] The Royal Proclamation, with its "line" beyond which settlement was forbidden, was not to their liking, but Washington regarded it as merely a temporary expedient. The Quebec Act of 1774 they regarded very differently. It, among other things, placed the lands between the Ohio River and the Great Lakes under the jurisdiction of the Governor and Council at Quebec. The land speculators reacted like a dog whose bone had been snatched away before he could begin to chew on it.

A year later, in April, came the first clash of arms between British troops and American colonials at Lexington and Concord.

not understood by Parkman, the event was no more a conspiracy than was British resistance to the American invasion of Quebec in 1775. The word "Uprising" in Peckham's title is singularly inappropriate, since it implies a revolt against legally established authority. The French had never dared to assert their sovereignty to the nations themselves, only to claim it in their dealings with the British. Thus the French could not have ceded a mirage sovereignty to Great Britain in 1763. In fact the Indian nations had merely taken up arms in self-defense to repel the invasion of their lands by the Americans.

[25] On the British use of bacteriological warfare see Eccles, *Essays on New France*, pp. 178–9; Francis Jennings, *Empire of Fortune* (New York, London, 1988), pp. 447–8.

[26] Robert J. Chaffin, "The Townshend Acts of 1767," *The William and Mary Quarterly*, Third Series, Vol. xxvii, No. 1, Jan. 1970, pp. 90–121.

[27] Jack M. Sosin, *Whitehall and the Wilderness* (Univ. Nebraska Press, 1961), p. 107.

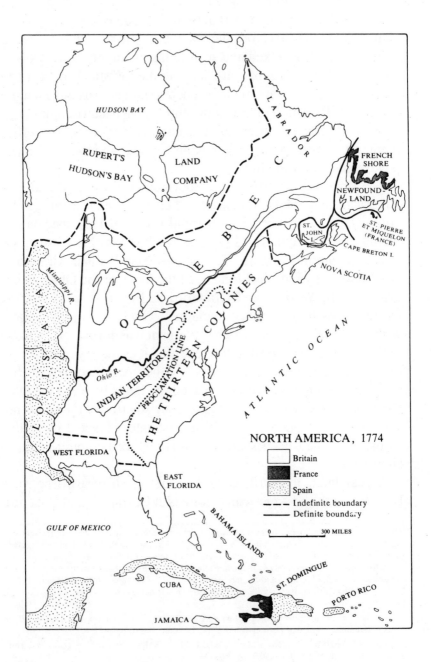

NORTH AMERICA, 1774

Britain
France
Spain
-- -- -- Indefinite boundary
——— Definite boundary

0   300 MILES

A month later, a rebel force surprised the weak British garrison at Fort Ticonderoga and took it. Then, in September, an American army invaded Quebec and, in mid-November, occupied Montreal. The Governor, Guy Carleton, escaped to Quebec, where he mustered a force of some 3,600 British regulars and militia. Another American army, or what was left of it after disease and desertion had taken their toll, under the command of Benedict Arnold, appeared at Lévis, across the river from Quebec, there to be joined by General Richard Montgomery's motley force, come from Montreal. Together they numbered about 1,000 untrained, ill-disciplined men.

Montgomery submitted a bombastic demand to Carleton that he surrender the city. Carleton treated the missive with contempt. The Americans made one attempt to take the city by assault; it failed miserably, cost Montgomery his life, and merely served to demonstrate their military ineptitude. Carleton had only to sit tight and wait whilst the American forces wasted away during the long winter. As soon as the St Lawrence was free of ice he could expect a British fleet with reinforcements to appear. The vanguard arrived on 6 May, whereupon the smallpox-ridden, panic-stricken, American army fled back by the centuries-old Lake Champlain invasion route.[28]

In France, the government was studying events in America with keen interest. Choiseul had been dismissed from office in 1770, but the foreign policy he had drafted was continued. The Family Compact with Spain was maintained, continental entanglements were avoided, and Britain was kept isolated. That last was by no means a difficult task. By trampling on the maritime rights of the neutral powers in the past war, interfering in continental affairs that were not their concern, and their habitual arrogance, the British had no allies, not a friend in the world. Their old allies, Austria and Prussia, had both been alienated, as had Russia, Holland, and Sweden.

In 1774, Louis XV died unexpectedly. His successor, the well-meaning but overly indulgent Louis XVI, appointed Charles Gravier comte de Vergennes to the office of minister of foreign

---

[28] The best study to date of the American invasion of Canada is Robert McConnell Hatch, *Thrust for Canada. The American Attempt on Quebec in 1775–1776* (Boston, 1979).

affairs. Vergennes, who had been ambassador to the Grande Porte (Turkey) and to Sweden, was a firm believer in Choiseul's policy: Britain was the enemy that had to be humbled and, it was becoming apparent, just as Choiseul had predicted, America might well provide the means.

In December 1774, some Americans who happened to be in London had approached a member of the French embassy's staff and pleaded for aid, should the colonies take up arms against the mother country. Vergennes declined to bite, but the following year, in September, he took the first step on a slippery slope. He sent a special agent, M. Archard Bonvouloir, to Philadelphia, to encourage the colonists to press on. Bonvouloir was also instructed to tell the American insurgents that their ships could make use of French ports. Subsequently, despite the objections of the Controller General of finance, who feared national bankruptcy, Louis XVI acquiesced in an appropriation of a million livres to furnish arms to the American rebels. To avoid the British government's using this as pretext to declare war, for which France was not yet prepared, a subterfuge was used. A private company, Roderique Hortalez, was established, to ship arms and supplies to the Americans. Pierre-Augustin Caron de Beaumarchais, author of the opera *The Barber of Seville*, who had performed diplomatic chores for the government from time to time, was appointed the director of the Company. Spain, at Vergenne's request, added another million livres to the Company's funds. It was this aid that kept Washington's forces in the field. The following year, France and Spain provided a further million livres each and the belligerent status of the United States was recognized.

In June 1777, an army commanded by General John Burgoyne, 7,400 strong, headed south from the St Lawrence to Lake Champlain. The intention was to gain command of the Hudson River and cut New England off from New York. By the time Burgoyne reached the Hudson, his army had been reduced to 4,812. He there found himself cut off and surrounded by 21,000 American provincial troops and militia. Unable to advance or retreat, Burgoyne proposed to General Horatio Gates a Convention whereby his troops would lay down their arms, be granted the honours of war, then return to England to serve no more in America. The alternative was that the British army would fight its way through the American lines and back to Canada. Faced with Burgoyne's proposal, or a bloodbath, Gates accepted the terms. Then, as soon as the British troops were disarmed, the Americans refused to honour the Convention of Saratoga. The troops were marched off to a prison camp on orders of the Continental Congress.[29]

Following the spurious American victory at Saratoga, Vergennes became extremely fearful that Britain would offer the Americans terms that they would be glad to accept; namely, de facto independence with merely nominal sovereignty resting with the British Crown—ironically the status that Canada enjoys today —on condition that the Americans join with the British in a war against France and Spain to strip them of their American colonies. He became convinced that war with Britain was now inevitable, hence it would be far better to have it with the Americans as allies rather than foes. His intelligence agents reported from London that Parliament was divided; the Chatham faction wanted to grant acceptable terms to the Americans, then wage a combined war on the Bourbon powers. Lord North wanted to crush the American rebellion first, then wage war with France and Spain. Vergennes admitted to his ambassador at Madrid that he was getting nowhere in his discussions with the American Commissioners and was convinced that the only way to prevent an Anglo-American reconciliation and alliance against France and Spain was a Franco-American alliance, with a French guarantee of American independence.[30] Therefore, Louis XVI was persuaded to sign,

---

[29] As one American historian cynically put it: "Congress was neither honourable nor foolish enough to keep it." Charles Royster, *A Revolutionary People at War* (New York & London) 1979, p. 176. This was not the first time, nor would it be the last, that the Americans sacrificed honour on the altar of expediency. See Hatch, *Thrust for Canada*, pp. 188–208.

[30] Paris, Min. Aff. Étrangères, Série Espagne, vol. 588, ff 22–36, Lu au Roi le 7 Janvier 1778 et envoyé en Espagne le lendemain; ff 17–21, Vergennes à M. le Cte. de Montmorin, No. 13, Versailles le 8 janvier 1778; ff 77–79, Vergennes à M. le Cte de Montmorin, lettre sécrete. No. 15, Versailles le 16 janvier 1778; ff 372–3, Vergennes à Montmorin, Versailles le 10 mars 1778; ff 375–7, Vergennes à Montmorin, Versailles le 10 mars 1778; f 389, Vergennes à Montmorin, Versailles le 17 mars 1778. But see Jonathan R. Dull, *A Diplomatic History of the American Revolution* (New Haven & London, 1985), pp. 89–96, where it is argued that it was recent American defeats, their manifest military weakness, that convinced Vergennes that the independence of the United States of America could not be achieved without open French military support. Vergenne's correspondence with the French ambassador at Madrid demonstrates clearly that the argument is false.

on 6 February 1778, two treaties with the American Continental Congress: the Treaty of Amity and Commerce, and the Treaty of Alliance. The latter treaty stated that its purpose was to maintain the independence of the United States. It went on to state that, were the Americans to conquer British territory to the north, or the Bermudas, they should retain it. Most significantly, Article 6 declared that France renounced forever the Bermudas and those parts of North America claimed by France prior to 1763. This last was intended to allay American fears of a renewed French presence on their northern border, which might well have driven them back into the arms of Britain.[31] The treaty also stated categorically that neither party would treat for a truce, or for peace, with Great Britain without first obtaining the other's formal consent.

The French had no desire to reconquer Canada, nor to see the Americans garner it. Their main aim all along was the destruction of the British Empire. Their immediate intention was that Canada and Nova Scotia should remain under the British Crown when the United States gained their independence. Then the British and Americans would be constantly at each other's throats; the British forced to maintain a large military establishment in Canada, at great expense, to keep the Americans in check. The maintenance of this balance of North American power would thus reduce Britain's strength elsewhere, and also the possibility of an American assault on Louisiana. Once again then, New France, or rather its shade, would play its old fortress role of tying down large British forces in America, but this time at no cost to France and at a very heavy cost to Britain. It would also, the French hoped, render the Americans more reliant on them for future support, move them out of the British economic orbit and into that of France. Spain also wanted Great Britain to retain Canada and Acadia, since that would keep the British and the Americans at loggerheads.[32] The Spaniards then feared the prospect of an independent United States more than they did Great Britain, and as events were to prove, with cause.

---

[31] Trudel, Louis XVI, *Le congrès américain et le Canada*, pp. 113–4.

[32] Ministère des affaires étrangères, Correspondance politique, Série Espagne, vol. 591, ff 83–88, Montmorin à Vergennes, À l'Escurial ce 19 oct. 1778 — reçue le 31.

In 1778, the marquis de Lafayette proposed an expedition to conquer Canada, to compensate for recent American reverses, claiming that, were six to ten thousand French troops and a naval squadron to support the American army, it would then merely be a matter of marching. The Canadians, he maintained, once they saw the white uniforms of France, would flock to the French colours to drive out their British oppressors.[33] He obviously was unaware that the comte d'Estaing, Admiral of the French fleet recently arrived at Delaware Bay with 12 ships of the line and four frigates, had implicit instructions from Vergennes not to lend more than token support to an American attempt to conquer Canada. Nor would France provide troops for the venture. When the proposal was put to the Continental Congress, its members showed a marked lack of enthusiasm. Washington and his staff opined that another attempt to take Canada should not be undertaken before the British armies had been driven off the continent.

The truth was, the Americans feared that, were a French army and navy to reconquer Canada then, despite the terms of the Franco-American Alliance, France would retain it. The Americans dreaded that, and Vergennes had no desire whatsoever to see the Americans dominate North America, and thereby possibly upset the delicate balance of power in Europe, which was, after all, his main concern. Moreover, it was plain that the Canadians would not aid an American invasion. They had seen one American army flee in total disarray in 1776, and the treatment they had received at the hands of the Americans during their brief occupation of the province had done nothing to make them desire its recurrence. When forced to choose between two evils, British or American domination, they were certain, reluctantly to choose the former.

In June 1778, hostilities began between Great Britain and France. Spain declared war the following year. Russia, Denmark, and Sweden formed the League of Armed Neutrality; a blunt warning to Britain not to trample on their maritime rights as it had done in the past. The Dutch, who were supplying the Americans from their West Indies islands, were a greater menace to Britain as a neutral power than they could be as belligerents, thus,

---

[33] Trudel, op. cit., pp. 149–199.

in December 1780, the Royal Navy began attacking their ships. The war in America then escalated into a global conflict and the American theatre, so far as the British were concerned, became little more than a sideshow. The Mediterranean, the Caribbean, India, and the threat of a Franco-Spanish invasion of England loomed far larger.

By 1780, the rebel American cause appeared doomed, as Washington's armies suffered one crushing defeat after another. His southern army was destroyed, his northern army reduced to some 10,500 men, with a desertion rate of 20-25%, whilst Generals Clinton and Cornwallis had 30,000 British and German regulars in the field. Only French financial aid and supplies kept the American forces active; loans and subsidies amounted to forty-eight million livres by 1782, plus considerably more for naval support. In 1781, Vergennes noted that the American war had cost France over two hundred million livres a year.[34] At the same time, the American Congress could not bring itself to levy a national tax to finance the war. Why, the delegates of Rhode Island and then of Virginia demanded, should they submit to be taxed by Congress when they had all risen in revolt against the attempts of the English Parliament to levy taxes on them? Some of the New York delegates were even more vociferous, declaring that France was trying to get them out of England's clutches only to subject them to the revolting yoke of a Virginia farmer.[35]

In May 1780, the first detachment of a proposed 8,000 man expeditionary force, 5,500 in all, under the command of the vicomte de Rochambeau, sailed for America. As usual, in the northern American latitudes, the French convoy baffled the Royal Navy and arrived unscathed at Newport, Rhode Island.[36] Fortu-

---

[34] Ministère des affaires étrangères, Correspondance politique, Série Etats-Unis, vol. 22, f 211, Vergennes à La Luzerne, Versailles, 7 sept. 1781.

[35] ibid., vol. 18, ff 8–12, Le Luzerne à Vergennes, Phil. 1 août 1781 reçu le 13 8bre; ibid., vol. 22, ff 368-9, Vergennes à La Luzerne, Versailles le 14 8bre 1782; ibid., f (manque) La Luzerne à Vergennes, Phil. 10 7bre 1782 reçu le 26 9bre; ibid., f 407, La Luzerne à Vergennes, Phil., no date, but the vote in the Rhode Island Assembly which rejected the motion to agree to a 5% tax on imports, prizes, and their cargoes, was taken on 1 nov. 1782; ibid., ff 581-2, Vergennes à La Luzerne, Versailles le 21 xbre 1752; ibid., vol. 23, ff 62-6, La Luzerne à Mr Morris, Philad. 18 janvier 1783; ibid., f 218, La Luzerne à Vergennes, 5 mars 1783 — reçu le 18 mai; ibid., vol. 22, ff 193-5, La Luzerne à Vergennes, Philadelphie 5 sept. 1783 — reçu le 6 9bre.

[36] On the relative merits of the French and British navies, see A. Goodwin (ed.), The New Cambridge Modern History VIII The American and French Revolutions 1763-93 (Cambridge, 1981), pp. 174-90.

nately for the American cause, the British fleet failed to attack before the French army was securedly ensconced, their gun batteries in place, General Clinton later wailed that, had the enemy been attacked promptly, the failing, flickering embers of the Revolution could have been stamped out, there and then.[37]

Rochambeau and his army were there because Vergennes and the comte de Floridablanca, the Spanish foreign minister, were convinced that American independence could not be achieved without the direct military intervention of France and Spain. Some members of the French Council of State did not think that the war in America should be continued; to them the game did not appear to be worth the candle; they advised that negotiations for peace with Great Britain be undertaken. Vergennes refused to give way. He, indeed, wanted an honourable peace, but it had to include the independence of the United States of America: he would settle for nothing less.

Rochambeau's troops received a frosty welcome from the Americans, as always suspicious and hostile towards Papists and subjects of a crowned monarch: it was bred in the bone. In consequence, relations between the officers of the two armies deteriorated rapidly. The French were appalled by the unmilitary bearing of the American troops, their slovenliness, their manifest lack of training and discipline. The American militia, the French quickly concluded, were worthless, more of a logistical encumbrance than a military asset.[38] They were also upset by the gouging of the local merchants, who charged outrageous prices for anything that they had to sell. Ironically, a British army just some fifteen years previous, sent to protect the subjects of the British Crown against the French, the Canadians, and the Indian nations, had had the same experience.[39]

---

[37] William B. Wilcox (ed.), *The American Rebellion, Sir Henry Clinton's Narrative of his Campaigns, 1775–1782, with an appendix of original documents* (New Haven, 1954), pp. 207–8.

[38] Howard C. Rice, Jr. and Anne S.K. Brown (eds. and translators), *The American Campaigns of Rochambeau's Army 1780, 1781, 1782, 1783* (Princetown NJ, Providence RI, 1972), Vol. I, pp. 33, 78, 152. See also Vincennes, Service historique de l'armée, Série A4, carton 48 ff, pp. 394 ff. Letter of a French officer serving with the American army. Au camp de le Grand Caroline du Nord le 21 oct. 1780; *ibid.*, f 287, Rochambeau à La Luzerne, New Port, 4 août 1780; *ibid.*, f 167, Rochambeau à Washington, New Port 3 7bre 1780.

[39] Sylvester K. Stevens and Donald H. Kent (eds.), *The Papers of Col. Henry Bouquet*, Series 21631 & 21632 (Harrisburg, 1941), passim.

Upon taking quick stock of the sitution, Rochambeau began to fear that the Americans were about to throw in the towel. Five days after he arrived, he sent his son off to France in a fast frigate, bearing an urgent appeal for troop reinforcements, ships and money, since the Americans could provide nothing and so far had proven that they were not to be depended on. He, like Vergennes and Floridablanca, must have been forced to conclude that if the enemy were to be defeated — for that was his responsibility — then the French army and navy would have to do it.[40] A few months later, in January 1781, the armies of New Jersey and Pennsylvania mutinied. These mutinies, given the overall situation, were far more serious than the endemic mutinies of the past. They gave Rochambeau and his officers pause.

Then, suddenly, everything changed. A tactical opportunity presented itself and the French, taking a reckless gamble, seized on it. In March, Admiral le comte de Grasse sailed for the West Indies with twenty ships of the line, to support the Spaniards against British assaults on their respective possessions. It was also intended that assaults should be made on Jamaica and Florida. De Grasse's orders were very flexible. He was given a free hand to take his forces to mainland America, if the circumstances appeared propitious and the Spanish commander in the Caribbean theatre concurred. There was a revealing codicil to those instructions: were the American military forces to disintegrate and the French army then be left alone to face the might of the British armies, de Grasse had to be prepared to snatch Rochambeau's troops away to safety to the West Indies.[41]

Meanwhile, the chevalier de La Luzerne, French minister plenipotentiary to the Continental Congress, urged Barras, commander of the French naval squadron at Newport, to take his ships and Rochambeau's army to support the Americans in the south before Cornwallis crushed them, as he had those in Georgia and the Carolinas. La Luzerne feared that some of the demoral-

---

[40] Piers Mackesy, *The War for America 1775–1783* (London, 1964), p. 387; Henri Doniol (ed.), *Histoire de la participation de la France à l'établissement des Etats-Unis d'Amérique: Correspondance diplomatique et documents* (Paris, 1886–99), Vol. IV, pp. 549–550.

[41] Mackesy, op. cit., pp. 384–7; Dull, *A Diplomatic History of the American Revolution*, pp. 118–9.

ized American leaders were prepared to enter into peace negotiations with Great Britain, hoping to save their necks from the rope and to retain possession of the territory they still controlled.[42]

Rochambeau had been instructed by the Council of State to merge his army with that of the Americans under Washington's command. On 6 May, Rochambeau's son arrived back from France with the disappointing news that no more troops would be sent to Newport, but he did bring six million livres for the American army's long overdue pay, and word that the French forces in the West Indies would cooperate in the forthcoming offensive. The French government was convinced that a hard blow had to be struck at the British before it was too late. Washington was eager to launch an assault on New York, claiming that to march the armies south would result in a heavy loss of men to disease, and that was something he could not afford. Rochambeau was of the opinion that a combined operation with de Grasse's fleet against Cornwallis at the Chesapeake offered the best opportunity for a victory. His maxim was the eminently sound one that the conquest of towns and countryside would not force the enemy to give up, the destruction of his armies would.

In June, Rochambeau received word from de Grasse that he hoped to be off the American coast by mid-July. Washington and Rochambeau and their staffs surveyed the British fortifications at New York, and concluded that they were too strong to warrant attempting an assault. The American cause could not afford another costly defeat. On 15 August, Rochambeau received confirmation that de Grasse expected to be at the Chesapeake shortly, with some 25 ships of the line, 3,200 troops, and 1,200,000 badly needed livres. De Grasse warned, however, that he had to return to the Caribbean by mid-October to rejoin the Spanish forces. Meanwhile, he had taken a dangerous gamble by ordering the annual convoy of Antilles produce to remain in port, placing it at risk to an attack by Rodney's fleet. This was something that

---

[42] Mackesy, op. cit., pp. 413–4; Jonathan R. Dull, *The French Navy and American Independence* (Princetown, 1975), pp. 238–246; Ministère des affaires étrangères, Correspondance politique, Série États-Unis, vol. 18, f 147, La Luzerne à Vergennes, Phil. 25 août 1781 reçu le 8 8bre; *ibid.*, f. 224, id à id, Phil. 8 7bre 1781; ibid., f 227, La Luzerne à Vergennes, Phil. 8 7bre 1781.

no British admiral would have dared to do, hence the British commanders never dreamed that de Grasse would.[43]

Washington grudgingly gave way to Rochambeau and agreed that the allied armies would march south to Virginia. From this point on, the French were completely in command of the campaign.[44] On 19 August, the French army set off from Phillipsburg on the Hudson. It had tarried long enough near New York to persuade Clinton that an assault on Staten Island was impending, hence he could not spare any of his troops to support Cornwallis; not, that is, until it was too late. The French artillery, the great siege train, was transported by Barras's ships along with some of the troops. By 26 September, the French army was encamped at Williamsburg where Lafayette, with a small motley force, awaited them.

A few miles away, at Yorktown, Cornwallis's troops were digging entrenchments in the soft earth and constructing redoubts, whilst waiting for the New York fleet to bring reinforcements and block the bay to any French ships that might venture south from Newport. Were those British ships to have been in place, Cornwallis and his army would have had nothing to fear. Cornwallis could then have transported his army by sea, or marched it north to New York, or south to Charleston.

As events turned out, Admiral Thomas Graves, with 19 ships of the line and one of 50 guns, on arrival at the mouth of the Chesapeake, found himself facing not just Barras's squadron but also the entire French West Indies fleet: 24 ships of the line, 1,800 guns, better and heavier ones, against his 1,400. The ensuing battle on 5 September was, in one sense, a draw. Neither fleet was able to destroy the other; both were badly mauled, but the

---

[43] Mackesy, op. cit., p. 419; Vincennes, Service historique de l'armée, Série A4, carton 48, f 178, Idées mises sous les yeux de Son Excellence le général Washington par M. le Comte de Rochambeau et le chevalier de Ternay. Réponses du général Washington, 22 7bre 1780; Ministère des affaires étrangères, Correspondance politique, Série États-Unis, vol. 19, ff 6 ff. La Luzerne à Vergennes, Phil. 2 oct. 1781 reçu le 18 9bre.

[44] On this fine point the journal of Second Lieutenant Jean-Baptiste-Antoine de Verger is particularly revealing. See Rice & Brown, *The American Campaigns of Rochambeau's Army.* See also Vincennes. Service historique de l'armée. Série A4, carton 49a, ff 204–207. Le siège de Yorktown 19 8bre 1781; Ministère des affaires étrangères. Correspondance politique. Série États Unis, vol. 18, ff 89–92. Journal des opérations du corps français commandé par M. le Comte de Rochambeau depuis le 15 aout 1781; *ibid.*, vol. 19, ff 6 ff, La Luzerne à Vergennes, Philadelphie, 2 oct. 1781, reçu le 18 9bre.

French remained in control of the bay. The British were unable to renew the engagement, and had to retire to New York to refit. The French had, in fact, won the day. The Royal Navy could now do nothing for Cornwallis, the French fleet everything for Rochambeau and Washington. Cornwallis was trapped, with just over 6,000 rank and file, including four Loyalist regiments. Opposing him were 7,800 French, 5,800 American Continentals, and 3,000 Virginia militia, fit only for digging entrenchments.

On 7 September, seven of Barras's ships sailed up the James River and landed the guns and supplies at Trebell's Landing, a few miles from Williamsburg. By the 28th, the allies had advanced from that unimposing town, driven the British out of their forward posts, and established themselves in front of the British lines. From this point on, the siege was directed by the French corp of engineers, an elite unit, employing eighteenth-century textbook military tactics. Neither Washington nor any other American officer had had any training for, or experience with, this type of set-piece warfare. The only engineers the American army had were French officers, seconded to it. The work thus proceeded in methodical fashion: first the artillery park was established, then the first parallel of entrenchments and gun emplacements were dug and the batteries sited; cannons, mortars, howitzers. Two British redoubts were stormed, then the second parallel was dug, 300 paces closer to the British entrenchments. The French siege train then, at short range, steadily, night and day, pounded the British position to pieces.

Cornwallis, his situation utterly hopeless, his army reduced to 3,273 men fit for duty, on 17 October offered to capitulate. It clearly made no sense whatsoever to go on. Two days later, the Articles of Capitulation were signed. The British army marched out and laid down its arms. This crucial and decisive Franco-American victory — certainly one of the more momentous in the history of western civilization — had been achieved by incredible tactical timing. The French fleets at Newport and the West Indies, some 2,000 kilometres apart, arriving together off the Chesapeake, ahead of the Royal Navy, and just as the French and American armies reached Williamsburg.

The victory won, the French officers entertained their British

and Hessian comrades in arms. As Lieutenant le comte de Cler-
mont-Crèvecoeur put it in his journal, "The American officers,
on seeing this, were outraged that the French showed a marked
preference for the company of their erstwhile foes."[45] They were
undoubtedly irked even more when they learned that Cornwallis,
upon finding himself with insufficient funds to pay his troops,
appealed to the French colonels, who pooled their resources and
loaned him 300,000 livres. Some months later, when Rochambeau's army camped near Peekskill on the Hudson and built huts
for themselves, the local farmers demanded an exorbitant sum
for damages they claimed had been done to their fields and fences.
The local sheriff asked to speak to Rochambeau, clapped his hand
on the General's shoulder, and declared him to be under arrest.
Since the claim for damages had not been settled, he declared,
the General would have to be lodged in gaol until it was. General
Washington had to send a squad of dragoons to put an end to that
nonsense. Rochambeau dismissed the incident, but he must have
wondered, what next?[46]

After Yorktown, the Americans pressed Rochambeau to join
his army with theirs in an assault on Canada. He demurred,
stating that he would first have to have the authorization of the
Conseil d'État. Before leaving France, he had been instructed
that on no account should he aid the Americans in their intended
conquest of Canada.[47] Congress then had to abandon the project,
for Washington's troops were no match for the 7,000 odd British
regulars stationed in Quebec to guard against just such an even-

---

[45] Rice & Brown, The American Campaigns of Rochambeau's Army, Vol. I, p. 64. See also
ibid, pp. 150–1. Verger's journal.

[46] Ibid., p. 167.

[47] Trudel, Louis XVI, Le congrès américain et le Canada, pp. 149–155. Yet, some in the French
camp still dreamed of evicting the British from North America. The comte d'Estaing, Admiral,
in November 1782, submitted to the Minister of War a plan for the ensuing year's campaigns:
The French and Spanish forces were to be massed for an assault on Gibraltar to delude the British.
Meanwhile, the French and Spanish fleets were to combine their forces for an assault on Jamaica.
That island taken, the Bourbon fleets would sail north, assail and capture Halifax, Newfoundland,
Île Saint-Jean. All that somehow miraculously accomplished, Spain would then retain the Bourbon
conquests since Spain had no treaty with the Americans, as did France, which precluded her from
regaining her old colonies. It was also expected that Washington's army would conquer Canada.
As a prerequisite to this scheme, Spain would be obliged to share the Grand Banks fisheries with
France: presumably, Britain and the United States would be excluded from the Banks. One can
speculate that if this memoir were brought to the attention of Vergennes he quickly filed it in his
wastepaper basket. See Vincennes. Service historique de l'armée. SérieA 4, carton 49ª, ff 274–
325. Mémoire en forme de Plan de la Campagne en Amérique en 1783. Du 28 novembre 1782.

tuality. What the Americans could not gain by force of arms, they were soon to attempt to acquire by guile.

The situation world-wide in 1782 was that the British still had 30,000 troops in America, held Quebec, Nova Scotia, New York, Charleston, Savannah, and St Augustine; de Grasse's fleet had been shattered by Admiral Rodney in the battle of the Saints off Guadeloupe in April, and de Grasse taken prisoner. The American forces were in poor shape and France teetered on the brink of bankruptcy. The British taxpayers, however, had had enough. The national debt had climbed to unthinkable heights, the war had lasted seven years and nothing appeared to have been achieved. Minorca, its garrison decimated by scurvy, had been forced to surrender, West Florida and Tobago had been lost, Fort Prince of Wales and York Factory in Hudson Bay had been destroyed by the comte de La Pérouse's expedition, and what was most menacing was the combined French and Spanish fleet cruising in the Channel with 15,000 troops assembled ready to be taken on board. Thus, when a resolution was introduced in the House of Commons on 4 March declaring that all who sought to continue to prosecute the war against the American colonies should be regarded as enemies of their country, it passed. The opposition then succeeded in forcing Lord North's government to resign. The Rockingham faction acceded to power, determined to end the war in America and concentrate the country's resources against the European foes who, for the first time since 1588, posed a serious threat of invasion.[48]

The new government, with the devious Earl of Shelburne serving as secretary of state for home, colonial, and Irish affairs, made contact with the American commissioners in Paris, using a wealthy British merchant, Richard Oswald, as emissary. The commissioners agreed to enter into negotiations for a separate peace treaty, this despite the fact that their official instructions and the Treaty of Alliance specifically forbade them to do any such thing. In addition to Britain's recognition of the independence of the United States of America, they demanded that they be granted the access to the Newfoundland fisheries that they had

---

[48] Mackesy, *The War for America*, pp. 460–70.

previously enjoyed as British subjects; similarly they expected to be granted access to the British West Indies markets. It was their territorial demands that were startling; they demanded that Britain cede Canada to them—that is, the Provinces of Quebec and Nova Scotia as then constituted—plus the territory south of the Ohio between the Appalachians and the Mississippi, with the right of free navigation on that river. Benjamin Franklin was particularly insistent on the cession of Canada, declaring that it was the only way there could be a reconciliation of England and America. The cession would, he claimed, constitute to a degree, reparations for the injuries inflicted on the Americans by British aggression. Without the cession of Canada, relations between America and Britain would remain soured, leading to endless acts of hostility and the reforging of the French alliance. In short, the Americans were determined to have Canada, better then for Britain to relinquish it graciously rather than wait for it eventually to be taken by force.[49]

Coming from delegates of a divided people, who could never have hoped to achieve independence by their own unaided military efforts, and were to receive it only as the result of a brilliant French military victory, to make such demands was, to say the least, extraordinary. That they were extraordinary men goes without saying, but that they could seriously expect Britain to accede to such outrageous demands, boggles the mind. The Americans had no viable claims to any territory beyond that which they had held in 1750, yet here they were demanding that half the continent be handed over to them.

Shelburne, if not the British people, who were not consulted at this stage, was perfectly willing to recognize the independence of Britain's American colonies. He had two aims: to drive a wedge between France and the United States and to break up their alliance. He also wanted a reconciliation with the Americans for purely economic reasons. The American market, present and potential, for cheap British goods was, in his view, well worth the swallowing of pride, since it required merely the cession to the Americans of the lands of the original occupants, lands that

---

[49] On these negotiations, see Trudel, op. cit., pp. 200–210.

had been theirs for millennia. That this would be a betrayal of Britain's Indian allies, who were now doomed to virtual extinction, meant nothing to Shelburne.[50] In similar fashion he betrayed the Loyalists, making only a feeble attempt to obtain compensation for them from the Americans, knowing full well that the American rebels would never honour the agreement.

He did draw back when Franklin demanded that Canada and Nova Scotia be ceded. Neither his cabinet colleagues nor Parliament could have been expected to swallow that. Access to the Newfoundland fisheries he was willing to grant, to make sure that New England did not reject the proposed peace treaty. The New Englanders were convinced that the cod of the Grand Banks had been put there by God for their express use. It would, therefore, have required a naval squadron at Newfoundland on a permanent basis to keep the Americans out. Nor would Shelburne grant the Americans access to the British West Indies; that market had to be reserved for the merchants of Britain, Quebec, and Halifax. The American commissioners agreed to these generous terms and signed the Preliminaries of Peace, but craftily made them conditional on a peace treaty being concluded between France and Britain. When they would inform Vergennes of the treacherous action that they had taken, his hand would be forced. Were France not to agree to a peace treaty with Great Britain, then Vergennes could be sure that the Americans, consulting only their own interests, would ratify a separate peace with Britain and cease hostilities. That would place Rochambeau's troops in jeopardy once again, and then free the British armies in America for service elsewhere. France wanted the Americans to continue to tie down the British armies in America while Spain again sought to take Gibraltar, and France to take Jamaica. Given what the Americans expected to gain, and what their allies had provided them to that end, it was not too much to ask.

On 29 November, Franklin unabashedly informed Vergennes of what he and his fellow Commissioners had done. Vergennes was outraged, but he could not have been surprised; he had long known that they were not to be trusted. Yet in his view it was, at

---

[50] See Jack M. Sosin, *The Revolutionary Frontier 1763–1788* (New York 1967), pp. 145–150.

the very least, an act of bad faith.[51] He now feared that France would rue the day that it had assured the independence of the United States. The Spanish ambassador to France, when informed of what had transpired, was of the same opinion.[52]

All that Vergennes could now do was to try to salvage what he could from the debacle for France. He was astounded by the terms that Shelburne had granted the Americans, in particular the trans-Appalachian West and access to the Newfoundland fisheries. He considered that Britain had not negotiated a peace treaty but had capitulated to the Americans. It was, he wryly commented, *un paix du marchand*, not *un paix du Roi*. He thought that Shelburne's failure to protect and gain compensation for the Loyalists was dishonourable. He sought, in vain, to have Shelburne rescind the cession of the western lands south of the Great Lakes. He wanted that region between the mountains and the Mississippi reserved for the Indian nations, whose lands, after all, they were, to serve as a buffer zone between the new republic and Louisiana. He had struggled, successfully, to ensure the independence of the United States of America, but he wanted it confined to the territory the British colonies had occupied before the war. An independent America, yes, but not one that would become powerful enough to threaten French and Spanish interests in the western hemisphere.[53] As for American access to the Newfoundland fisheries, one of his war aims had been the acquisition of the island and total control over the fishing grounds. That had not come to pass, and he resented the fact that French fishermen

[51] Ministère des affaires étrangères. Correspondance politique. Série États-Unis, vol. 22, f 500. Franklin à Vergennes, Passy, Nov. 29 1782; *ibid.*, f 539, Vergennes à Franklin, Versailles le 15 x^bre 1782; *ibid.*, ff 556-7, Franklin à Vergennes, Passy, le 17 x^bre 1782; *ibid.*, ff 562-3, Vergennes à La Luzerne, Versailles 19 x^bre 1782; Trudel, op. cit., pp. 216-219.

[52] Philippe Sagnac, *La fin de l'ancien régime et la révolution américaine (1763-1789)*, (Paris 1947), p. 375; Trudel, op. cit., pp. 215-219.

[53] Ministère des affaires étrangères, Correspondance politique, Série Espagne, vol. 591, f 109, Vergennes à Montmorin, 30 oct. 1778; ibid., Série États-Unis, vol. 22, ff 200-204, Idée Sur la manière de déterminer et fixer les limites entre l'Espagne et les États-Unis du coté de l'Ohio et vers le Mississippi. (Envoiée copie à M. Jay le 7bre 1782.); *ibid.*, f 309, 1782 Mémoire. Concernant les terrains situées à l'est du Mississippi . . . ; *ibid.*, Série États-Unis, vol. 22 f 231, La Luzerne à Vergennes, Phil. 12 7bre 1782, reçu 26 9bre; *ibid.*, ff 316-318, Mémoire Concernant les terrains situés à l'est du Mississippi . . . Résumé; *ibid.*, ff 369-370, Vergennes à La Luzerne, Versailles le 14 8bre 1782.

would now have to compete there with, not only the British but also the burgeoning American fishing fleets.[54]

In this war, the only ones who gained were some of the Americans who were possessed of white skins and, ironically, in the short term, the British. The Indian nations who occupied lands treacherously ceded by Britain to the Americans were now doomed. France gained its main objective, the loss to Britain of its old American colonies; and that the French could regard as a humiliating defeat. They thus now had some solace for the defeat that they had suffered in the Seven Years' War, but that was all, and purchased at a horrendous price all too soon to be exacted. Immediately after the peace treaties were signed, British ships began pouring goods into American ports whilst Beaumarchais was struggling to recover what he claimed was owed to him by the American Congress.[55] Just as Shelburne had anticipated, trade with the American republic grew by leaps and bounds, vastly exceeding what it had been before the war, as the western territories were settled and immigrants poured in, creating a vast new market for British goods. In that sense, Britain lost nothing by granting her colonies their independence. Earlier French hopes of capturing that market proved to be utterly illusory.[56]

There can be no question but that the United States of America owes its independence, its emergence as a nation, mainly to French support; financial, logistical, and direct military aid. It was the French navy, French guns and troops, that effected the crucial victory at Yorktown. Rochambeau's army could have defeated that of Cornwallis by themselves; Washington's troops most certainly could not have so done. The independence of the British colonies in America was bound to come, sooner or later, just as did that of Canada, but not necessarily when or in the way that it actually did. Whether or not the American Revolution was

---

[54] Orville T. Murphy, "The Comte de Vergennes, the Newfoundland Fisheries and the Peace Negotiations of 1783: A Reconsideration," *Canadian Historical Review*, XLVI, No. 1, March 1965, pp. 33 & 42; William C. Stinchcombe, *The American Revolution and the French Alliance* (Syracuse N.Y., 1969), p. 191.

[55] Richard Alden, *The American Revolution 1775–1783* (New York 1954), p. 183; A. Goodwin (ed.), *The New Cambridge Modern History VIII*, pp. 37, 40, 43–5.

[56] Dull, A *Diplomatic History of the American Revolution*, pp. 161–2.

a "Good Thing" should be, not an accepted, indisputable fact, but a moot question for historians to ponder.

The war over, independence gained, the Americans displayed a singular lack of gratitude to the French. The Treaty of Alliance had served its purpose, their purpose, hence it could now be tossed into discard.[57] Thus when the treaty was put to the test in 1793, the Americans, without a qualm, abrogated it. To their generation, independence had clearly been ordained from on high from the moment the first English invaders landed on the shores of what came to be known as Virginia and New England. The preordained end justified the means.

---

[57] Stinchcombe, *The American Revolution and the French Alliance*, pp. 199–209.

. Jean-Baptiste Hertel, seigneur
e Rouville. Captain in Troupes
e la Marine, chevalier of the or-
er of St. Louis

2. The Marquis de Montcalm

All photographs are by courtesy of the Public Archives of Canada unless otherwise indicated.

. Brigadier General James Murray,
rst British governor of Quebec

4. Monseigneur François de Laval, Bishop of Quebec, 1674-1688

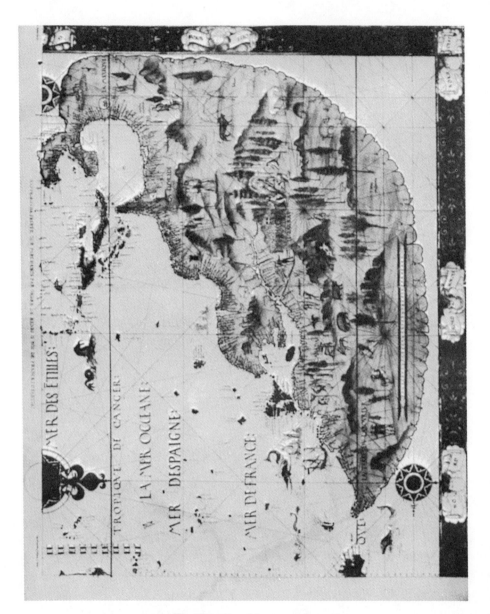

5. The Desceliers Mappemonde, 1550

7. Section of map by Père François Joseph Bressani. Novae Franciae Accurata Delineotia, 1757

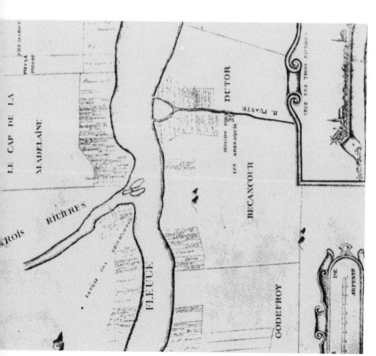

6. Seigneurial settlements at Trois Rivières, 1709. Section of map by Gédeon de Catalogne and Jean-Baptiste Decouagne. The narrow strip field division remains to this day.

8. De l'Isle map, 1750

9. View of Quebec from the northeast. By Richard Short, 1761

10. The Hôtel-Dieu, Quebec

11.   Eighteenth-century *habitant* home, Charlesbourg, Quebec

12.   Street scene, Quebec, at night. Painting by Clarence A. Gagnon
      (The National Gallery of Canada, Ottawa)

13. Eighteenth-century parish church, Saint-Laurent, Ile d'Orléans

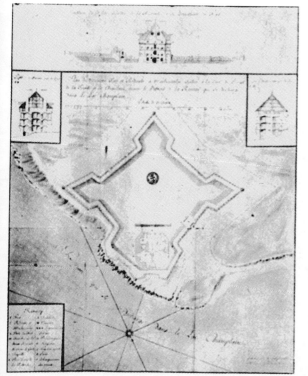

14. Fort St. Fréderic, Lake Champlain. By Chaussegros de Léry, 1757

15.   View of Trois Rivières. By James Peachey, *circa* 1781-1793

16.   Montreal, 1761. By Thomas Patten

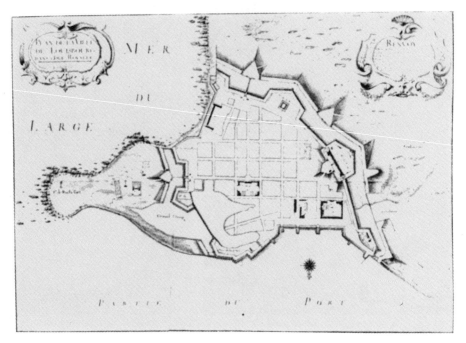

17.   Plan of Fortress of Louisbourg, 1744

(Department of Indian Affairs and Northern Development, Government of Canada)

18.   Reconstructed barracks and King's Bastion, Louisbourg

(Department of Indian Affairs and Northern Development)

19. French faïence excavated at Louisbourg

(Department of Indian Affairs and Northern Development)

20. Canadian silver, eighteenth century

(McCord Museum, McGill University, Montreal)

21. Superior Council Chamber, Louisbourg

(Department of Indian Affairs and Northern Development)

22. Canadian *habitants*. By J. Crawford Young *circa* 1825-1830

(McCord Museum, McGill University)

23. Brigadier George Townshend cartoon of Major General James Wolfe at Quebec

(McCord Museum, McGill University)

24. Canadian Indians. By J. Crawford Young, *circa* 1825-1830

(McCord Museum, McGill University)

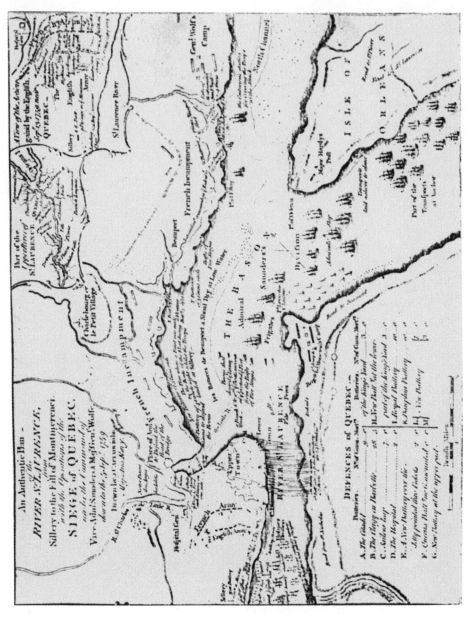

25.   The Siege of Quebec, 1759

26. Destruction of lower town, Quebec, by English bombardment, as depicted by Richard Short, 1759

27. Interior, Jesuit Church, Quebec, 1759. By Richard Short

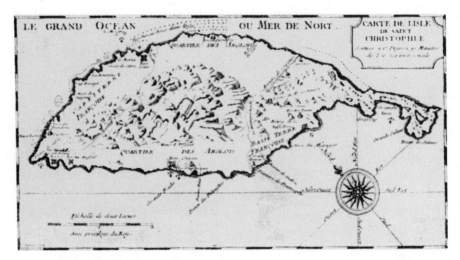

28. Map, St. Christophe. From J.-B. Labatt, *Nouveau Voyage aux Iles de l'Amérique* (1722)

29. Map, St. Domingue. From J.-B. Labatt, *Nouveau Voyage aux Iles de l'Amérique* (1722)

30. Tobacco manufacture. From J.-B. Labatt, *Nouveau Voyage aux Iles de l'Amérique* (1722)

31. Sugar mill. From J.-B. Labatt, *Nouveau Voyage aux Iles de l'Amérique* (1722)

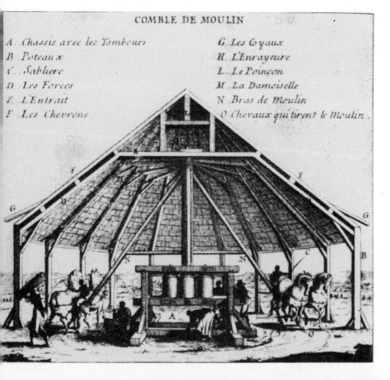

COMBLE DE MOULIN

A. Chassis avec les Tambours   G. Les Goyaux

B. Poteaux   H. L'Enrayeure

C. Sabliere   L. Le Poinçon

D. Les Forces   M. La Damoiselle

E. L'Entrait   N. Bras de Moulin

F. Les Chevrons   O. Chevaux qui tirent le Moulin.

32. Jean Baptiste Le Moyne de Bienville, Governor of Louisiana

(Collection of the Louisiana State Museum)

33. Pierre Le Moyne d'Iberville, founder of Louisiana

(Collection of the Louisiana State Museum)

34. Don Alexandro O'Reilly, Governor of Louisiana 1769-1770

(Collection of the Louisiana State Museum)

35. Colonial regime house, New Orleans
(Courtesy of the Louisiana State Museum)

Epilogue

In 1763 the vast, sprawling French empire in North America had ceased to exist. Nor did France have any desire to recover the lost territories. In 1777, the French foreign minister, the comte de Vergennes, informed the French ambassador at Madrid: "France possesses colonies that suffice for its population and its economy. More would be a liability rather than a benefit."[1] The French in America then numbered roughly 125,000, but the vast majority were no longer subjects of the French Crown.

The Caribbean remnant of the old Empire quickly regained its old dominance of the European market for its produce. Its economy waxed richer than ever before, but in other ways all was not well. The land in the older settled areas was beginning to be worked out. The only solution to meet the demands of the growing European market while production was falling, was to work the slaves harder. This caused more of them to flee to the mountains to join the *marrons*, at the risk of appalling torture if recaptured. Some of these *marron* bands now numbered in the thousands, and the danger of a slave insurrection increased greatly. At the same time the *philosophes* were attacking the institution itself. Unlike the Americans, they found it impossible to reconcile slavery with the rights of man.

---

[1] Henri Doniol (ed.), *Histoire de la participation de la France à l'établissement des États-Unis d'Amérique: Correspondance diplomatique et documents*, II, pp. 274–5, Vergennes au marquis d'Ossun, Versailles, 26 avril 1777.

The mulattos too were forced into opposition to the existing regime. Their resentment toward their white superiors, whose values they shared and whose social status they sought to achieve, was heightened by the 1766 decree of the Ministry of Marine which declared that no one with a slave ancestor could be granted equality with white subjects. Five years later they were barred from the professions and all public offices, some of which they already held. Then, in 1778, a new ordinance forbade marriage between white and coloured. The free mulattos, now comprising a large segment of the population, were forced to accept that only the abolition of slavery would allow them to achieve the equality they craved.

The *petits blancs*, doctors, surgeons, notaries, junior officials, the scorned salaried employees of the *grands blancs*, none of them retained any loyalty to the mother country. They could not go back to France without suffering economic hardship and a grave reduction in their standard of living. Their first loyalty now was to their island way of life and their own interests. In fact the only ones who retained their loyalty to the French Crown were the *grands blancs*, who regarded the islands only as a source of wealth. But they too had their grievances. They desired military and naval protection, but wished the economic restraints of the metropolis lifted and freedom to trade where they would. They preferred to regulate their own affairs without interference by edicts from France enforced by appointed officials. By 1790 the planters of Saint-Domingue were claiming that no decree of the metropolitan government was valid unless it had been approved by their representatives. When they had a bad year they bitterly resented being called on to pay their debts by their merchant suppliers in France. In short, the pattern of the American Revolution was being repeated in the French West Indies. With the destruction of the monarchy in 1793 the last ties of sentiment were severed.[2]

In Louisiana under Spanish rule the situation was in marked contrast to that of Canada under the British. After crushing the revolt in 1769, General O'Reilly governed the province with a light hand. He retained a garrison of only twelve hundred sol-

---

[2] See Gaston-Martin, *Histoire de l'Esclavage dans le Colonies françaises* (Paris, 1948).

diers, suppressed the Conseil Supérieur, and replaced it with a *Cabildo* performing much the same function and staffed by French colonists. The other administrative posts went almost exclusively to the new, French-speaking subjects of His Most Catholic Majesty. To protect the northern and western frontiers against assaults by the Indian tribes, O'Reilly retained the French officials as his agents, avoiding the mistake made by the English when they took over from the French, and continued the paternalistic policy of his predecessors, including the distribution of presents which the Indians regarded as tribute, not charity. Although there had never been any love lost between the French and the Spanish, the French preferred the Spanish to the English, who had taken over the old posts on the east side of the Mississippi. The presence of several hundred Acadian refugees who had made their way to Louisiana after being dumped in the colonies along the Atlantic seaboard, ensured that hatred of the English would endure a while longer. The new town of Saint-Louis-des-Illinois was established on the west bank of the Mississippi, and to it flocked the French from the old Illinois settlements, now on British territory.

Spain was determined to retain Louisiana as a buffer to protect Mexico from English colonial expansion. It retained the loyalty of the French by its lenient administration, which was carried on by O'Reilly's successor, Don Luis de Unzaga, who took over in 1770. Taxes were kept low; 3 million livres a year of Crown funds were spent on the colony, and a revenue was obtained from it of less than a million livres. But the greatest benefit of all was that Louisiana at long last had a viable market for its produce. In 1772, France imposed heavy duties on imports from the Spanish colonies, but this was more than compensated for by the contraband trade with the English colonies, and direct commerce with Cuba and Santo Domingo.[3]

---

[3] See Baron Marc de Villiers du Terrage, *Les dernières années de la Louisiane française* (Paris, 1904), pp. 318–370.

During the twenty-four years of Spanish rule the French of Louisiana had little cause for complaint. They retained their place in the administration, they were not ousted from control of the economy, their social structure was not disrupted, and no attempt was made to assimilate them. Moreover, the French and Spanish had some things in common: among the dominant group, much the same social values, and perhaps most important of all, the same religion. The Louisianans, like the Canadians, and the Acadians before them, were treated as pawns by the governments of Louis XV and XVI. A French subject in Louisiana, without his having been conquered, or in any way consulted, suffered that same experience as did the Canadians, not once, but three times. In 1762 a Louisianan became a Spanish subject and was not made aware of it until two years later; in 1800 Napoleon reclaimed him for France, then three years later he learned that the Emperor had sold his homeland to the United States of America.[4] The population of the colony was then 50,000 odd, more than half being slaves. Many of the French Creoles bitterly resented their forced change of allegiance and what it brought in its train. They were not to be treated as citizens, having equal rights in the country that had usurped them. In 1803, Gouverneur Morris wrote: "I always thought that when we should acquire Canada and Louisiana it would be proper to govern them as provinces and allow them no voice in our councils."[5] When the Louisianans subsequently sought statehood for the New Orleans region, President Thomas Jefferson declared that liberty would be wasted on the Creoles since "the principles of a popular Government are utterly beyond their comprehension." Not one in fifty, he added, "understand the English language." Congress then dutifully declared that Louisiana would be administered as a conquered country.[6] In the event, the Louisiana Creoles were soon swamped

---

[4] For the details of this sordid transaction, see Alexander DeConde, *This Affair of Louisiana* (New York, 1976). The Canadians may have been momentarily in danger of being traded away in similar fashion by Great Britain to Russia. In 1796, Britain, hard pressed financially, was desperately seeking means to win Russia over to the anti-French alliance, but could not afford the Russian terms. The well-informed Austrian ambassador to the Court of St. James's got wind of a proposal made in the Cabinet to offer Canada to Russia. Manifestly, it was rejected. See Karl F. Helleiner, "An Abortive Plan to Give up Canada," *Canadian Historical Review*, XLII, pp. 46-9.

[5] DeConde, *This Affair of Louisiana*, p. 210.

[6] DeConde, *op cit.*, pp. 211-212.

by the hordes of Americans who swarmed across the Mississippi and set about the final onslaught on the Indian nations. Within a few generations, the French in Louisiana were submerged and assimilated by sheer weight of numbers, until only mere vestiges of their old culture and way of life remained.

To the north the provinces of British North America were to form the basis of a new nation, a nation born out of defeat: defeat of the French by the British, and of the British by the French and the Americans. Some 37,000 American Loyalists removed to these provinces. The majority settled in the Maritimes, but about 6,000 entered Quebec and were subsequently settled to the west of the Canadian seigneuries in what is today Ontario. To accommodate them, Quebec was divided into two colonies, Lower and Upper Canada, each with its own government. Lower Canada, with a French majority of 145,000 but an economically dominant English minority numbering only ten thousand, retained the old French civil law and gained an elected assembly. Executive power and control of the all-important patronage remained vested in the governor and his predominantly Anglo-Canadian-appointed executive council for another half-century. Thus the French and the English were arrayed against each other in the political arena of Lower Canada.[7]

The French Canadians, concentrated in their seigneuries, bound together by their language, their old culture, and their religion — which now assumed far greater importance in their lives than it had since the early seventeenth century — successfully resisted the continual fumbling efforts of the Anglo-Canadians and British officials to assimilate them, to make them over into English-speaking Protestants, or at least to exorcize their divisive language. All that this accomplished was to strengthen what the conquerors sought to eradicate.

The French Revolution and the long, bitter struggle against Napoleonic Europe exacerbated the racial hostility in Lower Canada. The Revolution also weakened the lingering cultural and sentimental ties with France. The Roman Catholic clergy

---

[7] For general treatments of the period after 1791 see Mason Wade, *The French Canadians, 1760–1967* (2 vols., Toronto, 1968); Susan Mann Trofimenkoff, *The Dream of Nation. A Social and Intellectual History of Quebec* (Toronto, 1983); Fernand Ouellet, *Lower Canada 1791–1840. Social Change and Nationalism* (Translated and adapted by Patricia Claxton) (Toronto, 1980).

regarded with horror the assault on the Church by the revolutionary regime, and even came to think that perhaps the Conquest had been a blessing in disguise, intended by God to save the French Canadians from atheism. Now more isolated than ever, the Canadians found themselves without friends or allies abroad, and constantly threatened by the growing English-speaking population that regarded them as a bone in the country's throat. Their isolation was completed in 1821 when the Hudson's Bay Company finally won its 150-year-old struggle with the Montreal fur traders. In that year the North West Company, driven to the wall, was absorbed by "The Adventurers of England Trading into Hudson's Bay." The western furs no longer moved in the great canoe brigades of the voyageurs over Grand Portage, through the Great Lakes to Montreal, but by York boat to the waiting ships in the Bay.[8] The French Canadians were now cut off from the vast spaces of the West which they had always regarded as their country, where their language was the lingua franca, where they were free of the racial friction, the petty oppressions and frustration, the restrictive atmosphere of Lower Canada. More than ever before they were turned in on themselves.

With their numbers doubling every generation, every twenty-seven years, the pressure on the available land became great. This situation was made much worse by land jobbers and speculators. Large sections of land were denied to the French Canadians by various means and "were deliberately used to enrich the English and commercial minority and to build up the English population against the Canadian."[9] With land out of reach and other economic opportunities more and more restricted, the French Canadians were increasingly reduced to the role of proletariat, obliged to sell their labour cheap to English capitalists. This trend culminated in the mass exodus of hundreds of thousands of their number to the mill towns of New England,[10] a sorry

---

[8] See Donald Creighton, *The Commercial Empire of the St. Lawrence* (Toronto, 1956), pp. 175–202, a brief, colourful account with a strong economic determinist slant. A more detailed narrative account of the struggle between the rival fur trade organizations is contained in E. E. Rich, *The Fur Trade and the North West to 1857* (Toronto, 1967).

[9] W. L. Morton, *The Kingdom of Canada* (Toronto, 1963), p. 192.

[10] See "L'émigration des Canadiens français aux États-Unis," two articles by Albert Faucher and Gilles Paquet in *Recherches Sociographiques* (Laval Univ. Press), V. 3 (sept.–déc., 1964).

ending for the descendants of men who had once held half the continent in fee.

In the Legislative Assembly, new leaders of the emerging French-Canadian nation had come to the fore. These men came not from among the old seigneurial families but from the ranks of the *habitants*. They were men who had managed to acquire an education and, unable to compete with the established English commercial group, turned to the professions, became lawyers, notaries, doctors, journalists, then moved into politics. They quickly mastered parliamentary methods and tactics, to the fury of the English members of the assembly who found themselves all too often bested in debate. These new leaders were not uninfluenced by events in Europe, the resurgence of nationalism in Italy, Poland, the Germanies, and the revolutions of 1830. It was among this new middle class that French-Canadian nationalism was born, brought into being as a reaction to English attitudes.

Then, half a century after the revolt in Louisiana against foreign rule, worsening economic conditions, the bitter struggle to destroy the entrenched political power of the English oligarchy, and inflamed racial hostility brought events to the breaking point. In 1837 armed rebellion flared up in the Montreal region. The rebel or *Patriote* forces, badly organized and worse led, were swiftly and savagely crushed by British regular troops and the English-Canadian militia. French-Canadian villages were pillaged and burned, churches desecrated. The legacy of bitterness this created was to endure for generations. Most of the leaders and a few of their followers sought sanctuary in the United States. Of the 753 prisoners taken, twelve were eventually hanged and fifty-eight transported to the Australian penal colonies. The English of Montreal protested what they considered this far too lenient treatment.[11] But French-Canadian nationalism now had its martyrs.

The English, however, as Lord Durham's famous *Report* made plain, were still convinced that the French Canadians must be assimilated, for their own good.[12] That *Report* merely strength-

[11] For a succinct account of the rebellion see Mason Wade, *The French Canadians*, Chap. IV. For French-Canadian historians it is not easy to view this episode with detachment; for a detailed account see G. Filteau, *Histoire des Patriotes* (3 vols., Montréal, 1938–42).

[12] See Gerald M. Craig (ed.), *Lord Durham's Report* (Toronto, 1963).

ened the French Canadians in their resolve to retain their language, their culture, and their institutions. Over the ensuing years this national spirit waxed and waned, sometimes seeming only a vague malaise, sometimes apparently conjured out of existence by graver external threats to the entire country, but always reappearing. The frame of reference and the vocabulary have kept changing, but for over two centuries the desire of the French Canadians to be their own masters has remained constant. That spirit, a sense of their great past—*Je me souviens*, the motto of present-day Quebec—a few islands in the Caribbean, two off the coast of Newfoundland, are all that remain of France in North America.

Bibliographical Essay

Manuscript Sources

The primary source material on French activities in the Americas is abundant, more particularly for the period after 1663, but very dispersed. Unfortunately, little of the correspondence or accounts of the private commercial companies is known to have survived; thus, the main sources for the period prior to the establishment of royal government in 1663 are the correspondence of the missionaries, the journals of some of the leading figures such as Cartier and Champlain, and the reports by Spanish officials on French encroachments on territory claimed by Spain. The misinformation contained in the last is sometimes very revealing.

In 1671, Colbert took steps to have all official correspondence conserved in an orderly fashion, and some earlier material was included. The great bulk of the correspondence between colonial officials and the Ministry of Marine is now contained in various archives in France, the principal depositories being the Archives Nationales, the Bibliothèque Nationale, the Service historique de l'Armée, Vincennes, and the Archives du Ministère des Affaires Étrangères. Certain of the archives in the *départements*, e.g., those of the French ports, La Rochelle, Bordeaux, Rouen, Nantes, Honfleur, contain material pertinent to the colonies, much of it as yet not investigated.

As scholars extend the scope of their inquiries, more material is being brought to light; this is also true, but to a lesser extent, in the onetime colonies themselves. Recently a treasure trove was discovered in the British High Court of Admiralty, consisting of thousands of letters captured at sea during the eighteenth-century wars. (See Julian Gwyn, "Untapped Source for the Study of French West Indies in the Eighteenth Century," *Histoire Sociale: Social History*, 3, Ottawa, Apr. 1969.) In Canada, when in 1760 the French officials returned to France, all but documents of local interest, mainly those dealing with property and the records of the law courts, they took back with them. This also occurred in Louisiana after the cession of that colony to Spain. As for the West Indies, the records of the original company, the Compagnie des Îles de l'Amérique, have disappeared, and whatever documents were retained on the islands have suffered the ravages of the climate, insects, war, insurrection, and such disasters as that which destroyed Saint-Pierre, Martinique, in 1902.

The most extensive collection of manuscript material, outside of France, remains in Canada. The principal depositories are the Archives nationales du Québec at Quebec, Montreal and Trois Rivières. The Archives du Séminaire de Québec has a very rich collection and also a card-index catalogue; a card for every document, cross-indexed. The Séminaire de Saint-Sulpice at Montréal, quondam seigneurs of the island and district of Montreal also has a vast collection of documents. At the Université de Montréal the Baby Collection, well-housed, contains a great many important documents, particularly eighteenth-century private correspondence. The archives of the archbishoprics of Quebec and Montreal and of the women's orders are very rich sources. Finally, the National Archives of Canada—formerly the Public Archives of Canada—contains transcripts and microfilm of much of the material pertaining to Canada in various French archives; in addition there are some very important collections of documents, such as the Lévis collection of journals, letters, and dispatches pertaining to the War of the Conquest (1755–1760), and the Beauharnois collection.

Until recently, historians of the French colonial period devoted themselves mainly to narrative accounts and biographies. Within the past decade the trend has been toward social history, more particularly to quantitative analyses and demographic studies. The influence of the École des Hautes Études at the Sorbonne has been very marked. Thus, instead of mining the official correspondence or pawing over the slag heap at the pit head, historians today are studying the notarial *greffes*, the records of the law courts, and the rich collections pertaining to some of the seigneuries. Both in Canada and in Louisiana a superabundance of such material awaits investigation.

Guides to Manuscript Material

Among the many such aids the more useful are Henry Putney Beers, *The French in North America: A Bibliographical Guide to French Archives, Reproductions and Research Missions* (Baton Rouge, 1957) and his *The French and British in the Old Northwest: A Bibliographical Guide to Archives and Manuscript Sources* (Detroit, 1964). Very valuable for correspondence from the Ministry of Marine to the colonies is "Étienne Taillemite, *Inventaire analytique de la correspondance générale avec les colonies, Série B* (Paris, 1959). The National Archives of Canada has begun publication of an inventory of its manuscript material, original documents, transcripts, and microfilm; the first deals with the French regime, *Public Archives of Canada Manuscript Division: General Inventory Manuscripts Volume 1 MG1–MG10* (Ottawa, 1971). Archival sources in Quebec are listed in *L'État général des Archives publiques et privées du Québec* (Ministère des Affaires culturelles, Québec, 1968). Invaluable is Pierre-Georges and Antoine Roy (eds.), *Inventaire des greffes des notaires du régime français conservés aux archives judiciaires* (21 vols., Québec, 1943–64). Also useful is the earlier selective inventory by Pierre-Georges Roy, *Inventaire d'une collection des pièces judiciaires, notariales etc., etc., Conservées aux Archives judiciaires de Québec* (2 vols., Beauceville, 1917), and Pierre-Georges Roy, *Inventaire des Ordonnances des Intendants de la Nouvelle-France conservées aux Archives provinciales de Québec* (4 vols., Beauceville, 1919), and Pierre-Georges Roy, *Inventaire des Insinuations de la Prévôté de Québec* (3 vols., Beauceville, 1936–39). For the early sixteenth century, B. Hoffman, *Cabot to*

Cartier: Sources for a Historical Ethnography of North Eastern North America (Toronto, 1961) is more than an analysis of source material; it makes a case.

For the West Indies, see 'Les Sources' in Gabriel Debien, *Les Esclaves aux Antilles françaises* (Basse Terre, Guadeloupe et Fort de France, Martinique, 1974) pp. 9–38. The article by Winston de Ville, "Manuscript Sources in Louisiana for the History of the French in the Mississippi Valley," in John Francis McDermott (ed.), *The French in the Mississippi Valley* (Univ. of Illinois Press, Urbana, 1965), makes plain the problems created for the historian of colonial Louisiana by archival neglect. Fortunately, this situation is being rectified. The work being done at the University of Southwestern Louisiana is worthy of note.

Printed Source Material

A vast amount of the primary source material concerning the history of New France has been published in France, Canada, and the United States, but relatively little on the West Indies. The *Rapport de l'Archiviste de la Province de Québec*, published annually since 1920, until recently, its title was changed to *Rapport des Archives du Québec*, contains transcripts of series of documents, including the correspondence of governors and intendants, a great many memoirs, and calendars of trading licences for the West. Regrettably, the transcripts in the earlier volumes were not without error, some obvious, some not. An excellent index to the first 42 volumes of this invaluable collection, *Table des Matières des Rapports des Archives du Québec*, was published by L'Imprimeur de sa Majesté la Reine (Québec, 1965). The records of the Conseil Souverain to 1716, unfortunately not in their entirety, were published under the title *Jugements et Délibérations du Conseil Souverain de la Nouvelle-France* (6 vols., Québec, 1885–91). In 1703 the title of this high court was changed to Conseil Supérieur; the calendar of its judgments and deliberations, *Inventaire des jugements et délibérations du Conseil Supérieur de la Nouvelle-France de 1717 à 1760*, ed. by P.-G. Roy (7 vols., Beauceville, 1932–35) is useful. Three volumes that are also valuable are *Édits et ordonnances royaux, déclara-*

tions et arrêts du Conseil d'État du Roi concernant le Canada (Québec, 1854); *Arrêts et Règlements du Conseil Supérieur de Québec, et ordonnances et jugements des intendants du Canada* (Québec, 1855); *Complément des ordonnances et jugements des gouverneurs et intendants du Canada, précédé des commissions des dits gouverneurs et intendants et des différents officiers civils et de justice* (Québec, 1856). The *Collection des manuscrits contenants lettres, mémoires et autres documents historiques relatifs à la Nouvelle-France* (4 vols., Québec, 1883–85) is a historical dog's breakfast. Much more valuable is the calendar by E.-Z. Massicotte, *Montréal sous le régime français: Répertoire des Arrêts, Édits, Mandements, Ordonnances et Règlements conservés dans les Archives du Palais de justice de Montréal, 1640–1760* (Montréal, 1919). The judgments rendered and legislation enacted by the Conseil Supérieur and its successor, the *Cabildo*, of Louisiana have been published in translation in the *Louisiana Historical Quarterly*, over the years. Various of the earlier *Annual Reports of the Public Archives of Canada* contain transcripts of documents and series of documents; the calendars of documents published in these *Reports* are too brief to be of real value and are quite untrustworthy. On clerical affairs in New France, the selection by Mgr. H. Tetu and Mgr. C.-O. Gagnon (eds.), *Mandements, lettres pastorales et circulaires des évêques de Québec* (7 vols., Québec, 1887), is rather selective but very useful. For too long a standby among slovenly colonial historians is *Documents Relative to the Colonial History of the State of New York* (15 vols., Albany, 1856–83), ed. by E. B. O'Callaghan, B. Fernow, John Romeyn Brodhead. Brodhead collected the transcripts of the documents, Fernow edited those dealing with New Amsterdam, and Edmund Bailey O'Callaghan, a doctor and newspaper editor in Montreal who had to flee Lower Canada after participating in the 1837 rebellion, translated and edited the French documents. Both the transcription and translation are unreliable, enlivened by the occasional howler. The same stricture applies to *Documentary History of the State of New York*, ed. by E. B. O'Callaghan (4 vols., Albany, 1850).

Other printed source materials dealing with specific topics or limited periods are cited under the separate chapter listings below.

Imperial Background

Until very recently, historians, and more particularly Canadian historians, treated New France as though it had existed *in vacuo*, with little regard for the parent society whence it derived. Today, however, as historians turn their attention increasingly to quantitative as well as qualitative studies of colonial society, they find themselves obliged to use the parent society and its institutions as a point of departure. One conclusion to emerge is that society and institutions in the French colonies, particularly Canada, were much more closely integrated in the imperial system than was the case with the other European colonies in the Americas. Thus, whatever throws light on France during the old regime reflects on the colonies. The work done on all aspects of the history of France is, of course, immense and steadily increases. Only a few of the studies with greater relevance to the colonies can be mentioned here.

For the general background, the series edited by E. Lavisse, *Histoire de France* (9 vols., Paris, 1902–11), although dated, is still useful as a work of general reference. Marcel Marion, *Dictionnaire des Institutions de la France aux XVIIe et XVIIIe siècles* (Paris, 1923; reissued 1968), is indispensable; also very useful, if somewhat dated, is R. Doucet, *Les institutions de la France au XVIe siècle* (2 vols., Paris, 1948). *The Cambridge Economic History of Europe*, Vol. VI, ed. by E. E. Rich and C. H. Wilson (Cambridge Univ. Press, 1967), contains much of value. A. Goodwin (ed.), *The New Cambridge Modern History*, vols. III– VIII (Cambridge, 1970–1971) is an excellent reference work, better on the British than the French side of the hill. The reverse has to be said of the equally valuable series *Histoire Général des Civilisations*, Tome IV. Roland Mousnier, *Les XVIe et XVIIe siècles*, (Paris, 1954); Tome V, Roland Mousnier, Ernest Labrousse, Marc Bouloiseau, *Le XVIIIe siècle* (Paris, 1955). The A. de Boislisle edition of *Mémoires de St. Simon* (41 vols., Paris, 1879) contains a great wealth of invaluable information on individuals and institutions in its footnotes and appendixes, which make up the bulk of this massive work on the age of Louis XIV. Major works by Pierre and Huguette Chaunu, *Séville et l'Atlantique*

(1504–1650) (10 vols., Paris, 1955–59), and Fernand Braudel, *Civilisation matérielle et capitalisme (XVᵉ–XVIIIᵉ siècle)* (Paris, 1967), particularly the latter, are essential to place the history of the colonies in their broader context. These magisterial works also have the salutary effect of inculcating scholastic humility.

On French society, Philippe Sagnac, *La formation de la société française moderne (1661–1789)* (2 vols., Paris, 1940–46), is now somewhat dated, but still sound and a pleasure to read. The classic study by Marc Bloch, *Les caractères originaux de l'histoire rurale française* (Paris, 1952), cannot be ignored. Nor can Maurice Magendie, *La politesse mondaine et les théories de l'honnêteté, en France au XVIIᵉ siècle, de 1600 à 1660* (2 vols., Paris, 1925). An excellent critical commentary on the more recent work done on social and economic history is the volume in the series *Nouvelle Clio*, Robert Mandrou, *La France aux XVIIᵉ et XVIIIᵉ siècles* (Paris, 1967). Two more general works provide a good introduction to the France of the sixteenth and seventeenth centuries: Robert Mandrou, *Introduction à la France moderne, Essai de psychologie historique, 1500–1640* (Paris, 1961), and Pierre Goubert, *Louis XIV et vingt millions de Français* (Paris, 1966). The new series *Histoire économique et sociale de la France*, 4 vols., ed. by Fernand Braudel and Ernest Labrousse, sums up in magisterial fashion the results of research completed to date.

Secondary Sources: General Histories

The first modern history of New France of any signficance was that by F.-X. Garneau, *Histoire du Canada depuis sa découverte jusqu'à nos jours* (3 vols., Quebec, 1845–48). Written to refute the statement in Lord Durham's famous report that the French Canadians were a people without a history and without a culture, it has a strong nationalist bias, and the earlier part was largely based on the eighteenth-century history by P. F.-X. de Charlevoix, *Histoire et description générale de la Nouvelle France . . .* (3 vols., Paris, 1744). Many of the latter's errors and misconceptions were incorporated and thereby reinforced. *Cours d'histoire du Canada* (2 vols., Quebec, 1861–65), was written by F.-B. Ferland, a cleric who also relied heavily on Charlevoix and exaggerated the role played by the clergy. On a much higher level of scholarship are the works by the Jesuit historian Camille de Rochemonteix, *Les Jésuites et la Nouvelle-France au XVIIe siècle* (3 vols., Paris, 1895–96) and *Les Jésuites et la Nouvelle-France au XVIIIe siècle* (2 vols., Paris, 1906). Francis Parkman's epic series *France and England in North America* (Boston, 1851–84) was for too long regarded as the definitive history of the period. For the better part of a century his highly coloured interpretation of events, so persuasive to Americans and Anglo-Canadians who shared his conviction of the superiority of their institutions and way of life, inhibited original research, since it was believed that he had said all there was to say on the subject. This thralldom has finally been removed, and Parkman's works must now be regarded as period literary pieces, of interest to the student of historiography rather than the student of history.

Only those interested in Whig interpretations of history need consult William Kingsford, *The History of Canada* (10 vols., London, 1887–98). The four chapters dealing with New France in *The Cambridge History of the British Empire*, Vol. VI, *Canada and Newfoundland* (London, 1930), are hopelessly dated; so too is Adam Shortt and A. G. Doughty (eds.), *Canada and Its Provinces: A History of the Canadian People and Their Institutions* (23 vols., Toronto, 1914–17). The too frequently cited George M. Wrong, *The Rise and Fall of New France* (2 vols., Toronto, 1928), is little more than paraphrased Parkman but contrives to be pedestrian as well as riddled with errors and misconceptions. Abbé Ivanhoë Caron's slim study, *La colonisation du Canada sous la domination française* (Quebec, 1916), is dated. The thesis sustained at the Sorbonne by Émile Salone, *La Colonisation de la Nouvelle-France* (Paris, 1905; reprinted Trois Rivières, 1970), can still be read with profit. The writings of Abbé Lionel-Adolphe Groulx, with their strong nationalist and clerical theme, had a profound effect in French Canada; in particular, his *Histoire du Canada français depuis la découverte* (2 vols., Montreal, 1962). A valiant attempt at a Marxist interpretation of the history of Canada was made by Stanley Ryerson, *The Founding of Canada: Beginnings to 1815* (Toronto, 1960). Gustave Lanctot, *Histoire du Canada* (3 vols., Montréal, 1959–64), covering only the

French regime, has been published in English translation as *A History of Canada* (3 vols., Harvard Univ. Press, 1963–65). It is a discursive, detailed, narrative account with little analysis and some dubious hypotheses presented as established fact. W. J. Eccles, *The Canadian Frontier, 1534–1760* (New York, 1969), places the problems of the frontier within the broad context of the colony's history. The article by J. M. S. Careless, "Frontierism, Metropolitanism and Canadian History," *The Canadian Historical Review*, XXXV (Mar. 1954), is valuable on this topic. Still useful is J. B. Brebner, *The Explorers of North America, 1492–1806* (London, 1933). Two other useful reference works are the analysis of the institutions of New France by Marcel Trudel, *Introduction to the History of New France* (Toronto, 1968), and the historiographical study, which discusses many of the works cited here, by Yves F. Zoltvany, *The Government of New France: Royal, Clerical, or Class Rule?* (Toronto, 1971). In a class by itself is the massive genealogical dictionary by C. Tanguay, *Dictionnaire généalogique des familles canadiennes depuis la fondation de la colonie jusqu'à nos jours* (7 vols., Montréal, 1871–79). also invaluable is the *Dictionary of Canadian Biography*, Vols. I–IV (Toronto, 1966–1979). Finally, the leading journals are *The Canadian Historical Review* and *Revue de l'Histoire de l'Amérique Française*, both of which include checklists of publications as they appear. The journal variously entitled *Revue de l'Histoire des Colonies Françaises, Revue d'Histoire des Colonies, Revue Française d'Histoire d'Outre-Mer*, and the new Canadian journal *Social History: Histoire Sociale* should be consulted. A mine of miscellaneous articles, of widely varying quality, genealogical notes, transcripts of documents, and articles is contained in *Bulletin des recherches historiques* (Lévis and Québec), Vol. I, 1895– . (Index, 1895–1925, Beauceville, 1925–1926, 4 vols.) In American journals, such as *The William and Mary Quarterly*, the occasional article dealing with the French colonies appears from time to time. In recent years the history of the colonial period has begun to spill over national borders. The student of the history of New France cannot afford to ignore the American journals.

Mention must be made of that essential tool of the historian, the atlas. Three that are of great value for the student of the history of New France are R. Cole Harris (ed.), Geoffrey J. Matthews (cartographer), *Historical Atlas of Canada* (Toronto, 1988), Marcel Trudel, *Atlas de la Nouvelle-France. An Atlas of New France* (Québec, 1968), and Helen Hornbeck Tanner, *Atlas of Great Lakes Indian History* (Univ. Oklahoma Press, 1984).

Unlike French Canada, the French West Indies and Louisiana did not develop native schools of history. The history of Louisiana became merely a fragment of that of the burgeoning United States, and that of the French colonies and ex-colonies in the West Indies has been written mainly by non-creole historians, most of them metropolitan Frenchmen. It may be significant that French historians have to date shown more interest in the West Indies than in either Canada or Louisiana. The best general history of Louisiana is the very detailed, discursive study, based almost entirely on primary sources, by Marcel Giraud, *Histoire de la Louisiane française* (Paris 1953, 1958, 1966, 1974). The four volumes that have appeared cover the history of the colony to 1723. The first volume has been translated by Joseph C. Lambert, *A History of French Louisiana*, Volume One. The Reign of Louis XIV, 1698–1715 (Baton Rouge, 1974). The translation is very poor. See also Guy Frégault, *Pierre Le Moyne d'Iberville* (Montréal & Paris, 1968); Guy Frégault, *Le Grand Marquis: Pierre de Rigaud de Vaudreuil et la Louisiane* (Montréal, 1962); Gaillard McWilliams (translator & editor), *Iberville's Gulf Journals* (Univ. Alabama Press, 1981). The translation and annotation are excellent but the introduction by Tennant S. McWilliams is riddled with errors and misconceptions. John G. Clark, *New Orleans, 1718–1812. An Economic History* (Baton Rouge, 1970); Jay Higginbotham, *Old Mobile. Fort Louis de la Louisiane* (Mobile Museum, 1977), a work marred by appalling literary style; the author apparently felt compelled to split every infinitive. Marc de Villiers du Terrage, *The Last Years of French Louisiana* (translated by Hosea Phillips, edited and annotated by Carl A. Brasseaux and Glen R. Conrad. Lafayette LA, 1982), a dated but basic work.

For the West Indies, Herbert Ingram Priestley, *France Overseas Through the Old Regime: A Study of European Expansion*

(New York, 1939) contains much useful material. Arthur Percival Newton, *The European Nations in the West Indies, 1493-1688* (London, 1933) almost overlooks the French. Nellis M. Crouse, *French Pioneers in the West Indies, 1634-1664* (New York, 1940) and *The French Struggle for the West Indies* (New York, 1943) are superficial narrative accounts of events. The best survey to date, despite its title, is Gaston-Martin, *Histoire de l'Esclavage dans les Colonies françaises* (Paris, 1948).

Chapter One: 1500-1632

Much of the relatively scanty primary source material for this early period has been printed. Among the more important items are, for Canada, H. P. Biggar, *The Precursors of Jacques Cartier, 1497-1534* (Ottawa, 1911); and by the same editor, *The Voyages of Jacques Cartier: Published from the Originals with Translations, Notes and Appendices* (Ottawa, 1924) contains the best edition of Cartier's journal. H. P. Biggar, *A Collection of Documents Relating to Jacques Cartier and the Sieur de Roberval* (Ottawa, 1930) is drawn mainly from the Spanish archives at Simancas.

On Brazil, Jean de Léry, *Histoire d'un voyage fait en la terre de Brésil, autrement dite Amérique contenant choses curieuses et remarquable en ce pais-là* (La Rochelle, 1578), is basic. André Thevet's *Cosmographie Universelle* (1575) contains little but fascinating descriptions of the flora, fauna, and Indians; Vol. 2 was republished in the series *Pays d'Outre Mer, Deuxième Série, Les Classiques de la Colonisation, Les Français en Amérique pendant la deuxième moitiè du XVIᵉ siècle: Le Brésil et les Brésiliens par André Thevet*, choix de textes et notes par Suzanne Lussagnet, introduction par Ch.-A. Julien (Paris, 1953). In that same randomly entitled but valuable series has also appeared *Les Français en Floride*, textes de Jean Ribault, René de Laudonnière, Nicolas Le Challeux et Dominique de Gourgues, choisis et annotés par Suzanne Lussagnet, introduction par Ch.-A. Julien (Paris, 1958).

The best modern histories of this period to date are Ch.-A. Julien, *Les voyages de découverte et les premiers établissements (XVᵉ-XVIᵉ siècles)* (Paris, 1948), and Marcel Trudel, *Histoire de la Nouvelle-France*, Vol. I, *Les vaines tentatives, 1524–1603* (Montréal, 1963).

On the early history of Acadia, the printed source material is not abundant. The Jesuit *Relations* are a main source, and there have been several editions. The most complete, containing the original text and an English translation, is Reuben Gold Thwaites (ed.), *The Jesuit Relations and Allied Documents* (73 vols., Cleveland, 1896–1901). Joseph P. Donnelly, S.J., *Thwaites Jesuit Relations: Errata and Addenda* (Chicago, 1967), clears up many obscure theological points that may have puzzled seminarians and also includes a brief but useful history of the *Relations*. The publication of a new edition of the *Relations* and supporting documents has been undertaken by the Society of Jesus; Vol. 23 of the *Missiones Occidentales* series is the first of a continuing series of source material dealing with the order in North America. *Monumenta Novae Franciae*, Vol. I., *La première mission d'Acadie (1602–1616)* ed. by Lucien Campeau, S.I. (Rome and Québec, 1967) sets a standard for scholarship rarely attained; the book-length introduction is valuable as a critical history of the early period. Four volumes of this series have so far appeared; Vol. V is on press. Several editions of Champlain's journals have appeared; that published by the Champlain Society, *The Works of Samuel de Champlain*, ed. by George M. Wrong (6 vols., Toronto, 1922–35), contains an English translation. The Champlain Society has also published Marc Lescarbot, *The History of New France*, ed. by W. L. Grant and H. P. Biggar (3 vols., Toronto, 1907–14), and Nicolas Denys, *The Description and Natural History of the Coasts of North America (Acadia)*, trans. and ed. by W. F. Ganong (2 vols., Toronto, 1908).

There is a marked lack of good monographs on the history of Acadia, perhaps because the scanty source material demands much more exhaustive analysis than that for the later periods. Marcel Trudel's account in Vol. I of his *Histoire de la Nouvelle-France* (cited above) provides a good framework. J. B. Brebner, *New England's Outpost: Acadia Before the Conquest of Canada* (New York, 1927) is still useful. Alfred Goldsworthy Bailey, *The Conflict of European and Eastern Algonkian Cultures, 1504–1700* (Saint John, N.B., 1937; 2d ed., Toronto, 1969), is a scholarly treatment of the topic. French-Indian relations are also studied in some depth by Lucien Campeau in the preface to his *Monumenta Novae Franciae*, Vol. I, *La première mission d'Acadie*, cited above. Andrew Hill Clark, *Acadia: The Geography of Early Nova Scotia to 1760* (Madison, Wisc., 1968) is a useful work by a historical geographer concerned with what the people did with the land.

With the establishment of the colony at Quebec the amount of source material and the number of secondary accounts increase. Among the main printed sources are Champlain's journals, cited above. They must, however, be subjected to greater critical scrutiny than has been the case to date; some of his accounts of events strain credulity to the limit, for example, his account of his clash with the Mohawks in 1609. Throwing much new light on this period is *Nouveaux documents sur Champlain et son époque*, Vol. I, *1560–1622*, collected and ed. by Robert Le Blant and René Baudry (Publications des Archives publiques du Canada, No. 15, Ottawa, 1967). Gabriel Sagard, *The Long Journey to the Country of the Hurons*, trans. and ed. by George M. Wrong (Champlain Society Publications, Toronto, 1939) is invaluable for its revealing glimpse of European reaction to Indian culture. Chrestien Le Clercq, Récollet, *Premier établissement de la foy dans la Nouvelle France* (Paris, 1691) is rather tendentious. So too is Sixte Le Tac, R.P., *Histoire chronologique de la Nouvelle France ou Canada* (written 1689, pub. Paris, 1888), which covers the period 1504–1632 and makes explicit the hostility of the Récollets toward the Jesuits; the appendix contains useful documents. Chrestien Le Clercq's *Nouvelle relation de la Gaspésie*, ed. and trans. by W. F. Ganong for the Champlain Society, is entitled *New Relation of Gaspésia with the Customs and Religion of the Gaspésian Indians* (Toronto, 1910). Other contemporary histories that can be treated, warily, as primary material are Gabriel Sagard, *Histoire du Canada et voyages que les Frères Mineurs Recollects y ont faicts pour la conversion des Infidelles* (Paris, 1636; republished in 4 vols., ed. by Edwin Tross, Paris, 1866); François Du Creux, S.J., *Historiae Canadensis seu Novae-Franciae libri decem ad annum usque Christi MDCLVI* (Paris, 1664). The Champlain Society published this work, ed.

by J. B. Conacher, trans. by Percy J. Robinson, under the title *The History of Canada or New France* (2 vols., Toronto, 1951–52).

Again, the best detailed modern narrative history of the period is by Marcel Trudel, *Histoire de la Nouvelle-France*, Vol. II, *Le Comptoir, 1604–1627* (Montréal, 1966). The biography of Champlain by Morris Bishop, *Champlain: The Life of Fortitude* (New York, 1948) is written with exemplary flair, but is uncritical; it is, however, superior to the panegyric by N.-E. Dionne, *Samuel Champlain: Fondateur de Québec et Père de la Nouvelle-France: Histoire de sa vie et de ses voyages* (2 vols., Québec, 1891). A scholarly, critical, biography of Champlain remains to be written, as does a critical, annotated edition of his journals.

Chapter Two: 1632–1663

In addition to the printed primary source material cited for Chapter 1, the following are useful: Pierre Boucher, *Histoire véritable et naturelle des moeurs et productions du pays de la Nouvelle-France, vulgairement dicte le Canada* (Paris, 1664; Montreal, 1882; Boucherville, 1964); Ralph Flenley (trans. and ed.), *A History of Montreal, 1640–1672: From the French of Dollier de Casson* (Toronto, 1928); Marie Morin, *Annales de l'Hôtel-Dieu de Montréal*, collated and annotated by A. Fauteux, E.-Z. Massicotte, C. Bertrand; introd. by E. Morin (Montréal, 1921); *Histoire de l'Hôtel-Dieu de Québec* (Montauban, 1751; republished, ed. by Dom Jamet, Quebec, 1939); *Word from New France: The Selected Letters of Marie de l'Incarnation*, trans. and ed. by Joyce Marshall (Toronto, 1967). There are two collections, in the original French, of Marie de l'Incarnation's letters: *Lettres de la vénérable Mère Marie de l'Incarnation, première supérieure des Ursulines de la Nouvelle-France, divisées en deux parties*, ed. by Dom Claude Martin (Paris, 1681), and *Lettres de la révérende Mère Marie de l'Incarnation (née Marie Guyard), première supérieure du Monastère des Ursulines de Québec*, ed. by P.-F. Richaudeau (2 vols., Paris, Tournai, Leipzig, 1876). The latter of the two is the superior — see the comments by Joyce Marshall in her introduction. In the *Rapport des Archives du Québec*, Tome

41 (1963) is printed the journal of the Jesuits in New France for 1634–35.

There are not a few studies of aspects of the period of varying quality. For the confused situation in Acadia see the relevant chapters in Gustave Lanctot, *Histoire du Canada: Des origines au régime royale* (Montréal, 1959), trans. by Josephine Hambleton, *A History of Canada, Volume One: from Its Origins to the Royal Regime, 1663* (Cambridge, Mass., 1963), and also J. B. Brebner, *New England's Outpost: Acadia Before the Conquest of Canada* (New York, 1927): John G. Reid, *Acadia, Maine, and New Scotland* (Toronto, 1976) indicates where further research is required. On the French West Indies, the basic work for the early period is the scholarly study by Jacques de Dampierre, *Essai sur les sources de l'Histoire des Antilles françaises (1492–1664)* (Paris, 1904). The narrative account by Nellis M. Crouse, *French Pioneers in the West Indies, 1624–1664* (New York, 1940) is superficial. On Richelieu's policy for the islands, Bernard Schnapper, ''À propos de la doctrine et de la politique coloniale de Richelieu,'' *Revenue d'Histoire des Colonies*, XLII (1954), pp. 314–328, is useful.

For Canada, a useful narrative outline is contained in Gustave Lanctot's *Histoire du Canada*, cited above. A detailed account of events is given in R. P. Camille de Rochemonteix, *Les Jésuites de la Nouvelle-France au XVIIᵉ siècle* (3 vols., Paris, 1896). J. H. Kennedy, *Jesuit and Savage in New France* (New Haven, 1950) attempts the extremely difficult task of explaining the psychological problems involved. In this problem of clashing cultural values, the article by André Vachon, ''L'eau de vie dans la société indienne,'' *Canadian Historical Association Report, 1960*, goes deeper than the title suggests and is very perceptive. An intriguing work is that by François-Marc Gagnon, *La conversion par l'image* (Montreal, 1975).

On the relations of the Hurons and Iroquois with the French, Dutch, and English, George T. Hunt, *The Wars of the Iroquois* (Madison Wisc., 1940) gives an economic interpretation of the so called ''beaver wars'' which is now discredited, as also is Bruce G. Trigger, *Natives and Newcomers. Canada's ''Heroic Age'' Reconsidered* (Kingston & Montreal, 1985) a flawed and pretentious work. Much better, but very prolix, is Trigger's major work *The Children of Aataentsic. A History of the Huron People to 1660*, 2 vols., (Montreal & London, 1976). Conrad Heidenreich's *Huronia. A History and Geography of the Huron Indians 1600–1650* (Toronto, 1971) is a major work by a historical geographer.

In recent years, American ethnohistorians have broken the bounds of the history of Indian-European relations and set new scholarly standards, as they incorporate the findings of historians, geographers, anthropologists, and archeologists into their reconstruction of the past. Much of their work is relevant to New France. Only a few works can be mentioned here but they lead on to others: James Axtell, *The Invasion Within* (Oxford & New York, 1985); Neal Salisbury, *Manitou and Providence* (New York & Oxford, 1982); Robert F. Berkhofer, Jr., *The White Man's Indian* (New York & Toronto, 1978); and the combative Francis Jennings' *The Invasion of America. Indians, Colonialism, and the Cant of Conquest* (Chapel Hill NC, 1975); regarded as heresy by some, it did have a salutary effect and still stands up.

Also valuable is Elisabeth Tooker, *An Ethnography of the Huron Indians, 1615–1649* (Bureau of American Ethnology, Bulletin No. 190, Washington D.C., 1964).

The main causes, events, and consequences attendant on the foundation of Montreal have been elucidated, but much more remains to be done on this "New Jerusalem." In fact, New France still awaits its Perry Miller. A narrative account of events is contained in Gustave Lanctot, *Montreal under Maisonneuve, 1642–1665*, trans. from the French by Alta Lind Cook (Toronto, 1969). Roland-J. Auger, *La grande recrue de 1653* (Montréal, 1955), contains much useful information on the early settlers, and some trivia. Étienne-Michel Faillon, *Histoire de la colonie française en Canada* (3 vols., Montreal 1875–66) is a very detailed account by a Sulpician who ascribed too much to the intervention of Providence, but he did cite his documentary sources. An excellent corrective to Faillon is the two articles by E. R. Adair, "France and the Beginnings of New France," *The Canadian Historical Review*, XXV (Sept. 1944), pp. 246–278; "The Evolution of Montreal under the French Regime," *The*

Canadian Historical Association Report, 1942, pp. 20–41. The multivolume works of Marcel Trudel's *Histoire de la Nouvelle-France* put all previous works in the shade. In particular see *Histoire de la Nouvelle-France I: Les vaines tentatives 1524–1603* (Montréal & Paris, 1963); *Histoire de la Nouvelle-France II: Le Comptoir 1604–1627* (Montréal & Paris, 1966); *Histoire de la Nouvelle-France III: La Seigneurie des Cent-Associés 1627–1663 tome I: Les événements* (Montréal, 1979); *Histoire de la Nouvelle-France III: La seigneurie des cent-associés, tome II: La société* (Montréal, 1983); *Montréal. La formation d'une société 1642–1663* (Montréal, 1976). Another major work on the founding and early years of Montreal is Louise Dechêne, *Habitants et marchands de Montréal au XVIIe siècle* (Paris & Montréal, 1974). Using the renowned but demanding methods of the *Annales* school of historians, the author has produced a most impressive study of seventeenth-century Montreal. Unfortunately, due perhaps to haste, it is flawed by a few serious misinterpretations of evidence. A revised edition would be a major contribution to the history of New France. An example of the new approach to social history is the brief article by Marcel Trudel, "Les débuts d'une société: Montréal, 1642–1663 — Étude de certains comportements sociaux," *Revue d'Histoire de l'Amérique française*, XXIII (Sept. 1969), pp. 185–207.

Chapter Three: 1663–1685

With the advent of royal government in the colonies and the establishment of a centralized administrative system, correspondence and records multiplied. Moreover, when, on Colbert's orders, an archive was established, the bulk of this material was preserved. In the colonies the intendants saw to it that the notaries and officers of the law courts maintained proper registers. Some of this material, mostly official correspondence, has been printed. A rich selection was published in Pierre Clément (ed.), *Lettres, instructions et mémoires de Colbert* (7 vols., Paris, 1861–73). The voluminous correspondence of the intendant Jean Talon and the governor general Frontenac appears in the *Rapport de l'Archiviste de la Province de Québec, 1926–1927, 1930–1931*. Care has to be exercised in making use of Pierre Margry (ed.), *Mémoires et documents pour servir à l'histoire des origines françaises des pays d'outre mer: Découvertes et établissements des Français dans l'ouest et dans le sud de l'Amérique septentrionale* (6 vols., Paris, 1876); Margry took liberties with some of the texts to enhance the reputation of La Salle. Emma Helen Blair (ed.), *The Indian Tribes of the Upper Mississippi Valley and Region of the Great Lakes* (2 vols., Cleveland, 1911–12), translated some of the more significant French accounts. The account by the Sulpician at Montreal, François Vachon de Belmont, *Histoire du Canada par M. l'Abbé de Belmont, d'après un manuscrit à la bibliothèque du Roi à Paris* (n.p., n.d.) was also printed in *Literary and Historical Society of Quebec, Historical Documents*, Ser. 1, No. 2 (Quebec, 1840). The colourful Pierre Esprit Radisson's account of his role in the establishment of both the French and the English Hudson's Bay companies was published by the Prince Society of Boston, *Radisson's Voyages* (Boston, 1885). A new revised edition which replaces the pagination in what the editor claims to be the correct order, thereby reconciling obvious inconsistencies in the text, is Arthur T. Adams (ed.), *The Explorations of Pierre Esprit Radisson* (Minneapolis, 1961).

There have been two general studies of the period in recent years. Gustave Lanctot, *Histoire du Canada* Vol. II, *Du régime royal au Traité d'Utrecht (1663–1713)*, (Montréal, 1960); in translation by Josephine Hambleton, *A History of Canada*, Vol. II, *From the Royal Régime to the Treaty of Utrecht, 1663–1713)* (Harvard Univ. Press, 1964) is a detailed narrative account that goes little beyond the earlier works. W. J. Eccles, *Canada under Louis XIV, 1663–1701* (Toronto, 1964), is more analytical, stressing social and institutional development, but it is now dated.

Among the few worthwhile monographs are Stewart L. Mims, *Colbert's West Indian Policy* (New Haven, 1912), which deals with the establishment, operation, and demise of Colbert's Compagnie de l'Occident. The administrative framework of New France was first analyzed by Gustave Lanctot, *L'administration de la Nouvelle France* (Paris, 1929), and it is still useful. More succinct, but very cogent, is the article by André Vachon in the introduction to Vol. II of *The Dictionary of Canadian Biography,*

1701–1740, also published as a separate pamphlet, *L'administration de la Nouvelle-France, 1627–1760* (Univ. of Toronto Press and Les Presses de l'Université Laval, Toronto and Québec, 1970). The significant article by J. F. Bosher, "Government and Private Interests in New France," *Canadian Public Administration* (June 1967), pp. 244–257, throws light in a murky corner. There have been two studies of the Sovereign Council: J. Delalande, *Le Conseil souverain de la Nouvelle France* (Quebec, 1927), and Raymond Du Bois Cahall, *The Sovereign Council of New France* (New York, 1915). The latter is much the better of the two, but a reappraisal of the council is needed.

For the seigneurial system, William Bennet Munro, *The Seigneurial System in Canada: A Study in French Colonial Policy* (New York, 1907), is outdated and contains errors of fact and erroneous interpretations. Dorothy A. Heneker, *The Seigneurial Regime in Canada* (Quebec, 1927) has been superseded by Richard Colebrook Harris, *The Seigneurial System in Early Canada* (Univ. of Wisconsin Press and Les Presses de l'Université Laval, Madison, Milwaukee, London, Quebec, 1966). The pamphlet by Marcel Trudel, "The Seigneurial Regime" (The Canadian Historical Association Booklets, No. 6, Ottawa, 1967) provides a useful summary of the main features of the land tenure system and their continued historical significance.

Some of the leading personalities of the period have found biographers; others, equally important in their day, have not. Those who did have come to dominate the period and obscure those who did not, in general histories. Most of these biographies are of the "life and times" variety, and too many of them are hagiographic rather than critical studies. Little of the primary source material escaped Thomas Chapais in his uncritical study, *Jean Talon, intendant de la Nouvelle-France (1665–1672)* (Québec, 1904), but he gave Talon credit for more than he deserved. This work is a case in point. Until very recently it was the only biography of an intendant of New France; thus Talon came religiously to be referred to as "the great intendant," while the names of two later intendants, Jean Bochart de Champigny and Gilles Hocquart, whose tenures of office were much more significant, remain virtually unknown. Talon spent five years in the colony, Champigny sixteen, and Hocquart seventeen. The same caveat applies to the office of governor general. Frontenac appears to be the dominant figure of his age because his biographers made him appear so. The first was Francis Parkman's *Count Frontenac and New France under Louis XIV* (Boston, 1877), which also exhibited Parkman's entrenched belief in the superiority of Anglo-American institutions and their manifest destiny to prevail over those of France and Rome. H. Lorin, *Le comte de Frontenac* (Paris, 1895), bitterly anticlerical, took serious liberties with the evidence to extol his hero and denounce the clergy. W. J. Eccles, *Frontenac: The Courtier Governor* (Toronto, 1959) is a more critical study. The Jesuits' side of the controversy is well-expressed by Jean Delanglez, *Frontenac and the Jesuits* (Chicago, 1939), and in a series of revisionist articles that appeared in *Mid-America* between 1937 and 1949. La Salle remains a controversial figure. Francis Parkman, *The Discovery of the Great West* (Boston, 1869) was more a projection of Parkman's own personality than of La Salle's. It remains a literary epic but has little merit as history. The article by William R. Taylor, "A Journey into the Human Mind: Motivation in Francis Parkman's La Salle," *William and Mary Quarterly*, 3d Ser., XVIII (1962), pp. 220–237, elucidates this strange problem. More critical of La Salle is E. B. Osler, *La Salle* (Toronto, 1967). It was, however, again Jean Delanglez who effectively destroyed the Parkman "great man" image of La Salle in *Some La Salle Journeys* (Chicago, 1938). This Jesuit historian also placed another of the western fur traders and explorers in clearer perspective in his *Life and Voyages of Louis Jolliet, 1645–1700* (Chicago, 1948). La Salle's lieutenant, Henri Tonti, is the subject of a brief preliminary study by E. R. M. Murphy, *Henri de Tonty: Fur Trader of the Mississippi* (Baltimore, 1941). The Jesuit co-discoverer of the Mississippi, Jacques Marquette, was made the subject of controversy by a Franciscan, Francis B. Steck, in his unconvincing *Marquette Legends*, ed. by August Reyling (New York, 1960). His charges are refuted in Raphael N. Hamilton, S.J., *Marquette's Explorations: The Narratives Reexamined* (Univ. of Wisconsin Press, Madison, Milwaukee, and London, 1970). The traditional estimate of Marquette has recently been given in Joseph P. Donnelly, *Jacques Marquette, S.J., 1637–1675* (Chicago, 1968). The biography of Radisson by Grace Lee Nute, *Caesars of the Wilderness, Médard Chouart, sieur des Groseilliers and Pierre Esprit Radisson, 1618–1710* (New York, 1943) is florid and dated. A revealing study of an important Canadian family is Micheline D'Allaire, *Montée et déclin d'une famille noble: Les Ruette d'Auteuil (1617–1737)* (Ville La Salle, 1980).

The role of the clergy within the colony is depicted in the detailed but rather superficial study by the Abbé Auguste Gosselin, *L'Eglise du Canada depuis Monseigneur de Laval jusqu'à la conquête*, Première partie, *Mgr. de Saint Vallier* (Quebec, 1911). Bishop St. Vallier was himself the author of *État Présent de l'Eglise et de la Colonie Française dans le Nouvelle-France* (Paris, 1688). Cornelius J. Jaenen's *The Role of the Church in New France* (Toronto, 1976) is a slight but useful work, obviously intended for an undergraduate audience.

Chapter Four: 1683–1713

The printed source material for this period is abundant. The *Documentary History of the State of New York*, 4 vols., and *Documents Relative to the Colonial History of the State of New York*, 15 vols., cited above, contain much of the official correspondence, both French and English. The editing is poor, the translation worse. Frontenac's correspondence with the court during his second term is contained in the *Rapport de l'Archiviste de la province de Québec, 1927–1928, 1928–1929*; that of Philippe de Rigaud de Vaudreuil in the *Rapports* for the years 1938–39, 1939–40, 1942–43, 1946–47, 1947–48. A selection of documents concerning French activities in the West is contained in E. C. Pease and R. C. Werner (eds.), *The French Foundations, 1680–1693* (Collection of the Illinois State Historical Library, Vol. I, Springfield, 1934). On the role of the Five Nations, documents dealing with their negotiations with Albany are contained in Peter Wraxall, *An Abridgement of the New York Indian Records*, ed. by C. H. McIlwain (Cambridge, Mass., 1915) and in *The Livingston Indian Records, 1666–1723*, ed. by Lawrence

H. Leder (The Pennsylvania Historical Association, Gettysburg, 1956). Cadwallader Colden, *The History of the Five Indian Nations*, Part I (London, 1727), Part II (London, 1747), gives the eighteenth-century New York view of events down to 1701. Francis Jennings et al (eds.), *The History and Culture of Iroquois Diplomacy* (Syracuse Univ. Press, 1985) contains some excellent and some shoddy articles. Le chevalier de Baugy, *Journal d'une expédition contre les Iroquis en 1687* (Paris, 1883) is an interesting account by a French officer who participated in the campaign. Another French officer—who turned renegade—published a colourful journal of his years in New France: Louis Armand de Lom d'Arce, baron de Lahontan, *Nouveaux voyages de Mr le baron de Lahontan dans l'Amérique Septentrionale* (2 vols., La Haye, 1709). The English edition of 1703 was republished, ed. by R. G. Thwaites, *New Voyages to North America* (2 vols., Chicago, 1905). Nothing Lahontan wrote can be accepted at face value; he wrote this journal years after the events described, his memory was frequently faulty, and he embellished the truth not a little. Two other valuable contemporary works are Nicholas Perrot, *Mémoires sur les moeurs, coustumes et relligion des sauvages de l'Amérique septentrionale* (Tailhan, ed., Leipzig and Paris, 1864), and M. de Bacqueville de la Potherie, *Histoire de l'Amérique septentrionale* (Paris, 1753), but both demand careful checking with other sources on events. Ernest Myrand, *1690 Sir William Phips devant Québec: Histoire d'un Siège* (Quebec, 1893) is a valuable collection of documents, both English and French. An account of the 1690 assault by a New England officer is that of Thomas Savage, *An Account of the Late Action of the New Englanders, under the Command of Sir William Phips, Against the French at Canada* (London, 1691).

For the general background to the quarter-century and more of conflict in North America, W. J. Eccles, *Frontenac: The Courtier Governor* (Toronto, 1959) covers King William's War. The 1700–1713 struggle is succinctly analyzed by Guy Frégault, "L'Empire britannique et la conquête du Canada (1700–1713)," in *Le XVIIIᵉ siècle canadien* (Montréal, 1968). Francis Parkman, *A Half Century of Conflict* (Boston, 1892), leaves no doubt which side he believed should win. Howard H. Peckham, *The Colonial*

Wars, 1689–1762 (Chicago, 1964) is a superficial account with an Anglo-American bias, too riddled with errors of fact to have any value. On the 1711 abortive assault on Canada, Gerald S. Graham, *The Walker Expedition to Quebec: 1711* (Champlain Society Publications, Toronto, 1953) reproduces the relevant documents and a trenchant analysis. The struggle for Hudson Bay is discussed by E. E. Rich, *The History of the Hudson's Bay Company, 1670–1870*, Vol. I, *1670–1763* (The Hudson's Bay Record Society, London, 1958). The role of Iberville in this theatre is described in Guy Frégault, *Iberville le conquérant* (Montréal, 1944). For the French Hudson's Bay Company see the unpublished M.A. thesis by Richard H. Borins, "La compagnie du Nord, 1682–1700" (McGill University, 1968). A first-hand account of the initial French attack on the English posts in the Bay is I. Caron (ed.), *Journal de l'Expédition du Chevalier de Troyes à la Baie d'Hudson* (Beauceville, 1918). For the struggle in Acadia see again J. B. Brebner, *New England's Outpost: Acadia Before the Conquest of Canada* (New York, 1927). See also John G. Reid, *Acadia, Maine, and New Scotland* (Toronto, 1976). French policy in Acadia at the beginning of the century is analyzed in Francis H. Hammang, *The Marquis de Vaudreuil: New France at the Beginning of the Eighteenth Century* (Louvain, 1938). Antony F. C. Wallace, "Origins of Iroquois Neutrality: The Grand Settlement of 1701," *Pennsylvania History*, XXIV (1957), pp. 223–235, is rather superficial but has the virtue of studying the event from the Iroquois point of view. Two excellent articles by Brian J. Given and Susan Johnson in Bruce Alden Cox (ed.), *Native People, Native Lands* (Ottawa, 1987) shatter some hoary myths. For the struggle in the West, see Yves F. Zoltvany, *Philippe de Rigaud de Vaudreuil. Governor of New France 1703–1725* (Toronto, 1974). The broader consequences of these wars on Canada are discussed in W. J. Eccles, "The Social, Economic, and Political Significance of the Military Establishment in New France," *The Canadian Historical Review*, LII (Mar. 1971), pp. 1–22.

On the economic aspects of this period, Guy Frégault's article "La compagnie de la colonie," in *Le XVIIIe siècle canadien* (Montréal, 1968) gives a clear analysis of the attempt by the

Canadians to manage the fur trade. Canadian finances are also analyzed by Guy Frégault in his article "Essai sur les finances canadiennes," in the same collected work. On this problem, and particularly the introduction of card money, Vol. I of *Documents Relating to Canadian Currency, Exchange and Finance During the French Period*, selected and edited with notes and introduction by Adam Shortt (Board of Historical Publications, Canadian Archives, 1925) should be consulted. The attempt to exploit the Canadian forest for ship masts, timber, and naval stores is discussed in P. W. Bamford, *Forests and French Sea Power* (Toronto, 1956). The article by A. R. M. Lower, "The Forest in New France: A Sketch of Lumbering in Canada before the English Conquest," *Canadian Historical Association Report, 1928* is worth consulting. The best study to date is Jacques Mathieu, *La construction navale royale à Québec, 1739-1759* (Cahiers d'histoire, no. 23, 1971. La Société historique de Québec).

Chapter Five: 1713-1744

This period in Canadian history, perhaps because there was little armed conflict, has not been as closely investigated by historians as the periods before and after. Several important topics are, however, presently being studied by younger historians. It is likely that their findings will require the jettisoning of some revered concepts, many of them stemming from the warped view of Canadian institutions and society expressed almost a century ago by Francis Parkman in *The Old Regime in Canada* (Boston, 1874). An excellent recent revisionist work is Dale Miquelon, *New France 1701-1744. A Supplement to Europe* (Toronto, 1987).

On the economy, the best study is still that by Miss A. J. E. Lunn, "Economic Development in New France, 1713-1760" (unpublished Ph.D. thesis, McGill University, 1942). Recently a French translation of this work appeared, *Développement économique de la Nouvelle-France 1713-1760* (Montréal, 1986). Her article on the Montreal-Albany contraband trade, "The Illegal Fur Trade out of New France, 1713-1760," *Canadian Historical*

Association Report, 1939, remains the best study of that important topic. Harold Adams Innis, *The Fur Trade in Canada* (Yale University Press, 1930. Revised 1956, reprinted Toronto, 1962) is now hopelessly dated. See W.J. Eccles "A Belated Review of Harold Adams Innis, *The Fur Trade in Canada*," *Canadian Historical Review*, LX, No. 4, 1979, pp. 419–441, also, Eccles "The Fur Trade and Eighteenth Century Imperialism," *The William and Mary Quarterly*, 3d Series, Vol. XV, July 1983, pp. 341–362. On the colony's iron foundry see Louise Trottier, *Les forges. Historiographie des Forges du Saint-Maurice* (Montréal, 1980). See also Joseph-Noel Fauteux, *Essai sur l'industrie au Canada sous le régime français* 2 vols. (Québec, 1927), a superficial but still useful survey. P. E. Renaud, *Les origines économiques du Canada* (Mamers, 1928) lacks cohesion but provides some detailed information.

Jean Hamelin, *Économie et société en Nouvelle-France*, (Québec, 1960) employs quantitative methods in an attempt to prove that the colony's economy was not viable; Cameron Nish, *Les bourgeois-gentilhommes de la Nouvelle-France, 1729–1748* (Montréal, 1968) attempts to prove the opposite. Superior works are Dale Miquelon, *Dugard of Rouen. French Trade to Canada and the West Indies, 1729–1770* (Montreal & London, 1978), Jacques Mathieu, *Le commerce entre la Nouvelle-France et les Antilles au XVIIIᵉ siècle* (Montréal, 1981), J. F. Bosher, *The Canada Merchants 1713–1763* (Oxford, 1987). See also the provocative article on the colony's economic development, L. R. MacDonald, "France and New France: the Internal Contradiction," *The Canadian Historical Review*, LII (June 1971).

On expansion in the West and the search for the western sea, A. S. Morton, *A History of the Canadian West to 1870–71* (London, 1939) is a superficial and dated survey. Yves F. Zoltvany, "The Frontier Policy of Philippe de Rigaud de Vaudreuil (1713–1725)," *The Canadian Historical Review*, XLVIII (Sept. 1967), puts that policy in a clear perspective. On the explorations of La Verendrye, L. J. Burpee (ed.), *Journals and Letters of Pierre Gaultier de Varennes de la Verendrye and His Sons* (Champlain Society Publications, Toronto, 1927) provides the basic documents, but the translation bears checking. Antoine Champagne,

Les La Verendrye et le poste de l'Ouest (Québec, 1968), is a rather uncritical study of the explorer but the best there is. For the social consequences of the French presence in the West, the magisterial study by Marcel Giraud, *Le Métis canadien: Son rôle dans l'histoire des provinces de l'Ouest* (2 vols., Paris, 1945) is fundamental. But see Sylvia Van Kirk, *Many Tender Ties*, Women in Fur-Trade Society, 1670-1870,'' (Winnipeg, nd) and the three articles by Harriet Gorham, George Herman Springer, and Jennifer Brown in Bruce Alden Cox (ed.), op. cit. On Franco-Indian relations see L. F. S. Upton, *Micmacs and Colonists: Indian-White Relations in the Maritimes, 1713-1867* (Vancouver, 1979) and W. J. Eccles ''Sovereignty-Association, 1500-1783,'' *Canadian Historical Review*, LXV, 4, 1984, pp. 466-510.

Government and the colonial administration in the eighteenth century are succinctly analyzed in the article by Guy Frégault, ''Politique et politiciens,'' in his *Le XVIIIe siècle canadien* (Montréal, 1968). R. La Roque de Roquebrune, ''La direction de la Nouvelle-France par le ministère de la marine,'' *Revue d'Histoire de l'Amérique française*, VI (1952-53) is also valuable. The intendant Dupuy and the administrative system in which he worked and came to grief is studied in depth by Jean-Claude Dubé, *Claude-Thomas Dupuy Intendant de la Nouvelle-France, 1678-1738* (Montréal, 1969). An important work on the role of women in New France is Micheline D'Allaire, *L'hôpital général de Québec, 1692-1764* (Montréal, 1971) A seminal article that ruffled a few Marxist feathers is Jan Noel, ''New France: les femmes favorisées,'' ATLANTIS VI, No. 2, Spring 1981, pp. 80-98. Poor relief measures are outlined in W. J. Eccles, ''Social Welfare Measures and Policies in New France,'' *XXXVI Congreso Internacional de Americanistas*, IV (Sevilla, 1966), pp. 9-20. The incidence of slavery in Canada is exhaustively studied by Marcel Trudel, *L'Esclavage au Canada français* (Québec, 1960). A very revealing work that broke new ground is the demographic analysis by Jacques Henripin, *La population canadienne au début du XVIIIe siècle* (Paris, 1954). Robert-Lionel Séguin, *La sorcellerie au Canada français du XVIIe au XIXe siècle* (Montréal, 1961) cannot be called profound, but does provide some useful material. The same has to be said of the same author's

La civilisation traditionelle de l' "habitant" aux XVIIe et XVIIIe
siècles (Montréal & Paris, 1967). Of the numerous accounts by
contemporary visitors to the colony, among the more valuable is
that by the Swedish professor of botany Peter Kalm; Adolph P.
Benson (ed.), *The America of 1750: The Travels in North America*
by Peter Kalm (New York, 1937; paperback ed., 2 vols., New
York, 1966). The history of Kalm's tour, and his account of his
travels, is presented in the scholarly and interesting study by
Martti Kerkkonen, *Peter Kalm's North American Journey: Its*
Ideological Background and Results (Studia Historica, I, Finnish
Historical Society, Helsinki, 1959). An observant French officer,
Louis Franquet, gave his impressions of the colony, *Voyages et*
mémoires sur le Canada (Quebec, 1889). A well-educated and
discerning private soldier in the colonial regulars wrote an interesting account of his experiences, *Voyage au Canada dans le*
Nord de l'Amérique septentrionale fait depuis l'an 1751 à 1761
par J. C. B. (Quebec, 1887). There is also much valuable comment on Canadian society in Pierre-François-Xavier de Charlevoix, S.J., *Histoire et description générale de la Nouvelle-France*
. . . (3 vols., Paris, 1744).

The visual arts of New France have received some attention.
Fortunately, the Federal Government and the Ministère des
Affaires culturelles du Quebec are at last making a concerted effort
to preserve and restore what remains of French regime edifices;
Louisbourg and La Place Royale in Quebec city are examples of
what can be done. The journal *Culture Vivante*, published by the
Ministère des Affaires culturelles du Québec merits perusal. Jean
Palardy, *The Early Furniture of French Canada*, trans. from the
French by Eric McLean (Toronto, 1963), is a superb study. Ram-
say Traquair, *The Old Silver of Quebec* (Toronto, 1940), although
anything but exhaustive, is useful. Of much greater scope is the
same author's *The Old Architecture of Quebec* (Toronto, 1947).
A pleasure to peruse is Peter N. Moogk, *Building a House in*
New France (Toronto, 1977). Also useful is Robert-Lionel
Séguin, *La maison en Nouvelle-France* (Musée national du Canada. Bulletin 226. Ottawa, 1968). For church architecture see
Alan Gowans, *Church Architecture in New France* (Toronto,
1955). Exhaustive and well-illustrated is André Charbonneau,

Yvon Desloges, Marc Lafrance, *Québec The Fortified City: From the 17th to the 19th century* (Ottawa, Parks Canada, 1982). Also very useful is Gerard Morisset, *L'architecture en Nouvelle-France* (Québec, 1949). Woodcarving, at which Canadian artisans excelled, is discussed by E. R. Adair, "French Canadian Art," *The Canadian Historical Association Report, 1929*. Robert-Lionel Séguin, *La civilisation traditionnelle de l'habitant aux XVIIᵉ et XVIIIᵉ siècles* (Montreal, 1967) contains a mass of poorly digested material.

There are only a few studies of Acadia and Nova Scotia circa 1713–1783 that have scholarly value. The works of J. B. Brebner, although now sadly dated, and those of the geographer Andrew Hill Clark, cited previously, are still basic: yet a caveat has to be entered; Clark was a geographer, and his work was flawed when he strove to be a historian, lacking the training that the historian's discipline requires. An exceptional study is L. F. S. Upton, *Micmacs and Colonists. Indian-White Relations in the Maritimes, 1713–1867*, (Vancouver B.C., 1979). On Louisbourg, J. S. McLennan, *Louisbourg from its Foundation to its Fall, 1713–1758*, (London, 1918; reprinted without appendices, Sydney, N.S., 1957) is still the basic work. On the construction of the fortress see Frederic G. Thorpe, *Les Remparts lointains* (Ottawa, 1985). An intriguing example of comparative history is John Robert McNeill, *Atlantic Empires of France and Spain. Louisbourg and Havana, 1700–1763* (Univ. Carolina Press, 1985). D. C. Harvey, *The French Regime in Prince Edward Island* (New Haven, 1926) still stands alone.

Chapter Six: 1683–1748

The essential guide to the history of the French West Indies is Jacques de Dampierre, *Essai sur les sources de l'Histoire des Antilles françaises (1492–1664)* (Paris, 1904). Owing to the destruction of documentary material the contemporary histories are invaluable. The most significant of them is P. J. B. Du Tertre, *Histoire générale des Antilles habitées par les Français divisée en deux tomes* (4 vols., Paris, 1667–71). Also informative on the flora, fauna, economy, and events is F. Jean-Baptiste Labat, *Nou-*

veaux Voyage aux Isles de l'Amérique (6 vols., Paris, 1722). P.-F.-X. de Charlevoix, *Histoire de l'Isle Espagnole ou de S. Domingue écrite particulièrement sur les mémoires mss. du P. J.-B. Le Pers, jésuite, missionaire à S. Domingue et sur les pièces originales qui se conservent au dépot de la marine* (2 vols., Paris, 1732) is exactly what the title indicates. Charlevoix was perhaps the first historian to make use of archival material. Raynal, *Histoire philosophique et politique des Îles françaises dans les Indes occidentales* (Lausanne, 1784) is more valuable for the eighteenth century than the early period. For a general description of Saint-Domingue and its ambience at its height, the study by the creole Moreau de Saint-Méry is valuable: *Description topographique, physique, civile, politique, et historique de la partie française de l'Isle Saint-Domingue: Avec des observations générales sur sa population, sur le caractère et les moeurs de ses divers habitans; sur son climat, sa culture, ses productions, son administration etc., etc.* (2 vols., Philadelphie, 1797–98; republished Paris, 1958, in 3 vols.). The important and extremely rare 1767 edition of *Le Code noir ou recueille des reglemens rendus jusqu'à présent* has been reproduced by the Sociétés d'histoire de la Guadeloupe et de la Martinique (Basse-Terre & Fort de France, 1980).

Of the modern works on the history of the Antilles, Alfred Martineau and L.-Ph. May, *Trois Siècles d'Histoire antillaise: Martinique et Guadeloupe de 1635 à nos Jours* (Paris, 1935) is a brief survey, containing little analysis, but with a chronological outline of main events at the end of each chapter, making it useful for quick reference. H. I. Priestley, *France Overseas Through the Old Regime: A Study of European Expansion* (New York, 1939) also provides the basic facts. W. Adolphe Roberts, *The French in the West Indies* (New York, 1942) is not a scholarly work and has little value. One of the more useful scholarly studies, which deals with far more than the title suggests, is Gaston-Martin, *Histoire de l'Esclavage dans les Colonies françaises* (Paris, 1948). Among the many works specifically on the institution of slavery, Antoine Gisler, C.S.S.P., *L'Esclavage aux Antilles françaises (XVIIᵉ–XIXᵉ siècle): Contribution au problème de l'esclavage* (Éditions Universitaires Fribourg, Suisse, 1965) is particularly valuable. So too is Gaston-Martin, *Nantes au XVIIIe Siècle: L'Ère des Négriers (1714–1774)* (Paris, 1931). The social conditions of slaves on one plantation is examined by Roseline Siguret, "Esclaves d'ingoteries et de cafétières au quartier de Jacmel (1757–1791)," *Revue française d'Outre-Mer*, LV, 199 (1968), pp. 190–230. The attitude of the plantation owners is clearly revealed in G. Debien, *Plantations et esclaves à Saint-Domingue* (Dakar, 1962).

Other aspects of the Martinique economy are dealt with in Louis-Philippe May, *Histoire économique de la Martinique, 1635–1763* (Paris, 1930). Clarence P. Gould, "Trade Between the Windward Islands and the Continental Colonies of the French, 1683–1763," *The Mississippi Valley Historical Review*, XXV, 4 (Mar. 1939), pp. 473–490, outlines the main difficulties that hampered that trade. On white immigration and West Indian colonial society, the book-length study by G. Debien is invaluable: "La société coloniale aux XVIIe et XVIIIe siècles: Les engagés pour les Antilles (1634–1715)," *Revue d'Histoire des Colonies françaises*, XXXVIII, 1 and 2 (1951), pp. 5–261. See also the study of an eighteenth-century Saint-Domingue coffee plantation by Gabriel Debien in his *Études Antillaises (XVIIIe Siècle)* (Paris, 1956) and his earlier work on the same subject, *Le peuplement des Antilles françaises au XVIIe siècle: Les engagés partis de La Rochelle (1683–1715)* (L'Institut français d'Archéologie orientale du Caire, 1942); and Lilianne Chauleau, *La Société à la Martinique au XVIIe siècle (1635–1713)* (Caen, 1966). Another scholarly and valuable work is the quantitative study by M. Delafosse, "La Rochelle et les îles au XVIIe siècle," *Revue d'Histoire des Colonies françaises*, XXXVI (1949), pp. 238–281. On the eighteenth-century conflict for control of the West Indies and their trade, the classic work, based mainly on English source material, is Richard Pares, *War and Trade in the West Indies, 1739–1763* (Oxford, 1936). For the French side of the maritime war see G. Lacour-Gayet, *La marine militaire de la France sous le regne de Louis XV* (Paris, 1902).

Two recent peripheral works that provide the requisite background for an understanding of the history of that part of the world are Franklin W. Knight, *The Caribbean* (New York, 1978) and Geoffrey J. Walker, *Spanish Politics and Imperial Trade 1700-1789* (London, 1979). No doubt there is a host more that has escaped my attention.

Louisiana, founded after the French had established an efficient archival system, offers an embarrassment of documentary riches. Unfortunately, the documents retained in the colony relating to the French and Spanish regimes were, until recently, not well cared for. On this sad score see Winston De Ville, "Manuscript Sources in Louisiana for the History of the French in the Mississippi Valley," in *The French in the Mississippi Valley*, ed. by John Francis McDermott (Univ. of Illinois Press, Urbana, 1965). The records of the Superior Council of Louisiana have been translated and printed, over the years, in the *Louisiana Historical Quarterly*. That journal has also printed the odd interesting document from time to time. Little or no account has yet been taken of the rich material for social history in the *greffes des notaires*.

Of the modern histories of Louisiana, Alcée Fortier, *A History of Louisiana* (New York, 1904) and Charles Gayerré, *Histoire de la Louisiane* (2 vols., New Orleans, 1846), have, happily, been superseded, most recently by the very detailed narrative histories of Marcel Giraud, *Histoire de la Louisiane française*, Vol. I, *Le Regne de Louis XIV* (Paris, 1953); Vol. II, *Années de transition (1715-1717)* (Paris, 1958); Vol. III, *L'Époque de John Law (1717-1720)* (Paris, 1966): Vol. IV, *La Louisiane après le système de Law* (1721-1723) (Paris, 1974). The article by the same author, "France and Louisiana in the Early Eighteenth Century," *Mississippi Valley Historical Review*, XXXVI, 4 (1949-50), pp. 657-674, is a brilliant analysis of the troubled early years of the colony. P. Heinrich, *La Louisiane sous la Compagnie des Indes (1717-1731)* (Paris, 1908) is still useful; so too is Baron Marc Villiers du Terrage, *Histoire de la fondation de la Nouvelle-Orléans 1712-1722* (Paris, 1817). Even more so is his *Les dernières années de la Louisiane française* (Paris, 1904), particularly for the account of the cession of the colony to Spain and the repercussions. On that issue E. Wilson Lyon, *Louisiana in French Diplomacy 1759-1804* (Univ. of Oklahoma Press, 1934) is a disappointingly superficial account. Just the reverse is the article by Pierre H. Boule, "French Reactions to the Louisiana Revolution of 1768,'' in *The French in the Missis-sippi Valley*, ed. by John Francis McDermott (Univ. of Illinois Press, Urbana, 1965). The same author's "Some Eighteenth Century French Views on Louisiana," in *Frenchmen and French Ways in the Mississippi Valley*, ed. by John Francis McDermott (Univ. of Illinois Press, Urbana, 1969), revises some widely held misconceptions. In that same volume the article by John C. Rule has value: "Jérôme Phélypeaux, comte de Pontchartrain, and the Establishment of Louisiana, 1696–1715.'' Patricia Dillion Woods, *French-Indian Relations on the Southern Frontier 1699–1762* (Ann Arbor, Michigan, 1980), a doctoral thesis that con-tributes little or nothing to knowledge; although superficial, it does provide a useful outline for the uninitiated.

On the economy of Louisiana, N. M. Miller Surrey, *The Com-merce of Louisiana During the French Regime, 1699–1763* (New York, 1916) is detailed but hardly a trenchant analysis of the evidence. The same author writes with more authority in her brief article, "The Development of Industries in Louisiana Dur-ing the French Regime, 1673–1763," *Mississippi Valley Histor-ical Review*, IX, 3 (Dec. 1922), pp. 227–235.

The relations of church and state are discussed with exemplary detachment by the Jesuit historian Charles Edward O'Neill, *Church and State in French Colonial Louisiana Policy and Pol-itics to 1732* (Yale Univ. Press, 1966). Another Jesuit historian, Jean Delanglez, broke new ground in his *The French Jesuits in Lower Louisiana (1700–1763)* (New Orleans, 1935). Few of the leading figures in the colony's history have been the subject of biographies; fewer still have been fortunate in their biographers. Two who were are Iberville and Vaudreuil: see Guy Frégault, *Iberville le conquérant* (Montréal, 1944); it is, however, now in need of revision in the light of work done by other scholars during the past quarter-century. The same stricture applies with greater force to Nellis M. Crouse, *Lemoyne d'Iberville: soldier of New France* (Cornell Univ. Press, Ithaca, N.Y., 1954). Guy Frégault, *Le Grand Marquis: Pierre de Rigaud de Vaudreuil et la Louisiane* (Montréal, 1952) is a sympathetic treatment of this controversial figure.

For the settlements in the Illinois country, Natalie Maree Belting, *Kaskaskia Under the French Regime* (Univ. of Illinois Press, Urbana, 1948) is basic. Two articles that have value are Charles E. Peterson, "The Houses of French St. Louis," and Samuel Wilson, Jr., "Colonial Fortifications and Military Architecture in the Mississippi Valley," in *The French in the Mississippi Valley*, ed. by John Francis McDermott (Univ. of Illinois Press, Urbana, 1965). The role of the region in Anglo-French imperial rivalry is treated in the now outdated C. W. Alvord, *The Illinois Country, 1673–1818* (Springfield, 1920) and Norman Ward Caldwell, *The French in the Mississippi Valley, 1740–1750,* (Univ. of Illinois Press, Urbana, 1941). For relations with Louisiana's neighbors see Henry Folmer, "Contraband Trade Between Louisiana and New Mexico in the XVIIIth Century," *New Mexico Historical Review* (1941), pp. 249–274, and *Franco-Spanish Rivalry in North America, 1564–1763* (Glendale, Cal., 1953). For a view of Louisiana strictly from the Anglo-American side of the frontier, see Verner W. Crane, *The Southern Frontier, 1670–1732* (Duke Univ. Press, Durham, N.C., 1928).

Chapter Seven: 1749–1763

The quantity of printed source material relating to the destruction of the French empire in North America is vast. Many of the leading participants wrote lengthy memoirs, journals, or letters during or after the events. Some of this material from the French side has been printed over the years in the annual *Rapport de l'Archiviste de la province de Québec*, in recent years entitled *Rapport des Archives Nationales du Québec*. It is listed in *Table des Matières des Rapports des Archives du Québec*, Tomes 1 à 42 *(1920–1964)* (Ministère des Affaires culturelles, Québec, 1965) under the headings Guerre, Journaux, Mémoires, Capitulations, Siège de Québec. The *Report of the Canadian Archives* for the years 1904, 1905, and 1929 also contain correspondence by leading figures in the conflict. Some official correspondence, both French and English—the latter in translation—is contained in *Documents Relative to the Colonial History of the State of New York* (cited above). Serious errors were made in both the transcription and the translation of the French documents. They should be used only as a last resort. A major collection is H.-R. Casgrain (ed.), *Collection des manuscrits du maréchal de Lévis* (12 vols., Montréal and Québec, 1889–95); the odd error in transcription has been noted. The original documents are in the National Archives of Canada. Also edited by H.-R. Casgrain, *Extraits des Archives des Ministères de la Marine et de la Guerre à Paris, Canada, Correspondance générale MM. Duquesne et Vaudreuil Gouverneurs généraux, 1755–1760* (Québec, 1890). Two journals by officers in the Troupes de Terre are G. de Malartic, *Journal des campagnes au Canada de 1755 à 1760 par le comte des Marès de Malartic* (Dijon, 1890) and Le Chevalier de la Pause, "Mémoire et observations sur mon voyage en Canada," in *Rapport de l'Archiviste de la province de Québec pour 1931–1932* (Québec, 1932).

Fernand Grenier (ed.), *Papiers Contrecoeur et autres documents concernant le conflit anglo-français sur l'Ohio de 1745 à 1756* (Québec, 1952) is a particularly well-edited and valuable selection from the documents in the Archives du Séminaire de Québec. Dealing with the war in the West in the *Illinois Historical Collection*, ed. by Theodore Calvin Pease and Raymond C. Werner, in translation, are Vol. XXVII, ed. by T. C. Pease, *Anglo-French Boundary Disputes in the West, 1759–1763* (Springfield, Ill., 1936) and Vol. XXIX, ed. by T. C. Pease and Ernestine Jenison, *Illinois on the Eve of the Seven Years' War, 1747–1755* (Springfield, Ill., 1940). A. G. Doughty and G. W. Parmalee, *The Siege of Quebec and the Battle of the Plains of Abraham* (6 vols., Quebec, 1901), comprises a useful batch of documents and a worthless editorial commentary.

From the British side of the hill, A. G. Doughty (ed.), *An Historical Journal of the Campaigns in North America for the Years 1757, 1758, 1759, and 1760, by Captain John Knox*, 3 vols., (Champlain Society Publications, Toronto, 1914–1916). Reprinted as *The Siege of Quebec and the Campaigns in North America 1757–1760*, Edited and introduced by Brian Connell (Pendragon House of Mississauga, 1980). The work has to be used with care; Knox wrote his self-serving account of events several years after they occurred, and credulity is frequently strained. *The Papers of Henry Bouquet*, Vol. II, *The Forbes Expedition*, ed. by S. K. Stevens, Donald H. Kent, and Autumn L. Leonard (The Pennsylvania Historical and Museum Commission, Harrisburg, 1951). Volume I has not yet appeared. A mimeographed edition of the "Papers of Col. Henry Bouquet" appeared in 19 "volumes" (W. P. A. Penn. Hist. Survey), same editors; J. C. Webster, *The Journal of Jeffrey Amherst* (Toronto, 1931); J. Sullivan, *The Papers of Sir William Johnson*, Vols. 1–3 (Albany, 1921–23); Charles Henry Lincoln, *Correspondence of William Shirley, Governor of Massachusetts and Military Commander in North America, 1731–1760* (2 vols., New York, 1912); Gertrude S. Kimball (ed.), *Correspondence of William Pitt When Secretary of State with Colonial Governors and Military and Naval Commanders in America* (2 vols., New York, 1906); Stanley M. Pargellis (ed.), *Military Affairs in North America, 1748–1765: Selected Documents from the Cumberland Papers in Windsor Castle* (New York, 1936); William Wood (ed.), *The Logs of the Conquest of Canada* (Champlain Society Publications, Toronto, 1909) contains selections from logs of the ships in the fleet at Louisbourg and Quebec. On the role of the Royal Navy see also C. H. Little, *Despatches of Vice-Admiral Charles Saunders, 1759–1760 — The Naval Side of the Capture of Quebec, Despatches of Rear-Admiral Philip Durell, 1758–1759, and Rear-Admiral Lord Colville, 1759–1761* (Maritime Museum of Canada, Halifax, 1958).

As I. K. Steele, in the preface to his brief study of the war, *Guerillas and Grenadiers* (Toronto, 1969), cogently points out, this period poses a problem for English-speaking Canadians: where should their sympathies lie? With the people who occupied much of what is today Canada, called themselves Canadian, and defended the country against external aggression for the better part of a century, or with their fellow nationals of the eighteenth century who conquered New France, thereby bringing present-day English Canada into being? American and British historians, for the most part, have felt no need to conceal their identification with the British cause. French historians have tended to ignore the event—in fact, to ignore Canada. French-Canadian historians can hardly be blamed for treating the Conquest as a disaster, yet

English Canadians sometimes regard that attitude as suspect, if not seditious. English-Canadian historians tend, either expressly or as an unstated and perhaps unconscious premise, to regard the outcome of the struggle as having been inevitable, since had it been different their world would not exist today, which is unthinkable. Thus most of the histories of the war written in English are anything but detached in their views, and some are unblushingly partisan.

Among the more partisan accounts are Francis Parkman, *A Half Century of Conflict* (Boston, 1892) and *Montcalm and Wolfe* (Boston, 1884). Parkman made it very plain that he regarded the struggle as one between the forces of light and those of darkness, with the final outcome never in doubt. He also played fast and loose with the evidence. On this question see W. J. Eccles, ''The History of New France According to Francis Parkman,'' *William and Mary Quarterly*, 3d Ser., XVIII, 2 (Apr. 1961), and Francis P. Jennings, ''A Vanishing Indian. Francis Parkman Versus His Sources,'' in *The Pennsylvania Magazine of History and Biography*, Vol. LXXXVII, No. 3, July 1963, pp. 306–323. L. H. Gipson, *The British Empire Before the American Revolution*, Vols. IV–VIII (New York, 1936–64), a global study, hence much must be forgiven, relies heavily on Parkman and is equally chauvinistic. Howard H. Peckham, *The Colonial Wars, 1689–1762* (Chicago, 1964) follows the same pattern and is worthless. Little better is Douglas Edward Leach, *Arms For Empire. A Military History of the British Colonies in North America, 1607–1763* (New York, 1973). The latter work is a prize example of Whig history; all things contrived to lead to one end, the independence of the United States. The same Whig flaw is manifest in Francis Jennings' rather tendentious *Empire of Fortune* (New York & London, 1988). Guy Frégault's *La guerre de la conquête* (Montréal, 1955), trans. by Margaret M. Cameron, *Canada: The War of the Conquest* (Toronto, 1969); once the best work on the war is now dated and seen to be flawed in its treatment of logistics. Bigot is no longer regarded as a corrupt scoundrel. In the English edition, in an otherwise felicitous translation, a serious error was made (p. 203), the cost to Britain for the conquest of Canada is given as ''four million pounds.'' The figure cited by Frégault was £80,000,000. On the vital question of logistics in the French camp, scholars should consult an unpublished Ph.D. thesis by André Coté, "Joseph-Michel Cadet (1719–1781), Munitionnaire du Roi en Nouvelle-France," (Université Laval, 1984). George F. G. Stanley, *New France: The Last Phase, 1744–1760* (Toronto, 1968) utilized mainly secondary and tertiary sources, hence some significant questions were begged, and old myths revived.

On the broader aspects of the conflict, Richard Waddington, *Louis XV et le renversement des alliances: Préliminaires de la Guerre de Sept Ans 1754–1756* (Paris, 1896) and *La Guerre de Sept Ans: Histoire diplomatique et militaire* (5 vols., Paris, 1899–1914) although dated are still very useful. So too, despite its blemishes, is Sir Julian S. Corbett, *England in the Seven Years' War* (2 vols., London, 1918). Perhaps the most useful study of the European background to the conflict, in English, is Walter L. Dorn, *Competition for Empire, 1740–1763* (New York, 1940); unfortunately, the treatment of events in North America, of necessity based on the mediocre, or worse, secondary sources then extant, is poor. A concise and very valuable study is Lee Kennet, *The French Armies in the Seven Years' War* (Duke Univ. Press, Durham, N.C., 1967). Also valuable is James Pritchard, *Louis XV's Navy 1748–1762* (McGill-Queen's University Press, 1987), as also is the unpublished Ph.D. thesis by Jay Cassel, "The Troupes de la Marine in Canada, 1683–1760: Men and Materiel," (University of Toronto, 1987). Invaluable is André Corvisier, *L'armée française de la fin du XVIIe siècle au ministère de Choiseul. Le soldat*, 2 vols. (Paris, 1964). The year 1959 saw a spate of books on the Quebec campaigns of 1759–60. Some were not written by historians, and sought to glorify Wolfe and British arms and appeal to a popular British audience. Others, although written by professional historians, show little evidence of acquaintance with the primary sources, more with dubious dated secondary and tertiary works. C. P. Stacey, *Quebec 1759: The Siege and the Battle* (Toronto, 1959) is the best of a bad lot, but viewing a British victory as inevitable led the author into committing some serious misreadings of the evidence. See also the introductory essays by W. J. Eccles "The French Forces in North America during the Seven Years' War," and C. P. Stacey, "The

British Forces in North America during the Seven Years' War,''
in *Dictionary of Canadian Biography* Vol. III (Toronto, 1974).
See also the biographies for the leading participants in that and
the succeeding volume.

The article, too long ignored, by E. R. Adair, ''The Military
Reputation of Major-General James Wolfe,'' *Canadian Histori-
cal Association Annual Report, 1936*, is still useful. So also are
the more recent articles by C. P. Stacey, ''The Anse au Foulon,
1759: Montcalm and Vaudreuil,'' *Canadian Historical Review*,
XLII (Mar. 1959) and ''Quebec, 1759: some New Documents,''
Canadian Historical Review, XLVII, 4 (Dec. 1966), pp. 344–
355, and D. Peter MacLeod, ''The Canadians against the French:
The Struggle for Control of the Expedition to Oswego in 1756,''
Ontario History, Vol. LXXX, No. 2, June 1988, pp. 143–157.
On military operations in the West Indies see Richard Pares, *War
and Trade in the West Indies, 1739–1763* (Oxford, 1936), and L.
H. Gipson, *The British Empire Before the American Revolution*,
Vols. V, VIII (New York, 1939–64).

There are biographies of some of the leading figures in the
conflict, but with one or two exceptions they leave much to be
desired. Most seek only to praise their subjects, e.g., W. T.
Waugh, *James Wolfe, Man and Soldier* (Montreal, 1928). The
bitter conflict between Vaudreuil and Montcalm has been per-
petuated by latter-day historians. H.-R. Casgrain, *Guerre du
Canada, 1756–1760: Montcalm et Lévis* (2 vols., Québec, 1891)
is strongly critical of Montcalm, extols Lévis and Vaudreuil.
Thomas Chapais, *Le Marquis de Montcalm (1721–1759)* (Québec, 1911) extols his subject. Guy Frégault, *Le Grand Marquis:
Pierre de Rigaud de Vaudreuil et la Louisiane* (Montréal, 1952),
is sympathetic but does not extend his study to Vaudreuil's
governor-generalship at Quebec. Guy Frégault, *François Bigot:
Administrateur français* (Montréal, 1948) is biased against Bigot,
who was a product of an inefficient system rather than a mal-
feasant, and was made a scapegoat by an unscrupulous minister.
For correctives see J. F. Bosher, *French Finances 1770–1795:
From Business to Bureaucracy* (Cambridge Univ. Press, 1970)
and André Coté's Ph.D., thesis cited above. J. C. Long, *Lord
Jeffrey Amherst, a Soldier of the King* (New York, 1933); the

title suggests the quality. Louis des Cognets, *Amherst and Canada* (Princeton, 1962) has merit. The article by Bernard Knollenberg, "General Amherst and Germ Warfare," *Mississippi Valley Historical Review*, XLI (1954–55) is revealing. On this nasty episode see also Francis Jennings, *Empire of Fortune* (New York, 1988), pp. 447–8.

Chapter Eight: 1760–1783

The military conquest of Canada, Great Britain's subsequent decision to retain that vaguely defined territory, and the French desire to be rid of it, led directly to the destruction of the first British Empire and of the North American Indian nations. The primary source material is very extensive, but, unfortunately, too many historians have approached it with preconceived answers rather than questions. The work of American historians on the so-called "Revolution" consists mainly of Whig history, depicted in tones of black and white: independence was inevitable and 'a good thing', those fighting for it fought in the right cause, the British were tyrants, and the misguided Loyalists traitors to the cause who deserved what they eventually got, despoilment and exile. An impartial search for the truth, viewing events from both sides of the hill, is conspicuous by its absence. What is badly needed is a detached approach to what was, in essence, a civil war.

The best study of the involved negotiations that concluded the Seven Years' War is still Zenab Esmat Rashed, *The Peace of Paris, 1763* (Liverpool, 1951). On Canada's role in the negotiations see Guy Frégault, *Canada: The War of the Conquest*, Part V, translated by Margaret M. Cameron (Toronto, 1969). It provides an excellent summary. The problems besetting the British after 1763 were global, and of their own contriving. They are put in clear perspective by Vincent T. Harlow, *The Founding of the Second British Empire, 1763–1793*, 2 vols. (London, 1952–64). Sir Lewis Namier's magisterial works, *The Structure of Politics at the Accession of George III*, 2nd ed., (London, 1957) and *England in the Age of the American Revolution* (London, 1961) are basic.

The role of France in the American war for independence can be viewed, fleetingly, in the diplomatic documents and correspondence selected by Henri Doniol, *Histoire de la participation de la France à l'établissement des États-Unis d'Amérique*, 5 vols., (Paris, 1886-92). An intriguing account of the renewed struggle between France and Britain, from the contemporary French point of view, is Pierre de Longchamps, *Histoire impartiale des événements militaires et politiques de la dernière guerre*, 3 vols., (Paris & Amsterdam, 1785). An excellent general survey of the era is still Philippe Sagnac, *La fin de l'ancien régime et la révolution américaine (1763-1789)* (Paris, 1947). For Vergenne's policy see Orville T. Murphy, *Charles Gravier, Comte de Vergennes* (Albany, 1982), Réné Pinon, "Louis XVI, Vergennes et la grande lutte contre l'Angleterre," *Revue d'histoire diplomatique*, XLIII (1929) pp. 37-64, and Marcel Trudel, *Louis XVI, le congrès américain et le Canada 1774-1789* (Québec, 1949). On the role of the French army in the American war see Lee Kennett, *The French Forces in America 1780-1783* (Westport Conn. & London, 1977) and on the vital role of the French navy see Jonathan R. Dull, *The French Navy and American Independence* (Princeton NJ, 1975). Of particular interest are the journals of officers in the French army serving in America, Howard C. Rice Jr., and Anne S. K. Brown (eds. & translators), *The American Campaigns of Rochambeau's Army 1780, 1781, 1782, 1783* (Princeton NJ & Providence RI, 1972). Of the hundreds of works written on the so-called American Revolution (Marxist historians would not agree that it was a revolution) three only will be singled out. Piers Mackesy, *The War for America 1775-1783* (London, 1964), written with singular detachment, indeed at times, restraint; Jonathan R. Dull, *A Diplomatic History of the American Revolution* (Yale Univ. Press, 1985); and John E. Ferling, *The First of Men: A Life of George Washington* (Univ. Tennessee Press, 1988).

On events in Canada, renamed Quebec by the British, among the more useful collections of primary source material in print are Adam Shortt and Arthur G. Doughty, *Documents Relating to the Constitutional History of Canada, 1759-1791* (Ottawa, 1918) and W. P. M. Kennedy and Gustave Lanctot, *Reports on the Laws of Quebec, 1767–1770* (Ottawa, 1931). *The Annual Report of the Public Archives of Canada* for 1913 and for 1914–1915 contain the provincial ordinances of the military regime along with the proclamations of the governors, and for 1904, a selection of "Documents Relating to the War of 1775." Another useful collection is *Blockade of Quebec by the American Revolutionists (Les Bastonnais)*, ed. by Fred C. Wurtele (Literary and Historical Society of Quebec, Historical Documents, 7th and 8th Ser., Quebec, 1905–6). The *Rapport de l'Archiviste de la Province de Québec, 1927–1928* and *1929–1930*, contains the reports of the commissioners on the state of the province in the wake of the American invasion. On the invasion itself an interesting collection of firsthand accounts from the British side is contained in *Invasion du Canada, collection de mémoires recueillis et annotés par M. l'abbé Verreau, prêtre* (Montréal, 1873). Of the secondary works dealing with what is perhaps the most crucial period in the history of North America, Alfred Leroy Burt, *The Old Province of Quebec* (Toronto & Minneapolis, 1933) for long regarded as the definitive work, is now sadly dated. Adopting the same basic Whig premises, stated and unstated, that the conquest of New France was merely the inevitable unfolding of events that led to the best of all possible worlds, namely Anglophone dominance of British North America, is Hilda Neatby, *Quebec: The Revolutionary Age, 1760–1791* (Toronto, 1966). In both works too many significant questions never crossed the minds of the authors, hence were not answered. Some of those questions, but by no means all, were asked and answered by the neo-nationalist school of Quebec historians; Maurice Séguin, *La nation canadienne et l'agriculture (1760–1850)*, (Trois-Rivières, 1970), Michel Brunet, *Les Canadiens après la conquête, 1759–1775* (Montréal, 1969), and by the same author *La présence anglaise et les Canadiens* (Montréal, 1958). In marked opposition to the nationalist interpretation is Fernand Ouellet; his massive quantitative study *Histoire économique et sociale du Québec, 1760–1850* (Montréal, 1966) is more economic than social. A once influential work, Donald Creighton, *The Commercial Empire of the St. Lawrence 1760–1850* (New York & Toronto, 1937) was reissued as *The Empire of the St. Lawrence* (Toronto, 1956) without revision. It sacrifices nothing to scholarly detachment, espousing blatantly the cause of the British merchants in Quebec, selecting and marshaling the evidence accordingly; written with great verve, the weighted use of adjectives has to be noted. Scholarship of a much higher order is to be found in two works by Marcel Trudel, *Le régime militaire dans le Gouvernment des Trois-Rivières 1760–1764* (Trois-Rivières, 1952); *L'Eglise canadienne sous le régime militaire, 1759–1764*, Vol. I, *Les problèmes* (Montréal, 1956); Vol. II, *Les institutions* (Québec, 1957). Jack M. Sosin, *Whitehall and the Wilderness* (Univ. of Nebraska Press, 1961) throws much light on the murky problems of the midwest, post 1760.

The American War for Independence, as it affected Canada, is dealt with in a narrative account by Gustave Lanctot, *Canada and the American Revolution, 1774–1783* (Toronto, 1967). The best account to date of the American invasion of Quebec is Robert McConnell Hatch, *Thrust for Canada: The American Attempt on Quebec in 1775–1776* (Boston, 1979). Victor Coffin, *The Province of Quebec and the Early American Revolution* (Madison, Wisc., 1896) argued unconvincingly that, had not the Americans outbungled the British, Quebec would have joined the United States. In a similar unconvincing fashion, Reginald Coupland, *The Quebec Act: A Study in Statesmanship* (Oxford, 1925) maintained that the refusal of the Canadians to support the American cause stemmed from their satisfaction with the Quebec Act. Justin H. Smith, *Our Struggle for the Fourteenth Colony: Canada and the American Revolution*, 2 vols. (New York, 1907) is a narrative account by an American historian of what went wrong. G. M. Wrong, *Canada and the American Revolution* (Toronto, 1935) is an account by a Canadian of what went right. Neither has much value.

For events in the French West Indies between the wars, the pertinent chapters should be consulted in H. I. Priestley, *France Overseas Through the Old Regime: A Study of European Expansion (New York, 1939)*; Gaston Martin, *Histoire de l'Esclavage dans les Colonies françaises* (Paris, 1948), and by the same author, *Nantes au XVIIIᵉ Siècle: L'Ère des Négriers (1714–1774)* (Paris, 1931); Gabriel Debien, *Études Antillaises (XVIIIᵉ Siècle)*

(Paris, 1956), is particularly valuable for this period. Also useful is his three-part article "Gens de couleur libres et colons de Saint-Dominigue devant la Constituante 1789–mars 1790," *Revue d'Histoire de l'Amérique française*, Sept. 1950 pp. 211–232; Dec. 1950, pp. 398–426; Mar. 1951, pp. 530–549.

The best general account of events in Louisiana after the cession to Spain is Baron Marc de Villiers du Terrage, *Les dernières années de la Louisiane française* (Paris, 1904). Pierre H. Boule, "Some Eighteenth Century French Views on Louisiana," in John Francis McDermott (ed.), *Frenchmen and French Ways in the Mississippi Valley* (Univ. of Illinois Press, 1969), refutes the view, in convincing fashion, that France had lost interest in the colony. On the "Revolution" of 1768, James E. Winston, "The Causes and Results of the Revolution of 1768 in Louisiana," *Louisiana Historical Quarterly*, XV (1932), pp. 182–213, sketches in the event. Much more percipient is the article by Pierre H. Boule, "French Reactions to the Louisiana Revolution of 1768," in John Francis McDermott (ed.), *The French in the Mississippi Valley* (Univ. of Illinois Press, 1965). See also David Ker Texada, *Alejandro O'Reilly and the New Orleans Rebels* (Lafayette LA, 1970), and Alexander De Conde, *This Affair of Louisiana* (New York, 1976).

Index